T0340388

Agritourism, Wine Tourism, and Craft Beer Tourism

This book delves into the development opportunities for peripheral areas explored through the emerging practices of agritourism, wine tourism, and craft beer tourism. It celebrates the entrepreneurial spirit of people living in peri-urban regions.

Peripheral areas tend to be far from urban hubs, providing essential services but also typically suffering from marginalisation and remoteness, despite the access to environmental, cultural, and social resources. In this sense, this book investigates the linkages between local agency and tourism in peripheral areas, the role of existing policies, and the evolving bottom-up practices in fostering local development. The basic aim is to disestablish the dichotomies that often emerge when dealing with issues of rural–urban and/or centre–periphery relationships; innovation vs tradition; authenticity vs mise en scène; agency vs inertia; and social, cultural, economic mobility vs immobility; etc. With focused attention on the possible compliance or conflicting strategies of local actors with the existing policies, the book considers how local actors and communities respond to the implications of peripherality in areas often impacted by marginalising processes.

Drawing upon case studies from North America and Europe, this book presents this connection as a global phenomenon which will be of interest to community and economic development planners and entrepreneurs.

Maria Giulia Pezzi, PhD in European Ethnography, is Post-Doctoral Research Fellow at Gran Sasso Science Institute (GSSI) as a member of the Social Sciences research unit, working on a research project on the development of peripheral areas in Italy, specifically in relation to the Italian National Strategy for Inner Areas. Her current research focuses on tourism policies and heritage-making strategies as development tools for rural areas, and on the role that local entrepreneurship can play in such processes from a bottom-up perspective.

Alessandra Faggian is a Professor of Applied Economics, Director of Social Sciences, and Vice Provost for Research at the Gran Sasso Science Institute, L'Aquila, Italy. She is past President of the North American Regional

Science Council (NARSC) and co-editor of "Journal in Regional Science". Dr Faggian's research interests lie in the fields of regional and urban economics, demography, labour economics, and economics of education.

Neil Reid, Ph.D., is a Professor of Geography and Planning at the University of Toledo. He holds MA degrees in Geography from the University of Glasgow and Miami University and a Ph.D. in Geography from Arizona State University. He is an economic geographer and regional scientist with research interests in industrial location, regional economic restructuring, and local economic development. His current research focuses on a number of areas including the health of metropolitan labour markets in the United States, policies to deal with decline in America's shrinking cities, and the economic development opportunities surrounding America's rapidly growing craft brewing industry.

The Dynamics of Economic Space
Series Editor: Nuri Yavan, Ankara University, Turkey

The IGU Commission on 'The Dynamics of Economic Space' aims to play a leading international role in the development, promulgation and dissemination of new ideas in economic geography. It has as its goal the development of a strong analytical perspective on the processes, problems and policies associated with the dynamics of local and regional economies as they are incorporated into the globalizing world economy. In recognition of the increasing complexity of the world economy, the Commission's interests include: industrial production; business, professional and financial services, and the broader service economy including e-business; corporations, corporate power, enterprise and entrepreneurship; the changing world of work and intensifying economic interconnectedness.

The Industrial Enterprise and its Environment
Spatial Perspectives
Edited by Sergio Conti, Edward J. Malecki and Päivi Oinas

Towards Coastal Resilience and Sustainability
Edited by C. Patrick Heidkamp and John Morrissey

Better Spending for Localizing Global Sustainable Development Goals
Examples from the Field
Edited by Fayyaz Baqir, Nipa Banerjee and Sanni Yaya

Agritourism, Wine Tourism, and Craft Beer Tourism
Local Responses to Peripherality Through Tourism Niches
Edited by Maria Giulia Pezzi, Alessandra Faggian, and Neil Reid

For more information about this series, please visit: https://www.routledge.com/The-Dynamics-of-Economic-Space/book-series/ASHSER1030

Agritourism, Wine Tourism, and Craft Beer Tourism

Local Responses to Peripherality Through Tourism Niches

**Edited by Maria Giulia Pezzi,
Alessandra Faggian, and Neil Reid**

LONDON AND NEW YORK

First published 2021
by Routledge
2 Park Square, Milton Park, Abingdon, Oxon OX14 4RN

and by Routledge
52 Vanderbilt Avenue, New York, NY 10017

Routledge is an imprint of the Taylor & Francis Group, an informa business

British Library Cataloguing-in-Publication Data
A catalogue record for this book is available from the British Library

Library of Congress Cataloging-in-Publication Data
Names: Pezzi, Maria Giulia, editor. | Faggian, Alessandra, editor. | Reid, Neil, 1963 July 7- editor.
Title: Agritourism, wine tourism, and craft beer tourism: local responses to peripherality through tourism niches / edited by Maria Giulia Pezzi, Alessandra Faggian, and Neil Reid.
Description: Abingdon, Oxon; New York: Routledge, 2020. | Series: The dynamics of economic space | Includes bibliographical references and index.
Identifiers: LCCN 2019050038 (print) | LCCN 2019050039 (ebook)
Subjects: LCSH: Agritourism. | Wine tourism. | Rural tourism. | Rural development.
Classification: LCC S565.88 A43 2020 (print) | LCC S565.88 (ebook) | DDC 630—dc23
LC record available at https://lccn.loc.gov/2019050038
LC ebook record available at https://lccn.loc.gov/2019050039

ISBN: 978-1-138-61441-3 (hbk)
ISBN: 978-0-367-50253-9 (pbk)
ISBN: 978-0-429-46410-2 (ebk)

Typeset in Times New Roman
by codeMantra

Contents

Figures

Maps

Tables

Contributors

Douglas Arbogast is an Adjunct Professor and a Rural Tourism Specialist in West Virginia University (WVU) Extension Service. He conducts research and delivers training on rural tourism development in destinations across the state, and works collaboratively with WVU faculty and students to promote the sustainable development of tourism in West Virginia. His research interests include rural tourism, sustainable tourism development, craft beer tourism, tourism planning, tourism management, and regional competitiveness.

Maria Giovanna Brandano is an Assistant Professor of Applied Economics at the Gran Sasso Science Institute (GSSI) in L'Aquila (Italy) and a research assistant at CRENoS (Centre for North South Economic Research – University of Cagliari and University of Sassari). Her main interests of research are applied economics, tourism economics, tourism externalities, cultural economics, wine economics, and policy evaluation, with particular focus on tourism taxation.

Mary Constantoglou holds a PhD in Tourism Planning with the use of GIS and fuzzy logic, a Master Degree (M.Sc.) in "Tourism Planning, Administration and Policy" and a B.Sc. in Environmental Science from the University of the Aegean, Greece. She is a lecturer at the Hellenic Open University, Postgraduate Program in "Management of Tourism Enterprises" and at the Open University of Cyprus, Postgraduate Program in "Cultural Policy and Development". She has also taught at the University of the Aegean in the Department of Cultural Technology and Communication. She has participated in international conferences and published in international scientific journals. She has implemented various projects such as MED, Interreg, Europe Aid, Erasmus +, Life, and LEADER co-funded by the European Commission, UNEP, etc. Her research interests are tourism planning, geographical information systems, spatial decision-making systems, and destination management.

Marcela Rebeca Contreras Loera, PhD in Organisational Studies, is a Postdoctoral Research Fellow in Social Sciences and a member of the

National Research System (Mexico), Level 1. She had been a visiting researcher in national and international universities in France, Poland, Chile, Brazil, Venezuela, Spain, and Mexico. She has published books, articles, and book chapters.

Andrew Crawley is an Assistant Professor of Economics at the University of Maine. Dr. Crawley leads the Regional Economic Modelling and Forecast Lab in the School of Economics which specialises in the creation and application of economic models primarily focused on regional labour markets. Dr. Crawley has a decade of experience building and maintaining regional economic models and has also developed new methods and techniques for the analysis of regional economic phenomenon from rurality to industrial agglomeration.

Marusca De Castris is currently an Associate Professor of Economic Statistics at the Department of Political Studies of Roma Tre University. She is a member of Roma Tre University Board of Quality Assurance. Her research interests are in the areas of casual inference, regional policy evaluation, rural development policy, and spatial economic analysis. She teaches courses in economic statistics and statistical methods for policy evaluation, and she is an experienced statistical and economic consultant for many public institutions. Her contributions have been published in academic journals of regional science and applied statistics. She is a member of the Editorial Board of the *Italian Journal of Regional Science.*

Claudio Detotto is currently an Associate Professor of Economics at the Laboratoire UMR CNRS 6240 of the University of Corsica (France) and a researcher at CRENoS (Centre for North South Economic Research) in Sardinia (Italy). His research interests mainly concern the applied economic analysis of crime, paying particular attention to the effect of crime on the economy, the negative externalities of tourism activity, and the measurement of economic efficiency and productivity by using the non-parametric approach of Data Envelopment Analysis (DEA).

Evelia de Jesus Izabal de la Garza, PhD in Regional Studies with emphasis on North America, A member of the National Research System (Mexico), Level C. She's been visiting researcher at University of Illinois at Urbana-Champaign, in the United States, and Universidad Autonoma Metropolitana, in México. She has written articles and book chapters.

Daniele Di Gennaro is a Research Assistant at the Department of Political Science at Roma Tre University. He received his Ph.D. degree in Economic Statistics with an emphasis on the evaluation of direct and indirect policies effects from Sapienza University of Rome and his M.A. degree in Economics from Sapienza University of Rome. In 2015, he was a visiting student at Purdue University. His research interests include spatial econometrics, causal inference, and the evaluation of both industrial and agricultural policies effectiveness.

Daniel Eades is an Associate Professor and Rural Development Specialist in West Virginia University Extension Service. His teaching and outreach activities engage government and community leaders in the process of data-driven economic development decision making. His research interests include rural and regional development economics, the community development process and community vitality, and community data analysis.

Todd Gabe is a Professor of Economics at the University of Maine, where he teaches and conducts research on a broad range of topics related to state and local economic development. He is an expert in the analysis of occupations and industries, with a focus on the importance of human capital to regions large and small. Gabe is the author of the 2017 book *The Pursuit of Economic Development—Growing Good Jobs in U.S. Cities and States*. Gabe has graduate degrees from The Ohio State University and the University of Minnesota, and he went to college at Furman University.

Simona Giordano has a Doctor of Philosophy in Economic Geography, and is a Honorary Fellow and subject expert in Economic Geography at the University of Bari "Aldo Moro" (Department of Economic Sciences and Mathematical Methods), and a Research Fellow within the project "PERFORM TECH" (PUGLIA EMERGING FOOD TECHNOLOGY) at the University of Bari "Aldo Moro" (Department of Agricultural and Environmental Sciences). She's Senior Credit and Financial Analyst, CPA, Master of Science MIEM – MBA in International Economics and Management (Focus in Money, Banking and Finance) at the SDA – University Luigi Bocconi in Milan.

Rebecca Hill is a Research Scientist with the Department of Agricultural and Resource Economics at Colorado State University. Rebecca received her Ph.D. in Agricultural and Natural Resource Economics in 2012 and since that time has specialised in research broadly related to agritourism, outdoor recreation, water resources, local foods, and economic impact analysis.

Stella Kostopoulou is an Associate Professor of Regional and Tourism Development, Aristotle University of Thessaloniki (AUTh), Department of Economics. She has also taught at Cyprus University of Technology, Hellenic Open University, International Hellenic University, Democritus University of Thrace, and University of Thessaly, and gave invited lectures at universities abroad (Peking University, La Trobe University, York University, Moscow-MGIMO). She is the Director of the "Master on Tourism and Local Development", President of the "European Interdisciplinary Silk Road Tourism Centre"-AUTh, Departmental ECTS/Erasmus Coordinator and Institutional Coordinator for the Agreement AUTh-Chinese Academy of Social Sciences. She has participated in international conferences and published in international scientific journals on regional economics and planning, tourism, cultural industries, and local development.

Jason Kozlowski is a labour historian and labour educator in West Virginia University Extensive Service's Institute for Labor Studies and Research (ILSR). He conducts teaching and research programmes for labour unions and labour-management programs on labour relations and workplace concerns around the state. In addition, he develops and disseminates applied and academic research on historical and contemporary issues such as pertinent economic and policy matters.

André Magrinho is the Deputy Chairman of Portuguese Industrial Association Foundation, and a member of the Board of CINEL – Professional Training Center of Electronics, Energy, Telecommunications, and Information Technology Industries. He holds a PhD in Management from the University of Beira Interior (UBI), Portugal, and a Master in Economics from Lisbon School of Economics and Management. He is a professor in areas of management and economics at the Universidade Lusófona de Humanidades e Tecnologias, Lisbon, and a researcher at CIPES-Center for Research in Politics, Economics and Society. Among other subjects, he has published on competitive intelligence, innovation systems, and economic diplomacy.

Innisfree McKinnon is an Assistant Professor of Geography at the University of Wisconsin-Stout. Her research focuses on urban–rural interactions, political ecology, and critical GIS. She uses a variety of methods including qualitative methods, visual ethnography, and GIS.

Colleen C. Myles is an Assistant Professor in the Department of Geography at Texas State University in San Marcos, TX. She has a PhD in Geography and an MS in Community Development from the University of California, Davis. She is a rural geographer and political ecologist with specialties in land and environmental management; (ex)urbanisation; (rural) sustainability and tourism; wine, beer, and cider geographies (aka "fermented landscapes"); and food/agriculture (urban, peri-urban, and sustainable).

Joana Neves is the Head at AICEP – Trade & Investment Agency to South Korea. She's Founder and Director of the Knowledge and Business Intelligence Unit, the first to be created in the Ministry of Economy, Portugal. She holds a Ph.D in Management from Universidade Lusíada, Lisboa, and she acquired a solid applied background on tourism through her academic and professional experiences. She wrote a book on mature tourist motivations in the Portuguese domestic market, and authored or co-authored some papers focusing on tourism and consumer behaviour issues. She has a relevant teaching experience on these topics in Portugal as well as in Spain.

Joaquim Ramos Silva was Head of the Department of Economics, 2014–2018. At Lisbon School of Economics and Management, Universidade de Lisboa. He holds a PhD in Economic Analysis and Policy from École des Hautes Études en Sciences Sociales, Paris. Moreover, he is Member of SOCIUS/CSG – Research in Social Sciences and Management. His research has focused on various topics within international economics, and he has conducted studies on global, Portuguese and Brazilian economies. He is the author of around eighty scholarly papers in edited books and refereed journals, among others, in *Tourism Management, Business Process Management Journal, Journal of Enterprise Information Management*, and *WMU Journal of Maritime Affairs*.

Annelie Sjölander-Lindqvist is an Associate Professor in Social Anthropology and Senior Lecturer in Human Ecology at the University of Gothenburg. Her research concerns gastronomy and tourism, conflicting values in areas of contested natural and cultural resources and landscape management, including the limits and possibilities of deliberative measures, the analysis of local identity, science, and politics in environmental contests and the link between place attachment, landscape dynamics, and resource management.

Wilhelm Skoglund is a Senior Lecturer in Business Administration at the Mid Sweden University in Östersund, Sweden. His research stretches from community entrepreneurship in rural and peripheral regions to development dimensions of the cultural and creative industries. Particularly, the intersection of gastronomy, cultural and creative industries, and sustainability has been in focus in the last few years, including studies of the UNESCO Creative Cities Network.

Dawn Thilmany is a Professor with Colorado State University since 1997, and specialises in economic development related to local, organic, and other value-added food market segments, as well as food market analysis and consumer behavior. She is Co-Director for CSU's Regional Economic Development Institute and Associate Head for the Department of Agricultural and Resource Economics, and serves on the leadership team for CSU Extension Food Systems programme. She has worked with the USDA in several roles, chaired the Colorado Food Systems Advisory Council, and served in several academic leadership positions within the agricultural economics and agribusiness field.

Michele Tobias earned a Ph.D. from the University of California, Davis in geography focusing on coastal plant biogeomorphology and geospatial methods. She is currently the GIS Data Curator in the University of California, Davis Library where she provides a variety of geospatial data services, teaches workshops on geospatial tools, and creates datasets needed by the broader research community, such as the American Viticultural Areas dataset. She is an active charter member of the Open Source Geospatial Foundation.

Nikolaos Trihas holds a Ph.D. in e-Tourism, a Master Degree (M.Sc.) in "Tourism Planning, Administration and Policy", and a B.Sc. in Business Administration from the University of the Aegean, Greece. Currently, he is a Lecturer in the Department of Business Administration at the Technological Educational Institute of Crete in Greece, at the Hellenic Open University (Postgraduate Program in "Management of Tourism Enterprises"), and the Advanced School of Tourism Education of Crete, where he lectures courses on marketing, management, and tourism. His research interests include e-tourism, special and alternative forms of tourism, and tourism marketing.

Anders Van Sandt received his Ph.D. in Agricultural and Natural Resource Economics from Colorado State University in 2018, and is now a Post Doctorate Extension Associate at Texas A&M University. Brought up in rural Oregon, Anders has a passion for rural economic development, including diversifying agricultural businesses to make them more resilient to market fluctuations. Anders is passionate about teaching and making sure his research has real-world applications for rural community stakeholders.

Marco Vannini is a Professor of Economics at the Department of Economics and Business, University of Sassari, where he teaches microeconomics and economic policy, and is a founder member of CRENoS (University of Cagliari and University of Sassari). His areas of expertise are finance and growth, illegal behavior and the enforcement of law, litigation process, environmental economics, and cultural economics. He enjoys wine and is a certified wine taster.

Smaragda Zagkotsi holds a PhD in Sociology of Tourism, a Master Degree (M.Sc.) in Tourism Planning, Administration and Policy, and a B.Sc. in Business Administration from the University of the Aegean, Greece. She is a Lecturer at the Hellenic Open University (Postgraduate Program in "Management of Tourism Enterprises"), where she deals with course module "DTE60-Management of Tourism and Tourism Services Providers". She has also taught at the University of the Aegean, Alexandreio Technological Institute of Thessaloniki, and Technological Institute of Thessaly. Her research interests include tourism social and labour mobility, special and alternative forms of tourism, and tourism development.

Preface

The idea for this edited book emerged from the desire to compile emerging research on local responses to the implications of peripherality, in particular in relation to tourism development, aiming to expand (geographically, theoretically, and empirically) the understanding of the roles played by local actors in sustainable regional development.

The volume specifically attempts to go beyond the common belief that areas are usually considered as peripheral (i.e. far from urban hubs providing essential services) due to social, economic and cultural marginalisation, by focusing attention on the possibilities arising from the engagement of local actors as agents of change. Questioning the possible compliance or conflicting strategies of local actors with existing policies in relation to tourism development, in areas impacted by such marginalising processes, allows the book to contribute to the debate by showing that current trends demonstrate the existence of high degrees of innovation capacity in peripheral areas.

Peripheral areas are generally considered to be endowed with a wealth of key environmental and cultural resources of many different kinds, which could be seen as a means to potentially attract tourists. Therefore, tourism development is often considered (rightly or wrongly) as a viable answer to the negative effects of peripherality (i.e. deanthropisation, lack of essential services). It is easy to see how, from a tourism perspective, local agricultural systems and local or localised products and cuisines constitute an opportunity to generate added value in areas otherwise economically marginal. Similarly, how local actors and communities respond to the implications of peripherality through a variety of strategies is a topic of increasing importance. Focusing on the role of local actors and their entrepreneurial ability is pivotal in understanding how forms of tourism based on agriculture, wine and craft beer, their products, and their production methods, can contribute to the social and economic well-being of peripheral areas, within a more generalised regional development perspective, that also taking into account the interrelation between bottom-up practices and the related policies.

Given the trans-disciplinary nature of these phenomena, we are aware of the fact that the linkages between local, place-based development, and tourism can be investigated in a multitude of ways and from an array of different theoretical perspectives: the volume, therefore, presents twelve contributions from disciplines such as Economics, Regional Science, Business and Management, Political Science, Social Anthropology, Geography, and Tourism Studies. Consequently, all contributions have been written and thought of as to make them accessible to a wider audience without losing analytical depth.

Acknowledgements

This edited book is a collective effort. We would like to thank Faye Leerink and staff at Routledge, for their encouragement, support, and professionality throughout the writing and editing process. Moreover, we are grateful to the reviewers who have provided valuable insights, comments, and criticism on each chapter, as well as to the anonymous reviewers of the book proposal.

Our thanks go also to the numerous colleagues at Gran Sasso Science Institute who have kindly provided remarks on earlier drafts of the completed manuscript.

The authors of Chapter 1 would like to thank the support of the Colorado Experiment Station and a grant from the Agriculture and Food Research Initiative (#2014-68006-21824) for conducting this research.

This research described in Chapter 2 has received support from the research agreement between the Italian Council for Agricultural Research and Analysis of the Agricultural Economy (CREA) and the Department of Political Studies (DISCIPOL) of Roma Tre University. The authors would like to thank Roberto Henke, Concetta Cardillo, Antonio Giampaolo, and Mauro Santangelo of the Centre for Policies and Bioeconomics (CREA-PB) for making FADN microdata available. We also gratefully acknowledge helpful comments from Guido Pellegrini and Francesco Vidoli, and the participants of the workshop "Externality, profitability and diversification of agricultural production: empirical evidence from the FADN sample", co-organised by CREA-PB and DISCIPOL on 10 January 2018. The authors are grateful to the Editors Maria Giulia Pezzi, Alessandra Faggian, and Neil Reid and to an anonymous referee for their useful comments. Opinions reflect those of the authors.

Chapter 9 deals with research supported by a West Virginia University Extension Service Faculty Seed Grant.

Introduction

Local responses to peripherality through tourism development

Maria Giulia Pezzi, Alessandra Faggian and Neil Reid

Peripheral areas and tourism development

For many years, the relationship between peripheral areas and tourism has fueled the academic debate from a variety of disciplines and perspectives, looking at different facets such as local development and growth (Abram, 1998; Andreoli & Silvestri, 2017; Wanhill, 1997), participation (Adell et al., 2015; Mayaka, Croy, & Cox, 2017; Salvatore, Chiodo, & Fantini, 2018; Smith & Robinson, 2006; Tosun, 2000), innovation (Backman, Klaesson, & Öner, 2017; Dinis, 2006; Mitra, 2012), entrepreneurship (Ana & Lubiński, 2018; Calzada, 2018; Di Bella, Petino, & Scrofani, 2019; Eimermann, Tillberg Mattsson, & Carson, 2018; Komppula, 2014) and culture and heritage conservation and regeneration (Bessière, 1998, 2013; Bujdosó et al., 2015; Madden & Shipley, 2012; Pfeilstetter, 2015).

This volume sets itself within this stream of research and debate, with the aim to analyze different modalities of local responses to the implications of peripherality. In particular, the goal is to investigate various tourism development policies put in place by local communities and informal actors as a form of reaction to ongoing processes of marginalization. In this sense, we perceive peripherality not as an obstacle to, but as a potential asset for tourism development, and at the same time, we see tourism as a promising development option for peripheral areas.

The primary aim of the book, indeed, is to show that local actors can be (and often are) active agents of change in regional development. The decision to focus on agricultural/gastronomic tourism comes from the fact that existing natural and cultural resources are often seen as the most immediate assets to rely on, due to the high potentiality of their attractive power in terms of tourism development, and to the relatively lower initial investments that these forms of tourism require. Therefore, the volume aims at expanding geographically, theoretically and empirically discussions of how local actors can play a role in sustainable local and regional development, looking in particular at the tourism sector.

In doing so, we decided to set our focus on one niche (see Novelli, 2005) – agritourism – and two sub-niches – wine tourism and craft beer tourism – which are relevant both due to their embeddedness with the rural character of peripheral areas, and their high tourism potential.

Before getting deeper into details on the characteristics and peculiarities of these three tourism niches, it is important to provide a definition of peripherality and marginality in relation to tourism, so as to make them operational for the full understanding of the 12 contributions included in this edited collection.

Characteristics of peripheral areas

The notion of periphery and peripherality has often been constructed in relation to, or in opposition to, that of cores, centers and urban hubs, as the etymology suggests: peripheral is something that edges something else, and that constitutes its boundary or its circumference. Yet, as Grabher (2018, p. 3) maintains, periphery and center cannot (and should not) be reduced to a static dualism, due to their highly relational and functional interconnectedness.

When applying the notion of periphery to geographical areas, the first and most straightforward definition is the Euclidean one that focuses on the distance from the core. Nevertheless, the periphery/core relationship has one further dimension, which is important to pinpoint here.

The second dimension is the relational one, as in the work of Simmel (1992, cited in Grabher, 2018), but also of Hall et al. (2013), which entails the possibility of negotiation among the two ends of this imaginary continuum between cores and peripheries. Indeed, as Weaver (Hall et al., 2013, p. 83) maintained, "periphery and core can co-exist in the same place". Additionally, the relational dimension has some further distinctive components, which do not mutually exclude each other, but rather concur in defining peripheral areas.

Many scholars, in fact, agree on the statement that the question of what makes a periphery peripheral is relative to the existence of (often unbalanced) power relationships between centers and peripheries affecting their mutual perceptions, representations, definitions and policy interventions (Ardener, 2012; Chaperon & Bramwell, 2013; Copus, 2001; Copus, Mantino, & Noguera, 2017; Kühn, 2015; Lai & Li, 2012; Leik & Lang, 2018; Pezzi & Urso, 2016; Steinführer et al., 2016). Willett and Lang (2018), for example, have relied on Foucauldian knowledge/power processes to explain how peripheries are produced in the dominant "central" discourse, in an attempt to reason on how local agency can be embedded back into peripheral identity construction.

It is within these frameworks that this edited collection inserts itself and aims to contribute to the discussion on the topic, particularly applied to tourism development and tourism studies.

One more element needs to be highlighted here, and that is the frequent over-imposition of the notion of peripherality on that of marginality (see, i.e. Cullen & Pretes, 2000). Although the two terms are often used as synonyms on the basis of their similar etymological origin (margin derives from Latin and means "edge"), ideas of marginality relate to "a condition of disadvantage that may arise from unfavorable environmental, cultural, social, economic and political factors", and therefore require to be addressed from the point of view of inequity and inequality (Hall et al., 2013, p. 74). Peripherality is related to a spatial organization that is constructed through mutual core-periphery discursive, perceptive and power relations, whereas marginality refers to a process in which different forces concur in creating a condition favoring regional weakness, rather than strength.

Again, peripherality and marginality shall not be considered as mutually exclusive categories, and indeed they can either coexist or not in a variety of degrees. Nevertheless, what is important to highlight here is that peripheral areas are prone to marginality and marginalizing processes, and therefore a series of top-down and bottom-up interventions can be put in place in an attempt to stop or revert such ongoing processes.

In this sense, tourism is one of the most common policy responses to peripherality, as it is widely recognized as a promising development option for destinations though the generation of revenues (Buhalis, 1999), due to the lack of alternative investment opportunities and due to their distance from the power-exerting centers.

Salvatore, Chiodo and Fantini (2018, p. 42) analyzed the transition of peripheries to new rural tourism products, and evidenced the fact that, in opposition to "mass tourism" destinations, peripheral areas have been experiencing a transformation that can be defined as "tourism transition". This entails a co-evolution (Brouder, 2014; Martin & Sunley, 2006) in the needs of different stakeholders, institutions, local actors relying on endogenous cultural elements that tend toward a kind of tourism development that shifts peripheries from places of dependency, to new planning models focusing on "community-based" tourism.

Value of peripheral areas for tourism development

When analyzing tourism potential in peripheral areas, one of the key questions is what is the intrinsic value of such areas for tourism development and tourism consumption? As already pointed out, tourism is often used as a way to ignite value in lands that would otherwise be perceived as valueless, due to marginalizing processes and loss in the demographic and economic bases. Tourism development strategies seeking to trigger such dynamics rely on a variety of innovation strategies, policy options and narratives (Smith, 2015), aiming to communicate the value of peripheral areas to potential visitors. Two elements seem to be prevailing, although they cannot be considered as omni-comprehensive: the first is that "it is worth asking whether peripheries have more in common with each other than with their respective cores" (Hall et al., 2013, p. 87), which seems to presuppose that "peripherality" is an attribute in itself that recalls in visitors a series of indexes of peripheral characteristics (i.e. wilderness, geographical remoteness) which are functions to specific tourism experiences; the second element is that it is common of destination marketers to claim that "we have something for everyone" (Smith, 2015, p. 227), which entails the dangers of a so-called narrative fallacy, that is the "tendency of people to impose a coherent, plausible story on a set of facts regardless of the veracity of the story" through "a form of post hoc rationalization" (ibidem). In this sense, an overarching argument of all the contributions contained in the edited book is that a place-based (Barca, McCann, & Rodríguez-Pose, 2012) development takes into account both the intrinsic land and landscape values of a territory, as well as its qualities. Consequently, it can be more effective in fostering sustainable forms of regional development through tourism, both from the side of tourists/consumers and from the side of locals/producers (see e.g. Mantegazzi et al., forthcoming; Salvatore et al., 2018). Indeed, place-based cultural factors are indeed significant drivers for development (Huggins & Thompson, 2015).

Travelers' motivations, moreover, are multifaceted, but yet can be reduced to two macro-elements: attraction to places and attraction to goods (Hall & Gössling, 2016a). In the specific case of food-related tourism, "the desire to experience a particular type of food or the produce of a specific region must be the major motivation for such travel" (Hall & Gössling, 2016b, p. 7). Locals' motivations to engage in tourism development strategies rely mainly on the prospective increase of revenues, and of linkages with new potential markets (Sidali, Kastenholz, & Bianchi, 2015).

Since most peripheral/rural communities do not have a sufficiently developed and comprehensive business infrastructure, and "entrepreneurship encourages regional interplay as well as regional identity" (Kline, Slocum, & Cavaliere, 2017, p. 6), it is our aim to maintain that the presence of small businesses fosters an entrepreneurial culture which addresses local needs through high degrees of innovation, in the final attempt to overcome the negative externalities of peripherality through local means. The thread connecting all the contributions in the book, therefore, consists of a wider reflection on grassroots development strategies, and on the significance that local entrepreneurs and innovators can have in providing local and localized responses to the implications of peripherality, intended not as a limitation to overcome, but as an asset to rely on.

Agritourism

The term agritourism refers to a form of tourism based upon the agricultural economy, aimed at generating values from tourism through the local agricultural system (Phillip, Hunter, & Blackstock, 2010). Hence, it can be defined as a form of tourism in which visitors stay with local people in rural areas and typically spend their time on farms or ranches, experiencing their everyday life and activities with recreational purposes.

Agritourism is a key component of tourism development in peripheral/rural areas: first of all, because agriculture is typically the sector that has shaped the spatial and economic development of these areas, and is often paired with a deeply rooted sense of place and place attachment (see, respectively, Jiang et al., 2017; Kastenholz & Figueiredo, 2014). Moreover, through the increasing relevance of neo-rural and neolocal movements (see, i.e. Bender & Kanitscheider, 2012; Holtkamp et al., 2016), agritourism and related tourism offerings are showing higher and higher degrees of innovation. These innovation processes do not only rely on technological innovations, but also on the types of food and raw materials produced, as well as on the organizational structures (i.e. cooperatives, community enterprises) and the greater attention to sustainability (see, i.e. Backman, Klaesson, & Öner, 2017). Local agricultural systems and local or localized products and cuisines (Bessiere & Tibere, 2013; Hall & Mitchell, 2000; Hall et al., 2008; Vittersø & Amilien, 2011), indeed, constitute an opportunity to generate added value in areas otherwise economically marginal. Innovation and entrepreneurial efforts in agritourism are often linked with developing a further array of potentialities for the emergence of more specific niches (as wine and beer tourism), and that is why the three sections are interlinked.

In any sense, what is important to highlight here is that agritourism is qualitatively different from mass tourism, inasmuch it is different in quantitative terms. Therefore, policy makers should design incentives that are specifically targeted, in order to meet the characteristics of each particular peripheral area, and serve as an alternative to the subsistence economy. In this sense, place-based approaches to tourism development seem to be, once again, a viable option to stimulate rural development and economic opportunities, which also consider cultural identities, rural communities and at the same time (partially) counterbalance land abandonment and requalify rural areas (see, i.e. Bender & Kanitscheider, 2012).

Rural entrepreneurship surely plays a pivotal role in such dynamics – as evidenced in Chapter 1 by Van Sandt, Thilmany and Hill – where place-based approaches in US's rural West stimulate endogenous development processes and agritourism initiatives, aimed at balancing the relationship between tourism and non-tourism activities in rural environments and consequently creating a trade-off among economic benefits and social costs.

Chapter 2 by De Castris and Di Gennaro encourages a wider reflection on place-based development looking at how the relationship between agricultural policies and rural entrepreneurship fosters local development in Italy. According to the authors, the high degree of complementarity between agritourism and agricultural activities can support the inversion of population decline in lagging regions, as well as the increase of investments and diversification. In doing so, they conclude that "one size fits all" policy interventions do not work in peripheral areas and therefore effective policies should be tailored on the specificities of each rural/peripheral area.

Community participation in agritourism development can help hinder the negative externalities of tourism consumption, through a reasoning on sustainability in the longer run.

Simona Giordano in Chapter 3, in this sense, looks at bottom-up strategies to foster local and agritourism development, while preserving biodiversity, in a protected park in Apulia (Italy), with a focus on family farming. In doing so, it evidences potentially conflicting strategies between the park's management and the tourism activities, often to be considered as incompatible with a protected area, providing a comprehensive analysis of the environmental sustainability of agritourism activities and farms and their strategies to achieve a positive management model of their activities.

Nevertheless, community participation is not devoid of skepticism and tendencies toward conformism, rather than innovation, that can challenge emerging entrepreneurial processes. Chapter 4 by de Jesus Izabal del la Garza and Contreras Loera presents an analysis of the current challenges of promoting tourism in a fishing community in Mexico, which relies both on potentially highly impactful cultural and natural resources for tourism, but also pays the dues of progressive processes of economic marginalization and lack of entrepreneurial stimulation. The contribution shows the importance of cultural and psychological barriers to tourism development in an area facing diminishing fishing opportunities due to environmental and regulatory factors.

Focusing on the role of local actors and their entrepreneurial ability is, therefore, pivotal in understanding how forms of tourism based on agriculture, on its products and its methods, can contribute to the social and economic well-being of peripheral areas, within a more generalized regional development perspective, which also considers the interrelation with bottom-up practices and the related top-down policies.

Wine tourism

Wine tourism is an important sub-niche of agritourism showing many similarities with it, peculiarly in regard to its linkages with the territory, reflected by the concept of *terroir* (Bessiere & Tibere, 2013): both agritourism and wine tourism show high significance for the local communities not only in a spatial sense, but also because they can represent a sense of local pride, a revival of the craft economy, a mobilization of endogenous potential and of local knowledge. All these elements can lead to a renewed social construction of peripherality, including its limitations, and its potentialities.

Next to more institutionalized wine regions (i.e. Burgundy in France, or Piedmont in Italy), new wine regions emerge seeking to capitalize on the cultural and economic cachet, as well as networking possibilities among wineries and other touristic destinations in the same area.

The importance of the relational component of tourism development in peripheral areas is pivotal to the case study presented in Chapter 5 by Myles, Tobias and McKinnon that relies on the emergence of Arizona's wine country: a spatial disconnect between where tourism dominates and where grapes and wine are produced reflects a spatial mismatch in tourism development possibilities and opportunities, as well as in regional development.

The authors introduce, in this sense, the distinction between *terroir* and *fermented landscapes*, the latter being defined as fermented-focused landscapes that have both symbolic and material significance in the way processes of fermentation drive social and environmental changes (Myles, forthcoming).

The significance of networking possibilities is particularly evident in the case of wine routes, as evidenced in Chapter 6 by Brandano, Detotto and Vannini, focusing on the island of Sardinia in Italy: either spontaneous or policy-induced, wine routes have emerged as the most relevant vehicle linking wine and tourism. They have two effects: existing activities become more profitable because the area becomes more appealing, thanks to the so-called localization effect; they open up new opportunities for businesses, thanks to a synergy effect. The formation of networks is beneficial for wineries, tourism businesses and local communities, not only for further tourism development, but also for regional development, as it fosters the creation of linkages where before there was fragmentation.

Costantoglou, Kostopoulou, Trihas and Zagotsi in Chapter 7 deal with the emergence of wine tourism regions in Greece, a country associated with wine production and consumption since ancient times, but that only recently has started to capitalize on this asset for business and development purposes within the wider tourism sector. The contribution looks, again, at local entrepreneurs and their motivations, evidencing their need to establish stronger linkages between them and local tourism stakeholders to build a long-term sustainable tourism offering which is coherent with what the wine regions have to offer and with their economic, cultural and social structures.

Finally, Chapter 8 by Neves, Magrinho and Silva focuses on the development of wine tourism in the peripheral area of Alentejo, Portugal. The area, historically to be considered as a lagging region, has witnessed progressive efforts to trigger development through the enhancement of those cultural and economic characteristics that show high potential for tourism development. The contribution analyzes the importance of adequate infrastructures in the development of a wine tourism market, but also expresses and substantiates the idea (inspired by Getz, 2000) that wine tourism can be viewed as a form of consumer behavior, as a local development strategy and as a direct selling opportunity for wineries, highly impacted by an emerging "tourism of taste", seeking to enhance other senses apart from the visual.

Craft beer tourism

Craft beer tourism is a sub-niche of agritourism that has emerged relatively recently in comparison with wine tourism, following the success of the so-called "craft beer revolution" (Reid & Gartell, 2015). There is a growing debate on the role of craft beverages in general, and on craft beer tourism in particular, in both urban regeneration and rural development (see, i.e. Dunn & Wickham, 2016; Gatrell, Reid, & Steiger, 2017; Gómez-Corona et al., 2016; Hede & Watne, 2013; Kline, Slocum, & Cavaliere, 2017; Plummer et al., 2005; Rogerson & Collins, 2015).

A key question in this regard is whether and how craft beer tourism is helping in redefining tourism destinations, particularly in relation to sense of place (Cross, 2001) and authenticity (Zhu, 2012).

According to many, the recent success of craft beer production is to be found in a renewed attention to neolocalism (Holtkamp et al., 2016) and in the forms of consumption associated with craft beers, often entailing unique experiences (Pine & Gilmore, 2014), i.e. within dedicated festivals and/or beer trails. Moreover, the number of craft breweries in rural areas is beginning to increase, due to the availability of raw materials.

In Chapter 9, Arbogast, Kozlowski and Eades have analyzed the linkages between tourism, authenticity and craft beer in West Virginia, USA, to demonstrate ways in which different stakeholders can cooperate effectively to build a tourism development model relying on breweries and craft beer consumption. In this case, as in many others in this edited book, cooperation as well as the creation of networks among producers is deemed to be an efficient and successful strategy to diversify the tourism brand and redefine the state's identity as a destination, fostering local development.

In this sense, the spatial distribution of craft breweries in the US has been widely analyzed in Chapter 10, by Crawley and Gabe, who demonstrated that breweries became more geographically dispersed across regions since 2001, although unevenly within the country. These results help our understanding of the relationship between the location of breweries and peripheral areas favorable for tourism development, in particular for what the authors define as "beercations": holidays built around visiting as many breweries as possible. Moreover, the authors recognize the challenges posed by the fact that the craft beer sector has gained momentum in the last decade, but is currently witnessing a relative decline as a result of stabilization of the market; therefore, identifying areas for potential further development of such a tourism niche becomes pivotal in the longer run.

Skoglund and Sjölander, in Chapter 11, present a study based in a peripheral region in northern Sweden, which is an interesting case because the area is currently developing a flourishing craft beer sector, after having witnessed a decline of large-scale brewing. In such a scenario, understanding the success and growth of craft beer production from the producers' perspective sheds light on the hindrances and opportunities provided by the relationship between entrepreneurial motivation and initiative, product heritage and identity, tourism, and local development in rural regions.

In the last contribution in this edited collection (Chapter 12), Pezzi focuses her attention on a recently established network of craft breweries, microbreweries and the so-called "agricultural craft breweries" in a peripheral area of the Marche region in Italy, created under the premises of a wider, state-led, development strategy aimed at triggering the development of peripheral areas in the country, through tourism, among other things. Through her analysis of the ongoing processes of craft beer culture and heritage-making strategies, as well as of the ideation of a coherent territorial marketing campaign, she identifies a number of advantages in the creation of a tourism-led development path that heavily relies on high-quality products, as craft beers have become to be perceived: recognition, attraction, differentiation, identification and incorporation of the taste of a place.

References

Abram, S. (1998). Introduction. Anthropological perspectives on local development. In S. Abram & J. Waldren (Eds.), *Anthropological Perspectives on Local Development* (pp. 1–17). London and New York: Routledge.

Adell, N., Bendix, R. F., Bortolotto, C., & Tauschek, M. (Eds.). (2015). *Between Imagined Communities and Communities of Practice: Participation, Territory and the Making of Heritage. Göttingen Studies in Cultural Property* (Vol. 8). Göttingen: Universitätsverlag Göttingen.

Ana, R., & Lubiński, O. (2018). Cuban private entrepreneurship – from periphery to key sector of the economy in tourism-oriented market socialism. *Regional Science Policy & Practice.* https://doi.org/10.1111/rsp3.12154

Andreoli, A., & Silvestri, F. (2017). Tourism as a driver of development in the Inner Areas. *IJPP – Italian Journal of Planning Practice, VII*(1), 80–99.

Ardener, E. (2012, June 19). Remote areas: Some theoretical considerations. *HAU: Journal of Ethnographic Theory.* https://doi.org/https://doi.org/10.14318/hau2.1.023

Backman, M., Klaesson, J., & Öner, Ö. (2017). Innovation in the hospitality industry. *Tourism Economics, 23*(8), 1591–1614. https://doi.org/10.1177/1354816617715159

Barca, F., McCann, P., & Rodríguez-Pose, A. (2012). The case for regional development intervention: Place-based versus place-neutral approaches. *Journal of Regional Science, 52*(1), 134–152. https://doi.org/10.1111/j.1467-9787.2011.00756.x

Bender, O., & Kanitscheider, S. (2012). New immigration into the European Alps: Emerging research issues. *Mountain Research and Development, 32*(2), 235–241. https://doi.org/10.1659/MRD-JOURNAL-D-12-00030.1

Bessière, J. (1998). Local development and heritage: Traditional food and cuisine as tourist attractions in rural areas. *Sociologia Ruralis, 38*(1), 21–34. https://doi.org/10.1111/1467-9523.00061

Bessière, J. (2013). 'Heritagisation', a challenge for tourism promotion and regional development: An example of food heritage. *Journal of Heritage Tourism, 8*(4), 275–291. https://doi.org/10.1080/1743873X.2013.770861

Bessiere, J., & Tibere, L. (2013). Traditional food and tourism: French tourist experience and food heritage in rural spaces. *Journal of the Science of Food and Agriculture, 93*(14), 3420–3425. https://doi.org/10.1002/jsfa.6284

Brouder, P. (2014). Evolutionary economic geography and tourism studies: Extant studies and future research directions. *Tourism Geographies, 16*(4), 540–545. https://doi.org/10.1080/14616688.2014.947314

Buhalis, D. (1999). Limits of tourism development in peripheral destinations: Problems and challenges. *Tourism Management, 20*(2), 183–185.

Bujdosó, Z., Dávid, L., Tőzsér, A., Kovács, G., Major-Kathi, V., Uakhitova, G., ... Vasvári, M. (2015). Basis of heritagization and cultural tourism development. *Procedia – Social and Behavioral Sciences, 188*, 307–315. https://doi.org/10.1016/j.sbspro.2015.03.399

Calzada, I. (2018). Local entrepreneurship through a multistakeholders' tourism living lab in the post-violence/peripheral era in the Basque Country. *Regional Science Policy & Practice*. https://doi.org/10.1111/rsp3.12130

Chaperon, S., & Bramwell, B. (2013). Dependency and agency in peripheral tourism development. *Annals of Tourism Research, 40*(1), 132–154. https://doi.org/10.1016/j.annals.2012.08.003

Copus, A. (2001). From core-periphery to polycentric development: Concepts of spatial and aspatial peripherality. *European Planning Studies, 9*(4), 539–552. https://doi.org/10.1080/713666491

Copus, A., Mantino, F., & Noguera, J. (2017). Inner peripheries: An oxymoron or a real challenge for territorial cohesion? *Italian Journal of Planning Practice, VII*(1), 24–49.

Cross, J. E. (2001). What is sense of place? In *Archives of the Twelfth Headwaters Conference*, Colorado State University Libraries (https://mountainscholar.org/handle/10217/180311).

Cullen, B., & Pretes, M. (2000). The meaning of marginality: Interpretations and perceptions in social science. *Social Science Journal, 37*(2), 215–229. https://doi.org/10.1016/S0362-3319(00)00056-2

Di Bella, A., Petino, G., & Scrofani, L. (2019). The Etna macro-region between peripheralization and innovation: Towards a smart territorial system based on tourism. *Regional Science Policy & Practice*. https://doi.org/10.1111/rsp3.12176

Dinis, A. (2006). Marketing and innovation: Useful tools for competitiveness in rural and peripheral areas. *European Planning Studies, 14*(1), 9–22. https://doi.org/10.1080/09654310500339083

Dunn, A., & Wickham, M. (2016). Craft brewery tourism best-practices: A research agenda. *Annals of Tourism Research, 56*. https://doi.org/10.1016/j.annals.2015.10.009

Eimermann, M., Tillberg Mattsson, K., & Carson, D. A. (2018). International tourism entrepreneurs in Swedish peripheries: Compliance and collision with public tourism strategies. *Regional Science Policy & Practice*. https://doi.org/10.1111/rsp3.12148

Gatrell, J. D., Reid, N., & Steiger, T. L. (2017). Branding spaces: Place, region, sustainability and the American craft beer industry. *Applied Geography, 90*, 1–32.

Getz, D. (2000). *Exploring Wine Tourism: Management, Development and Destinations*. New York: Cognizant Communication Corporation.

Gómez-Corona, C., Escalona-Buendía, H. B., García, M., Chollet, S., & Valentin, D. (2016). Craft vs. industrial: Habits, attitudes and motivations towards beer consumption in Mexico. *Appetite, 96*, 358–367. https://doi.org/10.1016/j.appet.2015.10.002

Grabher, G. (2018). Marginality as strategy: Leveraging peripherality for creativity. *Environment and Planning A, 50*(8), 1785–1794. https://doi.org/10.1177/0308518X18784021

Hall, C. M., & Gössling, S. (2016a). *Food Tourism and Regional Development: Networks, Products and Trajectories* (C. M. Hall & S. Gössling, Eds.). London and New York: Routledge.

Hall, C. M., & Gössling, S. (2016b). From food tourism and regional development to foood, tourism and regional development: Themes and issues in contemporary foodscapes. In M. C. Hall & S. Gössling (Eds.), *Food Tourism and Regional Development: Networks, Products and Trajectories* (pp. 3–58). London and New York: Routledge.

Hall, C. M., Harrison, D., Weaver, D., & Wall, G. (2013). Vanishing peripheries: Does tourism consume places? *Tourism Recreation Research, 38*(1), 71–92. https://doi.org/10.1080/02508281.2013.11081730

Hall, C. M., & Mitchell, R. (2000). "We are what we eat": Food, tourism, and globalization. *Tourism, Culture & Communication, 2*(64), 29–37.

Hall, C. M., Sharples, L., Mitchell, R., Macionis, N., & Cambourne, B. (2008). Food tourism around the world: Development, management and markets. *Elsevier*, 1–390. https://doi.org/10.1016/B978-0-7506-5503-3.50005-1

Hede, A.-M., & Watne, T. (2013). Leveraging the human side of the brand using a sense of place: Case studies of craft breweries. *Journal of Marketing Management, 29*(1–2), 207–224. https://doi.org/10.1080/0267257X.2012.762422

Holtkamp, C., Shelton, T., Daly, G., Hiner, C. C., & Hagelman, R. R. (2016). Assessing neolocalism in microbreweries. *Papers in Applied Geography, 2*(1), 66–78. https://doi.org/10.1080/23754931.2015.1114514

Huggins, R., & Thompson, P. (2015). Culture and place-based development: A socio-economic analysis. *Regional Studies, 49*(1), 130–159. https://doi.org/10.1080/0034 3404.2014.889817

Jiang, Y., Ramkissoon, H., Mavondo, F. T., & Feng, S. (2017). Authenticity: The link between destination image and place attachment. *Journal of Hospitality Marketing & Management, 26*(2), 105–124. https://doi.org/10.1080/19368623.2016.1185988

Kastenholz, E., & Figueiredo, E. (2014). Rural tourism experiences. Land, sense and experience-scapes in quest of new tourist spaces and sustainable community development. *Pasos: Revista de Turismo y Patrimonio Cultural, 12*(3), 511–514.

Kline, C., Slocum, S. L., & Cavaliere, C. T. (Eds.). (2017). *Craft Beverages and Tourism. Volume 1.* New York: Palgrave MacMillan.

Komppula, R. (2014). The role of individual entrepreneurs in the development of competitiveness for a rural tourism destination – A case study. *Tourism Management, 40*, 361–371. https://doi.org/10.1016/j.tourman.2013.07.007

Kühn, M. (2015). Peripheralization: Theoretical concepts explaining socio-spatial inequalities. *European Planning Studies, 23*(2), 367–378. https://doi.org/10.1080/0 9654313.2013.862518

Lai, K., & Li, Y. (2012). Core-periphery structure of destination image. Concept, Evidence and Implication. *Annals of Tourism Research, 39*(3), 1359–1379. https://doi.org/10.1016/j.annals.2012.02.008

Leik, B., & Lang, T. (2018). Re-thinking non-core regions: Planning strategies and practices beyond growth. *European Planning Studies, 2*(August), 0–30. https://doi.org/10.1080/09654313.2017.1363398

Madden, M., & Shipley, R. (2012). An analysis of the literature at the nexus of heritage, tourism, and local economic development. *Journal of Heritage Tourism, 7*(2), 103–112. https://doi.org/10.1080/1743873X.2011.632483

Mantegazzi, D., Pezzi, M. G., & Punziano, G. (forthcoming). Tourism planning and tourism development in the Italian Inner Areas: Assessing coherence in policy-making strategies. In Ö. Öner, M. Ferrante, & O. Fritz (Eds.), *Regional Science Perspectives in Tourism and Hospitality*. Dordrecht: Springer.

Martin, R., & Sunley, P. (2006). Path dependence and regional economic evolution. *Journal of Economic Geography, 6*(4), 395–437. https://doi.org/10.1093/jeg/lbl012

Mayaka, M., Croy, W. G., & Cox, J. W. (2017). Participation as motif in community-based tourism: A practice perspective. *Journal of Sustainable Tourism*, 1–17. https://doi.org/10.1080/09669582.2017.1359278

Mitra, J. (2012). *Entrepreneurship, Innovation and Regional Development : An Introduction*. New York: Routledge.

Myles, C. C., Ed. (forthcoming). *Fermented Landscapes: Considering How Processes of Fermentation Drive Social and Environmental Change in (un)Expected Places and Ways*. Lincoln: University of Nebraska Press.

Novelli, M. (Ed.). (2005). *Niche Tourism: Contemporary Issue, Trends and Cases.* Oxford: Elsevier.

Pezzi, M. G., & Urso, G. (2016). Peripheral areas: Conceptualizations and policies. Editorial note. *Italian Journal of Planning Practice, VI*(1), 1–19.

Pfeilstetter, R. (2015). Heritage entrepreneurship. Agency-driven promotion of the Mediterranean diet in Spain. *International Journal of Heritage Studies, 21*(3), 215–231. https://doi.org/10.1111/j.1467-8330.1974.tb00606.x

Phillip, S., Hunter, C., & Blackstock, K. (2010). A typology for defining agritourism. *Tourism Management, 31*(6), 754–758. https://doi.org/10.1016/j.tourman.2009.08.001

Pine, B. J., & Gilmore, J.H. (2014). A leader's guide to innovation in the experience economy. *Strategy and Leadership, 42*(1): 24–29.

Plummer, R., Telfer, D., Hashimoto, A., & Summers, R. (2005). Beer tourism in Canada along the Waterloo–Wellington Ale Trail. *Tourism Management, 26*(3), 447–458. https://doi.org/10.1016/J.TOURMAN.2003.12.002

Reid, N., & Gartell, J. D. (2015). Brewing Growth. *Economic Development Journal, 14*(4), 4–12.

Rogerson, C. M., & Collins, K. J. E. (2015). Developing beer tourism in South Africa: International perspectives. *African Journal of Hospitality, Tourism and Leisure, 4*(41), 241–258.

Salvatore, R., Chiodo, E., & Fantini, A. (2018). Tourism transition in peripheral rural areas: Theories, issues and strategies. *Annals of Tourism Research, 68*(218), 41–51. https://doi.org/10.1016/j.annals.2017.11.003

Sidali, K. L., Kastenholz, E., & Bianchi, R. (2015). Food tourism, niche markets and products in rural tourism: Combining the intimacy model and the experience economy as a rural development strategy. *Journal of Sustainable Tourism, 23*(8–9), 37–41. https://doi.org/10.1080/09669582.2013.836210

Smith, M. K., & Robinson, M. (2006). *Cultural Tourism in a Changing World: Politics, Participation and (re) presentation. Tourism and Ciltural Change* (Vol. 7). Clevedon: Channel View Publications. https://doi.org/10.1016/j.annals.2006.11.005

Smith, S. (2015). A sense of place: Place, culture and tourism. *Tourism Recreation Research, 40*(2), 220–233. https://doi.org/10.1080/02508281.2015.1049814

Steinführer, A., Reichert-schick, A., Mose, I., & Grabski-kieron, U. (2018). European rural peripheries revalued ? Introduction to this volume. In Grabski-Kieron, U., Mose, I., Reichert-Schick, A., & Steinführer, A. (Eds.) (2016). *European Rural Peripheries Revalued* (Vol. 1). Münster: LIT Verlag.

Tosun, C. (2000). Limits to community participation in the tourism development process in developing countries. *Tourism Management, 21*(6), 613–633. https://doi.org/10.1016/S0261-5177(00)00009-1

Vittersø, G., & Amilien, V. (2011). From tourist product to ordinary food? *Anthropology of Food* [Online], 8. http://aof.revues.org/6833

Wanhill, S. (1997). Peripheral area tourism: A European perspective. *Progress in Tourism and Hospitality Research, 3*, 47–70. https://doi.org/10.1002/(SICI)1099-1603(199703)3:1<47::AID-PTH38>3.0.CO;2-F

Willett, J., & Lang, T. (2018). Peripheralisation: A politics of place, affect, perception and representation. *Sociologia Ruralis, 58*(2), 258–275. https://doi.org/10.1111/soru.12161

Zhu, Y. (2012). Performing heritage: Rethinking authenticity in tourism. *Annals of Tourism Research, 39*(3), 1495–1513. https://doi.org/10.1016/j.annals.2012.04.003

Part I

Agritourism

1 Targeting agritourism to leverage the unique natural resources base and heritage of the rural west

Anders Van Sandt, Dawn Thilmany, and Rebecca Hill

Agricultural-based rural tourism, more commonly labeled as "agritourism," is becoming a popular form of outdoor and heritage-based recreation in the US. This growth follows the lead of Europe and other parts of the world that find agritourism's linkages to culture, food and heritage to be a draw for visitors. Between 2002 and 2012, the number of agritourism establishments has grown by 42% in the US according to the US Census of Agriculture (USDA), and this growth can be connected to an overall increased demand for outdoor recreation. A recent USDA-funded survey indicates that around 8% of the adult population of the US participated in agritourism in the Western US, which could be extrapolated to estimate that there are 19 million annual agritourists in the US (based on US Census population statistics).

For this chapter, we assume that agritourism encompasses a diverse set of activities including you-pick-pumpkin patches, corn mazes, farmers markets, dude ranches, on-farm wineries and breweries along with events such as farm dinners and on-farm weddings. Since American agriculture and the rural communities that rely on the agricultural sector have undergone a major structural shift (Hoppe, 2014), there has been an increasing focus on enterprise diversification activities, including regional food systems and agritourism, that allow rural areas to capture more economic returns from those in urban areas interested in agriculture (Low et al., 2015; Van Sandt et al., 2018b). Past research explored producers' motivations for adopting agritourism, its economic impacts, as well as the overall demand for agritourism across the US. As a way to explore the managerial implications and competitive strategies that may be most effective for rural entrepreneurs focused on agritourism economic development strategies, this chapter explores both data from a travel cost model of visitors to the Western US and some specific case studies of communities that are leveraging the drivers discovered by the research. The overall goal of the chapter is to evaluate and compare the relative demand and elasticities for a variety of agritourism enterprises in the US, with a particular focus on how place matters, and opportunities to differentiate one's regional opportunities to travelers across a variety of peripheral areas.

Agritourism and rural development in the US

In the US, there is an increasing interest in rural economic development and specifically the roles that economic sectors that complement traditional base industries (such as farming and forestry) can play in the sustainable development of rural areas. Agritourism is one clear example. In addition to providing a diversification strategy that might supplement and smooth production income for US farmers, visitors to agritourism operations bring money to other businesses in rural communities. In short, the community development potential is also notable since visitors create economic impacts through their expenditures on lodging, dining, gas and other recreational expenditures while visiting the rural host community, and it follows that agritourism development strategies should be considered at the regional level.

Agritourism can be seen as an important asset in rural economic development, but by its very nature, the potential success of agritourism as a rural development tool is dependent on the unique geographical context of the rural community. A key example of this is the linkage between heritage tourism and agritourism, which can offer complementary experiences for travelers (Walden et al., 2013). For example, part of the Western US is known for its cowboy culture as well as its open spaces and scenic public lands, so it is logical that visitors to agritourism operations in that region may find higher value in activities that build on an experience that leverages these perceptions of regional heritage.

Agritourism is a unique form of rural entrepreneurship that is linked to a region's existing natural resource, economic and cultural base. Research has shown the important linkages between rural entrepreneurship, economic growth and rural poverty rates (Rupasingha and Goetz, 2013; Stephens and Partridge, 2011). Existing research on rural entrepreneurship has noted the important factors that enable a community to be able to make improvements in their wellbeing through entrepreneurship, together with the understanding that a community's existing natural capital is linked to their ability to improve their economic wellbeing (McGranahan et al., 2011). These linkages indicate that rural entrepreneurship has important policy implications and is an important tool in sustainable rural economic development initiatives. Still, there are differing views on the role of agritourism in community development outcomes. While some research has shown that rural tourism development has direct links to physical attributes of a region such as natural resources and amenities (Gartner, 2005), it may be that agritourism just as fully relies on adjacency to major transportation and population centers. It is likely that both play an important role, and in differing degrees, depending on the geographical region; so, place-based strategies are appropriate. One recent finding in the literature highlights agritourism's connection to place-based factors, including natural amenities and community assets. Evidence suggests that agritourism may be a complement to other types of outdoor recreation and tourism assets including National Parks Service lands (Van Sandt et al., 2018a, 2018b).

It appears that agricultural operators are more likely to adopt agritourism if they are located near a scenic byway, indicating that they are aware of the economic opportunities presented by the nearby flow of travelers seeking to explore a region (rather than taking freeways that offer more direct, efficient travel times). While some agritourism operations may be dependent on their proximity to urban markets or the flow of travelers passing through the area, Van Sandt et al. (2018a) also find evidence of agglomeration economies, indicating that individual agritourism establishments benefit from being located in a cluster of other agritourism businesses.

Data on past behavior of Western US agritourists

To develop a data-driven case study that could better inform those framing management strategies and policies to support agritourism development, a team of researchers from Colorado State University, University of California – Davis, University of Northern Colorado and the USDA Economic Research service secured a USDA National Institute of Food and Agriculture grant, "Place-Based Innovation: An Integrated Look at Agritourism in the Western U.S." in 2014. One goal of the project was to work with a national research organization to secure a rich dataset focused on agritourism travelers and to find trends in their past travel behavior (revealed preferences), while also soliciting information on a variety of preferences for future agritourism-related travel (stated preferences).

The traveler information was collected through an internet-based survey distributed by Taylor Nelson Sofres (TNS) in late April 2015. The survey used existing TNS participant panels to create a stratified regional and national sample of travelers, with a focus on agritourist to the Western Region, which included Montana, Wyoming, Colorado and Texas, as well as all states contiguous westward (Hawaii and Alaska were excluded). There were several benefits of collecting data through a research organization: one is the high response rate that pre-recruitment and incentives provide. Another benefit is a more balanced sample due to TNS's large and established panel of respondents. While participation in agritourism has been increasing over the years, without such a large set of potential respondents, finding our goal of 1,000 recent agritourists who had visited a wide variety of venues would be prohibitively difficult. Given a relatively low incidence rate within TNS's large established panel (8%), the final survey included 1,000 travelers who had visited agritourism sites in the Western Region, with an additional 500 non-agritourism travelers to serve as a comparative group. The entire survey, which included a choice experiment with 12 choice situations, was estimated to take participants 15–20 minutes to complete.

One unique goal of our survey was to gain an understanding of the varying degree of a traveler's motivations, and specifically whether the agritourism destination was the primary reason for their travel or if it represented a complementary or impulse excursion from their main trip. Combined, the surveys indicated that for the majority of agritourism visitors (72%), the agritourism site was the primary purpose of their trip. For the other 28% of respondents, agritourism represented a complementary excursion from their main trip (Van Sandt et al., 2018b). Since a sizeable share of visitors are drawn by other recreation assets, considering the full suite of activities a community and a region offer to attract travelers, it is important to understand the potential that can be achieved through coordinated agritourism development.

Learning from traveler behavior: travel cost methods applied to agritourism

Given the goal to explore the linkages between economic values that visitors receive from their agritourism trip and how these values are linked to different community attributes, we creatively match travel survey data with spatial factors of the areas where tourists traveled. One key element of the survey is a travel cost analysis that allows us to construct and compare the demand for a variety of different agritourism activities and characteristics based on the assumption that time spent traveling to a destination indicates something about the opportunity costs of that excursion, above and beyond any direct costs paid by the traveler. The travel cost method (TCM) has been used since the 1970s as a tool to estimate consumer surplus (CS) for a variety of natural resource sites and locations, and seemed particularly appropriate for this analysis as it allows for spatial variation.

Although less direct than an economic impact or cost analysis, CS is relevant because it signals untapped market potential since it is the estimated dollar value of the benefit to the consumer from participating in an activity, beyond any fees paid. Since the TCM captures the benefit consumers received by treating the cost of traveling to the site as a proxy for what the consumer was willing to pay for the activity in question, it is particularly useful for peripheral areas, where potential barriers related to being remote may otherwise be left unexamined. For this analysis, relevant survey data on agritourists includes the number of trips an individual took, the expenditures incurred while on these trips, as well as the distance they traveled. Using a seminal methodological approach, this data allows one to estimate a demand curve and then to infer the relative price sensitivity among agritourists from a variety of types of trips (through the estimation of price elasticities).

However, some special measures were taken to account for varying motivations among travelers. The standard form of the TCM assumes that costs related to travel are always incurred for a single-purpose recreation trip, but is not always realistic, especially for rural, peripheral areas. Assuming travelers travel longer distances to reach rural areas, they may choose to bundle multiple destinations and activities in a single trip in order to maximize their utility relative to the travel costs necessary to reach more remote destinations. This can make it difficult to isolate the benefits that are generated from an agritourism trip from those benefits generated from other destinations in the broader tourism sector.

If one assumes that, for some set of travelers, the natural and heritage resource base of an area is a strong attractor, multi-destination trips and linkages with other tourism assets are important factors in understanding the potential success of agritourism for a community and farm enterprise. To account for the multiple destinations and activities that agritourists participate in, the survey specifically solicited detailed information on incremental travel costs incurred. Then, survey findings were analyzed along with information on specific agritourism sites and visitor types to group findings as a strategy to disentangle different motivations and how they may influence the value of site attributes.

As a first step, agritourists' costs were treated differently if they identified an agritourism destination as the primary purpose of their travel (referred to as PP travelers). Then, as a complementary analysis, findings on how travelers to multiple destinations (referred to as MD travelers) may value agritourism activities differently provide an interesting comparison to the primary traveler results (Van Sandt and Thilmany, 2018). There are a broad range of activities that can be considered agritourism; the four different agritourism activity categories that were evaluated are defined as follows:

1 **On-Farm Direct Sales (DTC)**: U-pick, farm stand, farm store selling fresh fruits, nuts, vegetables, herbs, nursery products, Christmas trees, flowers, meats, eggs or processed fruit or vegetable products, dairy, fibers, wine, beer, spirits, juices, oil, baked goods, soaps, lotions or other farm-produced products.
2 **Entertainment/Special Events (Ent & Events)**: weddings, wine tours, farm dinners, family reunions, retreats, festivals, barn dances, corn or other mazes, haunted houses, sports events, games, hay rides, train rides, concerts, pig races, pony rides, etc.
3 **Outdoor Recreation (Out Rec)**: bicycle rides, picnicking, swimming, hunting, fishing, bird watching, photography hikes/classes, snowmobiling, horseback riding and skeet shooting taking place on a farm or ranch.
4 **Educational Activities (Edu)**: farm or ranch work experience, historical excursions, artisan food demonstrations, food preservation classes, camps, classes, tours, tastings, demonstrations, workshops, petting zoos, egg gathering, etc.

An important note related to these four different agritourism activities is that often an agritourism enterprise will offer more than one of these choices, and subsequently, agritourists in our survey often report being involved in multiple activities. Thus, "part-worth" CS estimates and elasticities that embody a consumer's experience with a specific activity in a specific region were estimated to separate out different regions' and activities' effects on demand (Tables 1.2 and 1.3). The fact that these are part-worth estimates implies that some estimates for an activity or a region may be positive or negative, signaling agritourism experiences that are more elastic or inelastic (since a traveler would consider the sum of their part-worth CS estimates).

While it is understandable that agritourism demand varies across regions, differences in agritourists' behavior are unlikely to adhere to administrative boundaries, such as state lines. Given this issue, we developed seven different "agritourism zones" identified by including 13 variables from secondary data sources that were found to be important factors in agritourism enterprise location decisions (see Bagi and Reeder, 2012; Van Sandt et al., 2018b) using principal components analysis (PCA)[1] to develop an "agritourism score" for each county. These "scores" were then used to inform the visual identification of seven agritourism regions in the Western US: the Northwest, Northern Plains, Mountain, Southern Plains, Southwest, Central and Northern California. The percentage of survey visitors to each region differed with only 1.64% of agritourists taking trips to the Central region and 26.17% of agritourists taking trips to the Southwest region.[2] Not surprisingly, some of the frequency patterns align with population centers (Van Sandt et al., 2018a), but other differences in visitation rates are likely due to natural or man-made tourism attractions, travel infrastructure and the number of agritourism sites. Given the low incidence of agritourists in the Central and Northern Plains regions, these two regions were aggregated to provide more robust estimates.

Another interesting aspect of the PCA was that it allowed us to identify specific counties that were more conducive to agritourism, based on farm sales, population, agritourism revenues, distance from a population center, natural amenities, scenic byways, interstates, distance to a national park, as well as county's dependency on farm and recreation sectors. Given their intensity of those variables, and estimates of marginal effects, the darkly shaded counties are those that are especially conducive to agritourism.

From a rural development perspective, the most intriguing use of the elasticities derived from the CS values is their potential to identify regional comparative advantages. That is, if you were to establish a new site or promote a cluster of agritourism businesses, what activities should you offer, and to whom to increase your likelihood of success? These findings help to identify the set of activities that are likely to generate the greatest attraction or value to consumers.

For example, if one region seems to dominate as a magnet for agritourists, in this case by showing more inelastic demand (less price sensitivity) for an activity, other regions should recognize the competitive challenge and perhaps offer an alternative activity that plays to the strengths of their own farms, ranches and broader tourism enterprises. Beyond farms and ranches, tourism development practitioners can use these findings to more effectively invest resources in programming that will create the largest draw for tourists in their region.

A discussion of agritourism demand and values to agritourists

Given the diverse history, heritage and natural resources of the Western US, it is not surprising that demand for agritourism activities would differ depending on the region in which it is hosted. Based on travel cost survey data and TCM analysis, one can infer that demand for agritourism differs significantly across geographical regions and activity. For example, a niche destination, with unique offerings (world-class wines such as the Napa Valley) or locational assets (adjacent to a national park with private access to rivers or mountain trails), might make demand more inelastic, and subsequently, travelers' price sensitivity will be relatively low. In contrast, more conventional destinations, like a farm stands or pumpkin patches, can be found near many urban areas, but have enough similar offerings across destinations such that demand will vary little across the US.

A more detailed description of the travel cost modeling process and the estimation of CS and own-price elasticity estimates can be found in the Appendix and in Tables 1.2 and 1.3; we preserve this section for the discussion of the model's results[3] and present only those results that are statistically significant. The resulting CS estimates provide a basis for the price elasticities and figures presented to guide this discussion. Unlike a traditional elasticity, exploring the relationship between price and volume of sales, in this case, here it is defined as the percentage change in the number of visitors (independent of revenue) to an agritourism site from a 1% change in price (in this case, the imputed travel cost) for a certain region or activity to provide more managerial intuition.

It may be surprising to see positive part-worths in the case of demand (where higher prices generally mean lower demand), but it is important to remember that the overall elasticity for the whole trip is still negative. So, activity-specific part effects show how that price sensitivity will relatively increase or decrease relative to a "representative trip," allowing for a comparative analysis across regions and activities, depending on consumer preferences, perceived attributes of agritourism sites and the other substitute recreational experiences in the region. Overall, the range of partial own-price elasticities suggests that agritourism trips are relatively inelastic recreational experiences; however, differences still exist within regions and activities. Demand curves for different agritourism activities by traveler type are shown in Figure 1.1, while partial own-price elasticities are presented in Table 1.1.

Beyond seeing differences in demand curves across traveler activities (as seen in Figure 1.1a,b), some regions exhibit relatively flatter demand curves, suggesting more price sensitivity (for example, Central/Northern Plains region for primary travelers and Northern California for multi-destination travelers). The relatively flatter demand curves in these regions make sense if you consider that the very remote location of the Northern Plains implies a large travel cost to visit; so, travelers may be relatively sensitive to investing in travel time and miles. In contrast, for the small share of those

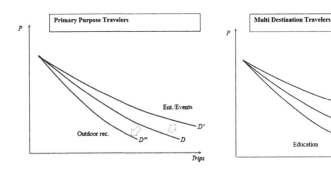

Figure 1.1 Demand curves for primary and multi-destination traveler activities.

Table 1.1 Partial own-price elasticities for Western US agritourists, by activity and region

Activity	Primary purpose	Multi-destination
Direct to consumer	0.0219	0.0245
Events and entertainment	0.1126	0.0440
Outdoor recreation	−0.0336	0.0277
Education	0.0243	−0.0004
Region		
Mountain	−0.0226	−0.0364
Southwest	−0.0335	−0.0421
Central/Northern Plains	0.0127	−0.0074
Northern California	−0.0457	0.0048
Northwest	−0.0061	−0.0113
Texas	−0.0191	−0.0303

All elasticities are calculated at the variable's means and results from Van Sandt and Thilmany (2018).

Source: Based on 2015 US traveler survey results, Van Sandt and Thilmany (2018).

Table 1.2 Primary purpose visitors' partial consumer's surplus estimates

	$Mntn^1$	SW^2	$CtNP^3$	$NoCal^4$	NW^5	$SoPlns^6$
DTC[A]	\$ 657.89[ALL]	\$ 518.13[ALL]	\$ −121.21	\$ 135.69[ALL]	\$ 362.32[ALL]	\$ 338.98[ALL]
Std. Error	*4.980704*	*2.194955*	*1.052026*	*0.308093*	*6.091764*	*0.900318*
Ent. & Events[B]	\$ −196.85	\$ −214.13	\$ −67.34	\$ 1,298.7[ALL]	\$ −260.42	\$ −273.97
Std. Error	*0.61573*	*0.529253*	*0.322723*	*9.276213*	*3.678631*	*1.928271*
Out Rec.[C]	\$ 140.65[ALL]	\$ 132.98[ALL]	\$ −375.94	\$ 77.16[ALL]	\$ 119.76[ALL]	\$ 117.10[ALL]
Std. Error	*0.227238*	*0.131972*	*12.73976*	*0.10614*	*0.650379*	*0.142181*
Edu[D]	\$ 917.43[ALL]	\$ 666.67[ALL]	\$ −115.21	\$ 144.09[ALL]	\$ 429.18[ALL]	\$ 396.83[ALL]
Std. Error	*10.75081*	*4.752308*	*0.941027*	*0.373352*	*8.699483*	*1.378283*

Note: Superscripts indicate whether there were significant differences across the CS estimates from other activities (A, B, C, D) and other regions (1, 2, 3, 4, 5, 6); ALL indicates that differences are significant across all other activities.

Table 1.3 Multi-destination visitors' partial consumer's surplus estimates

Model 8	Mntn[1]	SW[2]	CtNP[3]	NoCal[4]	NW[5]	SoPlns[6]
DTC[A]	$ 47.17[236,C]	$ 21.01[1356,BD]	$ 7.43[1256,D]	$ −10.48	$ 72.46[236,D]	$ 14.79[1235,BD]
Std. Error	*5.905498*	*0.40997*	*1.197091*	*4.906431*	*0.789432*	*0.376891*
Ent. & Events[B]	$ 263.16	$ 33.11[36,ACD]	$ 8.53[26D]	$ −8.87	$ −277.78	$ 19.92[23,ACD]
Std. Error	*2.383188*	*0.338322*	*1.863261*	*25.1675*	*0.538602*	*0.502403*
Outdoor Rec.[C]	$ 39.68[236,D]	$ 19.38[1356,BD]	$ 7.22[1256,D]	$ −10.94	$ 56.18[236,D]	$ 13.97[1235,BD]
Std. Error	*44.15173*	*1.041223*	*0.585101*	*0.967293*	*3.839151*	*0.232386*
Education[D]	$ 13.35[236,AC]	$ 9.87[ALL]	$ 5.31[ALL]	$ −23.98	$ 14.82[236,AC]	$ 8.24[ALL]
Std. Error	*7.331792*	*1.586491*	*0.468797*	*0.678145*	*10.9298*	*0.197574*

Note: Superscripts indicate whether there were significant differences across the CS estimates from other activities (A, B, C, D) and other regions (1, 2, 3, 4, 5, 6); ALL indicates that differences are significant across all other activities.

visiting Northern California who are not there specifically for agritourism, the perceived expensive nature of its sites may lead demand to be more elastic (Table 1.1).

It is interesting to note that the partial elasticities for activities are mostly positive, and that those activities typically associated with higher participation fees or with substitute recreational choices in the eyes of travelers, such as entertainment and events are relatively more elastic compared to outdoor recreation (which may have minimal user/entrance fees). Yet, for some outdoor activities that may have significant costs associated with them, such as guided hunting in the Mountain and Texas regions, outdoor recreation may be more price-inelastic given few substitute enterprises that offer the same experience.

There are several insights one can draw from these findings. First, estimates illustrate the notable visibility and reputation of some regions for some agritourism activities. As an example, the comparative advantage of Northern California with respect to drawing primary travelers is evident: the relatively large and negative elasticity for that region among primary purpose travelers suggests that the draw of that region is sufficient to garner interest, regardless of direct expenditures (cash costs) or distance (travel cost). Although a bit smaller, the Southwest and Mountain regions also have relatively inelastic demand estimates, which is unsurprising given the unique natural assets of that region (national parks, forests and monuments). But, unlike the Northern California, these regions also seem to have less price sensitivity among multi-destination travelers, consistent with the logic of agritourism benefitting from complementary recreational opportunities that may draw travelers to the region.

The patterns among activities are a little more nuanced, and worth discussion. Among primary travelers, almost all part-worth elasticities for activities are positive, suggesting that those participating will be more price sensitive in comparison to the one negative part-worth[4] (on outdoor recreation in this case). What this indicates is that those travelers coming with a goal of primarily participating in agritourism activities that are enhanced by the natural assets of the Western US are the least price sensitive. Or, in short, there is the greatest opportunity to further develop enterprises and revenues in the outdoor recreation space. In contrast, the other activities may still be in demand, but because they will be viewed as having at least some recreational substitute options, operators will need to be more careful to price their offerings competitively.

For multi-destination travelers, a similar pattern exists, but in this case, it is educational activities that may face more inelastic demand (although significantly negative, the effect is low in magnitude). Still, for other multi-destination activities, price sensitivity is an issue, and this finding is only more complicated when one realizes that the trip included agritourism as just one of a set of stops those travel parties chose. So, understanding broader travel behavior in one's region and community, perhaps through participation in regional tourism collaboratives, becomes even more critical to making good enterprise development and marketing choices.

Considering specific region and activity combinations provides additional context. For example, the Mountain region's comparative advantage in outdoor recreation holds for both primary and multiple-destination travelers. Of the agritourists surveyed, 19% of those indicating agritourism was a secondary destination listed a state or national park, beach or forest as their primary destination (Van Sandt et al., 2018b). In short, the agritourism industry in areas that are rich in other outdoor recreation tourism opportunities may benefit from linking and cross promoting with their natural resource sites to capture visits from tourists who are already traveling to the area. Each one of the seven regions likely has some subset of natural assets that could be considered as a key "attraction" to travelers to their area, even if not as pronounced as the Mountain, Southwest or Northwest regions with high-profile parks and recreational sectors. Figure 1.1 provides a visual context for these findings, as agritourism operations may face less price sensitivity from tourists seeking outdoor recreation as a primary draw for their travels if they are successful in converting them into multi-destination tourists. As one example, educational activities framed to complement nearby attractions (identifying birds or plants nearby a national forest, cooking classes associated with a major ethnic or Native settlement) can leverage the unique cultural and heritage assets of a community to draw in potential visitors. The Southwest and Mountain regions have reputations related to a rich cowboy culture and history, and were found to be highly valued by travelers (Van Sandt and Thilmany, 2018).

Across all regions, one thing that cannot be forgotten is the importance of a base population and travel infrastructure. The combined Central/Northern Plains had more elastic demand among both set of travelers, and this is likely due to this region's sparse population and relatively remote destinations. While both of these regions offer pristine landscapes and abundant outdoor recreation opportunities, the cost of traveling to a primary destination in these regions is less competitive, given the relatively easier accessibility to other regions with similar offerings. This does not mean that there is no potential for agritourism development in these rural communities; it just means that different strategies may need to be developed. What is clear from our TCM analysis and demand estimates for different types of agritourism visitors is that geographical context must be considered. Since there is no a one-size-fits-all strategy for agritourism development, identifying case studies that compare different approaches may provide important lessons to consider for entrepreneurs in this sector.

Two case studies exploring important linkages for agritourism success

While data-driven analysis and estimates can provide important indicators when investigating linkages between travelers, locations and activities, even greater insights can be gained when real-world qualitative examples are integrated into the discussion. Subsequently, part of the aforementioned USDA NIFA grant sought to evaluate two different case study regions with distinctly different agritourism strategies, one located in the Northern California, and the other, a comparative analysis of two communities in the Mountain and Northern Plains regions. In these case studies, we look at specific communities to explore results found by Van Sandt et al. (2018b). These results indicate that agritourism sites tend to earn more revenues when they are surrounded by a cluster of other agritourism sites to draw visitors to an area. Visitors are attracted by the choice of multiple activities within a small travel radius; so, agritourism may benefit from joint promotion, programming and information sharing.

The first case study focuses on Butte County which is a primarily rural county located on the eastern edge of Sacramento Valley in Northern California (Hardesty and Leff, 2018). Butte County tends to draw tourists because of its natural beauty and outdoor recreational activities. Existing natural resources that the community leverages include its proximity to two wildlife refuges, the North Table Mountain Ecological preserve, more than 50 waterfalls and a designated scenic byway. In addition, Butte County's chief economic driver is agriculture, with almonds and rice providing 77% of the county's agricultural income (Butte County Agricultural Commissioner, 2016). Given the region's natural outdoor recreation amenities and large agricultural economy, Butte County identified agritourism as a potential economic development driver for the region.

Agritourism development in the area faces several challenges including the commodity-based nature of their agricultural production (as opposed to vineyards which are prevalent in other areas of California) as well as the remoteness of the county. The community is approximately a 1.5-hour drive from a large urban center and a 2-hour drive from the nearest national park, Lassen National Park. This relative remoteness, partnered with its lack of clustered venues, represents challenges that the community faces in their development of an agritourism industry. In an effort to build their agritourism reputation, the County has organized festivals revolving around the apple harvest as well as a California nut festival, but has as of yet not fully developed the potential of these food heritage assets as a lever to strategically draw outside tourists. In addition, they have implemented three different local initiatives – the Sierra Oro Farm Trails Passport Weekend, Explore Butte County and Butte County's Unique Agriculture overlay – to increase agritourism activity in the region as a rural and community economic development strategy. Butte County was chosen for a case study as they have identified agritourism as an economic development strategy and begun to develop a plan to strengthen and promote agritourism as a visitor draw to the region.

For this case study, researchers interviewed agritourism operations and identified opportunities and challenges for the community. Some of the identified opportunities involve better leveraging the natural resources in the area, for example, installing kiosk stations promoting agritourism destinations at the existing, well-known and well-trafficked, tourist destinations. Identified challenges revolve around the remote location as well as community-level infrastructure needs, such as roads and road signs, for the region to support more tourists in the area. Survey results (survey conducted in 2015) indicated that currently in the county, operations offering agritourism were only open for agritourism activities 52 days a year, 85% of their agritourism came from direct sales (and none offered lodging or outdoor recreation activities) and that they earned less than $25,000 each in agritourism revenue. Overall, the conclusions from interviews with producers and other key stakeholders are that the community will need to address the location-based challenges that they face in order to ensure the successful expansion of agritourism in Butte County.

The second case study also illustrates how natural amenities can be important levers for community development, but compares two communities' ability to use these natural resources to their benefit and illustrates how the dynamics of agritourism may be dependent on a variety of other community characteristics (Gaede and Hill, 2018). The first region studied was a three-county area (Moffat, Rio Blanco and Routt) in the upper Northwest corner of Colorado. This region is endowed with beautiful mountain ranges as well as the popular tourist attraction, Dinosaur National Monument. The second region of interest is located relatively close by in Southwest Wyoming. Just like Northwest Colorado, Southwest Wyoming has a number of natural amenities including the Flaming Gorge National Recreation Area and Ashley National Forest, well known for its access to fishing. In addition, the area benefits from being adjacent to both an Interstate (I-80) and scenic byway that carry a stream of tourists on route to Yellowstone National Park.

While both regions have popular outdoor recreation-based sectors, because of their different community and regional assets, their current approaches to address opportunities and challenges for agritourism-based rural development appear very different. The Colorado Tourism Office has provided numerous resources for agritourism development and marketing and Northwestern Colorado to promote itself as a "hotspot" for agritourism. Specifically, the region has focused on agritourism related to the heritage of cattle and sheep ranches. Many of the ranches that are involved in agritourism in this area coordinate and train with the Colorado Department of Parks and Wildlife to become professionally licensed outfitters.

In contrast, just across the border in Southwest Wyoming, interviews with agritourists indicated that the promotion that attracted them to the site was discovered at the local level, commonly originating from the Chambers of Commerce in the nearby major cities. Unfortunately, such localized approaches may hinder the region's ability to tap into travelers that plan their itinerary ahead of the trip, thereby compromising their ability to tap the broader national and international markets. The Wyoming Office of Tourism is currently looking into a more coordinated approach for promotion. Those Southwest Wyoming ranchers who are entrepreneurial independently partnered with those offering hunting opportunities, a recreational enterprise that is very popular in Wyoming, but it seems that more could be done to make the region as a whole a better draw for agritourists.

Together with previous research findings on benefits to agglomeration among tourism destinations (Van Sandt et al., 2018a) and demand estimates presented earlier provides important context to the examples of how communities leverage, or could better leverage, the heritage, cultural and natural amenities in their region to support a successful agritourism industry. Unlike primary, extractive industries that will always feel the need to compete against globally derived prices that depend on cost competitiveness, agritourism allows communities to develop a differentiated economic model that can capture spending from outside the region if tourists see value in visiting. Moreover, given that successful tourism is likely to trigger further investment in natural resource improvements, infrastructure, cultural assets and public spaces, there may be benefits that outweigh the costs of such development to the citizens of the community.

Conclusions and looking forward

Agritourism has been shown to be an important driver of rural economic growth in several regions and can lead to positive outcomes for both agricultural operations and their surrounding communities. The connection agritourism has with rural development motivates the need to understand and strategically plan for how the unique natural resources and heritage of an area can help support the successful development or expansion of agritourism opportunities. It is our hope that the information gleaned about demand for agritourism and the values to tourists of their participation in different agritourism opportunities will enhance and inform the rural entrepreneurship and economic development field and practitioners.

Understanding the unique relationship between agritourism, place-based factors and resources, and the activities offered by farms and ranches can be used to help guide and better target policies and promotion activities in the Western US and other parts of the world with similar characteristics. As public and private entities make more investments in leveraging the interest in local foods, agriculture's heritage and the access to natural resources that farms and ranches steward, it is essential that traveler behavior and revealed demand are understood as key factors driving growth in this emerging sector. In our discussion, we also consider the challenges of tourism promotion and local development for those areas more distant from population centers and peripheral regions that would greatly benefit from economic flows and linkages to the purchasing power and disposable income aggregating in urban centers.

Appendix

Travel cost model estimation

The functional form for the travel cost method, which was used to develop estimates for part-worth CS and elasticities of demand estimates, regressed survey respondents' quantity of agritourism trips onto a set of demand determinants. This set of independent variables included interactions between the respondents' travel costs with the four different activity types and seven different agritourism regions, opportunity cost of time, intercept shifters for traveler type and activity type, McGranahan's natural amenities score, substitute prices, and respondents' gender, the natural log of income and age.[5] The opportunity cost of time was calculated by multiplying the respondent's travel time by one-third their wage rate.[6]

Due to the dependent variable being the quantity of agritourism trips taken by an agritourist survey respondent, a truncated negative binomial was employed to account for the count nature of the data and the presence of overdispersion. Employing the Newton Raphson search algorithm, the model was estimated via the maximum likelihood method and was statistically significant at the 1% level with a Wald Chi-squared test statistic of 149.76. Given the model was assumed to follow a truncated negative binomial distribution, the own-price elasticity of demand estimates were simply calculated by multiplying the coefficients for the TC interaction terms by the mean of that variable (Grogger and Carson, 1991). Part-worth CS estimates were calculated by taking the negative inverse of the relevant TC interaction term for each traveler type across regions and activities (Hill et al., 2014). While this calculation is slightly more complex than that for the elasticity estimates, it can be derived by taking the integral of the expected number of trips for the truncated negative binomial model between the choke-price and the market price (in this case, travel cost). Standard deviations were then developed for the CS estimates using Monte Carlo simulations to determine if the estimates were significantly different from one another, similar to Adamowicz et al. (1989).

Notes

1 The 13 county-level variables used in the PCA were average farm sales, population (2010), agritourism revenue/farm or ranch, total agritourism revenue, number of agritourism farms, travel time to a population of at least 250,000 from the county's population centroid, McGranahan's Natural Amenity Index, whether the county was farm dependent (2003), whether the county was recreation dependent (2004), miles of scenic byways per 100 square miles, miles of interstates per 100 square miles, travel time to a national parks service asset from the county's population centroid and the agritourism hot spot residuals from Van Sandt et al. (2018b). For more information on the relationship these variables share with agritourism enterprise location decisions, see Bagi and Reeder (2012) and Van Sandt et al. (2018b).

2 Survey visitation by region: Southwest 26.17%, Mountain 21.13%, Central 1.64%, Northern Plains 7.86%, Northern California 19.25%, Northwest 12.32% and Greater Texas 11.62%.

3 The appendices also include two tables with estimates of the per person consumer surplus (CS) results for the subset of travelers who denoted that the primary purpose of their trip was to participate in agritourism (primary purpose), and multiple-destination travelers (who denoted that their motivations were to visit a number of destinations on their trip, including at least one that is classified as agritourism).

4 Note that this interpretation is for a part-worth elasticity.

5 Similar to Benson et al. (2013), survey respondents' meals expenditures, recreation expenditures and shopping expenditures in the surrounding area of the agritourism site served as the substitute prices for agritourism activity.

6 A quarter of wage rate was also experimented with, but the differences between the two models were negligible.

References

Adamowicz, W.L., Fletcher, J.J., & Graham-Tomasi, T. (1989). Functional form and the statistical properties of welfare measures. *American Journal of Agricultural Economics*, 71, 414–421.

Bagi, F.S., & Reeder, R. (2012). Factors affecting farmer participation in agritourism. *Agricultural and Resource Economics Review*, 41(2), 189.

Benson, C., Watson, P., Taylor, G., Cook, P., & Hollenhorst, S. (2013). Who visits a national park and what do they get out of it? A joint visitor cluster analysis and travel cost model for Yellowstone National Park. *Environmental Management*, 52(4), 917–928.

Butte County Agricultural Commissioner (2016). Butte County 2016 Crop Report. Accessed 4/24/2020 https://www.buttecounty.net/Portals/2/CropReports/2016CropReport.pdf

Gaede, D., & Hill, R. (2018). Northwest Colorado and Southwest Wyoming Agritourism Case Study. *Working Paper*, http://agritourism.localfoodeconomics.com/publications

Gartner, W. (2005) A perspective on rural tourism development. *Journal of Regional Analysis and Policy*, 35(1), 33–42.

Grogger, J.T., & Carson, R.T. (1991). Models for truncated counts. *Journal of Applied Econometrics*, 6(3), 225–238.

Hardesty, S., & Leff, P. (2018). Butte County, California – Agritourism Development Case Study. *Working Paper*, http://agritourism.localfoodeconomics.com/publications

Hill, R., Loomis, J., Thilmany, D., & Sullins, M. (2014). Economic values of agritourism to visitors: a multi-destination hurdle travel cost model of demand. *Tourism Economics*, 20(5), 1047–1065.

Hoppe, R.A. (2014). Structure and finances of U.S. farms: Family farm report, 2014 edition. EIB-132. U.S. Department of Agriculture, Economic Research Service.

Low, S.A., Adalja, A., Beaulieu, E., Key, N., Martinez, S., Melton, A., Perez, A., Ralston, K., Stewart, H., Shuttles, S., Vogel, S. & Jablonski, B.B.R. (2015). Trends in U.S. local and regional food systems. Administrative Publication Number 067. Economic Research Service U.S. Department of Agriculture, Washington, DC.

McGranahan, D.A., Wojan, T.R., & Lambert, D.M. (2011). The rural growth trifecta: outdoor amenities, creative class and entrepreneurial context. *Journal of Economic Geography*, 11(3), 529–557.

Rupasingha, A., & Goetz, S.J. (2013). Self-employment and local economic performance: Evidence from US counties. *Papers in Regional Science* 92(1), 141–161.

Stephens, H.M., and Partridge, M.D. (2011). Do entrepreneurs enhance economic growth in lagging regions? *Growth and Change* 42(4), 431–465.

Van Sandt, A., Low, S.A., Jablonski, B., Weiler, S., & Thilmany, D. (2018a). Place-based factors and the success of farm-level entrepreneurship: A spatial interaction model of agritourism in the U.S. *Working Paper.*

Van Sandt, A., Low, S.A., & Thilmany, D. (2018b). Exploring regional patterns of agritourism in the U.S.: What's driving clusters of enterprises? *Agricultural and Resource Economics Review*, 47(3), 592–609. doi:10.1017/age.2017.36.

Van Sandt, A., & Thilmany, D. (2018). Navigating the corn maze: Examining multi-destination bias in heterogeneous agritourism-based travel cost models. *Working Paper.* Submitted to Tourism Economics on March 18, 2020.

Walden, J., Webb, A., Hobbs, D., & Hepler, K. (2013). "A Three Year Action Plan for Promotion of Agritourism in the State of Colorado" Colorado Come to Life, https://www.colorado.com/sites/default/master/files/HAgPLANFINAL.pdf

2 Do Rural Development Policies enhance performance of agritourism farms in Italy?

Marusca De Castris and Daniele Di Gennaro

Introduction

Since 2007, under Pillar II of the Common Agricultural Policy (CAP) 2007–2013, a new rural strategy emphasises the need of fostering rural development by supporting investments and rural tourism. This policy design focuses on the promotion of a substantial review of the traditional concept of farms and the empowerment of "alternative" rural activities. In this way, European policy-makers aim to stimulate the requalification of existing farms (including their related facilities) and the development of specific organisational skills to promote local development and to encourage employment, especially for women and young people. This strategy aims to counteract the increasing land abandonment consequential to urbanisation processes (Benayas et al. 2007; Dubois and Schmitz 2010).

Among the various alternatives for diversification activities, tourism has a prominent role to play. The definition of rural tourism, in its broader sense, relies on two distinct features: rural environment and the provision of additional revenues for businesses (Dară u et al. 2010). Under this perspective, environmental and economic features are combined in promoting the diversification of farms' activities. Diversification can occur in a twofold way, both on the demand (i.e. tourism flows) and supply (i.e. rural activities) sides.[1]

Indeed, rural tourism is not only a way of preventing the decline of traditional agricultural industries, especially in less favoured areas (Clarke 1999), but it provides an additional channel to diversify tourism products by proposing alternatives to traditional seasonal (i.e. seaside and mountain) and metropolitan destinations (Trunfio et al. 2006). Hernández et al. (2016), analysing the case of Catalonia, demonstrate how both seaside and rural tourism demands can be empowered by the presence of some common factors (i.e. services, cultural and natural attractions, etc.), while the supply of tourism services influences only seaside tourism showing the noncompetitive nature between rural and mass tourism.

However, small scale and lack of knowledge and experience in rural tourism, in the absence of an appropriate support, may arise potential problems (i.e. inefficiences, inability to promote their activity, lower than expected additional income), which make still uncertain the additional benefits of developing rural tourism activities (Slevin and Covin 1995; Tew and Barbieri 2012). Sharpley (2002), analysing the case of Cyprus, highlights how tourism activities have to be sustained by organisational and financial support to empower the role of tourism in rural areas.[2]

Looking at the supply side, rural tourism allows us to reach new agricultural markets and to revitalise cultural identities and customs (Karampela et al. 2016; Palka Lebek 2017). In other words, rural tourism makes it possible to increase products value by favouring new linkages with new potential markets (van der Ploeg et al. 2000). However, Mace (2005) underlines how the farmer's additional income coming from rural tourism is overall negligible, whereas the presence of different factors, like the improvement in the quality of life, may allow us to consider the farmer's benefits in a proper way.

To sum up, rural tourism may still be considered as a limited-scale phenomenon, but its empowerment requires a strong political and financial support to be sustainable. Policy interventions rely on two different levels: direct support to the formation and the empowerment of agritourism and aid to agricultural farms which may also be provided to agritourism units. For this reason, a counterfactual analysis aiming to evaluate the effectiveness of agricultural policies may not be limited to agritourism, since it would not be possible to distinguish between the overall, i.e. farms' aid, and the specific, i.e. agritourism support, effects of the policies. In other words, the evaluation of the effectiveness of policy instruments on agritourism activities has to consider both the overall impact on traditional farms and the differential effects on agritourism.

In doing so, the approach followed in this chapter consists of an empirical evaluation of the effects of the agricultural policies on both Farm Net Value Added (FNVA) and labour in Italy using a propensity score matching approach, by checking for the presence of heterogeneous effects between farms and agritourism units. This chapter is organised as follows. In the "Literature review" section, we present a discussion of the literature on rural tourism and agritourism; "The evolution of agritourism in Italy" section analyses agritourism in Italy, by focusing on regulation laws and the recent trends in agritourism supply; the "Rural Development Policies (RDPs) and agritourism" section discusses policy instruments devoted to Rural Development Policies (RDPs); the "Empirical evaluation strategy" section introduces data used in the empirical analysis of the chapter; the "Empirical analysis and results" section presents the empirical strategy; and the concluding section of the chapter is devoted to a discussion of the results.

Literature review

In the ever-increasing rural tourism framework, strong emphasis has been posed on providing evidences in favour of the benefits related to agritourism activities.[3] However, results are ambiguous and country-specific.

Indeed, a critical issue in agritourism literature is the lack of a world-wide agreed definition of this typology of farms. More in detail, while many countries favour scale economies by placing agritourism on an equal footing with non-agricultural commercial activities, Italy promotes the development of a small-scale agritourism by imposing strictly committing rules on these activities.[4]

Furthermore, major efforts are devoted to understand the relationship with environment (i.e. landscape) and rural areas,[5] while studies focusing on the effects on economic performance are still scarce. By focusing on the Italian case, the aim of this chapter is to show how the theoretical and normative framework behind the definition of agritourism can produce differentiated results.

By estimating a quantile regression model for Taiwanese agritourism, Hung et al. (2015) demonstrate how higher performance depends on different factors, like the availabiliy of a qualified human capital, economies of scale and a diversified production model. While performance is influenced by farm-specific features, agritourism supply depends on regional development and labour market characteristics, i.e. number of skilled workers and wages (Drăgoi et al. 2017). The strict dependence between the rural environment and the formation of agritourism hotspots is widely recognised in literature (Fleischer et al. 2018; Van Sandt et al. 2018), while the role played by regional planning and local policies as a possible instrument to foster both rural development and agritourism supply is not yet fully investigated (Marcouiller 2007; Presenza and Cipollina 2009).

This point is of particular relevance when we restrict our focus on the Italian case. Indeed, Italian agritourism units are defined at the national level, while regional derogations are possible, especially, in favour of less favoured areas. Furthermore, Italian agritourism is characterised by the limitations on farm size and the complementarity with agricultural production. In this sense, agritourism can be considered as a flexible tool able to reduce, at least partially, land abandonment and offer a substantial requalification of rural areas.

Ohe and Ciani (2010) demonstrate a growing trend in demand for Italian agritourism, both from domestic and international[6] markets. The effects are differentiated between different areas; Central regions account for the largest part of the agritourism demand, while Southern ones experience the largest growth during the period between 1997 and 2006. Demand has been fostered by the combination of different factors: mass tourism crisis, the emergence of new market segments and the choice of alternative locations (De Devitiis and Wanda Maietta 2013).

While the demand side is extensively analysed in literature, only few contributions focus on the supply of agritourism services (Brandano et al. 2016; Lupi et al. 2017). In this sense, this chapter aims to overcome the bias in literature on agritourism supply by analysing the differential impact of RDP between conventional and agritourism farms.

The evolution of agritourism in Italy

Agritourism regulation

The Italian definition of the word "agritourism" goes back to 1965, when the first National Association for Agritourism, Environment and Tourism (Agriturist) was founded. The idea behind the foundation of Agriturist relies on the enhancement of agricultural and rural tourism by promoting Italian food and wine excellences and rural heritage.

The first regulation law on agritourism activities appears only in 1985 (Law 730/1985). In its first definition, agritourism played a marginal role in farms' activities and was conceived as an instrument to sustain the farmers' income. However, the steady growth of this sector has required a further redefinition of the concept of agritourism. In this sense, Law 96/2006 (which has completely abrogated Law 730/1985) promotes "the development of appropriate forms of rural tourism devoted to favour agricultural activities and income differentiation, preserving rural landscape, sustain traditional and excellence production and promote the agricultural and forestry development" (Law 96/2006). This definition underlines how agritourism can now be considered the most prominent and radical product innovation in the Italian primary sector (Esposti 2006). Moreover, Santucci (2013) highligths that this definition relies on a distinction between different forms of rural tourism and agritourism, which has to be complementary to agricultural activities.

As previously mentioned, the law leaves a high degree of freedom to regional policy-makers in regulating how these activities have to be implemented. This has a twofold relevance in agritourism services. On the one hand, local authorities can correctly identify the possible strengths and deficiencies of rural areas. On the other, it has produced differentiated regional contexts.[7]

Summing up, Law 96/2006 produces a unique framework in international context. Indeed, few are the national policy-makers which directly regulate agritourism (i.e. Italy, Spain, Poland and Slovakia), while in many cases agritourism is defined by non-governmental associations, i.e. Germany, France and the United Kingdom (Streifeneder 2016). Furthermore, in many countries (China, Australia, etc.), agritourism activities are regulated by commercial laws. Overall, international framework, differently from the Italian case, rules out limitations on hosting size and on the strict complementarity with agricultural production.

Italian agritourism: regional diffusion

While law-making contributes to define Italian agritourism in a clear way, few are the statistical information published on this theme. In this paragraph, we analyse the data published by Italian Bureau of Statistics (ISTAT) from the 2010 Agricultural Census and the yearly "Report on Agritourism Activities". In Italy, agritourism supply quickly increased, from 19,973 units in 2010 to 22,238 units in 2015. Clearly, the increasing supply of agritourism activities is well portrayed in an increasing number of beds (238,323 in 2015, that adds 32,178 compared to 2010) and place settings (432,884 in 2015, that adds 47,414 compared to 2010).

Overall, the greater increase in agritourism supply is concentrated in Central Italy, Apulia (South) and in Northern wine excellence regions (i.e. South-Tirol, Veneto and Piedmont). The case of Apulia, a world-renowned region for the quality of its olive oil and wine, represents a clear example of agritourism late development: 687 is the number of agritourism reached in 2015 with a 5-year growth rate equal to 92%.

However, the increasing trend in agritourism supply raises an important issue related to the survival rate of these activities. Indeed, *"for the overall of Italian agritourism sector the 5-year survival rate is equal to 68%, 43% after 10 years and only 6% after 20 years"*.[8] Results are heterogeneous between different areas: agritourism in North-Eastern and Central regions shows a highest survival rate, while in the South, the probability slightly declines to zero after only 10 years. To sum up, regions with a higher agritourism survival rate are the ones with a long-term agritourism tradition and, by consequence, in which rural tourism is deeply embedded in a regional context. To further explore the differences existing between different areas, Figure 2.1 shows the regional distribution of agritourism supply.

Figure 2.1 highlights systematic differences in agritourism supply between Central and Northern Italian regions and the Southern ones. Tuscany (3487) and Trentino-South-Tirol (3517, mainly located in the South-Tirol area) are the regions with the highest number of agritourism, while fewer agritourism farms are located in Southern regions and coastal areas.[9] This point is confirmed by the distribution of agritourism farms by altimetric zones. Indeed, 85% of these activities are distributed between hill and mountain areas (ISTAT 2016). Clearly, the territorial distribution of the agritourism units highlights the connection with rural landscape.

While aggregated statistical information on agritourism highlights regional differences on the diffusion of these activities, in the next paragraph, looking at individual farm data, we present the major variables associated with the decision to supply agritourism activities.

Characteristics of Italian agritourism

In this paragraph, we introduce an empirical micro analysis in order to outline which factors can influence the decision of supplying agritourism activities in Italy. We present the estimates of a logit regression implemented at the farm level,[10] where the dependent variable is the dummy which identifies agritourism.[11] Logit estimates are in terms of odds ratio, i.e. fixing other variables; the parameter represents the constant effect of a predictor X on

Number of Agritourism
59 – 370
370 – 507
507 – 676
676 – 787
787 – 1.081
1.081 – 3.517

Figure 2.1 Systematic differences in agritourism supply between Central and Northern Italian regions, and the Southern ones.

the likelihood that an outcome (in our case, supplying agritourism activities) will occur relative to not occurring. This approach allows us to analyse how different farm and environmental characteristics related to the likelihood of providing agritourism activities.

The results (Table 2.1[12]) show how farms which have obtained rural development subsidies are 1.84 times more likely to provide agritourism services than those who are not subsidised. Furthermore, mixed farms (i.e. those adopting a type of farming combining different types of production, like cultivation and animal breeding) are associated with higher odds of being agritourism (+2.05 for mixed cropping and +3.73 for mixed crops), while farms in Southern and Insular Italian regions are less likely to implement agritourism. In addition, size[13] matters. Indeed, farms of smaller size are

Table 2.1 Likelihood of being an agritourism activity in the year 2014

Logit estimates. Dependent variable dummy agritourism

	Coeff.	S.E.
Presence of subsidies	1.84***	[0.29]
Farm characteristics		
Type of farming (°field crops)		
Horticulture	0.69	[0.34]
Permanent crops	1.32	[0.33]
Grazing livestock	2.08***	[0.51]
Granivores	1.67	[0.80]
Mixed cropping	2.05**	[0.62]
Mixed livestock holdings	1.2	[1.25]
Mixed crops	3.73***	[1.09]
NUTS I (°Central)		
Insular	0.14***	[0.07]
South	0.22***	[0.06]
North-West	0.75	[0.17]
North-East	1.43*	[0.29]
Economic size (°Big)		
Medium	2.03*	[0.81]
Small	2.56**	[1.10]
Workforce characteristics		
Low education	0.43***	[0.07]
Familiar	0.35***	[0.09]
Male	0.58***	[0.08]
Process certification	1.54**	[0.29]
Product certification	1.13	[0.35]
Conventional	0.60***	[0.10]
Municipalities characteristics		
Degree of urbanisation (°High)		
Medium	1.31	[0.55]
Rural	1.82	[0.75]
Seaside municipalities	1.51	[0.41]
Mountain municipality (°No)		
Partially	1.95***	[0.44]
Yes	1.72***	[0.31]
Constant	0.05***	[0.03]
Observations	5,923	
Log likelihood	−825.37	
Akaike inf. crit.	1,702.74	

Notes: Parameters are expressed in terms of odds ratio. SE = standard error. ° = reference group. Significance levels: ***0.01, **0.05, *0.1.

w2.56 times more likely to become an agritourism if compared with big farms. This highlights how these activities are, in overall, implemented by small-scale farmers aiming at an improvement of their economic condition.

Looking at farmers' characteristics, more qualified human capital is more likely to engage in agritourism activities. Interestingly, both male (0.58) and familiar (0.35) labour are less likely in agritourism farms if compared with traditional ones. This raises an interesting question about the possibility to enter in the agricultural labour market for both women and young people. In this sense, agritourism may constitute a relevant factor in fostering rural development by providing an additional source of employment and containing rural population decline.

The effects due to the certification of farms' process provide evidence in favour of the strong connection between agritourism and the environmental-friendly production processes, while in mountain areas, farms are 1.72 times more likely to supply agritourism activities. The commitment to the preservation of the landscape and the environment is considered crucial by farmers in order to meet the needs and tastes of consumers (LaPan and Barbieri 2014).

Rural Development Policies (RDPs) and agritourism

CAP is based on two fundamental lines of action, called "pillars". While Pillar I supports farmers' income through direct funding and facilitates the regulation for agricultural product market, Pillar II addresses measures aimed at fostering rural development. Furthermore, Pillar I is designed as a redistributive and financial instrument to provide an additional source of income to farmers. This has a twofold implication. On the one hand, Pillar I does not aim to promote productive investment and, therefore, it can't be considered as fostering rural development. On the other hand, financial support received through Pillar I has to be included in farmer incomes which is part of its gross production. Despite the relevance of Pillar I, in this chapter, we consider only policies included in Pillar II, which directly aims at the increase of employment in rural areas and the search for new opportunities for sustainable development.

In supporting rural development, Pillar II allows us to orient regional expenditures on the basis of local needs to address economic, social and environmental challenges. RDP programme is based on the three main objectives: improving the competitiveness of the agricultural sector (Axis 1); encouraging farmers to adopt favourable behaviour for the environment (Axis 2) and enhancing less favoured areas through investments, which may increase the quality of life, employment opportunities, tourism and the diversification of agricultural activity (Axis 3). Additionally, a fourth axis, called Leader, acts across the first three axes – in particular the third one – by applying strategies and development projects that are strongly targeted to territories which involved local institutions and established partnerships between public and private sectors. RDPs during the period 2007–2013 were governed by rules set out in Council Regulation (EC) No. 1698/2005. For the programming period 2007–2013, RDP through one fund, the so-called European Agricultural Fund for Rural Development (EAFRD), has provided an amount of EUR 96 billion. Interestingly, major resources were allocated to the regions characterised by structural development lag and adverse environmental features, i.e. Obj.1 Regions and Less Favoured Areas[14] (from now LFA).

Going in depth, Axis 1 is devoted to the modernisation of production processes by favouring investment on human and physical capital, while Axis 2 is directed to a more sustainable land use and protection of the environment. Latter measures aim to prevent land abandonment by encouraging the preservation and enhancement of the natural space and landscape. The main objective of Axis 3 is to ensure a "living countryside" by improving the social and economic contexts. Investments in rural economies and communities are essential to make rural areas more attractive for young people and women. In this regard, measures promoting employment opportunities and the strengthening of infrastructures and ICT are required.

Rural diversification and the empowerment of rural tourism are conceptually framed in Axis 3. In this sense, EU policy-makers recognise tourism and the possibility of supplying non-agricultural activities as an additional tool to foster rural areas. However, the strong connections between production, environmental characteristics and agritourism do not allow us to restrict our analysis only to Axis 3 Policies. Neglect to consider part of Pillar II axes does not allow us to properly evaluate the entire contribution of RDP. In other terms, although the four axes pose emphasis on different policy targets, they focus on the empowerment of the rural areas by promoting both productive investments and agricultural workforce regeneration.

In this chapter, we consider all the instruments comprised in RDP to take into account all the possible sources acting to foster rural development, and, in order to understand correctly the impact on lagging areas, we provide differentiated estimates for Southern regions, LFA and rural areas.

Data

The empirical analysis relies on the information extracted from the so-called RICA data warehouse, the Italian part of FADN.[15] RICA uses a stratified sampling method to ensure representativeness at the regional level, by type of farming and holding size. However, the RICA sample drawing is based on a rotating panel.[16] This provides temporal discontinuity of the observations and the impossibility to evaluate effects of long period. To overcome this limitation, we construct a panel dataset which consider all the farms tracked within the 3-year period between 2012 (pre-subsidy) and 2014 (post-subsidy), while the year 2013 corresponds to our subsidised period.[17] Table 2.2 presents the main statistics which characterised agricultural production distinguishing between the overall sample (RICA) and the dataset considered in our analysis (Panel). We get evidences in favour of the comparability between the unbalanced overall sample (RICA) and the balanced dataset considered in our analysis (Panel).[18]

Table 2.2 Summary statistics for the period 2012–2014

Variables	Overall sample			Panel sample		
	Mean		Median	Mean		Median
	All farms	of which agritourism		All farms	of which agritourism	
Gross production (€)	150,453	134,631	50,143	154,880	130,796	53,094
Labour unit	1.93	2.59	1.3	1.95	2.47	1.36
Land extension (ha)	33.42	43.67	14	32.56	40.28	14.2
Added value (€)	86,788	108,130	32,776	89,236	103,394	34,482
Farm net added value (€)	81,278	96,802	30,005	83,864	92,937	31,887
Fixed capital (€)	507,228	778,427	197,265	505,086	788,188	209,433
Land capital (€)	458,672	708,869	165,728	457,095	720,842	179,734
Observations	*33,133*	*1,128*	*33,133*	*19,503*	*643*	*19,503*

Overall, farms are characterised by a small size in both labour and FNVA. Moreover, Italian farms are capital intensive. Focusing on agritourism farms, they show greater land extension and workforce and, on the whole, better economic indicators. The comparison between conventional and agritourism farms provides some interesting insights. While agricultural farms are more focused on the production of agricultural products (i.e. higher gross production), agritourism farms have higher levels for added value, fixed and land capitals and in terms of land extension and labour units. This reveals how the supplementary activities provided by agritourism offer an additional channel to improve agricultural incomes, workforce and to requalify rural areas.

Empirical evaluation strategy

The aim of this chapter is to estimate the causal effect of RDP on incomes and labour for Italian farms, evaluating if the policy impact is different on agritourism farms than on agricultural farms. In other words, our empirical strategy relies on the presence of two different contrasts: units which receive (treated) or not (untreated) subsidies and between agricultural and agritourism farms. The comparison between the four different groups allows us to obtain heterogeneous causal estimates for agritourism and conventional farms. A higher impact means that agritourism farms can better exploit the benefits of the policies by diversifying production and increasing the profitability of the holding. On the contrary, a lower impact would indicate the need for targeted interventions to agritourism and not to the undifferentiated ones, i.e. without a specific agritourism destination.

We consider all the farms in the dataset, while the potentially different impact on agritourism is taken into account by getting different treatment estimates for "conventional" and agritourism units. To do so, we identify an appropriate control group of units without policy support and, thus, provide evidences on the effectiveness of RDP by means of a counterfactual approach.

Our empirical evaluation strategy considers the combined effect of all policies on agritourism: therefore, we consider a farm as treated when it has received one or more subsidies from the RDP in 2013. Indeed, while Axis 3 is directly devoted to promote the diversification and foster non-agricultural activities, agritourism may apply, on the basis of their needs, to all of the policies included in Pillar II, i.e. RDP. In this sense, a consideration of the entire set of instruments in RDP allows us to provide the entire contribution of the policies on agritourism activities.

The chosen strategy considers the peculiarity of rural policy. Indeed, RDP generally uses a planned selection process to assign subsidies to the farms. The selection process is a relevant factor in evaluating policy effects. The difference between the averages of the outcome variable of treated and untreated groups is affected by the so-called selection bias, which certainly affects the estimates of the policy impact. In other words, the selection process leads to the existence of pre-treatment structural and economic differences between treated and untreated farms. Only a randomised assignment of the subsidies to the farms could ensure that the two groups are not different.

For example, a large farm characterised by high profit, high land use and intensive capital may achieve better results also in the absence of the subsidy. Similarly, a farm that receives a subsidy to become an agritourism may have different results on already consolidated local units. Each of these factors can influence farm performance. For these reasons, we adopt an evaluation strategy that aims to decrease the selection bias associated with observable and not observable farm's characteristics.

Our identification strategy is based on a matching approach to identify a control group of untreated farms which are similar to the treated units in all relevant pre-treatment characteristics. We assume that time is not relevant for the selection bias, i.e. farm subsidies have multi-yearly pay-outs and we consider payment of the year 2013, regardless of the assignment time. In this way, an overlapping area of farms with the same propensity to be treated is available and a matching estimator is a feasible instrument to determine the effects of RDP.

The matching estimator assumes that selection can be explained purely in terms of observable characteristics. In this case, the conditional independence assumption (CIA) holds, i.e. the outcomes of untreated farms are independent from the treatment conditioned to the observables' variables that characterised the farms before the policy. The consequence of CIA is that for each treated farm, the untreated unit with the same covariate realisation constitutes the correct counterfactual.

The ability of matching to reproduce an experimental framework depends on the availability of the counterfactual. Hence, the second matching assumption is that all treated units have a counterpart in the untreated population. The main advantage offered by the matching method is that it does not require any assumption on the functional form of the dependency between the outcome variable and the observed covariates. On the other hand, if there are a high number of covariates, it may be difficult to identify a non-subsidised farm to match with every subsidised farm, unless for very high sample size. This obstacle is overcome by the propensity score matching (Rosenbaum and Rubin 1983). The accurate use of a propensity score, similarly, needs that farms with the same propensity score must have the same distribution of observable (and unobservable) characteristics regardless of the treatment status. This assumption is called the "balancing hypothesis" and can be tested using the approach presented in Becker and Ichino (2002). When the CIA assumption holds and there is an overlap between both groups (Rosenbaum and Rubin 1983), the PSM estimator for the average treatment effect, known as ATE, can be written in general as follows:

$$ATE = E\left[Y(1) \mid D = 1; P(X)\right] - E\left[Y(0) \mid D = 1; P(X)\right]$$

where Y is the outcome variable (i.e. Farm Net Value Added, FNVA, or labour), D is a binary variable on the treatment of the policy and $P(X)$ is the propensity score estimated on the pre-treatment and structural covariates X. In this chapter, we follow a parametric approach, by estimating a propensity score weighted regression of the form:

$$Y = \beta_0 + \beta_1 D + \beta_2 \text{ Agritourism} + \beta_3 \text{ Agritourism} * D + \gamma X + \varepsilon$$

In the latter equation, X represents post-treatment covariates, β_1 provides an estimate of the ATE, β_2 is the conditional mean difference in outcome variable due agritourism, and β_3 represents the differential effect of the treatment for agritourism. Thus, the parameters of interest in the regression model are estimated in terms of shift from non-agritourism control farms. In other terms, this approach allows us to estimate the impact of supplying agritourism services and the causal effects of RDP for both agritourism and non-agritourism farms.

However, a more comprehensive evaluation of the impact of both RDP and agritourism services requires the estimation of the average marginal effects which are obtained by differentiating outcome variables over each variable. This operation allows us to disentangle the marginal effect of RDP and agritourism over the chosen outcomes, FNVA and labour.

Empirical analysis and results

In this chapter, we present the estimates of the impact of RDP focusing on the agritourism activity. Furthermore, to understand the strength and deficiencies of agritourism, we provide evidences on the features that may or may not affect the choice of providing agritourism activities. As previously explained, the presence of a selection bias may conduct to the impossibility of identifying a proper control group and, by consequence, a biased estimate of policy effects.

However, by using propensity score matching, we are able to control and attenuate the presence of bias due to differences on pre-treatment farm characteristics and construct a counterfactual group "similar" to the treated one. In estimating the propensity score, we take into account the following variables: land extension and capital, type of farming, Nuts-I localisation and a series of dummies which allows us to identify, respectively, agritourism, less-educated entrepreneurs and workforce, which is mainly composed by entrepreneurs, conventional farms and both product and process certification.[19]

Figure 2.2 highlights how propensity score's distributions for treated and controls overlap after the matching procedure. In other words, we are able to construct a control group of untreated units which does not differ (in a statistical sense), in terms of pre-treatment covariates, from the ones

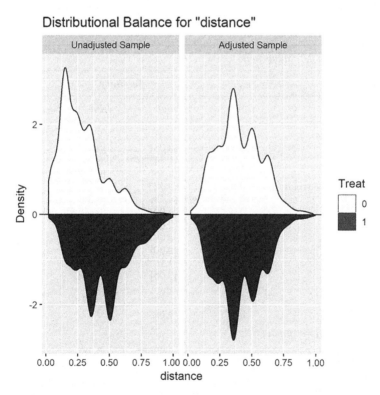

Figure 2.2 How propensity score distributions for treated and controls overlap after the matching procedure.

receiving policy support, i.e. the common support assumption is satisfied and this allows us to estimate the RDP effects.

Additional estimates are provided to take into account major areas in which RDP can play a determinant role, i.e. South, LFA and rural areas. Previous areas are defined as follows: South identifies all the farm located among South and Insular Italian regions (i.e. Nuts-I Classification); LFA comprise farms located in the different disadvantaged areas defined in Council Directive 75/268/EEC, while rural areas[20] are defined by using ISTAT classification on geographical characteristic of Italian municipalities. Farm and agritourism size are included by controlling for land extension, while differences due to other factors, i.e. capital and type of farming, are removed in propensity score estimation.

Table 2.3 resumes ATE estimates on farm labour units which are controlled for farm size. The effects of RDP on agricultural labour are negligible and not significant, while the specific effect of the subsidies on agritourism is negative, but again not significant. Interestingly, agritourism uses more labour, so the negative impact of the policies may suggest a substitution effect between labour and capital. Overall, the presence of an interaction

Table 2.3 Policy impact on farms' labour in the year 2014. ATE estimates by territory

Dependent Variable: labour unit

	Territory			
Variable	*Italy*	*South*	*LFA*	*Rural zones*
Subsidised farms	0.05	0.03	0.02	0.03
	[0.05]	[0.08]	[0.06]	[0.08]
Agritourism	0.49***	1.34***	0.24	0.55**
	[0.16]	[0.35]	[0.18]	[0.24]
Subsidised agritourism	−0.05	−0.90*	0.12	−0.19
	[0.24]	[0.53]	[0.25]	[0.34]
Land	0.01***	0.00***	0.00***	0.01***
	[0.00]	[0.00]	[0.00]	[0.00]
Added value	0.00***	0.00***	0.00***	0.00***
	[0.00]	[0.00]	[0.00]	[0.00]
Constant	1.22***	1.11***	0.99***	1.31***
	[0.04]	[0.05]	[0.04]	[0.05]
Observations	4,284	1,566	2,382	3,007
R^2	0.47	0.65	0.57	0.39
Adjusted R^2	0.47	0.65	0.57	0.39
Decomposition of marginal effects				
Agritourism	0.48***	0.98***	0.28*	0.48***
	[0.12]	[0.26]	[0.13]	[0.17]
Subsidised Farms	0.05	0.00	0.03	0.02
	[0.05]	[0.08]	[0.06]	[0.08]

Note: Standard errors in square bracket. Significance levels: ***0.01, **0.05, *0.1.

between agritourism and subsidies does not allow us to disentangle the contribution of each variable on labour units. To report the mean effects of the agritourism and policy factors across all farms, average marginal effects are estimated. The effects of agritourism are positive and significant (+0.48 units at national scale and +0.98 for Southern regions). This reflects a higher labour demand of agritourism to be able to provide the supplementary services related to these activities, i.e. hosting, food services, etc. Conversely, the effects of RDP on labour are negligible and not significant for all the cases considered. The inefficacy of the policy may be due to the short-time window between subsidies (2013) and post-treatment (2014).

Table 2.4 resumes ATE estimates on farm's FNVA, again controlled for farms' size. Interestingly, both RDP and agritourism activities have a negative and significant impact on FNVA, while the presence of subsidies in the agritourism farms has, overall, a positive effect, although not significant. The overall impact of the subsidies on agritourism is given by the sum of the general treatment effect on all the farms plus the specific impact on agritourism. Overall, the impact on agritourism is around zero, but it switches to positive and significant on Southern regions.[21] The negligible effects of

Table 2.4 Policy impact on farm's FNVA in the year 2014. ATE estimates by territory

Dependent variable: farm net value added

	Territory			
Variable	*Italy*	*South*	*LFA*	*Rural zones*
Subsidised farms	−21,881.18***	−5,453.15	905.16	−19,975.54**
	[6,572.67]	[5,403.15]	[3,698.03]	[8,951.26]
Agritourism	−49,537.38**	−106,852.20***	−3,673.49	−65,410.17**
	[19,782.90]	[24,820.85]	[11,561.30]	[27,227.08]
Subsidised agritourism	21,051.07	131,842.30***	−14,176.97	54,525.43
	[28,928.87]	[37,302.60]	[16,463.47]	[39,030.93]
Land	656.39***	296.06***	278.08***	1,244.79***
	[53.53]	[43.15]	[32.35]	[67.66]
Labour unit	70,460.00***	56,263.17***	47,913.00***	60,068.93***
	[1,494.99]	[1,120.51]	[929.80]	[1,802.39]
Constant	−61,120.35***	−50,809.89***	−32,880.57***	−66,649.53***
	[4,974.64]	[4,023.32]	[2,898.15]	[6,664.04]
Observations	4,284	1,566	2,382	3,007
R²	0.45	0.67	0.58	0.43
Adjusted R²	0.45	0.67	0.58	0.43
Decomposition of marginal effects				
Agritourism	−41,080.6***	−53,887.6***	−9,368.8	−43,505.8*
	[13,545.3]	[17,225.3]	[7664.0]	[18,618.0]
Subsidised farms	−20,962.3***	301.9	286.3	−17,595.5*
	[7,415.3]	[4,858.0]	[3,401.5]	[8,005.2]

Note: Standard errors in square brackets. ***0.01, **0.05, *0.1.

the subsidies may reflect the lack of an entrepreneurial capability in fostering economic performance which can be explained by normative limitation (i.e. absence of scale effects) and by the presence of a not yet consolidated agritourism market. Furthermore, not having selected between the different subsidies may have reduced their efficacy.

The marginal effects of agritourism and subsidies across all farms are in the bottom part of Table 2.4. Both factors affect FNVA negatively. There are several plausible explanations. On the one hand, the negative effects of agritourism on FNVA may be related to the positive effects on workforce. Indeed, more labour is negatively associated with FNVA when there is no appropriate improvement in production and technology.

On the other hand, negative effects of the public policy can be related to the fact that RDPs are devoted to address two different factors: adverse economic and environmental conditions (i.e. natural disasters) and the empowerment of farms by promoting productive investments. Additionally, subsidies on productive investments may require a longer time period for having a beneficial impact on farms' performance. Finally, policy selection processes may favour the participation in RDP by under-performing farms. All these factors may have a negative short-term impact on FNVA.

Conclusions

The strict complementarity between agritourism and agricultural activities may provide a support to prevent secular rural population decline and, in wider terms, to foster thriving rural areas. Furthermore, promoting rural development is a key-factor in the EU CAP. Indeed, EU policy-makers promote a series of interventions (Pillar II – RDP) devoted to increase farm investments and diversification, especially in LFA.

Although both agritourism and RDP seek the empowerment of rural areas, their scale of intervention and their principal aims differ. Indeed, agritourism provided by private farms promotes a revitalisation of landholders' rural assets by aiming at the maximisation of their own performance and profits, while RDP, intervening at an institutional level, aims at the global empowerment of the rural areas by offering an instrument for attracting labour and production capacities in the agricultural sector. Neglecting to consider the "two sides of the same coin" may not allow us to evaluate the "overall" effect of the policy on rural development. The evaluation of the effects of RDP on farm income and labour by allowing for different impacts for agricultural and agritourism farms constitutes the major innovation of this chapter.

Overall, agritourism units have lower FNVA than conventional farms, while the increase in labour demand due to the provision of additional touristic services is positively reflected in terms of employment. This provides evidences in support of the possibility offered by the agritourism to stimulate rural employment. Furthermore, RDP's effects on FNVA are negligible and in general even negative, in terms of labour, for agritourism. The latter results open the way to some interesting conjectures. The ineffectiveness of 2007–2013 RDP in Italy may reflect the still inadequate support to the diversification of agricultural activities and the regeneration of the rural areas. Indeed, during the period 2007–2013, CAP mainly addresses two distinct features: the decoupling reform and the financial global crisis. In this sense, while RDP targets were well-defined, major efforts were devoted to secure farmers' income and to preserve the competitiveness of agricultural markets. The lack of institutional support to RDP in 2007–2013 can be considered as the fundamental pillar for the redefinition of these instruments.

In this sense, the improvement of rural accessibility, production base and workforce has assumed a primary role under 2014–2020 RDP. In doing so, EU policy-makers have redefined priorities in RDP by including the promotion of social inclusion (i.e. poverty reduction and economic development), IT infrastructures, Start-up business aid and the development of non-agricultural activities. The novel policy framework aims to stimulate the agricultural sector not only through direct support to production, but also by focusing on the innovativeness and multifunctionality of farms.

To conclude, the effects of undifferentiated instruments of RDP applied to agritourism are small, although in some cases positive, especially in areas, such as those in the Southern regions, where financial constraints appear to be more severe. The conclusion is that in this case, a "one size fits all" policy approach does not work, which means that policy-makers must design incentives specifically targeted to the agritourism sector, supporting the various aspects of this multifunctional production model, entailing hosting, catering, entertainment aspects and the agricultural production.

Appendix I

List of variables and definitions

Dependent variables

Farm Net Value Added (FNVA): farm net income + non-EU subsidies – Taxes.
Labour Unit: the amount of work performed in the year by a full-time employee for a farm (1 Labour unit = 2,200 hours).
Agritourism: farms which provide agritourism services between 2012 and 2014. Binary variable equal 1 if there are agritourism activities.

Independent variables

Conventional: =1 if the farm is classified as "conventional".
Entrepreneurship =1 if the holding workforce is mainly constituted by entrepreneurs.
Land Capital: value of the land and buildings (Euro)
Land: utilised agricultural area (hectare)
Less Favoured Areas: 0. Non-LFA, 2. Partially; 3. Totally; 4. Areas affected by depopulation; 5. Areas with specific disadvantages.

Low Education: =1 if entrepreneur has a level of education below ISCED-3 (i.e. upper secondary education).

Nuts-I: 1. North-West; 2. North-East; 3. Centre; 4. South; 5. Insular.

Process Certification =1 if the farm provides a process certification, like environmental-friendly production process.

Product Certification: =1 if the farm provides a product certification, i.e. PDO (Protected Designation of Origin) or PGI (Protected Geographical Indication).

Economic Size: Big if Standard Production > 500,000 €; Medium if 25,000 € ≤ Standard Production ≤ 500,000 €, Small in the other cases.

Type of Farming: 1. Specialist field crops; 2. Specialist horticulture; 3. Specialist permanent crops; 4. Specialist grazing livestock; 5. Specialist granivores; 6. Mixed cropping; 7. Mixed livestock holdings; 8. Mixed crops – livestock.

Notes

1 The potential linkages between rural tourism and local development are explained in Postevoy (2017).
2 Further explanations, on the role of rural activities on tourism flows, rely on the behaviour of the consumers, i.e. guests. Different perspectives are presented in literature, including the willingness to get away from urban areas and have a contact with natural environment (Santana et al. 2015; Dubois et al. 2017), a social and direct interaction with the farm owner and other guests (Choo and Petrick 2014), and the possibility of having sports and/or didactic activities (Cha et al. 1995) and of tasting rural goods (Hultman et al. 2015).
3 Agritourism, sometimes confused with the broadest concept of rural tourism, can be considered as a subsample of rural tourism and it is represented by the farms which still produce agricultural goods and provide touristic services. This brief definition sums up the two major features of agritourism: the diversification (through tourism activities) and the strict connection and complementarity with farms product.
4 The definition of agritourism according to the Italian Law is discussed in Section "The evolution of agritourism in Italy".
5 Notwithstanding the relevant impact of agritourism in the improvement of landscape by promoting rural and agricultural requalification, our analysis will consider only the relationship between performance of agritourism and conventional farms.
6 The increase in international agritourism demand in Italy is usually considered as a consequence of the European Common Market, involving the free movement of people and the common currency. Santeramo and Morelli (2016) provide a further explanation by observing how high levels of urbanisation in domestic countries imply a higher demand for agritourism services.
7 As an example, while the majority of Italian regions limits the number of daily guests to a maximum of 30 units, Lombardy extends it to 60 units and particular derogations are permitted to the agritourism located in mountains and less favoured areas (i.e. Abruzzo).
8 Source: *Annual Report on Italian Agritourism* (ISTAT 2016). ISTAT estimates the survival rate of agritourism as the conditional probability of being an active unit when at least one other agritourism closes.
9 The localisation of agritourism activities has a clear relevance in terms of policies. Indeed, Common Agricultural Policy addresses the problem of rural

development by focusing on the less favoured areas (i.e. mountains and hills) and regions affected by structural lag (i.e. the South and islands).

10 For the sake of clarity, data used in this paragraph are presented in Section "Empirical evaluation strategy".

11 Lupi et al. (2017) propose a logit regression on the determinants of agritourism activities. Differently from our approach, they focus uniquely on the economic characteristics of agritourism.

12 See Appendix I for a description of the variables.

13 Economic size, differently from farm size, is defined on the basis of the value of Standard Productions: small for values under 25,000 Euro, medium between 25,000 and 500,000 Euro, and big in the other cases.

14 LFA include (1) mountain territories; (2) areas at risk of depopulation; (3) areas with specific limitations, i.e. natural conservation areas.

15 RICA is part of the European Farm Accountancy Data Network (FADN) and represents the only harmonised survey to collect micro-economic data on firms operating in agriculture. Italian RICA collects yearly information on about 11,000 farms sampled at the regional level. RICA's field of observation considers only farms with at least 1 hectare of UAA (utilised agricultural area) or a production value higher than 2,500 Euro.

16 The share of rotating farms between two different years is 20–25% of the total sample.

17 Considering 2013 as a treatment period allows us to take into account only the policies in the Framework Programme 2007–2013, thus avoiding the possibility of duplication due to the presence of different programming periods.

18 Tests, not reported here, reject the presence of differences, on average, between the Rica sample and the panel considered for our analysis.

19 Estimates of the propensity score are not reported here, but are available upon request.

20 Eurostat defines rural areas on the basis of the number of inhabitants per square kilometre. More in detail, an area is identified as rural if its population density is less than 300 inhabitants per square kilometre.

21 Given the few units of agritourism in our dataset, estimates on the South may only provide an indicative trend of the effects.

References

Becker, S. O., and Ichino, A. (2002). "Estimation of average treatment effects based on propensity scores." *The Stata Journal*, vol. 2, n.4: 358–377.

Benayas, J. M. R., Martins, A., Nicolau, J. M., and Schulz, J. J. (2007). "Abandonment of agricultural land: An overview of drivers and consequences." *CAB Reviews: Perspectives in Agriculture, Veterinary Science, Nutrition and Natural Resources*, vol. 2, n.57: 1–14.

Brandano, M. G., Osti, L., and Pulina, M. (2006). "An investigation on tourism farms in South Tyrol." *BEMPS –Bozen Economics and Management Paper Series* (35).

Cha, S., McCleary, K.W., and Uysal, M. (1995). "Travel motivations of Japanese overseas travelers: A factor-cluster segmentation approach." *Journal of Travel Research*, vol. 34, n.1: 33–39.

Choo, H., and Petrick, J. F. (2014). "Social interactions and intentions to revisit for agritourism service encounters." *Tourism Management*, vol. 40: 372–381.

Clarke, J. (1999). "Marketing structures for farm tourism: Beyond the individual provider of rural tourism." *Journal of Sustainable Tourism*, vol. 7, n.1: 26–47.

Dărău, A. P., Corneliu, M., Brad, M. L., and Avram, E., (2010) "The concept of rural tourism and agritourism." *Studia Universitatis Vasile Goldiș*, vol. 5, n.1: 39–42.

De Devitiis, B., and Maietta, O. W. (2013). "Regional patterns of structural change in Italian agriculture." In Ortiz-Miranda, D., Moragues-Faus, A., and Arnalte-Alegre, E. eds., *Agriculture in Mediterranean Europe: Between Old and New Paradigms (Research in Rural Sociology and Development, Vol. 19).* Emerald Group Publishing Limited, Bingley: 173–205.

Drăgoi, M. C., Iamandi, I., Munteanu, S. M., Ciobanu, R., Tartavulea, R. I., and Raluca G. L. (2017). "Incentives for developing resilient agritourism entrepreneurship in rural communities in Romania in a European context." *Sustainability*, vol. 9, n.12: 2205.

Dubois, C., Cawley, M., and Schmitz, S. (2017). "The tourist on the farm: A 'muddled'image." *Tourism Management*, vol. 59: 298–311.

Dubois, C., and Schmitz, S. (2010). "Which countryside for which agritourism? A comparative analysis." In Amit-Cohen, I., ed., *Sustainability in Transition and the Changing Faces of Rural Areas: Environmental, Social, Cultural and Economic Dimensions.* Bar Ilan University, Ramat Gan: 36.

Esposti, R. (2006). "Agriturismo al bivio." *Agriregioneuropa*, vol. 5: 28–30.

Fleischer, A., Tchetchik, A., Bar-Nahum, Z., and Evyatar T.(2018). "Is agriculture important to agritourism? The agritourism attraction market in Israel." *European Review of Agricultural Economics*, vol. 45, n.2: 273–296.

Hernández, J. M., Suárez-Vega, R., and Santana-Jiménez, Y. (2016). "The interrelationship between rural and mass tourism: The case of Catalonia, Spain." *Tourism Management*, vol. 54 (2016): 43–57.

Hultman, M., Kazeminia, A., and Ghasemi, V. (2015). "Intention to visit and willingness to pay premium for ecotourism: The impact of attitude, materialism, and motivation." *Journal of Business Research*, vol. 68, n.9: 1854–1861.

Hung, W., Ding, H., and Lin, S. (2016). "Determinants of performance for agritourism farms: An alternative approach." *Current Issues in Tourism*, vol. 19, n.13: 1281–1287.

ISTAT. (2016). *Rapporto annuale sulla multifunzionalità agricola e l'agriturismo.* Roma: ISTAT.

Karampela, S., Kizos, T., and Spilanis, I. (2016). "Evaluating the impact of agritourism on local development in small islands." *Island Studies Journal*, vol. 11, n.1: 161–176.

LaPan, C., and Barbieri, C. (2014). "The role of agritourism in heritage preservation." *Current Issues in Tourism*, vol. 17, n.8: 666–673.

Lupi, C., Giaccio, V., Mastronardi, L., Giannelli, A., and Scardera, A. (2017). "Exploring the features of agritourism and its contribution to rural development in Italy." *Land Use Policy*, vol. 64: 383–390.

Mace, D. (2005). "Factors motivating agritourism entrepreneurs." *Risk and Profit Conference*, Manhattan, KS.

Marcouiller, D. (2007). "'Boosting' tourism as rural public policy: Panacea or pandora's box?" *Journal of Regional Analysis and Policy*, vol. 37, n.1: 28–31.

Ohe, Y., and Ciani, A. (2010). "The demand trend of Italian agritourism." In Brebbia, C.A., and Pineda, F.D., eds, *Sustainable Tourism IV.* WIT Press, Southampton: 437–448.

Palka Lebek, E. (2017). "An exploration of the role of agritourism in revitalizing rural areas – The case study of South-East Poland." Zeszyty Naukowe Turystyka I Rekreacja, 141.

Postevoy, K. (2017). "Improving the competitiveness of rural areas in the aspect of rural tourism development." Doctoral dissertation.

Presenza, A., and Cipollina, M. (2009) "Analysis of links and features of tourism destination's stakeholders. An empirical investigation of a Southern Italian Region." The 2009 Naples forum on Services, Capri, 16–19 June.

Rosenbaum, P. R., and Rubin, D. B. (1983). "The central role of the propensity score in observational studies for causal effects." *Biometrika*, vol. 70, n.1: 41–55.

Santana-Jiménez, Y., Sun, Y., Hernández, J. M., and Suárez-Vega, R. (2015). "The influence of remoteness and isolation in the rural accommodation rental price among Eastern and Western destinations." *Journal of Travel Research*, vol. 54, n.3: 380–395.

Santeramo, F. G., and Morelli, M. (2016). "Modelling tourism flows through gravity models: A quantile regression approach." *Current Issues in Tourism*, vol. 19, n.11: 1077–1083.

Santucci, F. M. (2013). "Agritourism for rural development in Italy, Evolution, situation and perspectives." *British Journal of Economics, Management & Trade*, vol. 3: 186–200.

Sharpley, R. (2002). "Rural tourism and the challenge of tourism diversification: The case of Cyprus." *Tourism management*, vol. 23, n.3: 233–244.

Slevin, D. P., and Covin, J. G. (1995). "Entrepreneurship as firm behavior: A research model." *Advances in Entrepreneurship, Firm Emergence, and Growth*, vol. 2: 175–224.

Streifeneder, T. (2016). "Agriculture first: Assessing European policies and scientific typologies to define authentic agritourism and differentiate it from countryside tourism." *Tourism Management Perspectives*, vol. 20: 251–264.

Tew, C., and Barbieri, C. (2012). "The perceived benefits of agritourism: The provider's perspective." *Tourism Management*, vol. 33, n.1: 215–224.

Trunfio, M., Petruzzellis, L., and Nigro, C. (2006). "Tour operators and alternative tourism in Italy: Exploiting niche markets to increase international competitiveness." *International Journal of Contemporary Hospitality Management*, vol. 18, n.5: 426–438.

van der Ploeg, J. D., Renting, H., Brunori, G., Karlheinz K., Mannion, J., Marsden, T., de Roest, K., Sevilla-Guzmán, E., and Ventura F. (2000). "Rural development: From practices and policies towards theory." *Sociologia Ruralis*, vol. 40, n.4: 391–408.

Van Sandt, A., Low, S. A., and Thilmany, D. (2018). "Exploring regional patterns of agritourism in the US: What's driving clusters of enterprises?" *Agricultural and Resource Economics Review*, vol. 47, n.3: 1–18.

3 Rural development and sustainable tourism

A case for family farming in the Alta Murgia National Park (Italy)

Simona Giordano

Introduction: sustainability, a possible match between agriculture and tourism

The concept of sustainability starts from the main assumption that natural resources are exhaustible and, therefore, a system aimed at infinite growth is not feasible. This reflection was introduced at the first UN Environment Conference in 1972,[1] although only in 1987, with the publication of the so-called Brundtland report,[2] the objective of sustainable development was clearly defined as the new paradigm of development itself. Sustainability, from the point of view of environmental content, derives from the study of ecological systems and their properties such as load capacity, self-regulation possibilities, resilience and resistance, which, as a whole, affect the stability of the global ecosystem.

The achievement of environmental sustainability is at the basis of economic sustainability: the second cannot be achieved at the cost of the first (Khan 1995); it is a two-way interaction: the way in which the economy is managed impacts on the environment and the environmental quality impacts on economic results. With reference to agriculture, the attribution of the term "sustainable" to the actions implemented by farms has the aim of spreading some entrepreneurial choices taken by farmers for which a positive impact on the environment, on the territory and on limited resources is recognized.

Agricultural areas lend themselves to the development of rural tourism, including agritourism, both qualitatively and quantitatively different from the "traditional" mass tourism, a model that is related to the cultural values of a territory without generating great environmental impacts on it.

Agritourism,[3] understood as a productive activity linked to the territory of the countryside, allows rural populations to live within these areas, guarantees the protection of the territory and protects the agricultural and forest heritage. The last aspect assumes a particular role, especially in the areas most subject to depopulation, traditionally the rural ones devoted mainly to agriculture.

The birth of modern rurality on the one hand, the evolution of agricultural policy and the affirmation of rural development in Europe on the other are the premises that created a context in which, in recent years, greater attention has been paid to agricultural multifunctionality as a tool for economic growth, in terms of increased income and employment, available to local communities of the rural areas to diversify their activities and thus create an added value to be retained in the territory.

Certainly a complex phenomenon, rural tourism, and agritourism as a sub-part of it, is configured as a system of tourist offer represented by the territorial capital that through collaboration and interaction of all the actors involved, including local citizens, gains coherence and ability to attract (Balestrieri 2005; Saxena et al., 2007); it has an important role for rural development in an integrated, sustainable and endogenous way (Belletti 2010).

In the Apulia region, as mentioned earlier, an important initiative has been carried out by the Alta Murgia National Park, north of Bari[4]; the Park recognizes the fundamental role of farmers in protecting and managing the environment, through involving them in a number of actions for the protection of the Park and in keeping up the efficiency of the same farms.

As argued by Vedeld et al. (2012), protected areas aim at solving challenges of biodiversity conservation and at securing different environmental services, all with the aim of contributing to local livelihood improvements. Tensions between local people and park authorities are often strong and difficult to manage, as local people may perceive the area as a substantial constraint in their economic activities, in a context characterized by pressure over resource use. These tensions, within a long-term perspective, can be managed through an innovative approach to local development, in particular through local agriculture and sustainable tourism, certainly including agritourism.

The bad consequences brought by unmanaged tourism have more and more highlighted the importance of developing strategies carefully worked out to achieve sustainability in those natural areas usually devoted for tourism; consequently, the relationship between tourism, on the one side, and local agriculture and local people, on the other one, needs to be explored (Weaver 2005). As an example, it is vital to investigate whether an increased interest in local food traditions can really help to develop a sustainable tourism industry focusing not just on academic debates, but taking into consideration the responses of tourists and the opinions of local people (Sims 2009). Nowadays, rural areas are living a complex process of development and change that needs to be carefully dealt with in order to avoid the negative impact that can come from the inflow of tourists; this is particularly true with reference to protected areas (Lane 2005); sustainable tourism means first of all to re-establish a good relationship between the most important "actors" in this field, that is the tourism industry, the visitors or holiday-makers and the host areas with their habitats and their people. In the past years, the tourism industry has played the dominant part, with all the negative consequences on the environment. Sustainable tourism has to minimize the damage, both cultural and environmental, caused by unmanaged tourism, and must aim to ensure the satisfaction of visitors and above all an economic growth for the hosting region. In other words, it is the only way to obtain a perfect balance between the tourism potential growth and the need to safeguard the environment (Lane 2005).

In the Alta Murgia National Park, all the areas devoted to the promotion of traditional agricultural activities, together with the production of local traditional crafts, correspond to an area of 36.871 ha equal to 54% of the entire area of the Park.

Referring to the method proposed by McHarg, contained in his "Design with Nature" (1969), in the field of environmental planning, he outlines a "census of environmental resources" that serves the analysis of the natural and anthropological characteristics of the environment. In fact, according to the characteristics of the territory, the activities that can be carried out on it can be determined. Once the census has been carried out, the territory can be divided into areas with the same characteristics. For each area, it is possible to determine the resistance to transformations, the attitudes to the performance of particular functions and the susceptibility to the alterations suffered. In fact, these parameters depend strictly on the characteristics of the environment and therefore must be determined according to them. The identification of correct agricultural management practices passes through a pinpoint knowledge of the environmental resources present in the territory so as to increase the biological potential of these environmental systems, and to contribute to the protection of natural resources, it is necessary to provide for the use of agricultural land compatible with the conservation of species and habitats of species. The actions of the project "Agro-ecosystems: from the quality of the environment to the quality of production" have been developed, in the context outlined, with the aim to make the Park a place of "excellence".

The project: actions and best practices

The project "Agro-ecosystems: from the quality of the environment to the quality of production" arises from the need to compare the establishment of the Alta Murgia National Park with the agrozootechnical companies operating in the territory, in order to develop a model of sustainable management to be implemented in agricultural settings falling within valuable naturalistic areas. In fact, agriculture is the productive activity that, more than others, interferes with natural components and is affected by structural factors. On the territory of the Alta Murgia, which has always been characterized by a subsistence economy, linked above all to pastoralism, the productive realities are strongly affected by the natural characteristics such as climate, soil and water availability. At the end of the last century, in order to increase farms productivity and as a result of the EU price policy of cereals, a reduction was made in the area of natural meadows and pastures in the illusion of increasing the extension of arable land. These actions have partly modified the special characteristics of Alta Murgia, and accelerated the breeding crisis, especially sheep, which had until then determined the landscape and economy of Alta Murgia.

In 2004, the establishment of the national protected area, even if with a series of initial hostility and diffidence, allowed to start a process of safe-guarding and preserving the natural peculiarities and at the same time en-hancing the traditional economic activities, proposing new opportunities to operators. This is the starting point of a long journey started by the Park Authority, which also through this project aims to arrive at an efficient com-promise solution between strictly productive, and social and environmental objectives. The push toward the multifunctionality of the Alta Murgia farms allows the combination of the implementation of efficient production pro-cesses and the new demands of the community, combining the production of healthy food with the provision of a wide range of services and allowing the permanence of operators in the territory. The mentioned project, in fact, has allowed farmers to become aware of being the holders of a unique cul-ture and tradition and therefore to be the main players of the Alta Murgia National Park; farmers themselves will be able to participate in the sustain-able management of the territory through sharing the search for forms of sustainable economy.

Actions and methodology

The working methodology of the project was based on three main ac-tions, described as follows, coordinated by the "Laboratory of the Park".[5] The purpose, in general, is to come to develop a "business management model ideal and environmentally sustainable" both in valuable natural areas and in the territories used for agricultural and forestry equipment, and to draw up a "Catalog of the Park Friends Farms" in order to en-hance the productions and the tourist offers of the farms involved in the initiative. It reflects as well the need to adopt restoration strategies and actions based on a clear understanding of the context in which differ-ent agro-ecosystems evolve, first of all the wealth status of the farmers (Belem et al. 2011).

Activity 1: The farms friends of the Park. Research and history of the businesses in the area of Alta Murgia National Park through interviews with the owners of the sample farms, monitoring on the field and photo in-terpretation analysis of landscapes and naturalistic emergencies.

The choice of the companies to be sampled had, as a starting point, the consultation of the list of all the farms operating within the protected area, which had stipulated from the years 2010 to 2011 the "Convention for the correct environmental management of the territory"[6] with the Alta Murgia National Park Authority. Within this list, made up of over 300 companies, 172 have been identified with a business center within the Park area; these companies have been defined as "Park Friends farms".

Subsequently, the working group selected a sample of companies, among the 172 identified, which could be considered "representative" of the total number of farms operating in the Park territory. The choice of "representative companies" was the main design obstacle, as the Park covers a total area of about 68,000 ha and affects the territory of 2 provinces and 13 municipalities (Figure 3.1). In addition, the farms within the protected area show a considerable heterogeneity in terms of size, going from companies with a total extension not exceeding 20 ha, to companies of over 300 ha of extension.

For these reasons, it was decided to divide the total of the companies to be sampled into five dimensional classes, choosing within each class a number of companies that, in percentage, could be proportionally significant compared to the total. A second criterion of choice, beyond the dimensional one, has been the territorial distribution of the companies within the protected area, in relation to the territory of the single municipalities. Once the selection criterion has been identified, we have moved on to the identification of the dimensional classes; the 172 companies have thus been divided into 5 groups, on the basis of the extension of the company area contracted with the Park Authority, expressed in hectares:

- Group 1: 36 farms from 0 to 19.5 ha;
- Group 2: 50 farms from 20.46 to 49.64 ha;
- Group 3: 45 farms from 50.48 to 98.16 ha;
- Group 4: 38 farms from 101.82 to 340.42 ha;
- Group 5: 3 farms from 893.61 to 1139.45 ha.

Subsequently, established that 56 were to be the total of the companies to be sampled, the number of companies for each dimensional group was identified. The sample was defined as follows (Table 3.1):

- Group 1: 11 farms;
- Group 2: 16 farms;
- Group 3: 15 farms;
- Group 4: 13 farms;
- Group 5: 1 farm.

The next phase was the identification of companies based on their territorial distribution. The companies have been so selected within the area of the 13 municipal territories[7]:

- Altamura: 19;
- Andria: 4;
- Bitonto: 2;
- Cassano: 5;
- Corato: 5;

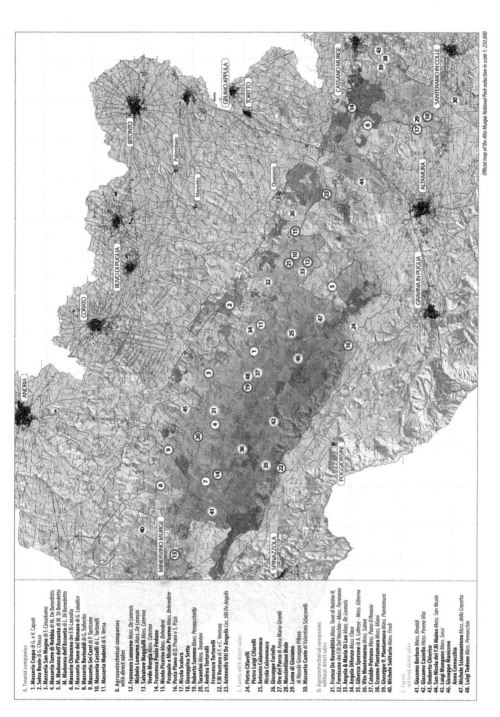

Figure 3.1 Map of the Park with location of companies.

Table 3.1 The 56 farms

n°	Farm	Block	n°	Farm	Block
1	Cifarelli Pietro	2	29	Lomurno Michele	3
2	Caputi Vittorio	4	30	Sette Giuseppina	2
3	Montemurno Vito	2	31	Solitario Michele	4
4	Tortorelli Luigi	2	32	Dileo Maria&Angela	3
5	Scalera Nicola	1	33	Cornacchia Anna	3
6	Berloco Giacomo	3	34	Casiello Giacomo	5
7	Debenedittis Michelangelo	1	35	Manicone Giuseppe	3
8	Tarricone Pasquale	4	36	Girardi Anna Maria	1
9	Cimadomo Francesco	4	37	Plantamura Erasmo	2
10	Patruno Cataldo	4	38	Dibenedetto Michele	3
11	Ventura Francesco e F.lli	3	39	F.lli Lanzolla	2
12	Sciannanteno Domenico/Michele	3	40	Maggiulli Salvatore	2
13	Pisani Domenico	4	41	Verna Saverio	4
14	Viti Deangelis Antonello	2	42	Lomurno Francesco	1
15	Pillera Nicola	1	43	Tortorelli Andrea	4
16	Summo Roberto	4	44	Maggiulli Annamaria	2
17	Colamonaco Nicola	2	45	Picerno Nicola	1
18	Colamonaco Antonio	3	46	Fariello Giuseppe	2
19	Sollecito Giovanna	4	47	Chierico Umberto	2
20	Lofrese Antonio	4	48	Plantamura Giuseppe Vito	1
21	Tortorelli Francesco	3	49	Picerno F.lli	2
22	Maino Giuseppe	3	50	Pedone Fracesco Paolo	3
23	Chicco Giuseppe	3	51	Sciacovelli Valentino	1
24	Mele Massimiliano	1	52	Mangano Luigi	2
25	Debenedittis Franco	4	53	Difonzo Rosa	3
26	Dibenedetto Leonardo	2	54	Tarantini Nicoletta	2
27	Loiudice Gianluca	3	55	Tedone	1
28	Del Vecchio Vincenzo	4	56	Cifarelli Pietro Luigi	1

Source: Official Alta Murgia National Park website.

- Gravina in Puglia: 4;
- Grumo Appula: 0;
- Minervino Murge: 4;
- Poggiorsini: 0;
- Ruvo di Puglia: 7;
- Santeramo in Colle: 2;
- Spinazzola: 3;
- Toritto: 1.

Including more than 10% of the entire surface of the protected area and affecting the areas of the 11 major municipalities of the Alta Murgia National Park,[8] the sample of the companies identified was considered representative of the entire area.

After this first phase of work, it was possible to move on to the development of a survey card in Excel format and to the "company visits" (Table 3.2). The card aims at reporting the data collected during the fieldwork, the

Table 3.2 Descriptive card (Excel format)

PAM_013 Az. Agr. Zoot. Posta Piano di Pisani D. & Piizzi S. Coc.	
Farm	Az. Agr. Zoot. Posta Piano di Pisani D. & Piizzi S. Coc.
SAU	150.63 ha
SAT	166.24 ha
Natural vegetation	62.44 ha
Town	Gravina in Puglia (Ba)
Agritourism	NO
Didactic farm	NO
Association/Territorial Consortium	NO
Organic agriculture	Yes
Livestock	Yes
Product transformation	Yes
Direct sale of products	Yes
Products	cheese
Main cultivations	cereals, legumes
Contacts	080/3252700 - 3487111347

Source: Official Alta Murgia National Park website.

interview with the farm owner[9] and the subsequent visit to each farm, so as to describe the "profile" of the single farm. The documentary material collected was subsequently filed using a logical pattern and the data sorted and digitized in a holding file.[10] Synthetic information was extrapolated and used to fill out a card and a descriptive text representative of each farm within the Catalog, from technical and practical information to more strictly functional details, useful to the practical use of the farm land and the surrounding area.

The resulting catalog[11] represents a fundamental tool to promote the same farms; aimed primarily at visitors and tourists, it classifies farms into five different categories based on the type of "offer of services". The categories identified were the following: (A) agritourism farms, (B) agrozootechnical companies with direct sales, (C) agricultural companies with direct sales, (D) agrozootechnical companies without direct sales and (E) agricultural companies without direct sales.

It is worth noting that the larger companies are generally agritouristic and agrozootechnical farms; many agritouristic farms also own farm animals and, therefore, have land used for grazing as for agrozootechnical companies. The companies that are on average smaller are those "with direct sales". These are small production companies that derive their income from the sale of their products directly to the consumer and on site, rather than from wholesale, part of the best practices described in the following paragraph (Hackl et al. 2007).

Activity 2: The Ideal farm. Definition of a methodology for monitoring and evaluating the actions to protect the geo-diversity and biodiversity carried out by the farms in the Park territory.

It is vital to note that the mentioned pursued methodology meets the following features:

1   Conciseness, as to the evaluation of the coherence of enterprise management systems (land use, crop choices, management techniques, aspects of flora and fauna) with the strategy of sustainable development decided by the Park.
2   Reproducibility, as to its applicability in any farm present in the Park, and to the comparability of results.
3   Sharing and appropriateness, i.e. it must not be imposed, but accepted by the farms in the Park.
4   Functionality and easiness, as to its capacity to adapt and improve the concrete conservation actions promoted by the Park Authority.

The final aim is to define the parameters to detect the mentioned "Ideal farm", i.e. a farm that, by means of its management strategies, is able to improve production performance and, at the same time, safeguard the territory (Blondel and Aronson 1995).

As to this action (Giordano 2017), a set of indicators was created, on the basis of theoretical models consistent with each other and with their practical application in the context of the Alta Murgia National Park. The set of indicators was based on four "dimensions": physical (water, soil, energy), ecological (biodiversity, habitat, ecosystem regulation), productive and economic (productive activities, waste management) and socio-cultural (learning and leisure, culture and landscape), all corresponding to respective domains in the agro-ecosystem (Pacini et al. 2009). Furthermore, for each of these dimensions, a precise number of systems can be identified (Lazzerini and Vazzana 2005). The indicators themselves are finally grouped according to the belonging systems and to the functions they represent. The functions are then categorized on the basis of studies of international importance such as the Millennium Ecosystem Assessment (De Groot et al. 2010) and interdisciplinary European research projects on the assessment of sustainable impact of land management policies (Pacini et al. 2011).

Subsequently, an evaluation system of indicators was developed, together with indexes according to their importance, as well as with the translation of the valuation rules in an automated program (DEXiSustainability companies Alta Murgia Park),[12] and the calculation process on the basis of data collected in 5 "case study" farms.[13] Then, for the evaluation of the agro-environmental sustainability of these selected farms, the application of the Program Dexi was carried out as an assessment tool of the mentioned "case study" farms, on the total number of farms involved in the project. In detail, in each of the dimensions of sustainability, the systems identified within each dimension and the eco-systemic functions, as well as to each indicator, the assignment of consistent weights.[14]

The approach used is based on a multi-criteria linear additive model that assumes that each of the indicators listed represents, through the level of its score, the performance produced by a company in relation to a particular eco-systemic function.

To each indicator corresponds a utility function of its own that represents the contribution that each farm gives with respect to each of the eco-systemic functions identified; the utility function is a linear function, or a function at fixed coefficients. Each coefficient depends, in the chosen model, on the number of indicators that contribute to the achievement of a given level of utility for the farmer/actor linked to an eco-systemic function. The model is additive in that the sum of the level of utility of the functions related to each indicator gives, as a result, the level of the eco-systemic function achieved by a single farm analyzed.

This result is then given by the sum of the products of the business performance (values of the indicators, standardized to sustainability scores between 0 and 1) multiplied by the relative weights (percentage calculated dividing by 100 the number of indicators of each eco-systemic function). Such method ensures equal distribution and importance to the various aspects to be measured; the calculation of the overall agro-environmental sustainability of a farm cannot be positive if one of the four dimensions (physical, ecological, productive-economic and socio-cultural) is negatively evaluated, in order to select only those companies really engaged in all the aspects taken into consideration. The overall sustainability of the 5 "case study" farms is shown below (Table 3.3).

Activity 3: The Park Places: twelve excursions among the most beautiful and significant places of the Alta Murgia National Park. The Park Laboratory.

Along with the Catalog, in order to promote the features of the farms, 12 tours whose itineraries start from farms were organized (Figure 3.2); participants had the opportunity to discover the naturalistic beauties of the "Murgia" area but also to approach those farms that brighten up the Park through the knowledge of the activities they play and their products.[15] This

Table 3.3 Evaluation of 5 "case study" farms

Farm	Aspect			
	Physical	*ECOLOGICAL*	*ECONOMIC*	*Socio-cultural*
Az. 01 Cifarelli	Medium	Low	High	Low
Az. 02 Caputi	Medium	High	High	High
Az. 24 De Benedittis	Low	High	High	Medium
Az. 03 Montemurno	High	Medium	High	High
Az. 40 Casiello	Medium	Medium	High	Low

Source: Official Alta Murgia National Park website.

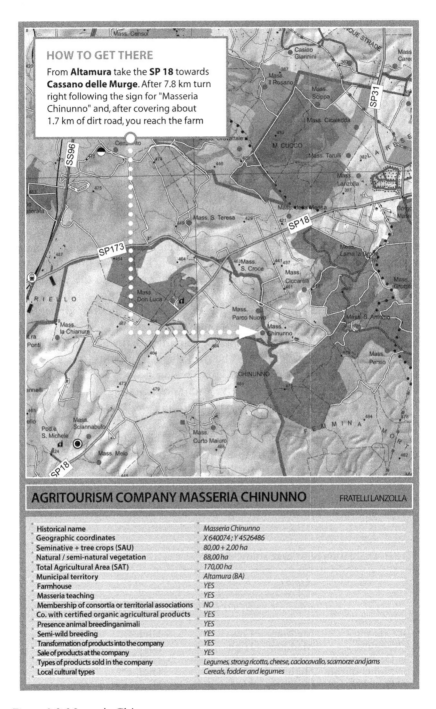

HOW TO GET THERE

From **Altamura** take the **SP 18** towards **Cassano delle Murge**. After 7.8 km turn right following the sign for "Masseria Chinunno" and, after covering about 1.7 km of dirt road, you reach the farm

AGRITOURISM COMPANY MASSERIA CHINUNNO   FRATELLI LANZOLLA

Historical name	*Masseria Chinunno*
Geographic coordinates	*X 640074; Y 4526486*
Seminative + tree crops (SAU)	*80,00 + 2,00 ha*
Natural / semi-natural vegetation	*88,00 ha*
Total Agricultural Area (SAT)	*170,00 ha*
Municipal territory	*Altamura (BA)*
Farmhouse	*YES*
Masseria teaching	*YES*
Membership of consortia or territorial associations	*NO*
Co. with certified organic agricultural products	*YES*
Presence animal breedinganimali	*YES*
Semi-wild breeding	*YES*
Transformation of products into the company	*YES*
Sale of products at the company	*YES*
Types of products sold in the company	*Legumes, strong ricotta, cheese, caciocavallo, scamorze and jams*
Local cultural types	*Cereals, fodder and legumes*

Figure 3.2 Masseria Chinunno.

action is an important local promozione tool, in particular, to bring citizens closer to the agro-operators, major knowers of the area.

In order to manage the organization of the general program, a "Laboratory" was set at the headquarters of the Officina del Piano "Don Francis Cassol" in Ruvo di Puglia. The function of the secretariat is to manage the project as a whole, from the contacts with farms to the overall organization of the project excursions.[16]

Best practices in the Alta Murgia National Park

All the data collected during the company visits, which led to the drafting of the Catalog, showed examples of sustainable agricultural practices, often applied by farmers in an unconscious way, simply for a "modus operandi" always followed in the family business, fundamental to promote multifunctionality and agritourism (Garrod 2006).

The mentioned direct sale, for example, once practiced routinely in the "Masserie"[17] of the Murgia: the farmer tries to "reduce" the steps of the commercial supply chain, recovering income, but above all, through direct contact with the consumer, manages to promote the quality of its products. Direct sale is among sustainable actions precisely because it reduces the frequency of transport to the distribution markets, moderates traffic and consequently pollution. Moreover, some of the companies interviewed have chosen to meet in consortia for the sale of their products, such as the Murgia Viva consortium, both for the promotion of their agricultural products and for the carrying out of educational activities, thus creating a virtuous process of sustainability, even social, through the relationship with local communities. It is also worth mentioning the 20 companies participating in the "Partnersheep" project, an initiative that aims to re-evaluate wool as a precious resource for various activities. Other companies show considerable attention and interest in reducing energy consumption, both through production with renewable sources and through energy savings; they play an important role in preserving the traditional, but also natural, agricultural landscape, through a series of action related to the safeguard of the so-called agro-biodiversity.[18] The agro-biodiversity reflects the existing dynamic relationships in each ecosystem between human activities, cultivated plants and domestic animals (Cromwell et al. 2003); as a result of its close and strong ties to food security, health, social equity, the fight against famine, environmental protection and sustainable rural development, agro-biodiversity is perceived as threatened and in need of protection by means of ad hoc innovative legal instruments both at national and international levels.

As a result, and perhaps for the first time, lawmakers are engaged in a major process of innovation that aims to protect and improve local and traditional agricultural systems seen as incubators of the agro-biodiversity itself and as basic elements of the cultural, historical and natural inheritance of each territory and rural space (Giordano 2017). The mentioned Catalog pays particular attention to organic farming, as an example of low environmental impact activities.

It is fundamental to note how the described project aims at creating a real network of farms aware of having the "strength" in promoting sustainable management in this Alta Murgia "territorial system", and at quantifying the positive effects of all the practices, through the search for eco-sustainability and biodiversity parameters that can be compared, to identify the mentioned "Ideal Farm" and create a quality label of the Alta Murgia National Park products.

SWOT analysis

It is worth noting that some crucial points, detected during the entire project, constitute hinge points on which to reflect in the light of a possible second phase of the project itself. These are related to issues strongly intertwined with those already analyzed throughout the present contribution:

- Infrastructural resources. The protected area is characterized by a good infrastructural situation; the farm territories are crossed by roads for a total, for the 56 companies taken into consideration, of 170.35 km. Nevertheless, there remains a significant gap compared to the national average situation. As to rural infrastructures concerning water distribution and the presence of artesian wells or other types of water supply, among the total number of selected companies, 71% of them are equipped with these systems.
- Hydrogeological instability. The hydrogeological instability phenomena show the condition of decay of the territory of some areas of the Alta Murgia National Park, concentrated in the top area of the plateau, in those with steeper slopes and in places where, over the years, successive interventions of stone clearance have taken place.
- Forests. The total forest area for the farms interviewed is 397.77 ha and is characterized by the attractive presence of young oak forests mixed with the Mediterranean scrub (over 150.77 ha), while the remaining 247 ha are made up of conifer reforestation. The territory of the Park and the selected farms shows a low degree of plant forest biodiversity, and, in general, a lack of integration between agriculture and forest activities.
- Organic farming. Organic operators, on the basis of the project elaboration, are 47 out of the 56 farms sampled; the distribution of surfaces, distinguished according to crop types, shows a prevalence of those under cereals with 4,115.54 ha out of a total of UAA (Utilized Agricultural Area) amounting to 5,387.49 ha, immediately followed by those dedicated to olive tree with a surface of 141.05 ha, and then almond trees with an area of 67.86 ha. However, we must point out, with regard to other stages of the "organic supply chain", a weakness and an insignificant role of the stages downstream of the agricultural production and, in particular, in the marketing sector (Caporali 2004, 2007).

- The characteristics of the food processing system. Agriculture in the Park area is characterized by a strong variety of production situations, with the vast majority of the farms managed directly by the owner. As to the distinction in the age of farmers, the project data show that 11 of the conductors are over 55 years old, while the number of those below the age of 35 is also equal to 11. There is, therefore, a lack of generational change situation, which is important both for the continuity and the introduction of innovations.
- Agriculture and other activities. Several farms take on other activities together with the production and marketing of farm products; the production diversification focuses on activities traditionally found in rural areas such as processing of agricultural products, direct sales on the farm and educational or tourist activities. Among the 56 farms, there are about 12 that offer farm holiday services and 31 that make direct sales of farm products. However, product diversification is not accompanied by marketing actions aimed at facilitating the integration of the supply of agricultural products and other farm activities with the resources in the area (Mangialardi 2011).

Valbuena et al. (2014) argue that the analysis of the diversity of local farms and of the agro-ecosystems in which they are present is vital to effectively design more sustainable management tools. The analysis of the strengths and weaknesses of the "altomurgiano" (i.e. from Alta Murgia) agro-livestock sector (SWOT analysis) has highlighted positive and negative "knots" with which the agricultural system must deal in order to promote a significant turnaround compared to also the most recent past. The SWOT analysis has highlighted, considering the socio-economic characteristics and their evolution, the need to adopt strategies able to improve the regional competitiveness of the area; a first objective is the improvement of the quality standards of agricultural products and of the integration of the supply chain, in order to allow the competitiveness in domestic and international markets, through interventions on productive structures and marketing strategies, mainly devoted to the revaluation of local food and wine products. Another goal is the promotion of innovation and integration along the supply chain, including technical and organizational innovations that improve the competitiveness of the different productive sectors. Investments in public infrastructures play, as well, a vital role mainly in support of marketing activities; important, ultimately, will be to improve the entrepreneurial and professional skills of local players, all combined with the aim of the conservation of biodiversity, key resource within a protected area. The primary sector, i.e. agriculture, strongly contributes through the diffusion of agro-forestry systems of high naturalistic value; the protection of biodiversity in agriculture is not just about habitats and wild species, but also about genetic diversity of the species cultivated. This involves the introduction or continuation of support for sustainable production methods, as well as the protection of animal and plant genetic resources and the overall diversification of agricultural activities toward the creation of new environmental services. The project "Agro-ecosystems, from the quality of the environment to the quality of the productions" plays a vital role, thanks to give to a group of farmers the awareness to be key players in local dynamics and in the decisions of the Park Board, as well as in the further development of the project itself.

Conclusions

Rural tourism is certainly not a panacea able to solve the problems of economic and social marginalization of marginal rural areas, and indeed the theme of economic, social and environmental sustainability of its development arises more precisely in the most fragile areas (Santilli 2005). Some themes appear to be priorities in defining a research agenda on the subject of sustainability in rural tourism: the actual role played by rural territorial capitals in the provision of rural tourism and the degree of endogeneity of rural tourism initiatives; the relationship between tourism activities and non-tourism activities in rural areas and the role played by tourism in the restructuring of the countryside; the trade-off between economic benefits and environmental and social costs, congestion in the use of resources and possible conflicts of use between local population and guests and participation in the benefits of tourism development by those who produce rural capitals and mechanisms for reproducing rural resources (Sharpley and Vass 2006). In any case, rural tourism can only represent an integrated and coordinated component within "ad hoc" rural development models and strategies specific to each territory, able to guarantee a balance between consumption and reproduction of rural collective resources through a participation of the various categories of bearers (Cawely and Gillmor 2008).

Rural and natural areas are easily damaged, and tourism can be a powerful agent for a negative change. Even protected national parks are in danger of deterioration because of the huge number of visitors and need policies of sustainable tourism to match development and conservation. Nevertheless, these areas also play an important role as repositories of natural and historical heritage, which makes them very important from a commercial point of view (Rössler 2005; Phillips 2005); in other words, what is usually referred to as "rurality" becomes a unique opportunity for selling holidays in the countryside, mainly to tourists looking for peaceful and quiet places, still unspoiled but with a good quality offer (Suess-Reyes and Fuetsch 2016).

Sustainable tourism must be dealt with in a different and more innovative way, taking into consideration not only the growth requirements of the tourism industry (capital investment plans and so on) but also, and above all, a wider analysis based on the social, economic and ecological needs of each area (McHarg, 1995). Local participation, derived mainly from farmers, is also to be stressed in any plan-making process and decision making (Lane 2005). Local agriculture and food play a very important role in sustainable tourism because of their appeal to the desire of visitors to live an "authentic" experience within their holiday (Sims 2009), establishing a stronger link between tourists and the culture and heritage of the area they are visiting, and providing stories and details that make them go beyond the simple taste of food. In the context of the Alta Murgia National Park, this resulted in the creation of the mentioned Catalog and in the so-called "Agro Stories".[19]

Once again, rural tourism is an effective tool that takes into consideration all the aspects and all the people in a territory: neither protection of the environment at the expense of business, nor benefiting businesses at the expense of local people, but creating a cultural economic and environmental milieu that is good for both visitors and local people, defined as "all-round sustainability" (Sims 2009). Successful sustainable tourism needs a long-term strategy and a government/private companies' partnership: the government has to ensure the majority of the financial resources in the first periods until the private companies have progressed enough to provide their part of funding; this is particularly true for rural areas, traditionally poorer (Hall et al. 2003). It is vital to adopt a wider perspective that starts from the analysis of the different needs of the area (cultural, economic, environmental and so on) and of how tourism can help to improve the local economy; the same strategy, then, develops, through the active participation of local people to plans and decisions, a long-term program able to protect the environment, to foster new local enterprises and to support local farming and agriculture, in a word the regional economy. As mentioned earlier, the role of protected areas in the preservation and sustainable use of agro-biodiversity is still under-estimated; still today, at the international scale, it is not possible to find a category of protected areas specifically dedicated to the safeguard of agro-biodiversity. This is true with reference to conservation "in situ" of wild species "relatives" of cultivated ones and to the management "on farm" of those agro-ecosystems with a high level of agro-biodiversity. According to the FAO Second Report on the state of the World's Plant Genetic Resources for Food and Agriculture,[20] a significant number of plant genetic resources for agriculture, among which wild species "relatives" of cultivated ones and plants harvested, are located outside protected areas (cultivated areas, orchards, meadows) and do not take benefit from any form of legal protection.[21] As a matter of fact, it is possible to observe a shift in the paradigm inherent in the conservation and preservation efforts, from the designation of exceptional natural sites without human presence (primary or quasi-primary zones) to the recognition of the value and importance of those sites of "natural heritage" in a landscape context entailing residential human presence. In other words, a greater attention is granted to the interaction between humans and nature, and the fundamental importance of those protected areas based on inhabited scenery is increasingly admitted and investigated. In the wake of this evolution, a new category of protected areas that may be labeled as "agro-biodiversity reserves" or "protected landscape with a high level of agro-biodiversity" can be established, peculiarly based on the management of biodiversity in agriculture and on the recognition and preservation of traditional techniques, practices and know-how, as well as on the mentioned multifunctionality, including agritourism initiatives.

Notes

1 Cf.: Sustainable Development Knowledge platform. "United Nations Conference on the Human Environment (Stockholm Conference)." https://sustainabledevelopment.un.org/milestones/humanenvironment (accessed February 20, 2018).
2 Cf.: UN Documents: Gathering a Body of Global Agreements. "Report ol the World Commission on Environment and Development: Our Common Future." http://www.un-documents.net/our-common-future.pdf (accessed February 13, 2018).
3 As to the Italian context, according to Law n.96, 20th of February 2006, "Agritourism Discipline", the agricultural activities must remain predominant with regard to hospitality; agritourism, therefore, perfectly represents the first true form of diversification and agricultural multifunctionality.
4 Parco Nazionale dell'Alta Murgia. http://www.parcoaltamurgia.gov.it/ (accessed February 2, 2018).
5 The "Laboratory of the Park", which will be discussed later and whose tasks relate to the logistical organization of the project in question, is based at the Workshop of the Plan for the Park "Don Francis Cassol" in Ruvo di Puglia (in the Province of Bari).
6 The "2010/2011 Convention for the correct environmental management of the Park territory" arises from the desire of the Park Board to set up with farmers and cattlemen working relationships for the proper management of the territory of the protected natural area. The text is available at:
Parco Nazionale dell'Alta Murgia. "Schema di convenzione per la realizzazione di interventi per la gestione ambientale da parte di privati nel territorio del Parco Nazionale dell'Alta Murgia." http://www.parcoaltamurgia.gov.it/images/convenzioneambientale/Schema_convenzione_gestione_def_23_03_2011.pdf (accessed February 2, 2018).
7 The municipalities that are part of the Park are Altamura, Andria, Bitonto, Cassano, Corato, Gravina in Apulia, Grumo Appula, Minervino Murge, Poggiorsini, Ruvo di Apulia, Santeramo in Colle, Spinazzola, and Toritto.
8 The town of Altamura is in first place with 12,000 ha.
9 The factors taken into account are farmland, crop types, presence of breeding animals, presence of valuable architectural artifacts, crop management and production companies of excellence, local products and high biodiversity value crops, the presence of karstic caves and peculiar views of the landscape, wildlife and flora life relevant stations, architectural and naturalistic emergencies, legends about places or people who have lived in it, and origin of place names.
10 Each monitored company has its own file, which consists of the Excel sheet of business survey; georeferenced photographs of the farm territory and the main structures; a technical report in Word format that describes extensively the farm in all its aspects ("Agrostorie"); a shapefile of "significant" business points manageable through GIS programs.
11 Cf.: Parco Nazionale dell'Alta Murgia. http://www.parcoaltamurgia.gov.it/ (accessed February 2, 2018). The Park website provides relevant information regarding the practices here described (accessed on 3/1/2018).
12 The Dexi-sustainability farms Alta Murgia Park program is built on the basis of an open-source software Dexi (http://wwwai.ijs.si/MarkoBohanec/dexi.html). The software comes with an original manual in English language.

13 One for each Group.
14 The assignment was carried out as proposed by Paracchini et al. (2011). An in-depth analysis can be found on the Park website at http://www.parcoaltamurgia.gov.it/
15 For all the excursions, a top limit of 50 people has been set up, in order to ensure the best possible service and guarantee a low level of inconvenience to the places visited.
16 In detail, it carried on the following tasks: to manage the relationships with the farms contacted (appointments, etc.); to contribute to the archiving of the material collected and of all the material collected throughout the project (photos, popularity cards, etc.); to provide logistical and organizational support to the organization of public events where required (spread promotional material, contact the speakers, organize and book meeting rooms, etc.); to collaborate in the monitoring of the Project; to manage the relationships with the press and media organs; to provide a logistical support to the correct carrying out of all the activities involved in the project.
17 A "Masseria" is a typical farm house.
18 The concept of agro-biodiversity has emerged in the last 15 years as the intersection between biodiversity and agriculture. According to the definition given by the FAO, "agro-biodiversity is the result of processes of natural selection and of the careful selection and developments in the inventiveness of farmers, herders and fishers over millennia. The agro-biodiversity is a vital by-product of biodiversity". Cf.: Food and Agriculture Organization of the United Nations (FAO). "What is agrobiodiversity?" in "Building on Gender, Agrobiodiversity and Local Knowledge." FAO, 2004. http://www.fao.org/docrep/007/y5609e/y5609e01.htm (accessed January 18, 2018). In the context of agro-biodiversity protection, a crucial role is played by the preservation of agro-ecosystems. Defined by the OECD as "an ecosystem subjected to agricultural management, connected to other ecosystems". Cf.: OECD. "Glossary of Statistical Terms. Agro-Ecosystem." http://stats.oecd.org/glossary/detail.asp?ID=82 (accessed February 18, 2018).
19 Cf.: Parco Nazionale dell'Alta Murgia. "Visitare il Parco." http://www.parcoaltamurgia.gov.it/index.php/visitare-il-parco/alta-murgia (accessed February 2, 2018).
20 Source: Food and Agriculture Organization of the United Nations (FAO). "The Second Report On The State Of The World's Plant Genetic Resources For Food And Agriculture, Synthetic Account." http://www.fao.org/docrep/013/i1500e/i1500e_brief.pdf (accessed January 26, 2018).
21 Taking into consideration farmers' rights is fundamental to allow the preservation and sustainability of agro-biodiversity. These mentioned rights are embedded in the preamble and in Article 9 of ITPGRFA (International Treaty on Plant Genetic Resources for Food and Agriculture). Cf.: Food and Agriculture Organization of the United Nations (FAO). "International Treaty on Plant Genetic Resources for Food and Agriculture." http://www.fao.org/plant-treaty/en/ (accessed February 2, 2018).

References

Balestrieri, Giovanni. *Il turismo rurale nello sviluppo integrato della Toscana*. Firenze: IRPET, Regione Toscana, 2005. http://www.irpet.it/storage/pubblicazioneallegato/49_Balestrieri.pdf

Belem, M., J. Bayala, and A. Kalinganire. "Defining the Poor by the Rural Communities of Burkina Faso: Implications for the Development of Sustainable Parkland Management." *Agroforest Systems*, 83, no. 3 (2011): 287–302. http://eprints.icrisat.ac.in/id/eprint/2959.

Belletti, Giovanni. "Ruralità e turismo." *Agriregionieuropa*, 6, no. 20 (March 2010). https://agriregionieuropa.univpm.it/it/content/article/31/20/ruralita-e-turismo.

Blondel, Jacques, and James Aronson. "Biodiversity and Ecosystem Function in the Mediterranean Basin: Human and Non-human Determinants." In *Mediterranean-Type Ecosystems: The Function of Biodiversity*, edited by George W. Davis, David M. Richardson, 43–120. Berlin: Springer-Verlag, 1995. doi:10.1007/978-3-642-78881-9.

Caporali, Fabio. *Agriculture and Health: The Challenge of Organic Farming.* Cento: Editeam, 2004.

Caporali, Fabio. "Agroecology as a Science of Integration for Sustainability in Agriculture." *Italian Journal of Agronomy*, 2 (2007): 73–82. agronomy.it/index. php/agro/article/download/ija.2007.73/.../0

Cawley, Mary, and Desmond A. Gillmor. "Integrated Rural Tourism: Concepts and Practice." *Annals of Tourism Research*, vol. 35, no. 2 (2008): 316–337. doi:10.1016/j. annals.2007.07.011

Cromwell, Elizabeth, David Cooper, and Patrick Mulvany. "Defining Agricultural Bio-diversity". Vol. 1, Chapter 1. In CIP-UPWARD. *Conservation and Sustainable Use of Agricultural Biodiversity: A Sourcebook.* Laguna: International Potato Center-Users Perspectives With Agricultural Research and Development. 2003. https://idl-bnc-idrc.dspacedirect.org/bitstream/handle/10625/36069/118718_v3.pdf

De Groot, R. S., R. Alkemande, L. Braat, L. Hein, and L. Willemen. "Challenges in Integrating the Concept of Ecosystem Services and Values in Landscape Planning, Management and Decision Making." *Ecological Complexity*, 7, no. 3 (2010): 260–272. doi:10.1016/j.ecocom.2009.10.006.

Garrod, Brian, Roz Wornell, and Ray Youell. "Re-conceptualising Rural Resources as Countryside Capital: The Case of Rural Tourism." *Journal of Rural Studies*, 22, no. 1 (2006): 117–128. http://course.sdu.edu.cn/G2S/ eWebEditor/uploadfile/20130509154805009.pdf.

Giordano, Simona. "Rural Poverty and Rural Development: A Case for Family Farming and Sustainable Tourism in the National Park of Gargano (Italy)." In VIII International Scientific Agricultural Symposium "Agrosym 2017", Jahorina, Bosnia and Herzegovina, October 2017. Book of Proceedings, ISBN 9789997671813.

Hackl Franz, Martin Halla, and Gerald J. Pruckner. "Local Compensation Payments for Agri-Environmental Externalities: A Panel Data Analysis of Bargaining Outcomes." *European Review of Agricultural Economics*, 34, no. 3 (2007): 295–320. doi:10.1093/erae/jbm022.

Hall Derek, Lesley Roberts, and Morag Mitchell. *New Directions in Rural Tourism.* Aldershot: Ashgate, 2003.

Khan M. Alid. "Sustainable Development: The Key Concepts, Issues and Implications. Keynote Paper Given at the International Sustainable Development Research Conference, 27–29 March 1995, Manchester, UK." *Sustainable Development*, 3, no. 2 (1995): 63–69. https://doi.org/10.1002/sd.3460030203.

Lane, Bernard. "Sustainable Rural Tourism Strategies: A Tool for Development and Conservation." *Revista Interamericana de Ambiente y Turismo*, vol. 1, no. 1 (August 2005): 12–18. A reprint from *Journal of Sustainable Tourism*, 2, no. 1–2 (1994): 102–111. doi:10.1080/09669589409510687.

Lazzerini, G., and C. Vazzana. "Indicatori agro-ambientali come strumenti di gestione aziendale e di valutazione della sostenibilità ambientale." Proceedings 36th National Meeting Italian Society of Agronomy, Foggia, Italy, 2005.

Mangialardi, Piergiorgio. *Agriturismo e ospitalità rurale. Come creare valore dal territorio*, Milano: Hoepli, 2011.

McHarg, Ian L. *Design with Nature*. Hoboken, NJ: Wiley, 1995.

Pacini, Gaio Cesare, Giulio Lazzerini, Paola Migliorini, and Concetta Vazzana. "An Indicator-based Framework to Evaluate Sustainability of Farming Systems: Review of Applications in Tuscany." *Italian Journal of Agronomy*, 4, no. 1 (2009): 23–39. http://www.agronomyjournal.it/index.php/agro/article/view/ija.2009.1.23/293.

Pacini, Gaio Cesare, Giulio Lazzerini, and Concetta Vazzana. "AESIS: A Support Tool for the Evaluation of Sustainability of Agroecosystems. Example of Applications to Organic and Integrated Farming Systems in Tuscany, Italy." *Italian Journal of Agronomy*, 6, no. 1 (February 2011): 11–18. doi:10.4081/ija.2011.e3

Paracchini, M.L., Pacini, C., Jones, M.L.M., Pérez-Soba, M. An aggregation framework to link indicators associated with multifunctional land use to the stakeholder evaluation of policy options. *Ecological Indicators* 11, no. 1 (2011): 71–80. doi:10.1016/j.ecolind.2009. 04.006.

Phillips, Adrian. "Landscape as a Meeting Ground: Category V Protected Landscapes/Seascapes and World Heritage Cultural Landscapes." In *The Protected Landscape Approach: Linking Nature, Culture and Community*, edited by Jessica Brown, Nora Mitchell, and Michael Beresford, 19–35. Gland and Cambridge: IUCN, 2005.

Rössler, Mechtild. "World Heritage Cultural Landscapes: A Global Perspective." In *The Protected Landscape Approach: Linking Nature, Culture and Community*, edited by Jessica Brown, Nora Mitchell, and Michael Beresford, 37–46. Gland and Cambridge: IUCN, 2005. https://portals.iucn.org/library/sites/library/files/documents/2005-006.pdf

Santilli Juliana. *Livro Socioambientalismo e Novos Direitos: Proteção Jurídica À Diversidade Biológica e Cultural*. Sao Paulo: Editora Peiropolis, ISA/IEB, 2005. http://www.ethno-terroirs.cnrs.fr/gestion/applis/apetit/fichiers/UNIVERSIDADEDEBRASILIA-SANTILLI_Juliana-Socioambientalismo-e-novos-direitos.pdf

Saxena, Gunjan, Gordon Clark, Tove Oliver, and Brian Ilbery. "Conceptualizing Integrated Rural Tourism." *Tourism Geographies*, vol. 9, no. 4 (2007): 347–370. https://doi.org/10.1080/14616680701647527

Sharpley, Richard, and AdrianVass. "Tourism, Farming and Diversification: An Attitudinal Study." *Tourism Management*, 27 (2006): 1040–1052. doi:10.1016/j.tourman.2005.10.025

Sims, Rebecca. "Food, Place and Authenticity: Local Food and the Sustainable Tourism Experience." *Journal of Sustainable Tourism*, 17, no. 3 (2009): 321–336. https://doi.org/10.1080/09669580802359293

Suess-Reyes, Julia, and Elena Fuetsch. "The Future of Family Farming: A Literature Review on Innovative, Sustainable and Succession-oriented Strategies." *Journal of Rural Studies*, 47 (2016): 24–140. https://doi.org/10.1016/j.jrurstud.2016.07.008

Valbuena, Diego, Jeron C. J. Groot, John Mukalamaj, Bruno Gérard, and Pablo Tittonell. "Improving Rural Livelihoods as a 'Moving Target': Trajectories of Change in Smallholder Farming Systems of Western Kenya." *Regional Environmental Change*, vol. 15, no. 7 (2014): 1395–1407. https://doi.org/10.1007/s10113-014-0702-0.

Vedeld, Paul, Abdallah Jumane, Gloria Wapalila, and Alexander Songorwa. "Protected Areas, Poverty and Conflicts. A Livelihood Case Study of Mikumi National Park, Tanzania." *Forest Policy and Economics*, 21 (August 2012): 20–31. doi:10.1016/j.forpol.2012.01.008. "The Distinctive Dynamics of Exurban Tourism",

Weaver, David. "The Distinctive Dynamics of Exurban Tourism." *International Journal of Tourism Research*, 7, no. 1 (January/February 2005): 23–33. PDF e-book. https://onlinelibrary.wiley.com/doi/pdf/10.1002/jtr.521

Sitography

Food and Agriculture Organization of the United Nations (FAO). "International Treaty on Plant Genetic Resources for Food and Agriculture." http://www.fao.org/plant-treaty/en/ (accessed February 2, 2018).

Food and Agriculture Organization of the United Nations (FAO). "The Second Report on the State of the World's Plant Genetic Resources for Food and Agriculture, Synthetic Account." http://www.fao.org/docrep/013/i1500e/i1500e_brief.pdf (accessed January 26, 2018).

Food and Agriculture Organization of the United Nations (FAO). "What is Agrobiodiversity?" in "Building on Gender, Agrobiodiversity and Local Knowledge." FAO, 2004. http://www.fao.org/docrep/007/y5609e/y5609e01.htm (accessed January 18, 2018).

OECD. "Glossary of Statistical Terms. Agro-Ecosystem." http://stats.oecd.org/glossary/detail.asp?ID=82 (accessed February 18, 2018).

Parco Nazionale del Gargano. http://www.parcogargano.gov.it/servizi/notizie/notizie_homepage.aspx (accessed January 1, 2018).

Parco Nazionale dell'Alta Murgia. "Schema di convenzione per la realizzazione di interventi per la gestione ambientale da parte di privati nel territorio del Parco Nazionale dell'Alta Murgia." http://www.parcoaltamurgia.gov.it/images/convenzioneambientale/Schema_convenzione_gestione_def_23_03_2011.pdf (accessed February 2, 2018).

Parco Nazionale dell'Alta Murgia. "Visitare il Parco." http://www.parcoaltamurgia.gov.it/index.php/visitare-il-parco/alta-murgia (accessed February 2, 2018).

Parco Nazionale dell'Alta Murgia. http://www.parcoaltamurgia.gov.it/ (accessed February 2, 2018).

Sustainable Development Knowlwdge platform. "United Nations Conference on the Human Environment (Stockholm Conference)." https://sustainabledevelopment.un.org/milestones/humanenvironment (accessed February 20, 2018).

UN Documents: Gathering a Body of Global Agreements. "Report of the World Commission on Environment and Development: Our Common Future." http://www.un-documents.net/our-common-future.pdf (accessed February 13, 2018).

4 Challenges of promoting tourism to encourage the local development of fishing communities

Evelia de Jesus Izabal de la Garza
and Marcela Rebeca Contreras Loera

Introduction

In Mexico, some factors have been affecting the fishing and rural sector development, such as low growth of agricultural and fishing activity, poverty of rural families, degradation of natural resources, an adverse economic environment, as well as a weak institutional framework (FAO and SAGARPA 2014).

Tourism is an important resource that has to be taken into consideration for developing rural areas (Gavrilă-Paven, Bârsan Mircea and Lia-Dorica 2015) and it is identified as an economic growth catalyst and as a development option for the economic and social regeneration of rural communities (Pezzi and Urso 2017).

In México, tourism is considered one of the driving forces of economic growth of the country, by contributing 8.7% of the national Gross Domestic Product (GDP) (INEGI 2018) worldwide. In 2016, Mexico advanced a position in the ranking of international tourists arrivals, being positioned at place number 8, and went up two positions in international tourism income, staying at place 14 (UNWTO 2017).

The composition of tourism GPD of Mexico and the tourist consumption for travel pattern in 2016 is summarized in Table 4.1.

However, rural tourism in México is incipient, and yet it receives little economic support compared to the tourism that is encouraged in the fully planned urban centers (Garduño 2009). Tourism attention in the country has focused mainly on the development of highly concentrated coastal complexes, so rural tourism should evolve to compete in the global tourism market and take advantage of its tourism potential, based on culture and nature, and thus contribute to the creation of sustainable employment and income opportunities for marginalized rural communities located in areas with abundant natural resources (OECD 2017).

In this context, this research focuses on determining if there are conditions for the development of tourism in a peripheral rural community, and in doing so it analyzes the case of a rural fishing community, which considers to take advantage of their natural and cultural resources for the

Table 4.1 Tourist GDP and tourist consumption in Mexico

		%
Tourist GDP	Accommodation services	28.8
	Passenger transport services	19.5
	Restaurants, bars and nightclubs	15.4
	Other services	15.3
	Goods and crafts	10.6
	Trade	7.4
	Cultural services	1.1
	Sports services	1.1
	Travel agency	0.8
Tourist consumption	Domestic tourism (national)	75.4%
	Receptive tourism (international)	16.2%
	Outbound tourism	8.4%

Source: Prepared by the authors with data from INEGI (2016).

development of tourism as an economic complementary activity, in the face of various problems affecting its economy. This chapter is organized into four sections: the first includes a theoretical review on rural local development and tourism as an alternative to promote it, then the methodological design and the results from field research are presented, among which are the challenges faced by the community under study, such as the lack of business mentality and problems of trust among its inhabitants. Finally, the conclusions derived from the whole investigation are exposed.

Local development and rural communities

Economic development is a multidimensional concept defined as a process that mainly focuses on the improvement of the living standards of a society that needs to enhance growth and technology levels, promotion of education and poverty reduction (Karlsson 1999; in Meyer, De Jongh and Meyer 2016).

In general, the local economic development is a process of growth and structural change that, through the use of the development potential existing in the territory, leads to raising the well-being of the population of a locality or a region (Aghon, Alburquerque and Cortes 2001, 21). However, Pike, Rodriguez-Pose and Tomaney (2006, 25) expose the lack of a homogeneous and generally accepted definition of local and regional development, and are also supported by Reese (1997) and Danson et al. (2000); they also explain that the elements considered to determine local and regional development change between countries, and within them; and that the particular notions of this development are determined by social groups and particular interests in specific places and periods. According to the authors, the definitions and conceptualizations of local and regional development differ geographically and change with time and historical context.

The debate about development policies, by academics and international organizations, shows great interest in the intervention of regional development, as well as the lack of a prevailing paradigm for that matter. It focuses on determining where efficiency should be concentrated: at the core or in the potential of each territory (Barca, McCann and Rodríguez-Pose 2012, 149).

Policymakers must seek to ensure that territorial strategies produce significant economic growth and social development, their efficiency can be maximized through capacity building at the local level, and the promotion of multilevel governance to enhance vertical and horizontal coordination (Rodriguez-Pose and Wilkie 2017).

Local and regional development has become a global challenge: it occurs in the middle of global flows of resources, finance and people. It is increasingly complex and interdependent; furthermore, in the midst of changing theories and ideologies influenced by particular governance and governance structures, they result in different types of political intervention (Pike, Rodriguez-Pose and Tomaney 2017).

In this context, Enríquez (2008) maintains that the processes of local development are endogenous, emerge from inside the territories from the development of the capacities that allow its emergence as a response to the current situation through which they live, revalue the set of local resources and seek optimal use of their potential.

Rural areas, as already mentioned earlier, survive many challenges, so a concept frequently associated with rural communities is that of resilience, which refers to the capacity of individuals or a community to cope with stress, overcome adversity or adapt positively to change (Fitri et al. 2015). At the human community level, resilience is the capacity of a place to maintain positive functional relationships in the presence of significant disturbances, resolve new issues and rebound from adversity with strengthened and more resourceful capabilities (Folke et al. 2002, in Fitri Amir et al. 2015, 118).

For Sánchez-Zamora, Gallardo-Cobos and Ceña-Delgado (2016, 103), community resilience focuses on the collective capacity of citizens to respond to change: based on a theoretical review, the authors identify two ways of approaching resilience from a territorial perspective, one raises a return to equilibrium prior to a disturbance, and another as a dynamic attribute associated with continuous adjustment processes, where resilience can be understood as the capacity of a territory to adapt its economic, social and natural conditions to the new conditions and maintain a continuous development over time. The latter notion is associated with innovation.

The environment of rural fishing activity is commonly defined through the concepts of vulnerability, risk, sustainability and resilience for the diverse economic and social affectations that are faced (Clay and Olson 2008). In recent years with evidence of rising global temperatures and extreme weather event, the concept of community resilience has become particularly salient (Newman et al. 2009, in Fitri Amir et al. 2015). In this context, the inhabitants of fishing communities perceive their areas as isolated; therefore, they accept tourist activities as an opportunity to have an additional contribution to their incomes and to spread their knowledge of their work, product and culture (Herrera-Racionero, Miret-Pastor and Lizcano 2018).

Rural tourism as an alternative local development strategy

Tourism refers to the temporary movement of people to destinations outside their places of work and normal residence, the activities involved during their stay in those destinations and the facilities created to meet their needs during their stay (Gunn and Var 2002, 9).

Tourism development depends on commercial, economic and logistical issues, such as the quality of the product, accessibility and infrastructure of the destination, availability of skills and interest of investors. In most of these aspects, rural areas may well be at a disadvantage compared to urbanized and more developed areas (Gavrilă-Paven et al. 2015, 1051). However, well-developed and focused rural tourism can become a new source of money and employment to eliminate the social isolation of rural communities (Dragi-Dimitrovski, Tomislav-Todorovic and Djordje-Valjarevic 2012). This requires well-developed and focused rural tourism to be able to become a new source of income and employment, as well as a resource to eliminate social isolation (Lane 1994, in Dragi-Dimitrovski et al. 2012).

The factors that motivate a community to develop rural tourism vary from one to another; some are motivated by economic problems, so they seek other commercial niches, while for others, their main reasons are based on the existence of favorable opportunities for their development (Streimikiene and Bilan 2015); however, the great challenge for these peripheral areas relies on not being guaranteed the supply of potential entrepreneurs who faced the threats and took advantage of the opportunities of these localities, as well as the lack of favorable conditions for innovation (Pezzi and Urso 2017).

Rural tourism is based on the development, use and enjoyment of alternative tourism products; it deploys a series of services and products that generate additional income, so it represents a complementary option, which gains competitiveness when the rural family is the entrepreneur, from territorial values; rural tourism should not be considered, exclusively, the engine of rural development (Pérez 2010). However, Hall et al. (2013) identified common characteristics of the regions considered peripheral, such as simple economies based on natural resources, low production of high-value products and services, limited transport infrastructure, among others, and found that tourism is one of the few economic policy responses for these regions due to the lack of development alternatives and other contingent and leveraged factors.

Tourism in rural areas and communities is a general trend in current tourism practices, outlining such a social change that allows the population of the city to find roots, cultural values, relaxation and tranquility (Dragulanescu and Maricica-Drutu 2012). Rural tourism is referring to all types of activities carried out by tourists in rural areas including the elements related to traditions, culture and hospitality of the people from rural villages; tourists are attracted to rural areas by their distinctive social and cultural heritage landscape qualities (Gavrilă-Paven et al. 2015, 1051).

The main factors in the motivation of rural tourism are the desire to escape from routine, the desire for pleasure and recreation, the search for an unforgettable experience of life, adventure, intellectual enrichment and the desire to learn more about nature, among others (Streimikiene and Bilan 2015). While tourist-fishing activities can be varied depending on the area, time of year, tourist profile, etc., activities such as guided visits to lighthouses, shipyards or along the coast can be organized. It is also possible to enjoy the gastronomy and seafood, stay in fishermen's houses, participate in workshops to learn about different fishing techniques, and learn to braid fishing nets or distinguish species of marine fauna. Activities at sea include the possibility to accompany the crew of a small-scale fishing boat on a fishing trip, during which tourists can enjoy, learn and value the marine environment and its resources (Molina, Gonzalez and Garcia 2010).

That is, rural tourism takes all the resources of the rural community, and combines and organizes them to generate tourism products that can offer different activities, that is, identifies the possibilities of the rural territory for the development of this new productive activity (Pérez 2010). Venegas (2009) mentions that to achieve long-term sustainability, tourism must (1) optimally use environmental resources, (2) respect the socio-cultural authenticity of communities and (3) ensure the viability of long-term investments, as well as a high level of tourist satisfaction based on innovative procedures.

The tourism contribution to rural development is important if local people participate, which can also help to protect the environment, the economy and cultural-historical traditions rural and local; alternative tourism can also help to develop other sectors of the local economy (Dragulanescu and Maricica-Drutu 2012). The tourism sector needs a great degree of involvement of the entrepreneur sector (Lordkipanidze and Backman 2005); that is, for the development of rural tourism, it is necessary that the communities have people with entrepreneurial characteristics.

Pérez (2010) identifies five main aspects to consider rural tourism as a strategic alternative to its development: (1) make a correct inventory to identify possible rural tourism products from the identification of possible attractions for tourists; (2) seek to develop rural tourism while maintaining the usual activity of the community: this is, consider tourism as complementary; (3) the increase in demand for rural products; (4) consider tourism as an alternative to non-agricultural rural employment, including women and young people in the communities; and (5) reduction of rural migration to urban areas.

Pérez (ibid.) suggests, first, not losing the essence of the communities or the activities of the place so that the product does not lose its originality and becomes a passing fad; on the other hand, he warns that an erroneous view of the tourism potential could cause oversized projects with negative effects on the environment (e.g. pollution), culture (e.g. loss of local identity) and local economic activity (e.g. increase in the cost of the life and in debt of the municipalities); finally, he underlines that a bad perception of the characteristics of the territory would derive from an inadequate elaboration of the tourist local offer, which might add negative impacts in its implementation.

Traditionally, the economic benefits provided by tourism have been emphasized; however, it is necessary to admit that tourism development also has a series of costs associated with the destination in which it takes place (Sancho 1998), such as the impact on the landscape and to the daily rhythm of rural life (Tervo-Kankare and Tuohino 2016). Damages to the environment, resources spent, corruption of local cultures and the exploitation of local workforce are possible scenarios resulting from ill-advised tourism promotion in rural areas (Fleischer and Felsenstein 2000).

In the conclusions of their article titled "Rural Tourism for Local Economic Development", Dragulanescu and Maricica-Drutu (2012) say that not all areas are suitable for economic development, not all communities wish to be developed or are suitable for development and not all forms of tourism activity are acceptable in every location; for better results, they suggest that the whole range of the stakeholders has to participate in the planning stage. In this regard, Pérez (2010) clarifies that rural tourism is not the only alternative for the local rural economy and not all rural areas are willing to develop such an economic activity, and the author says that the aims of the rural tourism as a development strategy must start from the integration with the rest of the economic activities of the communities to achieve a productive diversification of the rural area.

Methodology

This research focuses on determining if there are conditions for the development of tourism in a peripheral rural community, from the identification of community resources capable of being used to the development of this activity (Pérez 2010), and determining the feasibility of connecting local economic activity to tourism services (Lane 1994), as well as the internal challenges faced by the community, particularly in terms of entrepreneurship and innovation (Pezzi and Urso 2017).

The research was conducted under a qualitative and exploratory approach; for the identification of the resources of the community, it used the classification of resources suitable for tourist use raised in the Methodology for the Elaboration of the Inventory of Tourist Attractions proposed by the Ministry of Commerce, Industry and Tourism (MCIT) (2010) (see Figure 4.1).

The place under study is the rural community *Las Arenitas*, a fishing field located 81 km from Culiacan, the capital of the state of Sinaloa in Mexico, which is one of the 27 fishing fields that makes up the *Ensenada del Pabellón* on the Sinaloa coast (Ramirez-Rodriguez, Lopez-Ferreira and Hernandez-Herrera 2005) (Map 4.1). It has a total population of 1,838

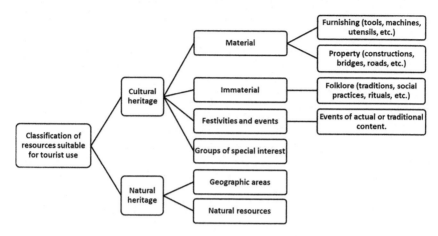

Figure 4.1 Classification of resources suitable for tourist use.
Source: Prepared by the authors with data from MCIT (2010).

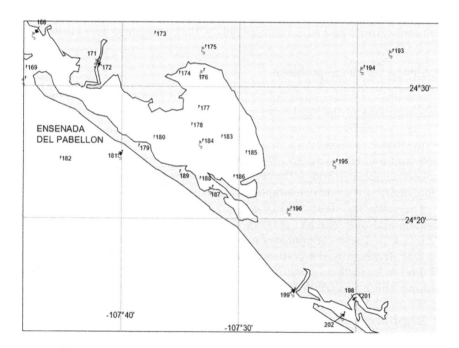

Map 4.1 Ensenada del Pabellón, in the state of Sinaloa, Mexico.
Source: Ramirez-Rodriguez, Lopez-Ferreira and Hernandez-Herrera (2005), used with permission.

inhabitants (913 men and 925 women), 452 private homes and 40.4% of its population (743 people) of 15 years or more have incomplete basic education (SEDESOL and CONEVAL 2014).

In 2010, its degree of marginalization was classified as "medium" by the National Marginalization Index of Mexico, which is determined by levels of literacy of the population, characteristics of the dwelling and housing amenities. In view of the foregoing, this index partly reflects the reality of the community, not considering other problems that it faces such as the temporality of its main economic activity, the unemployment arising, problems of insecurity and furtive fishing and a number of social problems, in which the abuse of drugs and alcohol stands out. The area was chosen as a case study due to the above-mentioned characteristics in light of the emergence of tourism as a possible secondary activity.

Data and information collection was performed through structured direct interviews to 18 key actors: authorities, leaders of fishing cooperatives, business owners, as well as residents living for more than 30 years in the community, during five community visits made from March to September 2017. Respondents were selected by the snowball effect. They were questioned about the economy of the region, problems of the fishing activity, consideration of tourism as a possible secondary activity, natural and cultural resources susceptible to the development of tourism in the locality, as well as challenges for its implementation; additionally, through observation, natural, cultural and social components of the community were identified.

Economy and local problems

The main economic activity of *Las Arenitas* is fishing, and to carry out this activity, many of the local fishermen are organized in fishing cooperatives. These cooperative societies are a form of social organization composed of individuals based on common interests and the principles of solidarity, self-help and mutual assistance, with the purpose of satisfying individual and collective needs, through the realization of economic activities of production, distribution and consumption of goods and services (DOF 2018).

The town has four fishing cooperatives, primarily targeting shrimp fishing, and only one has permits to capture shrimp, shark, fish and crab (Table 4.2). These cooperatives are part of 99 economic entities identified in *Las Arenitas* by the National Statistical Directory of Economic Units (DENUE by its Spanish acronym) of México: 93 of these engage in shrimp fishing; three to shrimp farming; two to the capture of fish, crustaceans, mollusks and other species; and one has a beer retail business (INEGI 2017).

Regarding the fishing seasons in Mexico, the National Commission of Aquaculture and Fisheries (CONAPESCA by its Spanish acronym) establishes the seasons and closed areas for fishing of different species of aquatic fauna, which vary every year. In the area, generally, the closure is six months (between February and September), which means that the closed fishing

Table 4.2 Fisheries cooperatives of *Las Arenitas*

Name of the cooperative	Foundation	Partners	Fishing permits
Boca del Río San Lorenzo (BdRSL)	1982	32	Shrimp
Ensenada del Tiburón (EdT)	1986	64	Shrimp
José Luis Castro Verduzco (JLCV)	1978	87	Shark
			Fish
			Crab
			Shrimp
Pescadores El Brinco (PEB)	1944	38	Shrimp

Source: Prepared by the authors with data from the Federation of Fishing Production Cooperatives Altata and Ensenada del Pabellón (2017).

seasons are long, and this also affects the local economy. In this situation, the residents seek to solve their shortcomings through self-employment activities in the community, as well as temporary jobs in packaging companies of agricultural products in other nearby places.

For its part, the Mexican government has supported programs to contribute to the satisfaction of the basic needs of the inhabitants, such as (1) Program for the Promotion of Fisheries and Aquaculture Productivity (PROPESCA by its Spanish acronym), which provides economic support to beneficiaries; their objective is that in times of low productivity or closure, fishermen acquire knowledge, training and preparation, to increase their safety of life at sea, for their personal development, to add value to their catches and thus obtain better income (National Commission of Aquaculture and Fisheries 2017); (2) the program of social inclusion, called PROS-PERA, which grants resources to Mexican families to strengthen their diet, health and education – it also links the beneficiaries with productive projects, labor options and financial services (Social Inclusion Program PROS-PERA 2016); and (3) the Temporary Employment Program, which seeks to contribute to the welfare of people who face a reduction in their income (with regard to this community due to fisheries closures), and of the population affected by emergencies (SEDESOL 2017).

Added to the problem of the reduction of income in closed seasons, fishing production has diminished. Interviewees refer to two causes: furtive fishing by people who come to the community in the fishing season, and using prohibited fishing gear. One of the inhabitants mentioned that those fishermen use boats handled by a single person, and use a type of fishing net that extends and sweeps everything; another problem identified is a kind of vegetation on the sea of the bay that prevents fishing where it occurs. In this regard, the local commissioner says: "the main problem of this community is that fishing is decreasing, goes from more to less, I think that fishing ceases to be an alternative, we have to look for others options that give us work, that we give welfare and development" (woman, Commissioner interviewed on March 15, 2017).

The vulnerability, risk and resilience characteristics of rural fishing activity (Clay and Olson 2008) are seen in the fishing community under study; its inhabitants have developed resilience to survive in adverse conditions. In this context, some of its leaders (authorities and managers of fishing cooperatives) see tourism as an alternative to face their economic problems (Streimikiene and Bilan 2015).

Rural tourism as a second economic activity

The main organizations of the community *Las Arenitas* are the fishing cooperatives; their leaders express their concern for the problem of fishing in the locality and, in general, consider the possibility of developing tourism activities in the region, although they clarify that it should be only a second income option for the inhabitants of the community, keeping fishing as their main economic activity. This coincides with one of the aspects to be considered for the development of rural tourism proposed by Pérez (2010) in the sense that the place where rural tourism develops should not lose its essence or its own activities and thus avoid the tourism product which loses originality and attractiveness.

The leaders of the fishing cooperatives (four presidents and four secretaries) agree on the need to look for new alternatives to improve the economy of *Las Arenitas*, by virtue of the various difficulties presented by the fishing activity, already described earlier (for example, low fishing production and closed time), which negatively affects the standard of living of the inhabitants; in this regard, they expressed some of the following expressions: "it is necessary because fishermen cannot cover their basic needs in the seasons when there is no work" (man, President of the cooperative "BdRSL", interviewed on May 26, 2017), "while the shrimp farms are not regularized, fishing is not profitable" (man, President of the cooperative "EdT" interviewed on May 26, 2017), "the situation is difficult because there is not the same production as the previous periods" (man, Secretary of the cooperative "EdT", interviewed on May 26, 2017), "working in fishing is exhausting and you do not have insurance" (man, President of the cooperative "PEB", interviewed on May 26, 2017), "sometimes the fishing activity becomes very difficult" (man, President of the cooperative "JLCV", interviewed on July 10, 2017), and "because they cannot fish all year long, they have to go to work elsewhere" (man, Secretary of the cooperative "JLCV" interviewed on July 10, 2017).

Regarding the development of tourism in the area, the leaders of the cooperatives expressed that it would be beneficial for the community, by the following: "tourism would be a new source for employment" (man, President of the cooperative "BdRSL", interviewed on May 26, 2017), "it would be of great help because the money is for the people of the same community, that is, in free time when there is no fishing, we can work in tourism" (man, President of the cooperative "EdT", interviewed on May 26, 2017), "it would be very good to create more sources of employment and that the whole community participates" (man, President of the cooperative "*PEB*", interviewed on May 26, 2017), and "it would be something very good for the community because there would be more sources for employment" (man, President of the cooperative "*JLCV*", interviewed on July 10, 2017).

To consider tourism as a second economic activity, it was necessary to identify the natural and cultural resources of the community, capable to be used for the development of tourism activity, which constitute their cultural and natural heritage (see Table 4.3).

The cultural heritage of *Las Arenitas* is made up of both tangible and intangible goods that are part of the daily life of the town, as well as its traditional and cultural activities, and the elements that still preserve its history.

Regarding historical attractions, three stand out: the remains of a ship in front of its coasts, a propeller recovered from it and the estate of the Redo family (although it is not properly in the community, it is nearby and is part of its history).

Remains of the sunken ship stand out in the sea, can be seen what its crow's nest was and at low tide it is possible to see a small part of what was the cabin, says one of the interviewees. The anecdotes regarding its origin and use are diverse; the most referenced suggest that the boat was owned by the Redo family (known to have been one of the most wealthy and influential families in the region); they got it as a gift from the former Mexican president Porfirio Diaz; according to these versions, the ship was used to transport cane liquor and to bring different species of trees and plants to the region. The interviewees explain that the owners chose the *Las Arenitas* route because there was a natural channel through which the ship could easily cross. Over the years, the ship along with other properties of the Redo family was abandoned, and over time, the ship was runs aground.

In 2013, one of the propellers of the ship, which weighs more than 13 tons, was extracted, and is currently on the sports field of the community. It is expected that these three vestiges and their legends serve as tourist attractions for the town.

Around the current cultural heritage is the multipurpose court, located in the center of the community, which is used as a meeting center; it is usually used to host sporting events, mainly soccer or basketball; it is also used to perform the community festivities.

Another important element is the four fishing cooperatives of the community; each one has work facilities, provided with the necessary equipment for their fishing work and for the subsequent processing of the captured products. The interviewed report that these facilities could also be used to offer tourist services, for example, workshops to learn the trade of fishing, sale of seafood, exhibitions of different fishing tools and tours to explain their use; however, everything requires aesthetic maintenance.

Additionally, the leaders of the fishing cooperatives say that these organizations have motor boats to carry out fishing activities, which could be

Table 4.3 Inventory of resources capable of tourist use

Heritage	Type	Element	Description
Cultural	Material	Sunken ship in early 20th century	From this sunken ship a part of the sea next to *Las Arenitas* can be appreciated. It is an evidence of local history and anecdotes.
		Propeller recovered from the sunken ship	This large-scale propeller is displayed on the multipurpose court, and next to the sunken ship is a historical hallmark of the place.
		The Redo's ranch	This ranch is not in the community itself but is part of the receivership and historical heritage of the region, on which there is a lot of legends.
		Multipurpose court	It is used as a coexistence area, both for sports events and festivities.
		Fishing cooperative facilities.	These are the work areas of the sea workers; they could also be used for tourist services: offer workshops to learn the trade of fishing, seafood sale, etc.
		Fishing instruments.	An exhibition and routes can be made in which the use of each element used in fishing is explained.
		Motor boats	They are used for fishing but could be used to make tours of the bay by visitors to the town
		Streets and rustic trails	Only the main street is paved, the rest is dirt paths.
		Households	Most are built of brick or block (some could provide accommodation service)
	Immaterial	Local gastronomy	Sinaloa gastronomy dishes made with local seafood: "pescado sarandeado", "ceviche", "caguamanta", "pata de mula", among others; The predominant local fruit could also be used for making Snacks.
	Festivities and events	Sailor's day	It is celebrated on May 31 and June 1, there are veteran football tournaments, cockfights, queens parade, dance and other activities.
		Day of the Virgin of Guadalupe	The celebration consists of a pilgrimage (tour of the community carried out by the residents) and kermes (popular open-air festival in which snacks are sold, contests, etc.).
	Groups of special interest	The fishermen and the population in general	The fishermen for their knowledge of the sea and their trade; the rest of the population for its simplicity and kindness.
Natural heritage	Geographic areas	Near islands.	Have bird colonies.
	Natural resources.	Flora	Various species such as: mangroves, coconut palms and fruit trees such as mangoes and papaya.
		Fauna	Birds, marine species, reptiles, even occasional sighting of dolphins.
		Landscapes	Beach, sea and blue sky, to which is added vegetation and local fauna.
		Fishery products	Shrimp, clams and various species of fish.

Source: Prepared by the authors (2018).

used to tour the bay for visitors from the locality (activity that is already performed sporadically).

Most of the streets and trails of *Las Arenitas* are rustic; only one street is paved, and the rest is dirt; this may be appropriate to reinforce its rural character; on the other hand, most homes are built with brick and block, but the community does not have accommodation spaces, although possibly some houses could provide this service if they are adapted for it.

By being a fishing community, they obviously capture various marine species that are appreciated to make gastronomic products, such as shrimp, clams and various fish species, with which are prepared dishes known and appreciated from Sinaloa gastronomy; in addition, in the community, it is possible to eat a type of clam known as "Pata de mula", which is difficult to find in other places.

In the community of *Las Arenitas*, the most important festivity is the Day of the Sailor, which is commemorated on June 1; every year, the celebration begins on May 31; there are veteran football tournaments, cockfights, queen pageant, dancing and other activities that extend until the next day.

As groups of special interest are the fishermen themselves for all that they contribute in the knowledge of the sea and its activity, as well as the rest of the inhabitants, who are characterized by their simplicity and kindness, they are always warm with those who visit them, both with acquaintances and with strangers.

Its geography highlights the existence of small islands in the vicinity, which have bird colonies; it has a great variety of flora and fauna. Regarding its flora, there are different species of mangroves, coconut palms and fruit trees such as mangoes and papaya. While its fauna are mainly birds, fishes, alligators and turtles, sometimes it is possible to watch dolphins in the sea. Other natural resources of the community are its landscapes of beach, sea and blue sky.

Las Arenitas currently receives some visitors, especially during the period from September to March when the shrimp season opens; the majority of visitors are fishermen from other regions that participate in the capture of the region. Also in December, the visits to the locality increase; mainly, the relatives of settlers who live in other regions of the country and abroad use to have get together with them during the Christmas holidays. Among the activities carried out by those who visit the community are travel by boat, visit the islands and eat seafood; this information could be relevant for the design of local tourism products.

The natural environment, as well as fishing products and local cuisine, would be the main attractions of the community, to which the remains of the sunken ship and its legend, as well as its community festivities could be added. Another factor that contributes to the possibility of developing the project is the simplicity and friendliness of its inhabitants; as a whole, it is constituted as the rural environment that has become a trend in current tourism practice mentioned by Dragulanescu and Maricica-Drutu (2012).

Challenges for the development of tourism in the community

Although the community has elements likely to have a tourism potential, they also face internal challenges for its implementation. The interviewees were questioned about it; the most outstanding fact is a tendency to be conformist of the inhabitants of the region. The interviewees agree that, despite their shortcomings and limitations, the inhabitants got used to survive through mutual support and government support programs.

The inhabitants are accustomed to surviving on the natural products they have: sea products and some fruits that are abundant in the locality. Some of the residents have temporary jobs in packaging companies of agricultural products, during the fishing season; they receive vegetables (like tomatoes, chili, etc.) which they share or exchange with their neighbors. With this and the support that they receive from government support programs, the population of *Las Arenitas* satisfies their basic needs in periods of vulnerability.

In this regard, the Commissioner mentions:

> generally people do not get involved in new projects, the inhabitants are conformist, to be honest, we are more accustomed to welfare programs than to be productive, to give me the pantry, give me the economic support, give me this or that, we do not try to find an activity to develop to produce and obtain a benefit.
>
> (Man, Commissioner, interviewed on September 4, 2017)

Regarding the development of entrepreneurial projects, the inhabitants of *Las Arenitas* generally support the ventures developed by external persons of the community; however, this radically changes when it is a new project of a member of the community; in these cases, not only the support is denied, but they also seek to discourage it. Several testimonies express the need to be cautious when trying to develop a business project by someone in the community; some of the interviewees mention that when the rest of the inhabitants find out, they begin to generate situations that reveal envy and try to block its realization.

In this regard, a resident comments that if someone from the community tries to start a business, others try to discourage him with expressions like: "he loses his time, he loses his money, that does not work here" (women, resident, interviewed on May 26, 2017). However, the opposite happens when an external person tries to put their business in *Las Arenitas*, in this case if it is supported. The interviewees agree that it may be because the inhabitants do not trust their own abilities. This may also be related to their low level of schooling.

Most of the inhabitants have become accustomed to survive in the current conditions and, although they often do not have economic resources, they know that in the community they have natural resources that provide them with food, as well as neighbors who are willing to help each other in the face of adversity. Added to this are government programs that provide them with money that complements their standard of living.

This adaptation derives from conformism that inhibits in most of them their entrepreneurial capacity, which is also reinforced by their low level of schooling; these characteristics cause that with the same intensity with which they trust each other in difficult times; they also hinder those who wish to undertake in the community.

In context, despite being a resilient community, according to what was proposed by Sánchez-Zamora et al. (2016), its resilience seeks to return to the familiar conditions when facing some disturbance; however, the search for new conditions to encourage their development is practically nil; that is, the innovative potential is limited by the community itself.

Conclusions

During the investigation, it was found that the community has natural and cultural resources that could serve as a base for the implementation of tourism in the region as a secondary activity, prioritizing fishing as its main economic activity and connecting it with the tourist activities that they develop, avoiding that the community loses its rural essence.

On the other hand, we identified several aspects that must be overcome if tourism is going to be considered as an economic activity, such as psychological and cultural barriers of the inhabitants that are adapted to their lifestyle (despite their shortcomings); they became accustomed to survive by the natural products of the region, to support each other to solve their feeding needs and to complement it with the governmental economic supports that they receive as help to vulnerable groups, which inhibits the development of an entrepreneurial and innovative culture.

In this context, although there are infrastructure conditions that could make the promotion of tourism activity in the community feasible, we conclude that the lack of an entrepreneurial society with the intention of overcoming its adversities beyond subsistence is the biggest challenge to overcome.

In addition, rural tourism in Mexico requires national attention (more focused on coastal complexes) through programs that encourage and promote it, take advantage of the potential of these regions and, simultaneously, move from welfare programs to alternatives that promote their development.

References

Aghon, Gabriel, Francisco Alburquerque, and Patricia Cortes. *Local Economic Development and Decentralization in Latin America: a Comparative Analysis.* Santiago de Chile: ECLAC/GTZ, 2001.

Barca, Fabrizio, Philip McCann, and Andrés Rodríguez-Pose. "The Case for Regional Development Intervention: Place-based versus Place-neutral Approaches." *Journal of Regional Science*, Vol. 52, No. 1, 2012: 134–152.

Clay, Patricia, and Julia Olson. «Defining "Fishing Communities": Vulnerability and the Magnuson-Stevens Fishery Conservation and Management Act1.» *Human Ecology Review*, Vol. 15, No. 2, 2008: 143–160.

Danson, Mike, Greta Cameron, and Henrik Halkier. *Governance, Institutional Change and Regional Development.* London: Ashgate, 2000.

DOF. *General Law of Cooperative Societies.* Mexico City, 2018. http://www.diputados. gob.mx/LeyesBiblio/pdf/143_190118.pdf: Official Gazette of the Federation.

Dragi-Dimitrovski, Darko, Aleksandar Tomislav-Todorovic, and Aleksandar Djordje-Valjarevic. "Rural tourism and Regional Development: Case Study of Development of Rural Tourism in the Region of Gruza, Serbia." *Procedia Environmental Sciences*, Vol. 14, No. 1, 2012: 288–297.

Dragulanescu, Irina-Virginia, and Ivan Maricica-Drutu. "Rural Tourism for Local Economic Development." *International Journal of Academic Research in Accounting, Finance and Management Sciences*, Vol. 2, No. 1, 2012: 196–203.

Enríquez, Alberto. "Desarrollo local: hacia nuevas rutas de desarrollo." In *Desarrollo Regional. Reflexiones para la gestión de los territorios*, edited by Adriana Abardía and Federico Morales, 11–33. Mexico City: Alternativas y Capacidades, A.C., 2008.

FAO, and SAGARPA. *"Diagnosis of the Rural and Fishing Sector 2012".* Ministry of Agriculture, Rural Development, Fisheries and Food, and the United Nations Organization for Food and Agriculture., Mexico City, 2014. http://www.fao.org/3/a-bc980s.pdf

Fitri Amir, Ahmad, Ammar Abd Ghapar, Salamiah A. Jamal, and Khairun Najiah Ahmad. «Sustainable Tourism Development: A Study on Community Resilience for Rural Tourism in Malaysia.» *Procedia - Social and Behavioral Sciences*, Vo. 168, No.1, 2015: 116–122.

Fleischer, Aliza, and Daniel Felsenstein. "Support for Rural Tourism. Does it Make a Difference?" *Annals of Tourism Research*, Vol. 27, No. 4, 2000: 1007–1024.

Garduño, Martha, Celia Guzmán, and Lilia Villarreal. "Rural Tourism: Community Participation and Federal Programs". *El Periplo Sustentable*, No. 17, 2009: 5–30.

Gavrilă-Paven, Ionela, Constantin Bârsan Mircea, and Dogaru Lia-Dorica. "Advantages and Limits for Tourism Development in Rural Area (Case Study Ampoi and MureúValleys)." *Procedia Economics and Finance*, Vol. 32, No. 1, 2015: 1050–1059.

Gunn, Clare, and Turgut Var. *Tourism Planning: Basics, Concepts, Cases.* New York: Routledge, 2002.

Hall, C.M., David Harrison, David Weaver, and Geofrey Wall. "Vanishing Peripheries: Does Tourism Consume Places?" *Tourism Recreation Research*, Vol. 38, No. 1, 2013: 71–92.

Herrera-Racionero, Paloma, Luis Miret-Pastor, and Emmanuel Lizcano. "Traveling with Tradition: Artisanal Fishermen and Fishing Tourism in Valencian Region (Spain)." *Cuadernos de Turismo No. 41*, 2018: 279–293.

INEGI. *National Statistical Directory of Economic Units.* DENUE. http://www.beta.inegi.org.mx/app/mapa/denue/# (accessed July 3, 2017).

INEGI. *System of National Accounts of Mexico: Satellite Account of Tourism in Mexico 2016.* Mexico: Base Year 2013 / National Institute of Statistics and Geography. INEGI, 2018. http://www.datatur.sectur.gob.mx/Documentos%20 compartidos/CSTM_Ed_2018.pdf

INEGI. *System of National Accounts of Mexico: Tourism Satellite Account of Mexico 2015: Preliminary: Base Year 2008.* Mexico: National Institute of Statistics and Geography, 2016. http://www.datatur.sectur.gob.mx/documentos%20 publicaciones/cstm_2015.pdf

Lane, Bernard. "What is Rural Tourism?" *Journal of Sustainable Tourism*, Vol. 2, 1994: 7–21.

Lordkipanidze, Maia, and Mikael Backman. "The Entrepreneurship Factor in Sustainable Tourism Development." *Journal of Cleaner Production*, Vol 13, No. 8, 2005: 787–798.

Meyer, D.F., J. De Jongh, and N. Meyer. "The Formulation of a Composite Regional Development Index." *International Journal of Business and Management Studies*, Vol. 8, No. 1, 2016: 100–116.

MCIT. Ministry of Commerce, Industry and Tourism. Methodology for the Preparation of the Inventory of Tourist Attractions. Bogotá, 2010. http://www.mincit.gov.co/loader.php?lServicio=Documentos&lFuncion=verPdf&id=40681&name=MethodologyInventoryTuristicos2010.pdf&prefix=file: Ministry of Commerce, Insudtry and Tourism.

Molina, Agustin, Jose Fernando Gonzalez, and Cesar Garcia. "El turismo pesquero como instrumento de apoyo al desarrollo sostenible en zonas litorales: la experiencia del proyecto Sagital." Paper presented at the *XIV International Congress on Project Engineering*, Madrid, Spain, June 30 – July 2, 2010: 1637–1648.

National Commission of Aquaculture and Fisheries. "CONAPESCA will Benefit 34,500 Fishermen with the PROPESCA Program." *gob.mx, 2017*.https://www.gob.mx/conapesca/articulos/la-conapesca-beneficiara-a-34-mil-500-pescadores-con-el-programa-propesca (accessed July 17, 2017).

OECD. *Tourism Policy Review of Mexico*, OECD Studies on Tourism, OECD Publishing, Paris, 2017. http://dx.doi.org/10.1787/9789264266575-en

Pérez, Samuel. "The Strategic Value of Rural Tourism as a Sustainable Alternative for a Territorial Rural Development." *Agronomía Colombiana*, Vol. 28, No. 3, 2010: 507–513.

Pezzi, Maria Giulia, and Giulia Urso. "Coping with Peripherality: Local Resilience between Policies and Practices. Editorial Note." *IJPP – Italian Journal of Planning Practice Vol VII*, No. 1, 2017: 1–23.

Pike, Andy, Andrés Rodríguez-Pose, and John Tomaney. *Local and Regional Development*. New York: Routledge, 2006.

Andy Pike, Andrés Rodríguez-Pose, and John Tomaney "Shifting horizons in local and regional development", Regional Studies, Vol. 51, No.1, 2017: 46-57

Ramirez-Rodriguez, Mauricio, Cesar Lopez-Ferreira, and Agustin Hernandez-Herrera. *Atlas of fishing locations in Mexico*. Mexico: National Polytechnic Institute, Interdisciplinary Center for Marine Sciences, National Commission of Aquaculture and Fisheries, 2005.

Reese, Laura A. *Local Economic Development Policy: The United States and Canada*. New York: Garland, 1997.

Rodriguez-Pose, Andres, and Callum Wilkie. "Revamping Local and Regional Development through Place-based Strategies." *Cityscape*, Vol. 19, No. 1, 2017: 151–170.

Sánchez-Zamora, Pedro, Rosa Gallardo-Cobos, and Felisa Ceña-Delgado. "The Notion of Resilience in the Analysis of the Rural Territorial Dynamics: An Approach to the Concept through a Territorial Approach." *Cuadernos de Desarrollo Rural*, Vol. 13, No. 77, 2016: 93–116. http://dx.doi.org/10.11144/Javeriana.cdr13-77.nrad

Sancho, Amparo. *Introduction to Tourism*. World Tourism Organization (UNWTO), 1998.

SEDESOL. "Temporary Employment Program". *gob.mx*. https://www.gob.mx/sedesol/acciones-y-programas/programa-de-empleo-temporal (accessed November 30, 2017), 2017.

SEDESOL, and CONEVAL. *Informe anual sobre la situación de pobreza y rezago social.* SEDESOL, 2014.

Social Inclusion Program PROSPERA. *"What is PROSPERA Social Inclusion Program?" gob.mx.* https://www.gob.mx/prospera/documentos/que-es-prospera (accessed July 18, 2016).

Streimikiene, Dalia, and Yuriy Bilan. "Review of Rural Tourism Development Theories." *Transformations in Business & Economics*, Vol. 14, No. 2 (35), 2015: 21–34.

Tervo-Kankare, Kaarina, and Anja Tuohino. "Defining 'Rurality' for Rural Well-being Tourism - Halfacree's Conceptual Triad of the Production of Rural Space in Practical-level Tourism Development in Northern Europe." *Nordia Geographical Publications*, Vol. 45, No. 2, 2016: 37–52.

UNWTO. *Landscape UNWTO of International Tourism.* World Tourism Organization UNWTO, 2017. https://www.e-unwto.org/doi/pdf/10.18111/9789284419043

Venegas, Sonia. "La competitividad e innovación de un turismo sustentable." In *Régimen Jurídico del Turismo y de la Zona Marítimo. Terrestre*, edited by Jorge Fernández and Javier Santiago, 251–274. México: Universidad Nacional Autónoma de México, 2009.

Part II
Wine tourism

5 'A big fish in a small pond'

How Arizona wine country was made

Colleen C. Myles, Michele Tobias
and Innisfree McKinnon

Introduction

Despite environmental and economic odds stacked against them, public and private actors (agricultural producers and advisors, entrepreneurs and investors, and fermentation craftspeople) have managed to construct a wine landscape in the high desert of Arizona in the Western United States. Due to the environmental and cultural landscapes of the state, the wine industry in Arizona is characterized by a spatial disconnect between where most wine grapes are grown (mainly in the south of the state in Cochise County/Willcox and Santa Cruz County/Sonoita-Elgin) and where wine tourism dominates (mainly in the more northern Yavapai County/Verde Valley). Arizona's notable tourist landmarks and the positioning of its two major urban centers (Phoenix and Tucson) make the north a more feasible and desirable tourism destination (Arizona Hospitality Research 2011; Fitch, Combrink & Pitts 2017). Nevertheless, wine grape growers in the south are actively seeking to capture a greater value from their grapes and associated wine landscapes, a challenging task given the difficulty of luring visitors without the appeal of other nearby tourist sites and amenities. This chapter examines the wine industry in Arizona as a classic fermented landscape (Myles forthcoming), one which demonstrates the symbolic and material significance of fermentation-focused landscape change. Using a variety of techniques, we explore how and why, in this place, various actors have pursued the production of wine grapes in a difficult environment and built a tourism destination based around the consumption of the rural landscape (Woods 2011).

Project purpose

In the world of wine, particular geological, hydrological, and climatic characteristics produce soil, drainage, sun exposure, and related microclimatic effects that significantly influence the quality of the grapes grown in a particular location. Winemakers then manipulate these characteristics to hide or highlight wine characteristics, building on the qualities cultivated in the vineyard to produce – hopefully! – a fine, fermented masterpiece. This whole package, both the physical environmental effects and the winemaking cultural traditions and practices, produces what is called *terroir* (Sommers 2008; Unwin 2012).

While wine grape production is well-established in some regions (Banks & Overton 2010; de Blij 1983; Dougherty 2012; Unwin 1991), as wine has become a cultural and status marker across the world, a number of new wine regions have emerged seeking to capitalize on the cultural and economic cachet such an industry can provide (Harvey, White & Frost 2014; Kline, Slocum & Cavaliere 2018). These emerging wine destinations can sometimes be successful, creating economic opportunities (Giuliani, Morrison & Rabellotti 2013) and actively (re)making place (Myles & Filan 2017; Myles & Filan forthcoming), while others languish, producing "landscapes of failure" (Overton forthcoming). With this perspective in mind, we examine the development of the nascent, but rapidly growing, "emerging" wine landscape in Arizona. Given the relatively obscure status of Arizona wine, we asked the following questions:

* What are the historical and contemporary drivers of Arizona wine/ grape production?
* How and why has the wine industry developed despite the physical challenges associated with wine grape growing in Arizona?
* How are growers and winemakers handling the spatial division between the best growing areas and the existing tourism and population centers?

Methods

This mixed method study encompasses qualitative, quantitative, and spatial analysis techniques to:

1   Establish baseline information regarding Arizona wine grape and wine production:
    a   Describe and map the notable environmental and geographic features in the state and especially in the regions of interest (e.g. population centers, tourist destinations, wineries and wine-based businesses, and relevant regulatory landscape traces like American Viticultural Area (AVA) boundaries).
2   Analyze the economic, environmental, and cultural contexts of and impetus for the wine industry in the state via targeted key informant interviews.

To these ends, we transcribed, coded, and analyzed a series of key informant interviews (12 interviews completed in June 2015 in the southern wine regions of the state[1]) and conducted a spatial analysis of the Arizona wine industry to investigate relevant environmental features, the locations and geographic dispersion of various types of permitted liquor establishments,

AVAs (Alcohol and Tobacco Tax and Trade Bureau 2017) boundaries, and populations centers. Specifically, the spatial analysis involved:

- *Determining grape-growing elevations:* The elevation dataset from PRISM was classified into three elevation categories based on the description of suitable elevations for growing table and wine grapes in Arizona from Crider (1923) in QGIS (QGIS Development Team 2018).
- *Locating business clusters:* The input data was a table of Arizona wine-producing and -selling permits collated from public liquor license data, which includes type of permit, business name, business owner, and address. Point locations (latitude and longitude) for the businesses were produced by geocoding the address data in the online geocoder Geocode.io. Geocoding is a spatial analysis process that estimates an address location based on a road network containing information about the address ranges present on each block. Once the approximate location of each business had been estimated, we looked for patterns in the permit types, locations, and business owners. To determine potential business clusters, the business location data was fed into R (R Core Team 2017). The physical distance between the points was estimated with the earth.dist() function from the fossil package (Vavrek 2011) and the distances were used to run a hierarchical clustering analysis (hclust() from the base R functionality) (R Core Team 2017). The spatial hierarchical clustering produced three clusters of four or more businesses.

These methods provided ample data to produce the findings presented herein. The next section of the chapter outlines the site and situation of wine in Arizona. The sections following will present the findings, discussion, and conclusions of the work.

Site and situation: the environmental and cultural contexts for wine in Arizona

Apparently Arizona is not yet identified as a culinary destination.
–Arizona Hospitality Research (2011: 61)

Despite its mild incredulity, Arizona does have a nascent, but notable, wine industry, which includes not just the production of wine grapes, but also the production of wine itself. According to the most recent report on wine tourism in the state (Fitch, Combrinch & Pitts 2017: 1), there are "three dominant wine growing regions of Arizona. These regions are Cochise County, Willcox; Santa Cruz County, Sonoita/Elgin; and Yavapai County, Verde Valley" (Map 5.1). In these places – though more vibrantly in some than others – there is also a budding wine tourism industry that makes a small but valuable contribution to the overall economy of the state. In 2017, the Arizona wine tourism industry created an estimated $56.2 million in total

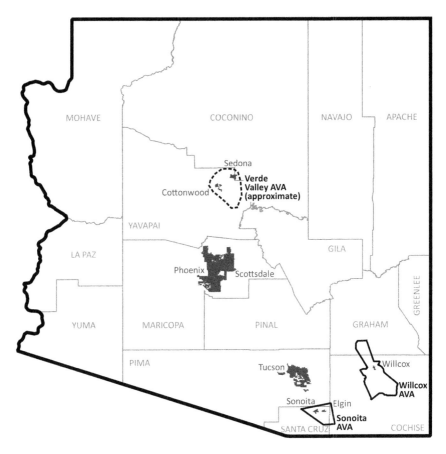

Map 5.1 Map of relevant geographies of Arizona, showing the major population
centers, county lines, and notable wine production and/or tourism sites.

economic output (plus an estimated 640 full-time equivalent jobs) (Fitch,
Combrinch & Pitts 2017). In addition, Arizona wine tourism expenditures
generated approximately $3.6 million in local and state taxes from indirect
and induced effects (Fitch, Combrinch & Pitts 2017).

Beyond the traditional economic measures of success for an industry, the
development of the wine industry also produces other more intangible benefits and changes within communities (Arizona Hospitality Research 2011: 10):

> While the economic benefits of the wine industry in Arizona may pale
> in comparison to other industries such as manufacturing or micro-
> electronics, the real strength of this niche market is in the value-added
> tourism experience. Wineries, vineyards and tasting rooms act as an
> attraction to tourists, providing a wine-related experience in a rural,

agricultural setting. All wineries in the state are located in rural counties (Santa Cruz, Cochise and Yavapai) and rural communities (Sonoita, Elgin, Jerome, Page Springs and Cottonwood). Tourism generated by wine production and tasting room visits therefore benefits rural communities disproportionally [sic], encouraging other tourism-related industries and strengthening the economic base of the local communities and regions.

In the findings and discussion sections of this chapter, we will evaluate and clarify some of the benefits and impacts of the kind of fermentation-focused tourism and development described in this report and in other public and private promotional materials (Arizona Experience 2018; Arizona Wine Growers Association 2017; Ducey 2016), but, before that, we will briefly describe the history and current status of wine grape growing and winemaking in the state of Arizona, with a focus on the three identified wine regions of the state.

History and current status of wine in Arizona

According to a 2017 report from the Arizona Office of Tourism (Fitch, Combrinch & Pitts 2017), Spanish Missionaries grew some of the first wine grapes in Arizona. However, only small amounts of wine were being produced for sale to local consumers by 1915, when Arizona enacted some of the strictest prohibition laws in the country. At that time, all wine production in the state was banned. It was not until 1970, that Gordon Dutt, a soil hydrologist at the University of Arizona, who had worked with wine growers in California through the University of California, Davis, began growing test plots in Arizona. Over the next decade, Dutt worked with the governor and a few other interested growers. In 1982, the first license was issued for wine production – but only after a fight in the legislature over legalization. Opposition from liquor distributors continued to severely restrict production (only 9 licenses had been issued by 2000). However, in 2005, the United States Supreme Court ruled that such restrictions were unconstitutional, which paved the way for the passage of less restrictive laws in 2006, which opened the state to increased local production. Since then, the industry has seen "steady growth in the last three decades" and describes how the character of the industry and the quality of the wines has developed (Arizona Hospitality Research 2011: 68):

> Arizona wines have improved in quality, with many wineries concentrating on high quality products with relatively low volumes, products that can demand a premium price in the marketplace. Wineries will also benefit from the increasing interest in Arizona-grown and locally-grown foods, that are gaining momentum statewide. Winemaking is an environmentally sustainable practice that helps to preserve open space, rural communities and values in counties where agriculture has been in a process of decline.

Tourism

The state tourism office has been eager to promote the wine industry as a part of Arizona's wider tourism strategy. The most recent "Guide to Arizona Agriculture" for the state (Ducey 2016) notes that the state is home to 97 wineries, with 300,000 gallons of wine produced in 2016. Promotional materials from the "Arizona Experience" website on "Arizona Wine Country" extol the virtues of Arizona wine, noting:

> Yes, world! Arizona is a great place to grow grapes! Moreover, celebrated winemakers have poured their considerable talent, energy, and expertise into creating an outstanding product. Though Arizona wines are flying below the national radar, bottle by bottle the state's winegrowers are introducing the vibrant tastes of Arizona wines to oenophiles around the world.
>
> (Arizona Experience 2018)

The Arizona Wine Growers Association (2017) goes on saying: "What makes Arizona so distinctive? You'd be surprised. Arizona is home to the perfect climate, elevation and weather to produce the very best wine making fruit."

In terms of tourism, in-state visitors make up the bulk of Arizona's wine tourists and most come from the large urban centers (Phoenix and Tucson) in the central part of the state (Fitch, Combrinch & Pitts 2017). These local tourists are not primarily interested in the quality of the wine consumed. Rather, the overall experience is key to most respondents (Arizona Hospitality Research 2011: 65). The top motivations offered by visitors were (1) to taste wine and (2) to relax and/or socialize (including enjoying "the beauty of rural Arizona vineyards" and "to have a different Arizona experience") (Arizona Hospitality Research 2011: 36). In general, Arizona wine tourists can be characterized as affluent urbanites, mainly hailing from Arizona's own urban centers, who are out to drink wine, and also to recreate and relax (Arizona Hospitality Research 2011).

Industry and entrepreneurship

Despite the rosy picture painted by tourism brochures, the industry has struggled somewhat with rapid growth and faced some serious challenges, including the ecological risks of growing grapes of consistent quantity and quality in Arizona; insufficient local grape production within regions, leading to a dependence on grapes or juice from other regions or out-of-state (the supply of which can be uncertain); a lack of skilled labor; restrictive regulations related to distribution (i.e. the imposition of the "three-tiered" distribution system vs promoting direct sales), zoning, and taxation; and economic hurdles, including difficulty obtaining financing for establishment or expansion of vineyard or winery operations (Fitch, Combrinch & Pitts 2017).

As suggested earlier, there are a number of factors that trouble Arizona wine/grape producers – a major one being financial. The biggest concern being the extensive capital required to establish a vineyard and/or winery. The heavy capital outlay and long rate of return limit who can participate in the industry. Fitch, Combrinch, and Pitts (2017: 9) describe some of the costs:

> Planting a vineyard typically costs between $25,000 to $35,000 per acre, not counting land acquisition and land preparation cost...It takes three to five years for new grapevines to generate the first usable crop and five to seven years to reach full production...In addition to the vineyards, a full scale winery can easily cost over $1 million to build and equip. With aging of wine before release, it is not unusual for a new winery to take seven years or more to generate its first dollar of income.

As one interviewee put it:

> With the wine industry...it's a rich man's hobby. You gotta have a lot of capital to get into it...A good way to make a million dollars in the wine-grape industry is to start with two [million dollars]. And then you widdle it down to one million dollars pretty fast.

> (R1, 20150605)

Market

Beyond the logistical challenges of growing the industry, Arizona wine must also place itself into the wider world of wine. The wine industry overall is shaped by geographic indicators, formal and semi-formal mechanisms for marking the origin and/or certifying the provenance of place-dependent foods (Fonte & Papadopoulos 2010; Morgan, Marsden & Murdoch 2009). Given the importance of place (terroir) to the product, schemes for organizing and ranking wine across the globe are relatively well-established. The French developed the first classification or appellation system to delineate and control (wine) growing regions in 1937, the Appellation d'Origine Contrôlée, but such systems are now used worldwide under various monikers (Dougherty 2012; Sommers 2008). The United States system (developed in 1980), which demarcates "special" or unique growing areas across the country, is regulated by creation and maintenance of AVAs (Alcohol and Tobacco Tax and Trade Bureau 2017). AVAs are wine regions producing a distinct character or quality of wine or having a particular reputation, and are defined by boundaries described based on publicly available maps (US Bureau of Alcohol Tobacco & Firearms 2018).

The industry's concern over its real and perceived legitimacy in the wider world of wine is revealed by comments like this from a state report: "While Arizona's wine industry is not nearly as large or well-known as that of Napa and Sonoma Counties in California, it has started to develop as a valid wine producer" (Arizona Hospitality Research 2011: 9). From a statement like this, it seems that, even in itself, the industry's validity is worth celebrating. Moreover, despite the fact that Arizona wine is otherwise relatively obscure, the industry is nevertheless notorious in some circle as the home of a literal rockstar winemaker and an expatriate film maker (Krecker 2017b). For example, the 2010 film, "Blood into Wine," featuring Maynard James Keenan (the lead singer of Tool) and Eric Glomsky, which "chronicles the development of the Northern Arizona wine industry," is mentioned on the very first page of the first report on Arizona's wine tourism industry (Arizona Hospitality Research 2011). Thus, it is no surprise that one popular writer, in telling the tale of Arizona wine, describes both the significant historical figures in the industry of the state and the "Arizona wine's early rockstars" (Krecker 2017a).

Famed or otherwise, growers and producers within Arizona are working to ensure their legitimacy and visibility through established means such as AVA designations. So far, Arizona has three recognized grape-growing regions, the Verde Valley region in roughly the center of the state and the Sonoita and Willcox regions in the southeast of the state (Arizona Wine Growers Association 2018). The Willcox region is the largest producer of wine grapes in the state. While Verde Valley has vineyards, much of the focus is on tourism and selling wine (Blake 2014). Both the Sonoita and Willcox regions are recognized by the US Alcohol and Tobacco Tax and Trade Bureau (TTB) as AVAs; Verde Valley has been proposed to the TTB as an AVA and the decision is pending for approval. These AVA regions are, in principle, established based on the physical characteristics of the local environment. Yet, they are also important markers of terroir and local distinction, which if recognized by consumers can provide a price premium which enables a sustainable wine tourism industry.

Although Arizona's growing population and established tourism industry provide potential opportunity for the local wine industry, growers and producers also face significant environmental, economic, and spatial challenges which we discuss below.

Findings and discussion

In Arizona, as elsewhere, the wine industry is composed of several interdependent parts: growing grapes, making wine, and selling the final product. Each of these component parts is made up of sub-parts, of course, including the land management and agricultural components of growing (quality) grapes; the precise methods and techniques required to ferment, age, and perfect the wine; or the nuances of both regulation and marketing required to get the product to the consumer. Interviews reflect the challenges for growers and producers of these various components – and the difficulties and opportunities associated with them in the Arizona context.

Through this analysis of wine grape production and winemaking in Arizona, we trace several compelling threads of interest to the geography of wine and wine tourism. First, the extreme environmental context of agricultural production in the state interacts with various social and political factors to produce a curious mix of notoriety and obscurity in the industry:

1 The context of *wine/grape production in Arizona is challenging* across several dimensions, such as the pool of knowledge (the "culture" of agriculture) is shallow due to the unique and unusual growing environment; the material costs of production are high; and the quality and quantity of the grapes are highly variable.

2 There is a clear *spatial mismatch* between the most prominent areas for the production of wine grapes and wine (in the south), and the most prominent wine tourism destinations (in the north). This north/south dynamic is evident in the locations of business (vineyards, wineries, tasting rooms), the sentiments of growers and producers themselves, and in the presentation of the Arizona wine industry by its proponents.

3 There are some *notable social/political drivers* of the shape or form of Arizona wine, including (changing) concepts of "Arizona made" and several relevant licensing rules and regulations.

4 Arizona wine inhabits a peculiar position somewhere between *notoriety and obscurity* driven by the high-profile winemaking of a certain (literal) rockstar (subject of the 2010 documentary *Blood Into Wine*) and a general incredulity – by the general public and winos alike – that wine can, or perhaps even should, be grown in the state.

This section outlines this series of findings, taking each theme in turn.

Arizona's challenging physical environment

Although Arizona has historically been a grape-growing region, commercial-level production of wine grapes in Arizona is relatively new. Statistics from the Bureau for Alcohol Tobacco and Firearms first begin recording wine production in the Fall of 1988, with approximately 40,000 gallons of wine produced that year. Growth has been significant over the last 30 years, with a recorded wine production in 2017 of almost 300,000 gallons. Although there are no comprehensive existing statistics on the growth of wine grape growing (unlike the documentation of the growing wine tourism industry), we compared the agricultural census in 1987 and 2012 to get a sense of how the industry has changed. In 1987, the census records 90 farms growing grapes in Arizona and 8,462 acres planted in grapes. By 2012, there were 178 farms growing grapes, but only 942 acres planted in grapes. This suggests that production of table grapes has largely been discontinued in Arizona, while increasing numbers of small vineyards have been planted in wine grapes over the last 30 years. This is confirmed by other sources as well (Arizona Hospitality Research 2011: 9):

> The local and regional grape content of Arizona wines has increased steadily as more acres are planted to vines. Verde Valley blends now contain 80-90% local grapes up from 50% a few years ago...The Arizona wineries, while still niche producers compared to California, have seen a steady improvement in both the quantity and quality of the wine produced.

Elevation & topography

Crider (1923) suggests that wine grapes are most successfully grown at elevations of 3,000–6,500 feet in Arizona, with those above 4,000 feet needing winter protection and are better suited for American grape classes. Lower elevations are better suited to table grapes. Topography can alter the effects of elevation, so local conditions are important to consider in siting a winery (Map 5.2A).

Temperature

Arizona has hot summers and cold winters, both of which can create unfavorable conditions for wine grapes, including vine desiccation (Mielke et al. 1980). However, the large difference in diurnal temperatures, the change from day to night, can produce (desirable) bold flavors in the resulting wine (Arizona Wine Growers Association 2018), though the impact may, in practice, be hard to manage (Map 5.2B).

Soils

Soils types vary across the state (Map 5.2C). The soils within each AVA mainly comprise one or two types, but they are different from each other and different from those found elsewhere in the state. Soil orders used for grape growing include Entisols, Aridisols, Alfisols, and Molisols; suborders of importance include Fluv, Arg, Torr, Xer, Calc, Dur, Hapl, and Ust (Mielke et al. 1980). Grapes can grow in a variety of soil types ranging from sandy to loamy to clay, but the soil quality affects the size, quality, and yield of the grapes. Sandy soils produce fruit that ripens earlier, but heavier soils produce larger yields (Crider 1923). Regardless of the soil type, vineyards should have well-drained soils and no hard pan because the shallow roots of the vines are negatively affected by long inundation (Crider 1923). Arizona soils have the necessary nutrients to successfully grow grapes, although fertilizing is necessary (Crider 1923).

Precipitation

Precipitation varies across the state from just a few inches to over two feet, with higher elevations typically receiving more than lower elevations (Map 5.2A and D). There are two rainy seasons – one in the winter and one in the summer (Arizona Wine Growers Association 2018). Wine grapes in

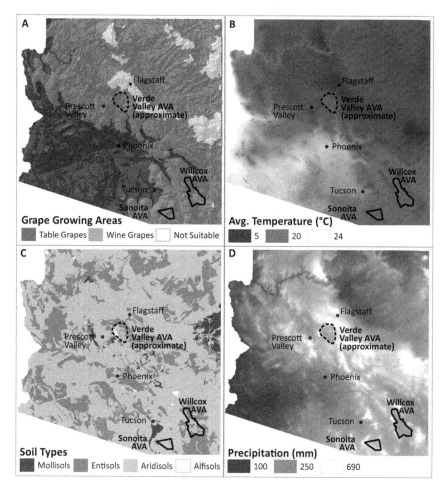

Map 5.2 Arizona's challenging physical environment. Map A: Areas suitable for wine and table grapes, based on elevation, as described by Crider (1923) (data: PRISM elevation dataset). Map B: Average diurnal temperature differences (data: Fick & Hijmans 2017). Map C: Major soil taxonomic order (data: NRCS SSURGO). Map D: Average annual precipitation (mm) from 1981 to 2010 (data: PRISM 30 year climate normals – precipitation). (All cartography by Dr. Michele Tobias.)

Sonoita require more water than the natural precipitation provides, so irrigation is necessary (Slack & Martin 1999).

Implications (for better or worse) for wine grape growing and winemaking in Arizona's "extreme" environments

Gordon Dutt, a pioneer for wine in Arizona and agricultural researcher at the University of Arizona, noted the similarities between the soil types in certain parts of Arizona (soil only, not climate or other [essential] factors) and Bordeaux, France. In the 1980s, after spreading the good word, Dutt decided to start a vineyard (and winery) himself – Sonoita Vineyards. Sonoita is now one of the most established and respected vineyards in the Arizona region. A representative points out that it is possible to grow world-class grapes, although the climate presents risks of crop loss:

> We, of course, make 100% Arizona wine. That was Gordon [Dutt]'s dream. He was like, 'In Arizona, we can make fabulous grapes here, world-class grapes here in Arizona, so there's no reason to import grapes from California.' So we have been making 100% Arizona wine since the inception. [If] we have a bad harvest or we have hail, we don't have wine for that vintage.
>
> (R9, 20150606)

The representative goes on to note that, when necessary, they will supplement their own grape supply, but only with grapes grown nearby. Indeed, "because the riskiest part of producing wine is growing grapes, Arizona winemakers want to defend the brand, and the slight premium, that comes with growing grapes in Arizona's rugged terrain" (Ingram 2015).

Although many winemakers, who are largely also growers, are committed to making wines that express the terroir of their region, not everyone in the industry is so committed. Some Arizona wineries have been able to take advantage of regulatory loopholes to produce Arizona-labeled wines even with grapes grown outside the state. Although efforts are being made to tighten the labeling requirements for Arizona wines (R8, 20150606), there is still room for winemakers to "split hairs" by using the "Arizona made" label without encroaching on any established guidelines (liquor license investigator, personal communication; 21 May 2018).

When pressed about the "Arizona grown" label, one producer lamented the potential damage done to the identity of Arizona wine when it is applied improperly:

> R9: If you're fermenting the grapes here, yes, you're producing it. But, ultimately, you're expressing the terroir of another place. [Customers] are looking at the pretty label on the front and it's an 'Arizona Merlot', but on the back it says that it's from California. That's a problem because then we're not showcasing the best that Arizona has to offer. California's been in the industry a long time and there's some lovely, lovely wines that come out of California...But I think we need...for the state hunker down and be like, you know, 'Let's express Arizona's terroir, not other places' terroir.' I think for any wine region they should really showcase themselves rather than other places.
>
> (R9, 20150606)

Growers, in our interviews, had mixed perspectives on the potential market for Arizona-grown grapes:

> I think growth is just out the door because we make just world class wines here in Arizona. In competitions I enter, international competitions, all the time I get silvers and golds. So our wine, it's not just beating against Arizona wine. It's beating against California, French, Canadian, Mexican. We have major growth opportunities. Some detriments, [are] when winemakers buy grapes from out of state and label it as an Arizona product. I think that's a detriment to Arizona because we need to we need to represent our terroir.
>
> (R9, 20150606)

Although the most recent wine tourism report noted that the availability of local (i.e. in-region) grapes was a challenge faced by the industry, some growers expressed that growth was slowing and they have started having difficulties selling all their grapes (R6 & R8, 20150606):

> R6: I think we've been through a really – I don't know if tsunami is the right term – but all of a sudden, like we said: 10 years ago, 9 wineries; today, over 90. I mean that's a massive expansion. Now most of them are small, but...the wine industry has grown. We really have to work hard now in finding customers. Because in 2005 or whenever, [when] the early innovators were getting started, they found it was a pretty ready market for anything that they could produce... Well, the thing that we've seen now is there's been enough expansion and we've kind of reached the tipping point where now there is enough fruit from Arizona and suddenly, you know, we had fruit that we couldn't sell last year. We have to adjust how much we produce or find markets for all of our fruit... The number of wineries has really shot up. The vineyard acreage has really increased. And it's satiated some of the demand that there was for locally grown grapes. I think we're going to kind of plateau here for a little while until we can develop the marketing aspects that we need.

However, the presence of locally produced and marketed fruit – specifically fruit from within the regional AVA – can be useful to growers. In reference to selling grapes, one grower stated (R9, 20150606): "Our little AVA is so small, some of the wineries that have a small vineyard and want to produce more Sonoita-grown grapes, they're gonna pick 'em up in a heartbeat because they want the AVA status on their bottle." These divergent perspectives show the tensions in the Arizona wine industry, particularly between growers and winemakers.

Besides the challenging climate, there are additional economic hurdles for growers and producers, given the smaller, less established nature of the industry in Arizona. In fact, two different growers specifically said "it's a nightmare" in reference to growing wine in Arizona. Two contributing factors are less local expertise among growers and winemakers, and the high costs involved in producing wine in a less established region. For example, in addition to the significant startup costs involved in establishing a vineyard, for small wineries, production costs (including inputs like bottles, corks, and labels) are relatively high in comparison to other more established growing regions (R9, 20150606). In other words, the small size of Arizona's wineries drives up input costs, but, on the upside, the high cost of establishing vineyards and wineries comes with a silver lining: "A huge plus is that people like to see where the grapes are grown and where their wine is made," which builds "long-term interest and loyalty on the part of consumers to visit and continually return to their favorite wineries" (Fitch, Combrinch & Pitts 2017: 9).

One interviewee, a vineyard manager, describes the challenge like this (R5, 20140606):

R5: It is a frontier setting. No one cares if you grow a 95-point wine in California.
It's more appealing to be a big fish in a small pond. That's why I decided to [come], among a lot of other things."

He goes on to describe growing in Arizona as a frontier:

R5: The really big hurdles that we face are Viticulture 101 stuff. We just need to get past that, so we can really figure out how to farm. I think it's exciting for people grow grapes in a frontier. And people grow grapes in extreme climates, extreme areas. I mean, they farm Mt. Edna which is an active volcano in Italy, and we share similar volcanic soils.

This grower was not the only one to note that skills and training acquired elsewhere were not sufficient in the Arizona context. Establishing "Viticulture 101" for Arizona is ongoing; one interviewee, associated with a well-established vineyard and winery, said that she had received formal viticulture and enology training, but she "had to kind of change it because we have different growing conditions here in Arizona to deal with" (R9, 20150606).

On top of the production challenges, there are also economic and spatial ones.

Revealing a spatial mismatch: the geographies of
wine production in Arizona

One of the unusual patterns we observed in the Arizona wine industry, given the challenges of grape growing and then producing and selling wine to local markets, was the spatial mismatch between where grapes are largely grown and where they are being marketed. Our analysis of the geographic locations of businesses holding a permit to produce or sell wine reveals three distinct geographic clusters of businesses, different from those marketed by the industry (Map 5.3). One exists in the general area of Verde Valley in the north near Flagstaff. Another encompasses the two existing AVAs in the south. And the third is coincident with the Phoenix-Mesa area, in between the other two areas. What is striking about these three areas is that companies often have locations in more than one of these clusters. It is fairly common for wine-producing locations in the southern cluster to have tasting room locations in at least one of the two more northern clusters.

Several of our interviewees noted this mismatch between population centers, where wineries and tasting rooms market to consumers, and the best growing regions (R9, 20150606).

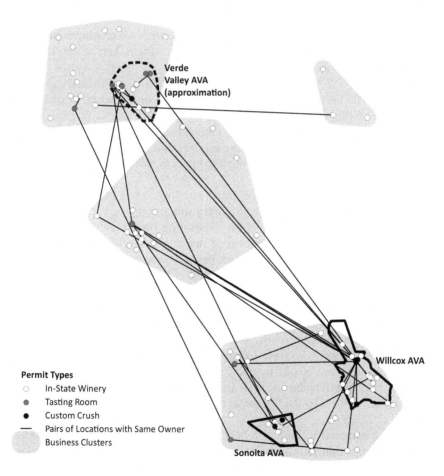

Map 5.3 Wine permit locations. (Cartography by Dr. Michele Tobias.)

Another set of respondents said (R6 & R8, 20150606):

R8: In the Verde Valley, you've got beautiful mountains. You've got the city of Cottonwood. So when they [tourists] go there, they've got, you know, theater and they've got movies and stores and everything else. We don't have any of that.

R6: And [in the Verde Valley] you're half an hour from Sedona which is a big, big time tourist center.

R8: Now the city of Cottonwood has really, really backed their industry and that's made a huge difference. When we first went to old town Cottonwood in about 2007 – it doesn't look anything like it did then. It was boarded up and everything else, and, now, it is a going strong.

R7: But then they can't grow the grapes as extensively.

R6: No.

R8: That's why we grow them here. But they've got the tourism.

Growers in the south, who potentially struggle to produce grapes in a risky environment, must also fight to become viable winemakers, given the marketing challenges (R6 & R8, 20150606):

R8: It's a little bit different because raising corn or soybeans or pistachios you're selling it to a broker.

R6: Yeah, they're commodity crops. You just –

R8: Once you sell it, it's gone. The wine is not that way. We thought the hard part is *producing* wine, [but] the hard part is *selling* wine.

Given that wine production, not grape growing, has a much larger potential for profit, there was a sense of frustration among the southern growers/producers about the limitations for expanding their businesses or adding the crucial value-added component of making and selling wine via direct sales to tourists, not just growing grapes. Growers/producers in the South understand their handicap (R6, 20150606):

> We probably are at a disadvantage here [in Cochise County], in this valley, because we're away from population centers. You know, if this valley was adjacent to the Phoenix area, it'd be a gold mine because we need people who want to buy wine to come buy wine. So one of our challenges, one of our primary challenges, is to be able to attract the people from the metropolitan areas, both Tucson and Phoenix, to make the drive down to the Wilcox area to buy wine.

Growers/producers in the south benefit from northern tourist regions, when those regions highlight the Arizona wine, but are also frustrated by the lack of local potential for tourism and tendencies among some wineries to market wine made from out-of-state grapes as Arizona made, potentially damaging the reputation of Arizona wines.

Arizona wine: caught somewhere between notoriety and obscurity

As has been described elsewhere in this chapter, the context for winemaking is difficult and expensive in Arizona and southern grower/producers are especially challenged. One set of wine grape growers and winemakers, who have struggled both with selling their surplus grapes and finding the right price point for their wines (at least something higher than their own cost of ~$15), offered this rationale for how/when one particular Arizona winery seems to garner top-notch prices for his product:

R8: Well, of course, you know who Maynard Keenan is.
INTERVIEWER: Yeah, his wines are like $65 or something, right?
R8: Yeah, but he is –
R7: He's a rock star.
R8: Yeah, he's very well-known. I guess he's also a very serious winemaker, too. I mean, he is the winemaker and I guess he's really good.
R6: He's done a good job. He's made some really good wines.

There is a delicate tension in this interaction; these growers and producers are seemingly simultaneously discomfited by their own inability to market their wines at high(er) prices but also resigned to the fact that, due to his notoriety, Maynard James Keenan, leader singer of Tool and focus of the documentary *Blood Into Wine*, can. And yet, his knack for making wine that is well-received is clearly of benefit to them as well. As another interviewee put it (R9, 20150606):

It took a really long time for the wine industry in Arizona to realize 'Oh, wow. Arizona makes really, really good wine' and then it started to catch on and now we've just blossomed. Also, the lead singer of Tool [Maynard Keenan], I think, is a big proponent of the industry here because he's got, you know, lots of money. He's got lots of high profile friends. I think that's also helped the industry really blossom because also now these people from California and elsewhere are like 'Oh, well, oh my gosh, Arizona makes really, really good wine. We need to go check this out.'

While numerous study participants lamented the reputation of Arizona wine – even Maynard James Keenan struggled at first to building credibility, given the state's reputation (Krecker 2017b) – they all also sang its praises, sharing stories of triumph despite low expectations. For example, this vineyard manager for a well-known Arizona winery said (R5, 20150606):

"I pour a lot of bottles of our stuff to my friends or people visiting or out of state or family, and I'll just stick it in a decanter, put the bottle away, and, like, 'Hey, try this. You know, this is a cool wine.' And they'll be like, 'Oh yeah, that's great' and I'm like, 'We brew it here' and they're like

'Holy crap.'" [There are] all these assumptions. It's the 'Arizona doesn't make good wine', you know, or *can't* make good wine. And then it's like, 'You can't grow grapes in Arizona. That doesn't make any sense.' But they don't get that...[even though] we don't have oak-tree studded mountains, it's the same type of climate and typography as parts of California [and Italy]. What really helps is [making] a really good wine, that some expert... at the next dinner party is like, 'I have this Arizona wine.'

In sum, the challenges for Arizona wine are multifaceted: a challenging climate for grape growing, perceptions (and reality) in regard to quality; a spatial mismatch between the (most) ideal growing areas (in the South) and the established population and tourism centers (in the North); and the limits of consumers' desires for (neo)local products (i.e. consumers' willingness to accept 'Arizona made' labeling despite lack of true terroir).

Conclusions

Using qualitative, quantitative, and spatial analysis techniques, this chapter outlined the historical and contemporary drivers of Arizona wine/grape production; how and why the wine industry developed despite the physical challenges associated with wine grape growing in Arizona; and the spatial patterns of wine grape and wine production in the state. The findings shared in this chapter reveal how, in various ways, actors have engaged in wine grape and wine production in a difficult environment and have cultivated tourism destinations based around the consumption of both wine and the rural landscape of Arizona. Growers and winemakers interviewed pursue wine production in this place precisely because it is difficult. Specifically, one respondent noted that a quality product is special when that product emerges from an unexpected place. This unlikeliness or unexpectedness of quality creates a value-added effect, which, hopefully, compensates for higher production costs. As such, stakeholders called the developing wine industry in Arizona "exciting" and poised for even more robust growth. Growers and producers in the state are persevering, despite these difficulties, to build on Arizona wine's notoriety in order to bring it out of obscurity.

Note

1 When cited in the chapter, interview respondents are denoted by their interview number preceded by the letter "R" in the text. For example, the second respondent would be noted as "R2" in the text.

References

Alcohol and Tobacco Tax and Trade Bureau (2017) "Wine Appellations of Origin" United States Department of the Treasury. https://www.ttb.gov/appellation/index.shtml#definition

Arizona Experience (2018) Arizona Wine Country: Arizona Wines. http://arizonaexperience.org/land/arizona-wines#quicktabs-arizona_wines=1

Arizona Hospitality Research & Resource Centre (2011) The Arizona Wine Tourism Industry. The W.A. Franke College of Business, Northern Arizona University. https://tourism.az.gov/wp-content/uploads/2019/06/3.4_NicheTourismStudies_Wine-Tourism-in-Arizona-Final-6-30-11.pdf (accessed 7/5/2018).

Arizona Wine Growers Association (2018) "Arizona Wine". http://arizonawine.org (accessed 8/3/2018).

Banks, G. and J. Overton (2010) Old World, New World, Third World? Reconceptualising the Worlds of Wine. *Journal of Wine Research* 21(1): 57–75.

Blake, C. (2014) *Arizona Grape-wine Industries Spur Growth, Respect.* Western Farm Press, Clarksdale (June 6, 2014). https://search.proquest.com/docview/1534248044/8A1BCCFE165D4C3APQ/1?accountid=14505

Crider, F.J. (1923) Establishing a Commercial Vineyard in Arizona. Bulletin (University of Arizona, Agricultural Experiment Station) No. 96. College of Agriculture, University of Arizona, Tucson. https://repository.arizona.edu/handle/10150/196603

de Blij, H. (1983) *Wine: A Geographic Appreciation.* Rowman & Allanheld, Totowa, NJ.

Dougherty, P.H. (Ed.) (2012) *The Geography of Wine: Regions, Terroir and Techniques.* Springer, New York, NY.

Ducey, D. (2016) "Guide to Arizona Agriculture". Arizona Department of Agriculture. https://agriculture.az.gov/sites/default/files/AZDA_GuideToAZAg-R5.pdf

Fitch, R., T. Combrink and T. Pitts (2017) The Arizona Wine Tourism Industry. Allianz Bank Business Outreach, University of Arizona. https://tourism.az.gov/wp-content/uploads/2019/06/3.4_NicheTourismStudies_AHRRC-AZWineTourismStudy-2017-report_07-18-17.pdf (accessed 8/11/2018).

Fonte, M. and A. G. Papadopoulos (2010) *Naming Food After Places: Food Relocalization and Knowledge Dynamics in Rural Development.* Ashgate, Farnham; Burlington, VT.

Giuliani, E., A. Morrison and R. Rabellotti (Eds.) (2013) *Innovation and Technological Catch Up: The Changing Geography of Wine Production.* Edward Elgar, Cheltenham.

Harvey, M., L. White and W. Frost (Eds.) (2014) *Wine and Identity: Branding, Heritage, Terroir.* Routledge, New York.

Ingram, P. (2015) "A Wine by Any Other Name." November 16, 2015. http://ediblebajaarizona.com/a-wine-by-any-other-name

Kline, C., S. L. Slocum and C. Cavaliere (Eds.) (2018) *Beers, Ciders and Spirits: Craft Beverages and Tourism in the U.S.* Palgrave, New York, NY.

Krecker, E. (2017a) *The Unexpected History of Arizona Wine, Part I. Grape Exploration.* Krecker & Company, LLC, Phoenix, AZ,.

Krecker, E. (2017b) *The Unexpected History of Arizona Wine, Part II. Grape Exploration.* Krecker & Company, LLC, Phoenix, AZ.

Mielke, E.A., G.R. Dutt, S.K. Hughes, W.H. Wolfe, G.J. Loeffler, R. Gomez, M.D. Bryant, J. Watson and S.H. Schick (1980) "Grape and Wine Production in the Four Corners Region. Technical Bulletin". University of Arizona, Agricultural Experiment Station. No. 239. College of Agriculture, University of Arizona, Tucson. https://repository.arizona.edu/handle/10150/602124

Morgan, K., T. Marsden and J. Murdoch (2009) *Worlds of Food: Place, Power, and Provenance in the Food Chain.* Oxford University Press, Oxford.

Myles, C. C. (Ed.) (forthcoming) *Fermented Landscapes: Considering How Processes of Fermentation Drive Social and Environmental Change in (un)expected Places and Ways.* University of Nebraska Press, Lincoln.

Myles, C. C. and T. Filan (2017) Boom-and-Bust: (Hi)stories of Landscape Production and Consumption in California's Sierra Nevada Foothills. *Polymath* 7(2): 76–89.

Myles, C. C. and T. Filan (forthcoming) Making (a) place: Wine, Society, and Environment in California's Sierra Nevada Foothills. Regional Studies, Regional Science.

Overton, J. (forthcoming) Landscapes of Failure? Why Some Wine Regions not Succeed. In *Fermented Landscapes: Considering How Processes of Fermentation Drive Social and Environmental Change in (un)expected Places and Ways* (C. Myles, Ed.), in review (under contract)). University of Nebraska Press, Lincoln.

QGIS Development Team (2018) QGIS Geographic Information System. Open Source Geospatial Foundation Project. Version 2.18.21. http://qgis.osgeo.org

R Core Team (2017) R: A Language and Environment for Statistical Computing. R Foundation for Statistical Computing, Vienna, Austria. https://www.R-project.org

Slack, D.C. and E.C. Martin (1999) Irrigation Water Requirements of Wine Grapes in the Sonoita Wine Growing Region of Arizona. Arizona College of Agriculture 1999 Wine Grape Research Report. http://citeseerx.ist.psu.edu/viewdoc/download?doi=10.1.1.513.996&rep=rep1&type=pdf

Sommers, B. J. (2008) *The Geography of Wine: How Landscapes, Cultures, Terroir, and the Weather make a Good Drop.* Plume, New York, NY.

Unwin, T. (1991) *Wine and the Vine: An Historical Geography of Viticulture and the Wine Trade.* Routledge, New York, NY.

Unwin, T. (2012) Terroir: At the Heart of Geography. In *The Geography of Wine: Regions, Terroir and Techniques* (P. H. Dougherty, Ed.). Springer, New York, NY, 37–48.

US Bureau of Alcohol Tobacco & Firearms (2018) Electronic Code of Federal Regulations – Title 27: Alcohol, Tobacco Products and Firearms; PART 9—American Viticultural Areas. https://www.ecfr.gov/cgi-bin/text-idx?c=ecfr&sid=057f99d79266 8247a3c45b4699417291&rgn=div5&view=text&node=27:1.0.1.1.7&idno=27

Vavrek, Matthew J. (2011) Fossil: Palaeoecological and Palaeogeographical Analysis Tools. *Palaeontologia Electronica*, 14:1T. http://palaeo-electronica.org/2011_1/238/index.html

Woods, M. (2011) The Local Politics of the Global Countryside: Boosterism, Aspirational Ruralism and the Contested Reconstitution of Queenstown, New Zealand. *GeoJournal* 76: 365–381. https://doi.org/10.1007/s10708-009-9268-7

6 Wine routes and efficiency of wineries in Sardinia

Maria Giovanna Brandano, Claudio Detotto and Marco Vannini

Introduction

Since the 1990s, wine tourism has grown steadily everywhere, not only in Europe but also across the wine-producing regions of the Northern and Southern Hemispheres. As of today, it represents a major segment of gastronomy tourism, or more generally of culture tourism, and it is widely believed to be an effective driver of local development. With few exceptions, however, the relationship between tourism and wine had long been neglected by governments, researchers and enterprises (Hall *et al.*, 2000). In this context, the wine route – either as a spontaneous partnership or as a policy-induced joint initiative among winegrowers, rural tourism businesses and public bodies or both – has emerged as the most relevant vehicle for linking wine and tourism, combining both the tangible and intangible dimensions of the wine tourist experience.

Around the world, one can find different types of wine routes. An example could be the "boutique winery" that broke out in Australia back in the 1960s and 1970s contributing to the rapid expansion of this New World's wine industry. This concept refers to many newly established small wineries that based their business on direct sales and visitations. They quickly became very popular and marked the beginnings of the Australian wine tourism. In the 1990s, Australian tourism bureaus acknowledged the importance of wine tourism as a regional development opportunity and started integrating wine tourism into the overall tourism product in a market mostly concentrated in metropolitan areas (Hall and Macionis, 1998). As regards Europe, perhaps the oldest wine routes are those located in Germany along the ancient Roman vineyards. They go back to the 1920s, and by the 1970s, every region had a wine itinerary. In France, the first modern wine routes were created in the 1960s in the Alsace region. Nowadays, wine routes are proliferating, given the desire to learn more about wine, the wish to discover the world of wine and its undisputed allure (Gatti and Incerti, 1997). In more recent years, official wine routes (also roads or trails), i.e. networks propelled by some local government or business association, backed by formal agreements among the parties, linking the actors of an area with the aim of creating value around the culture of wine, have been established in Portugal, Spain and Italy. Eastern European countries, such as Hungary, have followed suit. These developments are an integral part of today's wine tourism industry (Bruwer, 2003), but it is only in the last few decades, as stressed by Hall and Mitchell (2000), that wine and tourism have been linked for addressing the issue of global rural restructuring.

Italy, the first wine producer in the world in 2016 (OIV, 2017), is one of the few countries which has two national associations that *de facto* coordinate the wine tourism activities: Wine Tourism Movement (*Movimento del Turismo del Vino* – MTV) and Cities of Wine (*Città del Vino* – CW). The former, started in 1993 by a small group of winemakers that has now grown to more than 1,000 members across the country, prompted wine tourism not only by requiring associated members to stick and agree upon principles of cellar door hospitality, but also by promoting popular events like "Cantine aperte" (*Open Cellars*) or "Calici sotto le stelle" (*Wine glasses under the stars*). The latter, established shortly after the 1986 wine adulteration incident,[1] brought together a sizeable group of Italian local authorities from wine areas with the aim of carrying out communication, education and dissemination projects on the strategic role of quality winemaking for sustainable local development. Against this backdrop of growing attention to wine routes as instruments of wine tourism development, here we attempt to measure the impact of such routes on the efficiency of local winemakers. To this end, we take advantage of the difference-in-difference (DD) methodology, which evaluates the effectiveness of a programme by comparing the average outcome of participants (the treated group, in our case the wineries belonging to wine route areas) and non-participants (the non-treated or control group, here the wineries outside of the routes).

The chapter is organized as follows. After an illustration of the context of wine routes in Italy, we continue by a brief overview of the literature related to (a) wine and tourism and (b) efficiency of wineries, with a focus on DEA (data envelopment analysis). Afterwards, we describe the case study under analysis, the data and the methodology used. Finally, we discuss the results and provide the main conclusions.

Wines routes in Italy

Law n. 268 of 27 July 1999 and the associated Ministerial Decree of 12 July 2000 are the main pieces of legislation concerning the wine routes in Italy. They refer to wine routes as *"carefully signposted and publicized trail/roads, encompassing natural, cultural and environmental amenities, vineyards and wine cellars open to visitors. They constitute a tool for wine-oriented areas and their produce to be promoted, marketed and enjoyed as a tourist product"*. In light of these official acts, regions have the possibility to establish wine routes at the local level. By 2013, according to Cities of Wine, Italy boasted over 150 wine routes encompassing around 1,450 municipalities.

While these numbers kept growing, it is important to notice that around 50% of the wine routes are still in a starting phase. This is hardly surprising, given the significant coordination efforts and specific investments that local administrations have to make in order to attain fully functioning wine routes. Moreover, many of the targeted wine areas are located in regions which are lagging behind precisely because of the poor performance of local institutions at providing public goods and overcoming market failures. It is worth stressing that some regions, like Friuli Venezia Giulia, established some wine routes back in the 1970s, i.e. well before the 1999 act. Since then, the number of wine routes has continued to expand especially in the North (57 routes), followed by the South (41), the Centre (32) and the Islands (17). The regions with the highest number of wine routes are Tuscany (17) and Veneto (16), which are two of the most famous producers of Italian wine with protected names, i.e. Protected Denomination of Origin (PDO) and Protected Geographical Indication (PGI).

The regional distribution of wine routes along with the number of PDOs and PGIs is as follows:

- Aosta Valley: 1 (1 PDO)
- Piedmont: 7 (59 PDOs)
- Liguria: 1 (8 PDOs and 4 PGIs)
- Lombardy: 8 (26 PDOs and 15 PGIs)
- Veneto: 16 (43 PDOs and 10 PGIs)
- Friuli Venezia Giulia: 7 (16 PDOs and 3 PGIs)
- Trentino-South Tyrol: 6 (9 PDOs and 4 PGIs)
- Emilia Romagna: 11 (21 PDOs and 9 PGIs)
- Tuscany: 17 (52 PDOs and 6 PGIs)
- Marches: 7 (20 PDOs and 1 PGI)
- Umbria: 4 (15 PDOs and 6 PGIs)
- Lazio: 4 (30 PDOs and 6 PGIs)
- Abruzzo: 6 (9 PDOs and 8 PGIs)
- Molise: 1 (4 PDOs and 2 PGIs)
- Campania: 11 (19 PDOs and 10 PGIs)
- Basilicata: 1 (5 PDOs and 1 PGI)
- Apulia: 11 (32 PDOs and 6 PGIs)
- Calabria: 11 (9 PDOs and 10 PGIs)
- Sicily: 10 24 PDOs and 7 PGIs)
- Sardinia: 7 (18 PDOs and 15 PGIs)

As shown by Asero and Patti (2009), the number of wine routes per region is associated with the quality of wines. Indeed, the Spearman correlation between the ranking of regions per number of wine routes and the ranking of regions per number of wines registered as PDO and PGI is positive and statistically significant. In particular, the results for the year 2017 indicate a strong correlation for PDOs ($\rho = 0.71$) and a moderate correlation for PGIs ($\rho = 0.55$).

Overview of the literature

In recent years, the role of wine routes has been studied in relation to both the tourism sector and the wine industry (e.g. Brunori and Rossi, 2000 for Italy; Correia *et al.*, 2004 for Portugal; Bruwer, 2003 for South Africa and Peris-Ortiz *et al.*, 2016 for selected countries around the world). In this section, we briefly recall two sets of contributions that motivate and help to interpret our exercise, namely (a) wine routes and tourism and (b) efficiency of wineries.

Wine routes and tourism

In Italy, the first paper on wine routes and their socio-economic effects focuses on the case study of Tuscany (Brunori and Rossi, 2000). According to these authors, a successful wine route exerts a twofold effect on farms: on the one hand, existing activities become more profitable simply because the area and its products get more appealing to consumers (*localization effect*); on the other hand, it opens up new opportunities for their business (*synergy effect*). Moreover, when the wine route is effective, it adds value to the agricultural sector that drives the rural development. More recently, Santeramo *et al.* (2017) study the synergies between the wine and the tourism sectors through a standard gravity model over the period 2008–2012, in which domestic tourist arrivals in a region depend, in addition to mass and relative distance between generating and destination locations, on a number of key indicators of the wine industry. The authors find that PDOs and wine exhibitions positively affect tourism flows. On the contrary, the number of credited wineries and PGIs is negatively correlated with tourist arrivals at the regional level. Given the strong correlation between wine routes and quality denominations, one may be tempted to interpret the significant coefficient of PDOs as evidence that wine routes matter. But since the break in legislation occurred before the time span of the analysis, this interpretation is not warranted.

Turning to case studies outside Italy, Telfer (2001) examines the Niagara wine route by qualitative in-depth interviews conducted at 25 local wineries. The author finds that strategic collaborations between wineries, food industries and tour operators located in the region as well as aggressive marketing policies were crucial for additional on-site wine and related merchandise sales. By applying a similar methodology to a sample of South African wineries located in the most representative wine routes of the country, after remembering that all wine route estates are per se involved in wine tourism, Bruwer (2003) examines to what extent the structure of the wine industry leads towards a lesser or greater involvement in wine tourism. It is found that, unlike larger suppliers, smaller estates participate more actively in wine tourism through wine routes. But are wine routes effective in creating value for affiliated wineries? Correia *et al.* (2004) attempted to answer the question by collecting the opinions of winery managers around the Bairrada wine route, Portugal. Four years after 1999, when the wine route started, only 29% of the respondents believed that they achieved the initial goals. More recently, Hojman and Hunter-Jones (2012) analyse Chilean wine routes by investigating the role that wine tourism plays in the strategies of a winery. Authors find that two broad different strategies are prominent among wineries: some see wine tourism as a key link in a long-distance relationship strategy, with high-quality productions; others consider wine tourism a key element of survival. The latter strategy denotes poor performances in wine production or exports.

Efficiency of wineries

Efficiency studies of wineries based on the non-parametric method called DEA represent a relatively recent entry to wine economics (see the "Methodology" section for a snapshot of the technique). Several papers analyse specific case studies in Europe, traditionally the most productive continent, with Spain emerging as the most studied country in this context.

Arandia Miura and Aldanondo-Ochoa (2007) analyse 86 wineries in 2001 and find that organic wine producers are more efficient than conventional firms. Fernandez and Morala (2009) focus on the case of Castilla Leon region in the years 2006–2007. According to the DEA scores obtained from their sample, comprising 66 winemaking companies, about 23% of the companies are globally efficient in 2006 and 26% in 2007. Moreover, since the average scores of the inefficient firms in both years are similar and slightly over 0.82, there is room for improving technical efficiency. In order to investigate the efficiency of 1,222 Spanish wineries in 2007, Sellers-Rubio (2010) applies both traditional methods and DEA. Results from different approaches do not converge and no dominant measure emerges. More recently, the case of Spain has been revisited by Sellers-Rubio and Mas-Ruiz (2015) and Sellers-Rubio et al. (2016). The first work assesses the impact of PDO labels, a collective reputation indicator which is assumed to trigger investments, on the efficiency of wineries. Data include 1,257 wineries: 437 are not members of any PDO, 820 are members of at least one of the 58 PDOs represented in the sample and 110 are members of more than one PDO. Measured efficiency is rather modest for all firms in the sample; however, both the non-parametric test on the DEA scores and the post-DEA regression analysis show that PDO companies have significantly higher economic efficiency than the non-PDO companies. The second contribution, on the total productivity change in a sample of Spanish and Italian wineries in the period 2005–2013, shows a declining Malmquist productivity index in both countries[2].

The efficiency of the Portuguese wine industry is analysed through DEA also in the works of Barros and Santos (2007) and Henriques et al. (2009). The former compares the efficiency of private winemaking companies and co-operatives operating in the same market on the basis of a panel dataset for the period 1996–2000. Out of 27 decision-making units (DMUs), 7 are co-operatives. Their main result indicates that co-operatives are, on average, more efficient than their privately owned counterparts. Henriques *et al.* (2009), focusing on 22 wineries located in the Alentejo region for the years 2001 and 2004, after decomposing the calculated DEA efficiency scores into the three components (pure technical, scale and congestion efficiency), conclude that there is room to improve efficiency by mitigating scale and congestion inefficiencies.

The efficiency of Italian wineries, which are often organized as co-operatives, with vineyard owners as members/owners who deliver the grapes to the winery (cantina sociale) for the production of wine and subsequent marketing activities, is analysed by Brandano and Vannini (2011) and Brandano *et al.* (2018) with reference to Sardinia. They study the whole population of winemaking companies operating in the island, which comprises 22 conventional firms and 20 co-operatives, over the period 2004–2009. The post-DEA bootstrap regression analysis shows that co-operatives producers are less technically efficient than conventional firms. Galluzzo (2014) examines the technical and economic efficiencies of Italian wineries during the period 2008–2011. The dataset includes both organic and conventional producers in order to identify the most efficient group, which is found to be the conventional one. Sellers-Rubio and Alampi-Sottini (2016), by using a sample of 723 Italian wineries (both conventional and co-operatives) for the year 2013, find that size matters, positively affecting the economic performance of firms. Finally, Sellers-Rubio *et al.* (2016) compare Italian and Spanish wineries, relative to a common frontier, between 2005 and 2013. Italian wineries seem to be more efficient than the Spanish, even though the scores decline in both countries after 2010.

The non-parametric approach that characterizes the majority of studies described earlier, sometimes combined with post-DEA multivariate regressions, has been applied to measure the efficiency of wineries also in many non-European countries, like China (Liu and Lv, 2010), South Africa (Townsend *et al.*, 1998) and Turkey (Bayramoglu and Gundogmus, 2008).

All in all, these efficiency studies point out that significant improvements can be reached almost everywhere mostly by adjusting firm-level factors and/or changing the scale of production. Efficiency gains may also come from adopting quality denominations, from knowledge spillovers between local operators, as well as cellar doors relationship with customers. To our knowledge, however, despite the large number of internal and external factors considered, little is known about the overall impact on the outcome "efficiency of wineries" of the treatment "wine route". Taking advantage of our sample properties, in what follows we try to fill this gap by estimating a post-DEA DD model.

Case study and data

Up until 1999, when the legislation described in the "Wines routes in Italy" section finally passed, Sardinia did not boast any wine route. In line with the new regulation, in 2006, the Sardinian government stepped in and launched the wine routes programme (WRP), i.e. set a framework (see deliberation 45/14 of 2006), addressed to all interested and entitled parties, for establishing the wine routes. Accomplishing the task was easier said than done, owing to the richness of the local viticulture with its 14 core grapes and 18 quality appellations. Eventually, in 2009, seven routes were agreed upon as a result of a two-way process that involved both top-down initiatives by local authorities and bottom-up actions by winemakers, business associations and stakeholders. The grapes central to these routes are Cannonau, Vermentino, Carignano, Malvasia, Vernaccia and Nuragus. The first three, along with other grapes, are grown all over the island, while the remaining ones are only grown in specific territories. That is why the official names of the routes, listed below along with the associated provinces, sometimes omit the name of the core grape:

- Carignano del Sulcis (Carbonia – Iglesias Province);
- *Cannonau* (Nuoro and Ogliastra Provinces);
- *Provincia di Cagliari* (Cagliari Province);
- *Vernaccia di Oristano* and *Malvasia di Bosa* (Oristano Province);
- *Vermentino di Gallura D.O.C.G.* (Olbia – Tempio Province);
- *Sardegna Nord Ovest* (Sassari Province).

It is worth stressing that the WRP aimed at preserving and enhancing the production of quality wines, especially under the designation DOCG (Controlled and Guaranteed Denomination of Origin) and DOC (Controlled Designation of Origin). Further goals, spelled out in the framework regulation, are as follows: (a) to foster the social and economic growth of rural and inner areas (characterized by high rates of unemployment and demographic decline); (b) to increase the appeal of the designated territories as tourist destinations; and (c) to develop synergies with local popular culture, culinary traditions and sustainable management of environmental resources. In short, wine routes should act as magnets for attracting visitors and as a catalyst to economic development.

Map 6.1 shows the territories in which the wine routes are situated. It doesn't include the wine route of Vernaccia di Oristano which has not been implemented yet. It is interesting to note that most of these territories stretch from unique coastlines into wild mountainous interiors, providing diverse landscapes often encompassing off-the-beaten-track destinations.

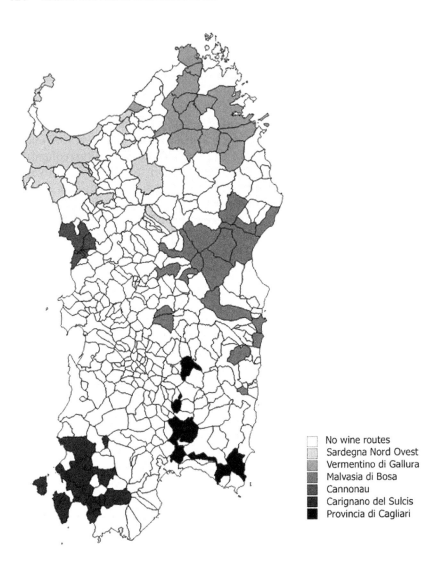

Map 6.1 Map of Sardinian wine routes. Year 2017.
Source: Authors elaboration.

Data

In order to analyse the efficiency of wineries and the impact of the WRP on local producers, we collected information about all Sardinian winemaking enterprises established as limited liability companies for the period 2004–2012. Business entities not considered in the study are mainly small winemakers producing for self-consumption organized as partnership or sole proprietorship. Unfortunately, the dataset is an unbalanced panel due to missing observations on some covariate. However, a large sub-panel (43 firms) is observed throughout the period of study for a total of 343 observations in the time span under analysis. The dataset includes both capitalist (or conventional) firms and agricultural (or winemaking) co-operatives. Accounting practices across the two types of organizations are not homogeneous. This refers in particular to the labour costs of the wine growers/members of the co-operatives, which are not explicitly considered in the co-operative income statement. However, since they are incorporated into the value of intermediate consumption, i.e. of the grapes delivered by members (vineyard owners) to the co-operative, we generate a composite variable, valid for all firm types, which reflects direct and indirect labour costs plus the value of any goods and services used as intermediate consumption.

In order to measure firm-level efficiency through DEA, we consider three inputs (labour, capital and land) and one output (sales revenue), all measured in monetary terms except for land. As in Brandano *et al.* (2018), labour is captured by the composite indicator (L) mentioned earlier, whereas capital (K) is the book value of buildings, machinery and other fixed assets except for land used in production. Land (T) indicates, for each unit and each year, the size in hectares of the vineyards. As for the outputs, we use companies' sales revenue (S) that represents the product between the price at which goods are sold and the number of units sold (Pulina *et al.*, 2010; Detotto *et al.*, 2014). Table 6.1 shows the descriptive statistics of the variables used.

We assess the technical efficiency of our firms with reference to a common production frontier estimated using DEA. The efficiency indicators derived from this calculation – the scores – are then further examined in a DD application aimed at gauging the effect of the WRP on the efficiency of wineries, controlling for additional environmental variables. To implement the latter design, which allows the estimation of the causal effect of a specific intervention or treatment (here the WRP) by comparing the changes in outcomes (here the efficiency of wineries) over time between a population that is exposed to the programme (the intervention or treated group, here the wineries belonging to a wine route) and a population that is not (the control or untreated group, here the wineries located outside the wine route areas), we generate a dummy variable, WINEROUTE$_{it}$, which takes 1 if the *i*-th winery belongs to a wine route in a given year *t* and 0 otherwise. The treatment time starts in 2009, when wine routes were implemented.

In detail, there are 21 treated wineries and 22 untreated. Table 6.1 depicts the descriptive statistics for both groups separately. Notice that the treated group shows higher values for all the variables observed, indicating that treated wineries are larger than the control group.

Table 6.1 Descriptive statistics: DEA inputs and output, Post-DEA covariates (# 343 obs.) and by group

Variable	Type	Measurement unit	Mean	sd
K	DEA Input	in thousands of €	3955.329	7884.839
L	DEA Input	in thousands of €	2766.499	3488.243
T	DEA Input	in hectares	263.921	272.664
S	DEA Output	in thousands of €	3183.25	4990.307
RAIN	POST-DEA covariate	Average precipitation at year t over average precipitation in year $t-1$ and $t-2$	$t-2d$ average	
TEMP	POST-DEA covariate	Average temperature at year t over average precipitation in year $t-1$ and $t-2$	$t-2d$ average	

	Untreated group					Treated group				
	Before the treatment (A)		After the treatment (B)		(1)	Before the treatment (C)		After the treatment (D)		(2)
	Mean	sd	Mean	sd	|test|	Mean	sd	Mean	sd	|test|
K	1552.65	275.65	1755.13	370.20	3.62*	5235.81	911.86	6584.80	1157.46	3.47*
L	915.695	79.269	1024.78	112.07	7.70*	4291.36	400.53	4132.25	443.62	5.89*
T	99.97	13.09	119.44	17.06	8.27*	372.17	28.35	412.26	32.01	7.29*
S	697.11	112.52	917.24	160.74	6.94*	5114.15	581.14	5115.12	652.22	5.42*
RAIN	−.4IN44	0.327	−.3274	0.489	0.785	−.4898	0.284	−.2847	0.539	0.317
TEMP	0.001	0.030	−.0301	0.119	0.082	0.001	0.029	−.0296	0.018	1.154

Notes: The variables K, L and S are expressed in real term (reference year 2010).
1 and 2 represent, respectively, the t-values of the tests on the difference between the following sample means: (A)−(C) and (B)−(D). * The difference between the means of the two groups (A and B) is significant at the 5% level or lower.

Methodology

Data envelopment analysis

The DEA approach measures the efficiency of a given DMU evaluating its performance relative to an estimated production frontier generated by the best performing units in the sample. Unlike the parametric approach, which requires the specification of the functional form of the production function and its disturbance term a priori, DEA is a flexible technique that, in a multiple input-output framework, focuses on a virtual single-input-output structure (Charnes *et al.*, 1978). Mathematically, the efficiency () of the *i*-th DMU is given by the following expression (see Simar and Wilson, 2000):

$$\hat{\theta} = \min \left\{ \theta > 0 \middle| y \le \sum_{i=1}^{n} \gamma_i y_i; \right.$$
$$\left. x \ge \sum_{i=1}^{n} \gamma_i x_i; \sum_{i=1}^{n} \gamma_i = 1; \ \gamma_i \ge 0, \quad i = 1,...n \right\} \tag{1}$$

where γ_i is a vector of nonnegative parameters, and y_i and x_i are the observed vectors of outputs and inputs of the *i*-th DMU, respectively. This calculation is repeated for each year included in the analysis. A given DMU is deemed technically efficient or inefficient as long as = 1 or < 1. In order to take into account both scale efficiency and pure technical efficiency, we adopt the variable return to scale (VRS) model. Furthermore, because wine firms have more control over their inputs than over their output (at least in the very short-run), the input-oriented model seemed more appropriate.

Difference-in-differences estimation

The DD method is largely used in observational settings to compare the outcomes overtime for two groups. In the simplest setup, in which outcomes are observed for two groups for two time periods, one of the groups, the treated one, is exposed to a treatment only after time *t*. The second group, called the control or untreated group, is not exposed to the treatment in either period. As long as the same units within a group are observed in all periods, the average gain in the control group is subtracted from the average gain in the treatment group. This removes biases in the after-treatment period comparisons between the treatment and control groups that could be the result from permanent differences between those groups, as well as biases from comparisons over time in the treatment group that could be the result of trends (Imbens and Wooldridge, 2007).

In a panel data framework, the DD model can be written as follows:

$$y_{it} = \lambda_t + \tau \, WINEROUTE_{it} + x_{it}\beta + u_i + \varepsilon_{it} \tag{2}$$

where y_{it} represents the DEA score for a given winery i at time t, as calculated in Equation (1). $WINEROUTE_{it}$ is the binary variable indicating the treatment and τ measures the gain in terms of DEA efficiency obtained by the firms after the implementation of the WRP. ε_{it} is a continuous *iid* random variable. Then, λ_t and u_i represent time and individual fixed effects.

Finally, x_{it} contains the constant term and a set of time-varying covariates that could affect firm's efficiency and β is a vector of parameters. These covariates measure factors outside the control of the DMUs like temperature ($TEMP_{it}$) and precipitations ($RAIN_{it}$). Climate is a factor of the outmost importance to the viability and success of the wine industry. In general, viticulture requires moderate climate oscillation. We control for these components, including local variations in temperature and rain precipitation between April and October. The two variables are calculated as the ratio between the annual average values at time t and the annual average values in the two years before. Values higher (lower) than 1 are associated with higher (lower) values of temperature and rain precipitation compared to past observations. The variables are observed at the municipality level and then attributed to the wineries according to their location. Table 6.1 shows descriptive statistics.

The nearest-neighbour matching

One of the possible drawbacks of the DD approach is related to the endogeneity of treatment. This issue can be due to individual self-selection or to the fact that some unobservable firm's characteristics can affect both the response variable and the likelihood to be treated. One solution is proposed by Wooldridge (2002, p. 285). Basically, the procedure requires to re-estimate Equation (2) by leading the treatment variable $WINEROUTE_{it+1}$ by one period. An alternative procedure is based on the nearest-neighbour matching approach (Abadie and Imbens, 2006). Since the treated and control groups seem to be highly different regarding their inputs and output (Table 6.1), the latter method allows to identify similar pairs of (treated and untreated) units according to their inputs levels. Similarity between firms is based on a weighted function of the inputs for each observation. The average treatment effect (ATE) is computed by taking the difference between the treated group and the potential similar group.

Results

DEA results

In the first step, we calculated the DEA efficiency indicator in each year. The results are shown in Table 6.2. The sample average efficiency score equals to 0.838 and no difference is detected between the two groups in

Table 6.2 DEA efficiency scores before and after the treatment

	All period		Before the treatment		After the treatment		|t-test|
	Mean	sd	Mean	sd	Mean	sd	
Treated group	0.843 (A)	0.013	0.851 (C)	0.014	0.834 (E)	0.023	0.622 (1)
Untreated group	0.832 (B)	0.016	0.860 (D)	0.018	0.791 (F)	0.030	2.086 (2)*
|t-test|	0.372 (3)		0.401 (4)		1.146 (5)		
Number of obs.	343		190		153		

Note: 1, 2, 3, 4 and 5 represent, respectively, the *t*-values of the tests on the difference between the following sample means: (C)–(E), (D)–(F), (A)–(B), (C)–(D) and (E)–(F).
* The difference between the means of two groups is significant at the 5% level or lower.

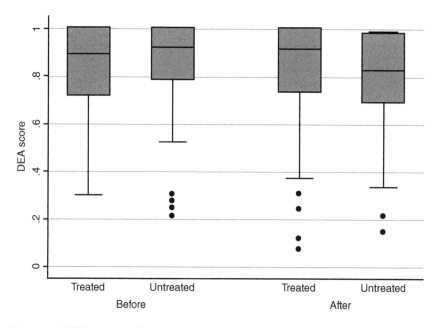

Figure 6.1 DEA scores efficiency before and after the treatment.

the overall period. However, looking at their performance before and after the treatment, one can notice that on average, their efficiency falls, with the decline being much more marked among the untreated wineries. This pattern becomes even more evident when depicted as in Figure 6.1. While the untreated firms are, on average, marginally more efficient before the implementation of the WRP (0.860 vs 0.851), afterwards they become the lagging group (0.791 vs 0.834).

Post-DEA results

The first set of findings refer to the DD model formulated in Equation (2) with a fixed-effects estimator. The WRP impact is significant in all the specifications and it ranges between 0.084 and 0.099, which means that it brought about an increase in wineries technical efficiency of about 0.1 units in terms of DEA scores (see Table 6.3). In column (3) of Table 6.3, we split the binary treatment variable into three ones in order to understand if its impact is constant over time or not. The findings confirm that the impact is higher and statistically significant only in 2011 and 2012. The rationale is that the implementation of the wine routes took some time to produce its effects.

Looking at the remaining covariates, *RAIN* and *TEMP* are significant. The interpretation is that positive variations in terms of rain precipitation or temperature compared to short-run average lead to an increase of DEA efficiency scores.

Table 6.3 POST-DEA regression results (FE model). Dependent variable: DEA

Variables	(1)	(2)	(3)	(4)	(5)	(6)	(7)
WINEROUTE	0.095**	0.099**		0.084**	0.095**	0.080*	0.160***
	(0.038)	(0.038)		(0.039)	(0.039)	(0.041)	0.051
WINEROUTE 2010			0.012				
			(0.028)				
WINEROUTE 2011			0.073*				
			(0.046)				
WINEROUTE 2012			0.206**				
			(0.076)				
RAIN				0.30***	0.132**	−0.016	0.017
				(0.063)	(0.061)	(0.030)	(0.027)
TEMP				0.076***	0.007	0.138**	0.082
				(0.017)	(0.021)	(0.062)	(0.069)
Trend	−0.130***			−0.078**			
	(0.033)			(0.030)			
Salest−1						0.000	
						(0.000)	
Constant	0.862***	0.845***	0.845***	0.871***	0.840***	0.839***	0.850***
	(0.005)	(0.017)	(0.017)	(0.006)	(0.021)	(0.033)	(0.023)
Year dummies	No	Yes	Yes	No	Yes	Yes	Yes
Observations	343	343	343	343	343	292	257
R-squared	0.091	0.343	0.372	0.159	0.345	0.359	0.361
Number of firms	43	43	43	43	43	43	31

Robust standard errors in parentheses.
*** $p < 0.01$, ** $p < 0.05$, * $p < 0.1$.

In column (6), winery size is also taken into account. To do, we include firm's sales: it is one year lagged in order to avoid any endogeneity issue. As a further robustness check, in the last column (7), the untreated sample group is restricted to wineries of less than 15 km – as the crow flies – distance from closest treated areas. The WRP effect is still confirmed.

Robustness checks

In line with the recommendations of Imbens and Wooldridge (2007), we test for the presence of individual trend components, and the null hypothesis of jointly zero coefficients cannot be rejected. This allows us to use the Fixed-effects approach instead of the First-difference estimator in Equation (2). The endogeneity of the treatment variable is also tested using Wooldridge procedure (2002), and the null hypothesis of endogeneity cannot be rejected. Finally, the Wooldridge test for autocorrelation confirms the absence of first-order autocorrelation (Wooldridge, 2002).

As indicated in Table 6.1, treated and control firms are characterized by different levels of inputs and output, with the former group handling significantly larger amounts than the latter. This difference could be an issue if we think that only the biggest firms entered the WRP leading to a treatment selection bias.[3] The result could bias our DD estimates.

In order to avoid (or reduce) this selection bias, we employed a nearest-neighbour matching approach: for each treated individual *i*, the control individual with the smallest distance from individual *i* is selected. The pairs selection is run according to the pre-treatment average period level of the following variables: the three inputs used in the DEA analysis, the DEA scores, the localization (by using latitude and longitude of wineries) and firm's ownership (co-operative or conventional proprietorship). The ATE is still significant (p-value = 0.076) and positive: the ATE coefficient equals 0.119 over the whole treatment period, while, as in the DD analysis, the ATE rises to 0.193 (p-value = 0.048) restricting the analysis only to the year 2012.

Conclusions

Wine tourism is widely acknowledged as an instrument for local development, and wine routes have increasingly been used not only to put rural areas on the map and make them accessible to visitors, but also to coalesce the efforts of private enterprises, public authorities and local stakeholders towards achieving sustainable development goals (SDGs). Indeed, even a passing glance at the 2030 Sustainable Development Agenda (17 SDGs and 169 targets) endorsed by the members of the United Nations reveals several links between policy interventions like the wine routes and the objectives of the Agenda. Here, we tried to assess the effect of such programme on the efficiency of wineries in rural areas. As long as these companies are central to these territories, any improvement in their performance is good news for local economic growth. Even more so if their success, magnified by the wine route, brings further external positive effects.

We pursued this task by means of a DD estimation approach, i.e. by mimicking an experimental research design using observational data. Our findings show that the WRP had a positive impact on the efficiency of Sardinian wineries measured by DEA scores. The estimations range between 0.095, when the standard DD approach is applied, and 0.119, when a propensity score matching technique, that accounts for the covariates that predict receiving the treatment, is used.

While our results seem to confirm empirically the beneficial effects of wine routes on a crucial driver of local economic development, a thorough assessment of the WRP would require investigating further dimensions, like, for instance, the environmental efficiency (or resource use efficiency) of winery operations not explicitly considered here.[4]

Notes

1 The incident, known as the "methanol wine scandal" after some dishonest bottlers added methyl to bulk wines to increase their alcoholic content and price, occurred in Piedmont in 1986 and caused 23 deaths, tens of people poisoned and an immediate collapse of wine exports (which fell by more than one-third).
2 The Malmquist index was introduced by Caves, Christensen and Diewert (1982). By using distance functions, this index allows changes in productivity to be broken down into technical and efficiency changes. The first one reflects the frontier shift over time, while the second represents deviations from the best practice frontier (Sellers-Rubio et al. 2016).
3 Similarly, we can think that wine routes programme follows big wineries, which means that policy makers decide the treatment zones according to the distribution of main Sardinian wineries.
4 Maria Giovanna Brandano and Marco Vannini thank Disea – University of Sassari for support under the Progetto di Eccellenza 2018–2022. Claudio Detotto gratefully acknowledges the Visiting Professor Programme 2017 of the University of Sassari.

References

Abadie, A., & Imbens, G.W. (2006). "Large sample properties of matching estimators for average treatment effects". *Econometrica* 74: 235–267. doi.org/10.1111/j.1468-0262.2006.00655.x

Arandia Miura, A., & Aldanondo-Ochoa, A. (2007). "Eficiencia técnica y medioambiental de las explotaciones vinícolas ecológicas versus convencionales". *Revista Española de Estudios Agrosociales y Pesqueros* 215–216: 155–184.

Asero, V., & Patti, S. (2009). "From wine production to wine tourism experience: The case of Italy". AAWE Working Paper No. 52.

Barros, C.P., & Gomes Santos., J.C. (2007). "Comparing the productive efficiency of cooperatives and private enterprises: The Portuguese wine industry as a case study". *Journal of Rural Cooperation* 35: 109–122.

Bayramoglu, Z., & Gundogmus, E. (2008). "Cost efficiency on organic farming: A comparison between organic and conventional raisin-producing households in Turkey". *Spanish Journal of Agricultural Research* 6(1): 3–11. doi:10.5424/sjar/2008061-289

Brandano, M.G., Detotto, C., & Vannini, M. (2018). "Comparative efficiency of producer cooperatives and conventional firms in a sample of quasi-twin companies". *Annals of Public and Cooperative Economics.* doi:10.1111/apce.12220.

Brandano, M.G., & Vannini, M. (2011). Economia del vino in Sardegna. In A. Saderi (Ed.), *Il vino in Sardegna, 3000 anni di storia, cultura, tradizione e innovazione* (pp. 449–465). Nuoro: Ilisso Edizioni.

Brunori, G., & Rossi, A. (2000). "Synergy and coherence through collective action: Some insights from wine routes in Tuscany". *Sociologia Ruralis* 40(4): 409–423. doi.org/10.1111/1467–9523.00157

Bruwer, J. (2003). "South African wine routes: Some perspectives on the wine tourism industry's structural dimensions and wine tourism product". *Tourism Management* 24: 423–435. doi.org/10.1016/S0261–5177(02)00105-X

Caves, D.W., Christensen, L.R., & Diewert, W.E. (1982), "The economic theory of index numbers and the measurement of input, output, and productivity". *Econometrica* 50 (6): 1393–1414.

Charnes, A., Cooper, W., & Rhodes, R. (1978). "Measuring the efficiency of decision making units". *European Journal of Operational Research* 2(6): 429–444. doi. org/10.1016/0377–2217(78)90138-8

Correia, L., Passos Ascençao, M.J., & Charters, S. (2004). "Wine routes in Portugal: A case study of the Bairrada wine route". *Journal of Wine Research* 15(1): 15–25. doi.org/10.1080/0957126042000300290

Detotto, C., Pulina, M., & Brida, J.G. (2014). "Assessing the productivity of the Italian hospitality sector: A post-WDEA pooled-truncated and spatial analysis". *Journal of Productivity Analysis* 42: 103.

Fernandez, Y., & Morala, B. (2009). "Estudio de la eficiencia en costes en las empresas del sector vinicola de la Comunidad Autonoma de Castilla y Leon (España)". *Revista del Instituto Internacional de Costos* 5: 31–51.

Galluzzo, N. (2014). "Analysis of efficiency in organic vine-growing farms using Italian F.A.D.N. Dataset". *European Journal of Business, Economics and Accountancy* 2(2): 73–83.

Gatti, S., & Incerti, F. (1997). "The Wine Routes as an Instrument for the Valorisation of Typical Products and Rural Areas". Paper presented at the "Typical and traditional productions: Rural effect and agro-industrial problems", 52nd EAAE Seminar – Parma 1997: 213–224.

Hall, M.C., & Macionis, N. (1998). "Wine tourism in Australia and New Zealand". In R.W. Butler, M.C. Hall and J. Jenkins (Eds.), *Tourism and recreation in rural areas* (pp. 267–298) Chichester: Wiley.

Hall, M.C., & Mitchell, R. (2000). "Wine Tourism in the Mediterranean. A Tool for Restructuring and Development". *Thunderbird International Business Review* 42(4): 445–465. doi.org/10.1002/1520–6874(200007/08)42:4<445::AID-TIE6>3.0.CO;2-H

Hall, M.C., Sharples, L., Cambourbe, B., & Macionis, N. 2000. *Wine Tourism Around the World.* Oxford: Elsevier Butterworth-Heinemann.

Henriques, P., Carvalho, M., & Fragoso, R. (2009). "Technical efficiency of Portuguese wine farms". *New Medit* 1: 4–9.

Hojman, D.E., & Hunter-Jones, P. (2012). "Wine tourism: Chilean wine regions and routes". *Journal of Business Research* 65: 13–21. doi.org/10.1016/j.jbusres.2011.07.009

Imbens, G., & Wooldridge, J. (2007). *What's New in Econometrics: Difference-in-Differences Estimation.* Lecture Notes 10. Cambridge, MA: National Bureau of Economic Research.

Ismea (2018). *Rapporto 2017 ISMEA* – Qualivita, Ismea Qualivita – Fondazione Qualivita, Roma.

Liu, H.Y., & Lv, K. (2010). "Productive efficiency and its influencing factors of wine-making firms in China. A research based on DEA-tobit approach". *Collected Essays on Finance and Economics* 2: 1–6.

OIV. 2017. *I dati sulla congiuntura vitivinicola mondiale 2017.* Organisation Internationale de la vigne et du vin, Paris, France.

Peris-Ortiz, M., Del Rio Rama, M.C., & Rueda-Armengot, C. (2016). *Wine and Tourism: A Strategic Segment for Suatainable Economic Development.* New York: Springer.

Pulina, M., Detotto, C., & Paba, A. (2010). "An investigation into the relationship between size and efficiency of the Italian hospitality sector: A window DEA approach". *European Journal of Operational Research* 20(4): 613–620. doi. org/10.1016/j.ejor.2009.11.006

Santeramo, F.G., Seccia, A., & Nardone., G. 2017. "The synergies of the Italian wine and tourism sector". *Wine Economics and Policy* 6: 71–74. doi.org/10.1016/j. wep.2016.11.004

Sellers-Rubio, R. (2010). "Evaluating the economic performance of Spanish wineries". *International Journal of Wine Business Research* 22(1): 73–84. doi. org/10.1108/17511061011035215

Sellers-Rubio, R., & Alampi-Sottini, V. (2016). "The influence of size on winery performance: Evidence from Italy". *Wine Economics and Policy* 5(1): 33–41. doi. org/10.1016/j.wep.2016.03.001

Sellers-Rubio, R., Alampi-Sottini, V., & Menghini, S. (2016). "Productivity growth in the winery sector: Evidence from Italy and Spain" *International Journal of Wine Business Research* 28(1): 59–75. doi.org/10.1108/IJWBR-05-2015-0019

Sellers-Rubio, R., & Mas-Ruiz, F. (2015). "Economic efficiency of members of protected designations of origin: Sharing reputation indicators in the experience goods of wine and cheese". *Review of Managerial Science* 9(1): 175–196.

Simar, L., & Wilson, P.W. (2000). "A general methodology for bootstrapping in non-parametric frontier models". *Journal of Applied Statistics* 27: 779–802. doi. org/10.1080/02664760050081951

Telfer, D.J. (2001). "Strategic alliances along the Niagara Wine Route". *Tourism Management* 22: 21–30. doi.org/10.1016/S0261-5177(00)00033-9

Townsend, R.F., Kirsten, J., & Vink, N. (1998). "Farm size, productivity and returns to scale in agriculture revisited: A case study of wine producers in South Africa" *Agricultural Economics* 19(1–2): 175–180. doi.org/10.1016/S0169-5150(98)00033-4

Wooldridge, J.M. (2002). *Econometric Analysis of Cross Section and Panel Data.* Cambridge, MA: MIT Press.

Web sites

"Le Strade del Vino in Italia", http://www.agriturist.it/it/le-strade-del-vino-in-italia/30-5303.html

"Le Strade del vino Sardegna Nord Ovest", http://www.stradevinosardegnanor-dovest.it

"Strade del vino", http://www.italianbestwine.it/strade-del-vino.php

"Turismo in Rete-Itinerari Tematici in Italia", https://www.tuttitalia.it/itinerari-tematici/

7 Wine tourism and local entrepreneurship in peripheral areas of Greece

A regional analysis

Mary Constantoglou, Stella Kostopoulou,
Nikolaos Trihas and Smaragda Zagkotsi

Introduction

Tourism is widely recognized as a promising development option for destinations through the generation of revenues and employment. This is particularly evident in peripheral destinations also due to the lack of alternative
investment and employment opportunities (Buhalis, 1999).

Wine tourism is a new form of tourism that combines participation of
the agricultural and the tourism sectors, where tourists visit vineyards to
taste or experience wine and wine-related activities (Hall et al., 2002). Wine
tourism offers many advantages to the local enterprises and wine-producing
regions in terms of sales, employment, income, etc. (O'Neill & Charters,
2000). The increasing importance of gastronomy has also helped in bringing
the wine product close to hospitality and tourism. Furthermore, the scenic
value of vineyards and their significance in preserving the cultural heritage
of rural areas emphasize the critical role of wine tourism in local development efforts (Alonso & O'Neill, 2009).

Since the 1990s, wine tourism has experienced a rapid growth rate worldwide in terms of industry, destination development, as well as academic interest. In many viticultural regions, wine tourism has been gaining increasing
popularity, and new wine tourism destinations have emerged, with private
and public stakeholders joining efforts to expand the benefits arisen from
inter-sectoral synergies (Alebaki et al., 2015; Getz & Brown, 2006; Williams,
2001). As Getz (2000) stresses out, wine tourism as an emerging form of tourism can be viewed as a form of consumer behavior, as a local developmental
strategy and as a direct selling opportunity for wineries. As a result of this
multi-purpose approach, a great variety of studies on different topics have
been introduced, including wine tourism culture, business, marketing and
tourist behavior (Carlsen & Charters, 2006; Mitchell & Hall, 2006).

Wine tourism is now an emerging field of research in the tourism literature (Ma et al., 2017). In wine tourism studies, information has been often
gathered from the wineries' perspective, rather than from the wine tourism
consumers (Mitchell et al, 2000; Tassiopoulos et al., 2004). Hence, as visitors'

expectations seem to vary from region to region, there is no unilateral definition or a definitive model of wine tourists (Charters & Ali-Knight, 2000, 2002; Thompson & Prideaux, 2009), and more research is needed to gain a deeper understanding on the topic (Alebaki & Iakovidou, 2010; Getz et al., 2008). Another stream of research that also needs further investigation focuses on wine tourism regions and destination attractiveness (e.g. Alonso & O'Neill, 2009; Bruwer, 2003; Carlsen & Charters, 2006; Charters & Menival, 2011; López-Guzmán et al., 2011; Stavrinoudis et al., 2012).

Even though winemaking activity has a long tradition in Europe, studies about wine tourism have been mainly conducted in the New World wine regions or countries (Charters & Ali-Knight, 2002; Getz & Brown, 2006). This includes also Greece, where relatively little research was conducted until recently (Alebaki & Iakovidou, 2010; Karafolas, 2007; Pitoska, 2008; Tsartas et al., 2008; Tzimitra-Kalogianni et al., 1999; Velissariou et al., 2009; Vlachvei & Notta, 2009; Vlachvei et al., 2009). Despite recent developments and growth of interest, much remains to be explored in the field of wine tourism in Greece, in terms of demand and supply. The present study aims to contribute to the emerging wine tourism research in Greece, gathering information about wine tourism involvement among winery operators in three regions, to add to the limited data of the newly established wine tourism market in Greece. By exploring the views and main problems of Greek winemakers from peripheral wine areas in three regions of Greece, this study seeks to shed more light on these areas from the winery operators' points of view.

Literature review

Wine tourism has been characterized as a form of cultural tourism and a type of special-interest tourism that is based on the desire to visit wine-producing regions or in which travelers are induced to visit wine-producing regions and wineries, while traveling for other reasons (Charters & Ali-Knight, 2002; Brown & Getz, 2005 cited in Alebaki & Iakovidou, 2010).

One may find many definitions concerning wine tourism; for example, Getz and Brown (2006, p. 147) define wine tourism as *"...simultaneously a form of consumer behaviour, a strategy by which destinations develop and market wine-related attractions and imagery, and a marketing opportunity for wineries to educate and to sell their products directly to consumers"*. Carlsen and Dowling (2001) further indicate that wine tourism integrates grape growing, winemaking, cellar door sales, food and beverage, accommodation and tours, thus forming a complete set of tourism experiences.

Currently, the wineries' visitor is rarely interested simply in wine tasting, but seeks for a total tourism experience (Charters & Ali-Knight, 2002; Getz et al., 2008). This includes activities closely related to tourism, like exploring the rural landscape and natural environment, local hospitality and gastronomy, communicating with local people, participating in cultural traditional festivals and with wine like meeting the winemakers and learning about wine (Alant & Bruwer, 2004; Charters & Ali-Knight, 2000; Mitchell et al., 2000).

Given the dynamics of the combination of wine and tourism industries, collaboration efforts between wineries and local tourism businesses worldwide have formed networks beneficial to wineries, tourism businesses and local communities (Beverland, 1998; Bruwer, 2003). Wine tourism networks may act as strong motivation for travelers (Velissariou et al., 2009), providing attractive offers for tourists, which, in turn, drive the economic development of the wine region (Charters & Menival, 2011; Hazard et al., 2016; Lopez-Guzman et al., 2011).

Wineries open to the public provide an additional activity for visitors, thereby adding value to the visitors' experience, enriching and differentiating the local tourism product, extending overnight stay, boosting employment and therefore strengthening the local economy (Alonso & O'Neill, 2009; Stavrinoudis et al., 2012). Moreover, wineries also provide critical benefits to the local communities in building or preserving the area's social fabric.

The wine tourism activities seem to alter year after year and become more promising for the future, as winemakers enrich the wine tourism experience with events connected with the wine culture and heritage of their region. Hummelbrunner and Miglbauer (1994) had pointed out that new cultural trends are re-orienting tourists' choices, transmitting peripheral areas into a new era, where these isolated areas have the opportunity to reconsider their position in positive terms. Wine tourism can therefore provide 'a sense of a place', helping rural areas create a unique profile with experiential value and authenticity based on the '*genius loci*'.

In Greece, the country's culture and tradition are historically associated with wine, dating back to ancient times, as numerous archaeological discoveries indicate. Today, wine production in Greece is widely expanded geographically throughout the country. With a wine production of 2.6 million hl in 2016, Greece is ranked 8th in Europe (15th in the world) in terms of volumes produced (OIV, 2018), representing about 1.7% of the European (1% of the world) wine production. Over time, wine production in Greece fluctuates and during the last few years is rather declining (Table 7.1). Regarding the regional distribution of vineyards, the largest areas are recorded in Peloponnese, followed by Western Greece and Crete (Figure 7.1). Greek wine industry consists of a large number of firms (approximately 700 wineries). The majority of firms are small-sized wineries with limited human and financial resources, while a small number of large and well-organized wineries cover a significant part of the domestic market. Greek wine, though not internationally recognized yet, has recently started to develop an increasing international awareness, and it seems that it is a challenging time for Greek wineries to explore their export potential, in addition to domestic consumption (Table 7.1) (Vlachos, 2017; Vlachvei & Notta, 2009).

Table 7.1 Wine statistics for Greece

Year	Surface area (in 1,000 ha)	Wine production (in 1,000 hl)	Exports (in 1,000 hl)	Imports (in 1,000 hl)	Consumption (in 1,000 hl)
1995	134,928	3,841	544,000	39,670	2,696
1996	132,318	4,109	485,000	39,570	2,636
1997	131,900	3,987	462,000	40,250	2,686
1998	129,527	3,826	593,000	46,640	2,927
1999	128,355	3,680	493,000	69,840	3,059
2000	130,800	3,558	429,740	62,870	2,861
2001	121,600	3,477	552,610	72,150	2,947
2002	122,000	3,085	290,710	107,180	2,466
2003	111,000	3,799	364,450	311,200	3,072
2004	111,500	4,248	350,600	244,000	3,300
2005	112,800	4,027	289,000	145,000	3,586
2006	111,700	3,938	320,000	159,000	3,200
2007	117,471	3,511	320,000	184,000	3,300
2008	115,127	3,868	340,000	184,000	3,200
2009	112,889	3,365	304,000	165,000	3,029
2010	112,272	2,950	370,000	107,000	3,248
2011	109,973	2,750	376,000	203,000	2,852
2012	110,000	3,115	289,000	174,000	3,068
2013	109,800	3,343	243,000	179,350	2,996
2014	109,500	2,800	281,000	155,000	2,639
2015	107,000	2,501	n.a.	n.a.	2,400
2016	105,000	2,581	n.a.	n.a.	2,300

Source: OIV, 2018.

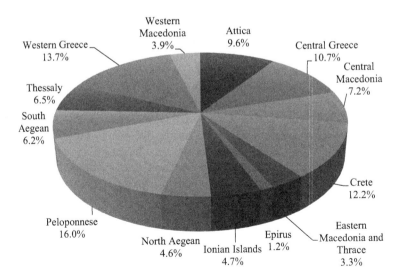

Figure 7.1 Distribution of vineyards in Greece per region.

Even though Greece is continuously improving and expanding as a wine-producing country and is a popular tourism destination, wine tourism is still a relatively new tourism activity, still lacking official data (Karafolas, 2007). Wine tourism in Greece is often considered as part of agritourism and only recently relevant studies started to approach the product as a special form of tourism (Alebaki & Iakovidou, 2010, 2011; Alebaki et al., 2015; Kilipiris & Karamanidis, 2010; Nella & Christou, 2014; Stavrinoudis et al., 2012; Tsartas et al., 2008).

Regarding the wine sector, Greek legislation is mainly based on the legal framework of the European Union, while it also addresses issues that continue to be regulated at a national level, consisting of a series of legislative measures (New Wines of Greece, 2018). According to the Greek National Strategic Plan for Tourism 2014–2020, one of the medium-term objectives is to provide incentives for the development of special forms of tourism, such as wine tourism. This goal has been supported by Law 4276/2014, which sets out the legal framework for wine tourism, e.g. the criteria that a winery has to meet in order to get the official certification from the Ministry of Tourism to act as a venue for wine tourists (Ministry of Tourism, 2018). These criteria are as follows: within the winery area, services provided may include touring, hosting, catering or all the aforementioned services, as well as facilities to ensure visitors' reception. The aforementioned criteria were recently reviewed by the Ministry of Tourism and the Ministry of Rural Development with Law 3233/2018, in order to enhance the quality of wine tourism services.

This chapter examines the characteristics of the supply of wine tourism in peripheral wine areas in three regions of Greece and especially the views of wine businessmen about the development of wine tourism. The study addresses survey questions in the context of the selected Greek wine regions, in order to explore the respondents' expectations, perceptions and motivations for being involved in wine tourism, the nature of the various business ventures, the wine tourism product offered, the potential differences among wineries' visitors and the contribution of wine tourism to the local economy. The answers to the aforementioned questions aim at highlighting the industry perceptions of wine tourism development and the potential regional peculiarities related to the stage of tourism development in the regions explored. The utility of this chapter lies in the comparative regional analysis approach to wine tourism development in Greece. The information gained could prove beneficial in helping to formulate suggestions for a more coordinated approach to wine tourism development. Research results may indicate weaknesses of the study areas that need to be improved, and act as examples for other wine areas in the world.

Survey area

The objective of this research is to explore wine tourism development among different peripheral areas in Greece. A research survey in three Greek regions (NUTS2 EU) was conducted, namely in the Regions of Central

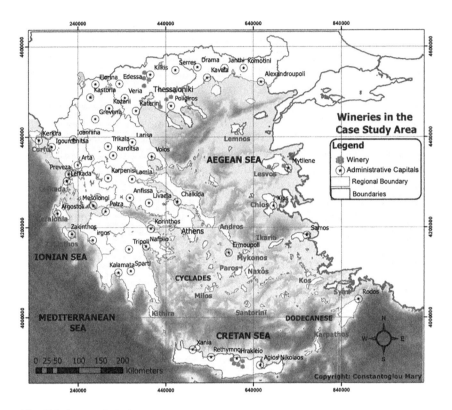

Map 7.1 Areas of study.

Macedonia, Crete and Northern Aegean. The chapter provides evidence from wine areas in the three regions of Greece, namely Goumenissa and Chalikidiki in the region of Central Macedonia, Lesvos in the region of Northern Aegean and Heraklion in the region of Crete (Map 7.1).

The significance of the areas under investigation as traditional Greek wine areas, in relation to the different types of tourism development identified, was the fundamental reason for being selected by the researchers. The wine areas selected include distinct geographic and socio-economic characteristics, and patterns of tourism development. They are indicated as peripheral areas mainly in spatial terms, in reference to their location on the fringes of the country (Herrschel, 2011, cited in Pezzi and Urso, 2016):

* The Region of Central Macedonia in Northern Greece, with almost 1.9 million inhabitants (Hellenic Statistical Authority, 2018), is the second most populous region in Greece, after Attica. Two wine areas with distinct characteristics were selected for study, namely Goumenissa and Chalikidiki.

Goumenissa is a famous wine-producing area, historically renowned for the quality of its wines. It is part of Kilkis Regional Unit, located at the Northern borders of the country. Goumenissa's vineyard extends to 2,727 ha, and is one of the 'Appellation of Controlled Origin' (A.O.C) wine zones in Greece (Ioannidis, 2016). While Goumenissa is a well-known vineyard area back from the 19th century, the 1990s and 2000s decades were crucial for the development of wine production in the area. During this period, 73% of vineyards were planted due to the recognition of wine 'Goumenissa' as V.Q.P.R.D. (Vin de Qualité Produit Dans Une Région Déterminées).

Chalkidiki Regional Unit, a popular mass tourism destination, is a peninsula lying ahead with three branches that sink into the Aegean Sea, Kassandra, Sithonia and Athos. The vines are cultivated at Sithonia, the central Chalkidiki area and at Mount Athos, an important center of Eastern Orthodox monasticism. The vineyard area is 7,500 ha, while 3,000 ha of them are undivided, consisting of the largest undivided vineyard in Europe. The total annual production of wine in the area is approximately 40,000 hl (Wine Roads of Northern Greece, 2018).

- The Region of Crete, the Southern end of Greece, with 623,065 inhabitants (Hellenic Statistical Authority, 2018), is the largest Greek island and the fifth largest in the Mediterranean, divided into four Regional Units: Heraklion, Chania, Rethymnon and Lasithi. The island is mainly a mass tourism destination: in 2017, 4,241,406 tourists arrived at the airports of Chania and Heraklion, 23.14% of the total arrivals by air in Greece (SETE, 2018). Crete is currently considered to be an active and dynamic area of quality wines production. With 4,200 ha of vineyards, 33 wineries and an annual production of 46,200 tons of wines grapes and 300,000 hl of wine, Crete is rapidly becoming a wine destination of high added value. The large number of local traditional varieties, the diversity and uniqueness of various wine areas, as well as the long Cretan wine tradition document Cretan wine's high-quality standing and ongoing growth (Wines of Crete, 2018).
- The Region of Northern Aegean, on the Eastern border zone of Greece, consists of three Regional Units: Samos, Chios and Lesvos. The island of Lesvos, with an area of 1,636 km^2 and 85,330 inhabitants (Hellenic Statistical Authority, 2018), is the third largest Greek island. The local economy is mainly based on agriculture, with an emphasis on olive oil production, and second on tourism (43,948 international arrivals by air in 2017). In recent years, efforts have been made by the two wineries operating on the island to revive local varieties and develop wine tourism.

In terms of tourism development, Goumenissa is considered to be at an early stage of tourism development, Lesvos at the developing stage, while Chalkidiki and Crete as mature mass tourism destinations. In terms of wine tourism development, all areas are identified as destinations at the developing stage, since mature wine tourism destinations require winemakers to get more involved in tourism activities related to wine (Alebaki et al., 2014). However, there are considerable differences among the wine areas explored. In Chalkidiki and the islands of Crete and Lesvos, wine areas are gifted with nearby beaches and tourist resorts. Goumenissa, being at a considerable distance from sun and sea tourism centers, is striving to become a magnet for visitors, using the wine, the wineries, the landscape and the local gastronomy as the core themes to attract visitors.

Research methodology

In this study, a qualitative research design with semi-structured face-to-face in-depth interviews of wineries' owners and/or managers was adopted. Although in wine tourism research information has been often gathered from the supply-side (Alebaki & Iakovidou, 2010; Mitchell et al., 2000; Tassiopoulos et al., 2004), qualitative research about a supply-side comparative regional analysis is rather limited in Greece. In this study, a qualitative approach was considered as an appropriate starting point, due to the lack of relevant data on wine tourism in the areas under investigation.

A first step in the data collection process consisted in contacting individually all winery operators in the selected areas. The total size of the initial sample was 46 wine establishments. In Central Macedonia, the sample consisted of the wineries participating in the 'Wine Roads of Northern Greece' Network: 7 wineries in Goumenissa and 15 in Chalkidiki. In Crete, the sample consisted of 22 wineries participating in the 'Wines of Crete' Network located in Heraklion. In Lesvos, both wineries operating in the island were included in the survey. All wineries of the sample were initially contacted by phone calls, in order to identify the owner's/manager's willingness to participate in the survey. Out of the 46 wineries included in the research survey, 13 accepted to participate, that means a response rate of 28%, which is considered to be a rather satisfactory percentage for this kind of research. Out of the 13 wineries participating in the survey, six wineries were located in Central Macedonia (out of 22 wineries in the region, response rate 27%), four in Goumenissa and two within the Regional Unit of Chalkidiki, five wineries were located in Crete in Heraklion (out of 22 wineries in the region, response rate 23%), and two in Lesvos (out of 2, response rate 100%).

The 13 wineries that accepted to participate were subsequently contacted by e-mail, consisting of an explanation of the study's goals and also a formal letter of invitation for operators to participate in the study and arrange the interview date. Face-to-face interviews with the owners and/or managers of the 13 wineries have been conducted in the wineries premises, during the period July-September 2016. Each interview lasted an average of 60 minutes. For the purpose of confidentiality, in the research survey results analysis, the six wineries from Central Macedonia are identified as M1, M2, M3, M4, M5 and M6, the five wineries from Crete are identified as C1, C2, C3, C4 and C5 and the two wineries from Lesvos are identified as L1 and L2.

Research results and discussion

Wineries' profile

Out of the 13 wineries of the sample, 46% are wineries that have been established after 2004, 39% were founded during the 1990s and only 15% were old traditional wineries with a history of more than 40 years. Regarding the legal status, 46% of the wineries were individual enterprises, while the rest of them were Société Anonyme (S.A.) or General Partnership (G.P.). Furthermore, 75% of the wineries are running winemaking process on a personal entrepreneurial basis, while the rest of them have a different corporate form like legal entities.

As for the demographics of the research survey sample, 63% of the respondents were over 50 years old, while 75% were men. Their education level was relatively high: 25% of the respondents hold a Bachelor degree, 38% of them have a Master Degree and 25% of them have a PhD. Therefore, the research clearly indicates that most of the owners and managers are middle-aged men and have a rather high educational background.

In reference to the number of labels that each winery is producing, 46% of the wineries within the survey areas produce six to eight labels. A percentage of 41% of the wineries cover 100 to 150 acres of vineyards, while only 8% of them are covering areas larger than 5,000 acres. In the latter category, wineries with a large volume of wine production are included, both in number of labels and in liters of wine produced (Table 7.2).

Wineries are operating with a rather low number of permanent personnel and usually employ seasonal workers during the harvest period. Only 23% of the wineries have more than 10 permanent and seasonal employees (a range from 25 to 40 seasonal employees), while 60% operate with no more than four permanent employees and five seasonal employees (Table 7.3).

Table 7.2 Vineyard area

Vineyard area (in acres)	Wineries (number)
up to 50	2
51–100	2
101–150	5
151–200	1
more than 201	2

Table 7.3 Number of employees

	Permanent positions	Seasonal positions
Up to 4	8	5
5–10	2	3
More than 10	2	4

Wineries in the survey areas are closely collaborating with local restaurants, hotels, retailers, wholesalers and transport companies in order to place and sell their products to the market. They also use web-developers and promotion companies in order to promote and properly advertise their wine products to the market.

Wine networks and synergies

Wineries' owners and/or managers in the survey areas generally believe that they should better collaborate with other local winemakers, in order to have better quality products and enhance production procedures, while they argue that they do not compete with each other.

A statement from a winery owner in Goumenissa (M3) illustrates the strong perception of collaboration and networking: "...*when a neighbor winery owner needs specific machinery, I can lend mine to him, and when I run out of bottles, I will borrow from a colleague. We believe that we have to promote Goumenissa's wine, while ensuring that all partner wineries will participate in the market. Since we are all running small to medium size wineries, it is of vital importance that we work together, having no competition between us*". In Lesvos, there are no networks of wine producers, mainly due to the small number of wineries currently in operation. In the other two survey regions (Crete and Central Macedonia) where networks are operating, wine producers characterized them as the 'backbone' of wine tourism. The majority (77%) of the respondents stated that they are members in many regional wine networks like 'Wine Network of Crete', 'Union of Wine Producers of Northern Greece', 'Association of Wine Producers of the Aegean Islands', and/or nationwide networks like 'Greek Wine Federation' and 'New Wines of Greece'.

However, some winemakers reported that they have dropped the networks they had been participating in, explaining that they left "...*because of the high membership fees, but will be enrolled again once they (the wineries) will recover economically...*" (M4), while other winemakers argued that they left "...*because their requests and opinions were not considered (by the networks) since they were small wineries*", stressing the point that "...*It is the large wineries whose opinion usually dominates the network*" (M6).

The role of wine networks is of crucial importance for the development of wine tourism, mainly due to the fact that there are no actions taken by the state and/or the regional authorities to support wine tourism, and as a result wine networks have to respond to obstacles and challenges met. Respondents mentioned that "...*all that has been accomplished in Greece in wine tourism is due to the wine networks...*" (M3), adding that "...*if there weren't such synergies, there would be no wine tourism at all...*" (M1).

Networks have a key role in the promotion of wine tourism by enabling the participating wine producers to develop actions that they would not be able to support independently, due to the high cost and the lack of know-how. Such actions include participation in exhibitions, hosting journalists and bloggers, the creation of promotional websites, the design of wine tourism maps, brochures and wine routes. The contribution of the networks to the organization of the wineries is also of vital importance in order for them to properly promote their wine tourism products. For example, they can provide technical and/or organizational support and consultation to wine producers, to enable them to be integrated in development programs and take advantage of funding sources to upgrade their vineyards and wineries, so as to be visited by tourists (Goumenissa), or to achieve the required operating standards (Crete) according to the Greek legislation.

Wine tourism and the profile of wine tourists

With regard to the break-down of the wineries' visitor groups, in terms of place of origin, the vast majority are from the USA and Europe, mainly from Germany, the UK, France, Belgium, Switzerland and Greece. Furthermore, research findings illustrate that wine tourism as a holidays activity is not included in the motives of young people, visitors are usually middle-aged married couples, with medium to high income, while all wineries emphasize the high educational level of visitors. A part of them could be characterized as 'conscious' wine tourists, with wide knowledge about wine, traveling around the world for this purpose and having visited more than one wineries during their trip in Greece. Similar results have also been indicated by other research (Yuan et. al., 2004).

Research results show that tourists visit the wineries either individually or in groups, with a cultural or educational purpose of visit. In regions with significant tourist development, like Crete or Chalkidiki, visitors can be distinguished into two groups: the wine 'connoisseurs' with a strong wine tourism motive, and those who are the leisure tourists that perceive the visit to a winery as part of their overall tourist experience. In contrast, in areas at an early stage of tourism development, like Goumenissa, independent tourists visit the wineries because they already know their products, they have already tasted their wine and they want to meet the producers in order to acquire knowledge about the wines varieties, the cultivation and production procedure and moreover to have a contact with local people and culture. There are also educational visits organized by University Departments for students on the specific field of study.

Regarding the characteristics and motives of wine tourists in the three regions, as described by the wine owners or managers, the results show that in Goumenissa, visitors may be characterized as 'wine lovers'. This follows the four types of visitors proposed by Alebaki and Iakovidou (2010): wine lovers, neophytes, occasional wine tourists and hangers-on. Goumenissa visitors are rather highly educated, with deep knowledge about wine, often have traveled around the world for this purpose, while their primary motive to visit a destination is the existence of a significant winery. On the contrary, wine tourists in popular tourism destinations like Crete and Chalkidiki can be characterized either as 'wine lovers' or as 'hangers-on' (Charters & Ali-Knight, 2002), that is, tourists seeking to enrich their activities during their holidays, without having a specific motivation associated with wine.

The wine tourism experience

The facilities available at the wineries participating in this survey research include vineyard walking, winery organized tours, wine tasting and cellar door sales. At first, visitors are offered a guided tour to the wineries and/ or walking the vineyards, while information is provided about the company and its products (labels, number of bottles, etc.), as well as about the history of wine in the area and its role for preserving the identity and the cultural heritage of the place. At the end of the tour, visitors are offered wine tasting, usually including 1–3 labels of different varieties and cellar door sales. Some wineries also provide restaurant facilities and/or organize special events.

A rather small number (23%) of wine producers offer organized wine tourism packages. Some of them have an exclusively commercial character, aiming to increase the company revenues (e.g. different prices of packages based on the number of labels tasting and variety of meals), while others offer an integrated wine tourism experience (e.g. touring the vineyards, visiting sites of interest associated with the history of wine in the region). A typical example is what a winemaker mentioned: *"...we end up the wine tour to a monastery dating back to 1800. Local people used to call the monastery 'vineyard', because illegal transactions of grapes were taking place there at those times. There we taste special labels of wines, together with light meals of local products like cheese, etc..."* (M1). Another wine producer mentioned: *"...we organize thematic events, e.g. 'the grape vine on Pella's gastronomy', where professional chefs prepare meals based on local products"* (M2).

In the survey areas, the 'Wine Roads of Northern Greece', the 'Wines of Crete' and the 'Aegean Islands Wine Producers Association' networks give the opportunity to visitors to participate in various activities which include tours, tasting, and competitions with awards (New Wines of Greece, 2017).

However, wine tourism activities' profits in the wineries that participated in the survey seem not to hold a considerable share in their overall revenues (5–10% of their annual turnover). This figure demonstrates that the main economic activity of wineries is the production and sales of wine, while there is a considerable potential for further development of wine tourism as an additional activity. A winemaker in Crete (C3) mentioned that *"...wine tourism is not very important in regard to the financial contribution for the winery... but we deeply believe in its potential and we expect that it will be an activity of major importance in the future...".*

Wine tourism and local development

The vast majority of respondents agreed that wine tourism activities have contributed to local development, that is, to the recognition and promotion of local wines, to the diversification of the area's tourism product and to the creation of new jobs. In all three study regions, wine producers perceive wine tourism as a promising activity that can offer significant benefits to the local communities. They actually describe wine tourism as a *"quality"*, *"innovative"* tourism product (L1, L2), addressed to *"people who respect the visited place"* (M6).

Winemakers conceive wine tourism as a special tourism product which is closely related to local production, boosting the development of other sectors of the local economy, while also highlighting the traditional authentic characteristics and the history of the place. Among the comments provided, a winemaker acknowledged the wine tourism role in *"...featuring the local production and the winery. The wine not only highlights the history of the area, but in a sense also provides the cultural geography of the place in a bottle. By getting to know the local products, like wine, olive oil, etc, the visitors may search for these products once they will be back home..."* (C1). Another respondent mentioned that *"...wine tourism development has considerable benefits; it promotes local products and protects local cultural heritage"* (C5).

More specifically, Cretan wine producers point out wine tourism as a means to diversify from mass tourism that is the dominant tourism product of Crete. As a wine producer commented: *"...wine tourism promotes and protects the unique elements of each region by contributing to the well-being of the local community without, however, wasting natural resources ... Wine tourism promotes the dissemination of the local cultural heritage, traditions and customs in contrast to mass tourism, which has gradually led to the commercialization of local tradition..."* (C2).

Wine producers, especially those operating in regions with popular tourism destinations (i.e. Chalkidiki and Crete), recognize that wine tourism can support balanced and sustainable regional development both for natural resources and local communities, a development process that builds on local products and initiates future demand, while offering authentic tourism experiences to visitors.

Future development and promotion of wine tourism

Winemakers recognize that wine tourism is an important alternative form of tourism, with significant potential for further development. Cretan winemakers believe that *"...there is a significant development of wine tourism in the island and more travel agents include visits to wineries in their tours"* (C2). In Lesvos, a winery owner stated that *"...we are not a well-established destination; if we were betterknown as a destination we also might have more visitors in the winery. Although wine lovers are increasing worldwide, they are still a minority group of visitors in Greece"* (L1).

Comments from winemakers in the survey areas also demonstrate that apart from actions implemented by wineries individually, only the wine networks represent an organized effort to promote wine tourism in Greece. Wineries often participate in international wine exhibitions and events addressed to targeted audience (wine lovers, journalists, bloggers, etc.). Additionally, they use the internet, as well as social media, to disseminate information about wine tourism activities.

A number of wine producers clearly recognize that for the further development and promotion of wine tourism in Greece, the establishment of synergies at the local, regional and national levels is required, with the involvement of local and regional authorities (e.g. municipalities) and the tourism industry. It is widely acknowledged by wine producers that actions by the state institutions are necessary, in addition to the individual efforts of wine producers: *"...there must be a national strategy for the promotion of wine tourism, while wine producers, must also draw their own strategies for promotion. It is a rather multi-level effort..."* (M5).

Additionally, of particular importance is the development of synergies between the wine and tourism sectors and all the stakeholders involved in order to establish wine tourism as a distinct tourist product. A winemaker pointed out that *"...in Greece, tourism agencies have not yet been involved in wine tourism, thus there is a missing link for the development of wine tourism. Networks do a great job.... but they cannot act as tourism agents ... instead they have to find a way to activate tourism agents to get interested in wine tourism..."* (M3). Another winemaker mentioned: *"...co-operation and coordinated actions are required between the wine industry, tourism agents, hospitality and catering industry, to create an attractive and competitive tourism product..."* (C3). Evidence from previous research with winemakers confirms the aforementioned factors as critical for the successful development of wine tourism (Alebaki et al., 2014; Telfer, 2001).

Difficulties and challenges of wine sector development

As reported by a number of wine producers, the current problems of the Greek wine sector derive mainly from the increase in taxation during the economic crisis period, i.e. increase in the Special Consumption Tax and the Value Added Tax up to 23%.

Wine producers in Goumenissa reported the difficulty in finding workers, especially during the harvest period, as well as the existence of bulk wine without a known trademark available at lower prices. Wine producers in Crete focus on issues of strategic planning and the promotion of wine culture. The main obstacles recognized include the lack of synergies at the local, regional and national levels among the local and regional authorities, the wine and tourism sectors and all the stakeholders involved, as well as the lack of a comprehensive national strategic planning and marketing. Furthermore, marketing efforts for the promotion of Greek wine abroad are characterized by lack of continuity and consistency. In addition to weak marketing, Greek wines are not competitive in the European market to the New World wines, which have lower prices (CP, 2018).

Conclusions

Wine tourism recorded a remarkable growth over the past few decades, creating challenges and opportunities for wineries to diversify in an effort to support their primary business activity of producing and selling wine, while also being viewed as a source for sustainable tourism development, supporting local producers and boosting local economies. In Greece, wine tourism appears to be at an initial stage; therefore, it is not surprising that wine tourism research has only taken place in recent years.

In this context, this chapter contributes to the existing body of wine tourism research, exploring current developments in three traditional Greek wine regions from the wine operators' perspectives. The study adds to the empirical supply-side literature on wine tourism, by providing further consideration for winemakers and tourism policy makers, while adding to the body of knowledge on wine tourism to stimulate further research in the field. Study results revealed some interesting information about wine tourism development in Greece that may allow for useful conclusions to be reached.

The Region of Central Macedonia is being identified as a wine tourism destination in a rapidly developing stage. In the Region of Crete, wine tourism is considered as an opponent of the dominant mass tourism model. According to the survey results, the regions' wine sector consists predominantly of small firms, engaged in wine tourism during the last few years. Winemakers involved in wine tourism acknowledge the multiple benefits derived from its further development. However, wine tourism is not yet considered as a significant activity for wineries, as far as its contribution to their annual turnover is concerned. Regarding the employment generated from wine tourism, research results also indicate that the development of wine tourism in the areas explored is not directly linked to a considerable contribution in employment.

Winemakers participating in the research, being members of wine networks, generally recognize their pivotal role in the development and promotion of wine tourism. According to respondents, one of the major obstacles for the development of wine sector in Greece is high taxation, with recently increased Special Consumption Tax and VAT in wine up to 23%. A generalized conclusion of the interviews is that wine tourism development in Greece, despite the difficulties mentioned earlier, has good perspectives, since wine producers already involved in wine tourism activities are willing to expand their business engagement in the field.

In this context, introducing local wine tourism packages and marketing strategies to inform and get familiarized groups of potential tourists, taking into account the special characteristics of the particular areas, e.g. local tangible and intangible cultural heritage, as well as wine wise features (local wine varieties, etc.), could help in maximizing the potential of the various tourist segments available. These actions could provide with an increasing resource for wine tourism that, in combination with gastronomy and the rural landscape, may become as or even more attractive than the traditional sun and beach tourism model (Alonso & O'Neill, 2009). However, to further develop wine tourism, wineries need national, regional and local agencies to stimulate such processes, investing in infrastructure, and promoting the local wine and gastronomy. It is also necessary that the state provides institutional support to the wine enterprises in the form of a specialized institution which will coordinate all actions related to wine tourism (Stavrinoudis et al., 2012).

Although this study provided valuable insights into the wine tourism sector in the regions explored, certain limitations to the findings of the research need to be recognized, concerning mainly data availability and number of areas explored. The research survey included only thirteen wineries in three regions of Greece. Nevertheless, there are many more wineries in other regions in the country, with various characteristics. While the number of participants was considered sufficient for this study, the authors acknowledge that the low response rate does not allow for making generalizations of the findings, since the results may not reflect the wine industry in Greece as a whole and may not be applicable to winemakers in other regions. Future research could involve a more comprehensive approach using a larger number of respondents to further explore wine tourism development in the regions under investigation. It could even widen the research survey to include also other stakeholders involved in wine tourism, such as local authorities, local tourism bodies, local wine networks and associations, the local community and the wine tourists themselves. The further exploration of the study regions would provide all stakeholders involved with valuable information that could assist the areas explored, that are making efforts to evolve as wine tourism destinations. Furthermore, future research could be enlarged by examining the perceptions and expectations of winemakers in other regions of Greece, with different geographic and economic characteristics, and patterns of tourism development. Growing research interest about wine tourism development can be of much assistance for the Greek wine regions and industry.

References

Alant, K. & Bruwer, J. (2004). Wine tourism behaviour in the context of motivational framework for wine regions and cellar doors. *Journal of Wine Research*, 15(1), 27–37.

Alebaki, M. & Iakovidou, O. (2010). Segmenting the Greek wine tourism market using a motivational approach. *New Medit*, 9(4), 31–40.

Alebaki, M. & Iakovidou, O. (2011). Market segmentation in wine tourism: A comparison of approaches. *TOURISMOS: An International Multidisciplinary Journal of Tourism*, 6(1), 123–140.

Alebaki, M., Iakovidou, O., & Menexes, G. (2014). Current state and potential of wine tourism in Northern Greece: Weighing winemakers' perceptions. *TOURISMOS: An International Multidisciplinary Journal of Tourism*, 9(2), 227–239.

Alebaki, M., Menexes, G., & Koutsouris, A. (2015). Developing a multidimensional framework for wine tourist behavior: Evidence from Greece. *Wine Economics and Policy*, 4(2), 98–109.

Alonso, A.D. & O'Neill, M. (2009). Wine tourism in Spain: The case of three wine regions. *TOURISM*, 57(4), 405–420.

Beverland, M. (1998). Wine tourism in New Zealand-maybe the industry has got it right. *International Journal of Wine Marketing*, 10(2), 24–33.

Brown, G. & Getz, D. (2005). Linking wine preferences to the choice of wine tourism destinations. *Journal of Travel Research*, 43, 266–276.

Bruwer, J. (2003). South African wine routes: some perspectives on the wine tourism industry's structural dimensions and wine tourism product. *Tourism Management*, 24(4), 423–435.

Buhalis, D. (1999). Limits of tourism development in peripheral destinations: problems and challenges. *Tourism Management*, 20(2), 183–185.

Carlsen, J. & Charters, S. (2006). Introduction. In: J. Carlsen and S. Charters (Eds.), *Global Wine Tourism: Research Management and Marketing* (pp. 1–16). London: CABI Publishing.

Carlsen, J. & Dowling, R. (2001). Regional wine tourism: a plan of development for Western Australia. *Tourism Recreation Research*, 26(2), 45–52.

Charters, S. & Ali-Knight, J. (2000). Wine tourism – a thirst for knowledge? *International Journal of Wine Marketing*, 12(3), 70–81.

Charters, S. & Ali-Knight, J. (2002). Who is the wine tourist? *Tourism Management*, 23(3), 311–319.

Charters, S. & Menival, D. (2011). Wine tourism in Champagne. *Journal of Hospitality & Tourism Research*, 35(1), 102–118.

CP - Critical Publics (2018). Greek Wine Industry, Global Public Rhetoric Analysis, Wines from Greece.

Getz, D. (2000). *Explore wine tourism: Management, development, destinations*. New York: Cognizant.

Getz, D. & Brown, G. (2006). Critical success factors for wine tourism regions: A demand analysis. *Tourism Management*, 27(1), 146–158.

Getz, D., Carlsen, J., Brown, G., & Havitz, M. (2008). Wine tourism and consumers. In: A.G. Woodside & D. Martin (Eds.) *Tourism Management: Analysis, Behaviour and Strategy* (pp. 245–268). Wallingford: CABI.

Hall, M., Longo, A.M., Mitchell, R., & Johnson, G. (2002). Wine tourism in New Zealand. In: C.M. Hall, L. Sharples, B. Cambourne and N. Macionis (Eds.), *Wine Tourism Around the World: Development, Management and Markets* (pp. 150–176), Oxford: Elsevier Science.

Hazard, W., Mohanty, A., Magrath, C., & Nogueira, T. (2016). *Wine Tourism Development in Northern Greece*. Thessaloniki: American Farm School-Perrotis College.

Hellenic Statistical Authority (2016). Research on Vineyards. Available at: http://www.statistics.gr/documents/20181/0922bf75-feba-4ba9-b199-d584138bee1d [accessed on 08/09/2018].

Hellenic Statistical Authority (2018). 2011 Population and housing census. Available at: http://www.statistics.gr/en/statistics/-/publication/SAM03/- [accessed on 05/03/2018].

Herrschel, T. (2011). Regional development, peripheralisation and marginalisation – and the role of governance. In T. Herrschel & P. Tallberg (Eds.), *The Role of Regions? Networks, Scale, Territory* (pp. 85–102). Kristianstad: Kristianstad Boktryckeri

Hummelbrunner, R. & Miglbauer, E. (1994). Tourism promotion and potential in peripheral areas: Tea Austrian case. *Journal of Sustainable Tourism*, 2(1–2), 41–50.

Ioannidis, V. (2016). The vineyard of Kilkis. Photographic guide. Region of Central Macedonia, Regional Unit of Kilkis.

Karafolas, S. (2007). Wine Roads in Greece: A Cooperation for the Development of Local Tourism in Rural Areas. *Journal of Rural Cooperation*, 35(1), 71–90.

Kilipiris, F.E. & Karamanidis, I.A. (2010). "Wine Roads of Northern Greece": A Tool for Promoting Oenogastronomy for the Areas of Epirus, Macedonia and Thrace. Tourism and Hospitality Proceedings 2010, 976–975.

López-Guzmán, T., Rodríguez-García, J., Sánchez-Cañizares, S., & Luján-García, M.J. (2011). The development of wine tourism in Spain. *International Journal of Wine Business Research,* 23(4), 374–386.

Ma, E., Duan, B., Shu, L., & Arcodia, Ch. (2017). Chinese visitors at Australia wineries: Preferences, motivations, and barriers, *Journal of Tourism, Heritage & Services Marketing*, 3(1), 3–8.

Ministry of Tourism (2018). Article 314 Wine Tourism. Available at: http://law.mintour.gov.gr/resources/96cc4b2d27397762438ef3b35dd5811e4f58ca82 [accessed on 04/09/2018].

Mitchell, R. & Hall, C.M. (2006). Wine tourism research: the state of play. *Tourism Review International*, 9(4), 307–332.

Mitchell, R., Hall, C.M., & McIntosh, A. (2000). Wine Tourism and Consumer Behaviour. In: C.M. Hall, E. Sharples, B. Cambourne, N. Macionis (Eds.), *Wine Tourism around the World: Development, Management and Markets* (pp. 115–135). Oxford: Butterworth-Heinemann.

Nella, A. & Christou, E.(2014). Segmenting wine tourists on the basis of involvement with wine. *Journal of Travel & Tourism Marketing,* 31(7), 783–798.

New Wines of Greece (2017). Open Cellar doors. Available at: http://www.newwinesofgreece.com/news_of_greek_wine/en_open_cellar_doors_may_2728_2017.html [accessed on 09/02/2018].

New Wines of Greece (2018). Greek law regarding the wine sector. Available at: http://www.newwinesofgreece.com/nomo8esia/en_greek_law_regarding_the_wine_sector.html [accessed on 04/09/2018].

OIV – International Organisation of Vine and Wine (2018). Statistics. Available at: http://www.oiv.int/en/databases-and-statistics/statistics [accessed on 03/09/2018].

O'Neill, M. & Charters, S. (2000). Service quality at the cellar door: Implications for Western Australia's developing wine tourism industry. *Managing Service Quality*, 10, 112–122.

Pezzi, M.G. & Urso, G. (2016). Peripheral areas: conceptualizations and policies. Introduction and editorial note. IJPP – *Italian Journal of Planning Practice*, VI(1), 1–19.

Pitoska, E. (2008). Networking of the wine-tourism small and medium sized enterprises and their contribution to the local development: The case of the 'wine roads' of Northern Greece. International Conference on Applied Economics–ICOAE 2008 (pp. 15–17).

SETE (2018) Statistics repository. Available at: http://sete.gr/en/ [accessed on 18/03/2018].

Stavrinoudis, T., Tsartas, P., & Chatzidakis, G. (2012). Study of the major supply factors and business choices affecting the growth rate of wine tourism in Greece. *Current Issues in Tourism*, 15(7), 627–647.

Tassiopoulos, D., Muntsu, N., & Haydam, N. (2004). Wine tourism in South Africa: a demographic and psychographic study. *Journal of Wine Research*, 15(1), 51–63.

Telfer, J.D. (2001). Strategic alliances along the Niagara Wine Route. *Tourism Management*, 22(1), 21–30.

Thompson, M. & Prideaux, B. (2009). Developing a food and wine segmentation and classifying destinations on the basis oftheir food and wine sectors. *Advances in Hospitality and Leisure*, 5, 163–183.

Tsartas, P., Stavrinoudis, T., & Chatzidakis, G. (2008). Wine tourism in Greece: Crucial parameters of demand and supply. First National Congress on wine tourism, Greek Wine Federation, Lemnos.

Tzimitra-Kalogianni, I., Papadaki-Klavdianou, A., Alexaki, A., & Tsakiridou, E. (1999). Wine routes in Northern Greece: consumer perceptions. *British Food Journal*, 101(11), 884–892.

Velissariou, E., Galagala, A., & Karathanos, A. (2009). Wine Tourism and Development of Planning a Wine Route Network-In the Region of Thessaly-In Greece. *TOURISMOS: An International Multidisciplinary Journal of Tourism*, 4(4), 311–330.

Vlachos, V. (2017). A macroeconomic estimation of wine production in Greece. *Wine Economics and Policy*, 6(1), 3–13.

Vlachvei, A. & Notta, O. (2009) Wine Routes in Greece: Producers' Perceptions andEconomic Implications. *International Journal of Arts and Sciences*, 3(2), 95–106.

Vlachvei, A., Notta, O., & Ananiadis, I. (2009). Does advertising matter? An application to the Greek wine industry. *British Food Journal*, 111(7), 686–698.

Williams, P. (2001). Positioning wine tourism destinations: An image analysis. *International Journal of Wine Marketing*, 13, 42–59.

Wine Roads of Northern Greece (2018) Wine routes. Available at: http://www.wineroads.gr/en/ [accessed on 18/03/2018].

Wines of Crete (2018). History of Wine in Crete. Available at: http://www.winesofcrete.gr/ [accessed on 18/03/2018].

Yuan, J., Cai, A.L., Morrison, M.A., & Linton, S. (2004). An analysis of wine festival attendees' motivation: A synergy of wine, travel and special events? *Journal of Vacation Marketing*, 11(1), 41–58.

8 The emergence of tourism niches in rural areas

The case of Wine Tourism in Alentejo, Portugal

Joana Neves, André Magrinho and Joaquim Ramos Silva

Introduction

Alentejo, located in southern Portugal, occupies more than a third of the national territory and is one of the regions that has experienced most changes in recent decades. As one of the oldest regions of the country, and generally not distant from the Metropolitan Area of Lisbon, some of its features do, however, characterise Alentejo as typically peripheral (for example, a very sharp decline in its population over recent decades, a long and painful process of agricultural restructuring and modernisation, which still retains a relatively high economic weighting, a scarcity of advanced manufacturing industries, etc.). On the other hand, the region is mostly homogeneous from the geographical and historical points of view: a large plain punctuated by soft hills with somewhat distanced villages and small towns featuring many vestiges of different eras, from neo-lithic times to Roman and Arabic settlements, the Christian Re-conquest, the medieval and modern ages (for example, ancient castles and fortresses are common across the landscape). Even its vegetation, where cork and holm oaks still occupy large areas, is also very distinctive on a global scale. However, in spite of all these and other endowments, Alentejo has long since lagged behind in terms of economic development. Nevertheless, as shown in the following, the region does have a long tradition in wine production and other potential tourist advantages.

The major investments put into modernising vineyards, wineries and other tourism facilities related to local food reflect the need to improve on its differentiation and strategic repositioning, while strengthening its economic and social base, in an attempt to generate greater wealth and prosperity through capitalising on the main advantages and opportunities held by the region. According to Alebaki and Iakovidou (2011), the tourism supply, based on aggregating distinct sectors such as tourism facilities and wine, has gained a rising profile as a catalyst for economic and social development. Additionally, fierce competition among international tourist destinations, unthinkable until very recently, highlights the need for new strategies and means of interaction between natural, historic and cultural resources and all of the main local, regional and national players, as well as with visitors.

When wine and vineyards play a determinant role as part of local livelihoods, they may serve as an instrument for the rebirth of local festivities and traditions contributing to the international appeal of destinations (Atout France, 2010). There are good examples of this in the "Old World" countries such as France, Italy or Portugal, but above all in the so-called "New World Countries" such as Australia, New Zealand, South Africa or the USA (California) as noted by Getz (2000). This mainly relates to the increasing demand for "tourism of taste", that is, tourism linked or motivated by wine and gastronomy, thereby reflecting one of the new tourism paradigms based on greater specialisation and sophistication. This means that the *"art de vivre"*, linked to pleasures of the senses, to tasting good food and wines, is now no longer confined to isolated social and cultural elites.

The concept of Wine Tourism emerged out of this context and, according to Silva (2012, p. 1), in addition to those already mentioned, other factors often get referenced as the reasons for growing demand. These include, for example, the social status linked to quality wines and their consumption by elites with specific lifestyles, as well as the interest of public figures in wine production, such as actors, filmmakers and singers (Gerard Depardieu in France, Francis Ford Coppola in California (USA) and Cliff Richard in Algarve, Portugal). Furthermore, there is also the association of world-famous architects in the design and planning of wineries and wine centres such as Frank Gehry for the Marques de Riscal winery in Rioja (Spain), or Siza Vieira for the Adega Maior winery in Alentejo, Portugal, which have all contributed to increasing and diversifying Wine Tourism demand.

In accordance with this constantly shifting picture, what were the impacts of these new trends on Alentejo as regards wine, food and tourism? How did the diverse stakeholders, local and national, private or public, react to these new opportunities for the region? How do they evaluate the experiences acquired in the meanwhile? In seeking to answer these questions, the present chapter assesses the evolution of this process and its main determinants with a particular focus on the role of Wine Tourism in the region's dynamics. More specifically, the aim of this work is twofold: (i) to understand the relevance of the wine industry to the development of Wine Tourism in Alentejo and (ii) to identify the policies pursued by the regional authorities that may have contributed to expanding and deepening a "competitive niche of Wine Tourism" composed of wine, food and the other critical factors to success provided by the region.

The chapter is structured as follows. After this introduction, we continue by refining the concept of Wine Tourism. Afterwards, we describe the main features of Wine Tourism development in Alentejo, considering not only the wine sector but also other critical factors such as the environmental and cultural heritage, and the development of tourism. The following step involves the presentation in detail of the methodology underpinning this research as well as the analysis of its results, particularly as regards evaluation, and the discussion. Finally, in the conclusion, we summarise the main findings of the work and prepare the ground for further research on the subject.

Wine Tourism: a concept under evolution

What actually is Wine Tourism? Even though lively debates have arisen involving tourism and wine sector professionals, government officials and academics, there is still no consensus over the definition and assertion of Wine Tourism as a tourist product in its own right, and with its inevitable corresponding linkage to other types of tourism. Table 8.1 summarises the main contributions of the literature on this subject.

Table 8.1 Wine Tourism concepts

Author (data)	*Wine Tourism's perspectives*
Johnson (1997)	Ecotourism/Food Tourism as forms of "Tourism of taste". Engagement with local lifestyle.
Macionis (1996); Selwyn (2000); Taylor (2006); Yuan et al. (2006); Getz and Brown (2006); Chiorino (2007)	Destinations supply.
Bruwer (2003)	Wine routes. Wine ludic aspects.
Hall et al. (2000); Getz (2000); Pikkemaat et al. (2009); Charters et al. (2009); Atout France (2010)	Travel motivations and experiences offered by destinations.
Cambourne et al. (2000); O'Neil and Charters (2000): OECD (2005); Novelli (2005)	Wine Tourism related to rural space, urban and cultural destinations, and special interest tourism.
Croce and Perri (2010)	Wine Tourism linked to active tourism, health tourism and industrial tourism.
Charters and Ali-Knight (2002); Getz and Brown (2006); Xu (2010)	Based on the demand (those who stay at wine estates and those who spend money on wine); Critical Success Factors.
Tassiopoulos and Haydam (2006); Galloway et al. (2008); Croce and Perri (2010); Alebaki and Iakovidou (2011)	Demand segmentation.
Hashimoto and Telfer (2003); Griffin and Loersch (2006); Charters and Fontaine (2006)	Human resources, training and qualification related to Wine Tourism.
PCT – TendenciesEnotur (2011)	Leisure activities/resources related to the indigenous wines and foods of destinations.
López-Guzmán et al. (2014)	Food and wine as new experiences that enhance other senses apart from the visual.

Source: Organised by the authors based on Silva (2012).

When referring to Wine Tourism, it is considered as complementary activities, those based on leisure and others related to both the tangible and intangible aspects of the wines and the indigenous gastronomy to any given territory (PCT – TendencièsEnotur, 2011). Novelli (2005) prefers to associate Wine Tourism with rural tourism because its environment is predominantly rural and mainly driven by agricultural products such as vineyards and wine. In turn, the OECD (2005) stresses the linkage between wine, gastronomic and cultural tourism, with this understood as an engine driving tourist flows interested in new cultures and "lifestyles", emphasising these facets in conjunction with identity transmission belts. Furthermore, Croce and Perri (2010) define the links between wine and food in a rural environment as obvious. According to López-Guzmán et al. (2014, p. 67), food and wine are new experiences for tourists enhancing other senses apart from the visual, such as taste or smell. In turn, Morpeth (2000) conveys how Wine Tourism may interlink with active tourism, through walking, horse and bicycle riding across wine routes (France, Italy and California), to health tourism through the provision of wine- and grape-based spa treatments (Portugal, France), and industrial tourism related to visits to historic wineries (port wine cellars in Gaia, Portugal, or some Napa Valley wineries in California, USA).

These different perspectives of Wine Tourism, depicting its main areas of linkage, clearly convey the conceptual evolution of the term. This correspondingly also means that Wine Tourism has moved on from merely focusing on wine products and beginning to involve other demands from tourists, related to new living experiences and lifestyles, as well as the other facilities offered by these destinations. This new reality requires the development of distinctive policies and strategies both for tourism and for economic development, backed and promoted at the local, regional and national levels, involving different players, both public and private (Metodijeski et al., 2017).

The development of Wine Tourism in Alentejo

Alentejo's territory is composed of four natural sub-regions (Map 8.1): Higher Alentejo (Alto Alentejo), Central Alentejo, Lower Alentejo (Baixo Alentejo) and Coastal Alentejo (Alentejo Litoral), with each considered for wine production as a PDO – Protected Designation of Origin (DOP: the acronym in Portuguese). The PDO designation spans the region where a wine is produced, processed and prepared, in accordance with recognised know-how.

Wine sector and wine routes

The geography of the territory, based on its microclimates with simultaneously Mediterranean and continental influences, is favourable to vine cultivation and the production of wine (IVV – "Instituto da Vinha e do Vinho", 2018).

Map 8.1 The four sub-regions of Alentejo.
Source: By courtesy of CCDR Alentejo – commission for coordination and development of the Alentejo region

According to this source, in 2016, the total area of vineyards in the region stood at 23,375 ha, which is about 12.3% of the continental Portugal land-mass (190,467 ha). In 2017, regional wine production achieved a total of 1,050,439 hl (15.7% of continental Portugal production) with a total of 1,676 economic actors involved in this industry. Today, Alentejo wines account for over 45% of the total wine consumed in Portugal and are the national market leader both in terms of volume and turnover.[1]

This high productivity in terms of hl/ha mainly stems from the restruc-turing experienced by regional wine sector. This process began in the 1980s with EU backing through co-financed programmes (e.g. LEADER, VITIS, PRODER, QREN), leading not only to improvements in traditional wine grape varieties, but also to the introduction of new grapes (including their crossing). On the whole, this led to a jump in both the quality and quantity of production through better-adapted varieties. Although there is still a margin for efficiency improvement (Henriques et al., 2009), the entire chain for wine production, upstream and downstream, from basic infrastructure to marketing received substantial improvements in efficiency and sustainability (Santos et al., 2019). Moreover, other factors also contributed to these results: higher levels of education among wine makers, with many new producers, or representing new generations in family wine businesses who have already acquired technical knowledge at high school and university levels (for example, in Alentejo, wine makers on average "double" the education level of other Portuguese wine regions); the size and structure of wine companies (80% are major companies with 19% either small or very small); as well as the collaborative working traditions among the largest regional wine companies (e.g. Borba, Reguengos, Redondo, Portalegre, Vidigueira or Alvito). From the latter point of view, not only in Alentejo but also in the rest of the country, the positive role of wine cooperatives must be highlighted (Barros and Santos, 2007), and they also evidence the deep social roots at the regional level (Figueiredo and Franco, 2018). Thus, all these factors facilitated an expressive transformation of Alentejo into a more competitive region in terms of its wine sector (CRVA – "Comissão Regional Vitivinícola do Alentejo", 2018).

Portugal, like other European countries, has long since displayed a natural vocation for Wine Tourism practices. This trend started out on some farms in the Douro Valley (North of Portugal) with track records in port wine producing. Since the second half of the 1990s, Wine Tourism has expanded practically throughout the entire country (see for the case of Bairrada in the centre of Portugal, Correia et al., 2004), with a particular focus on Alentejo. This also constitutes the point in time when the wine routes began to emerge (e.g. Alentejo Wine Route, Douro and Porto Wine Route, and Sparkling Wine Route, to name just a few). From a national perspective, this development has also been critical insofar as in the early post-war decades, Portuguese tourism was basically known for its "sun and sand" product concentrated on the coast, particularly in Algarve, in the far south of Portugal. Recourse to Wine Tourism, gastronomy and the relevance of cultural legacies (sites and traditions/customs) represent some of the most important vectors of this change, which demonstrated that opportunities also exist for inland and peripheral regions.

Alentejo Wine Route aims at promoting regional wines, boosting contacts between wine producers and consumers, as well as contributing to deepening knowledge about the sector. Since the 1990s, Alentejo Wine Route (2018) has reported clear growth in terms of the Wine Tourism facilities under operation, which we set out in Map 8.2. According to our own research presented below, the data we have collected confirm the existence of 65 wine facilities in 2017, covering wineries, wine tasting rooms, and specialised wine shops, among others. Map 8.2 also shows the three main paths of Alentejo Wine Route.

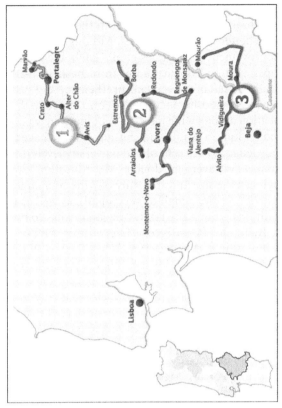

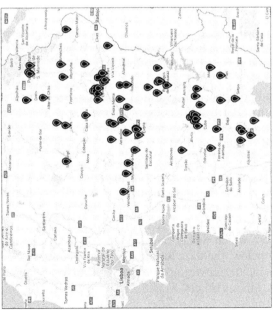

Map 8.2 Wine facilities (left) and wine routes (right) in Alentejo.

Source: By courtesy of CRVA – "Comissão Regional Vitivinícola do Alentejo" and "Club dos Vinhos Portugueses"

Environmental and cultural heritage

As referred to above, Alentejo's territory also concentrates vast and diversified environmental and cultural heritage, which in all its aspects is playing an increasing role in development of tourism (Noonan and Rizzo, 2017). Recognition of the intrinsic value of these regional assets becomes very clear when analysing the multiplicity of assets classified under specific frameworks of legal protection, such as Natura 2000 – the world's largest network of protected areas. This is a network of core breeding and resting sites for rare and threatened species, and some rare natural habitat types which are protected in their own right. In all, the sites of Natura 2000 and its Special Protection Areas, as well as other Natural Protected Areas cover 1.063 thousand hectares in Alentejo. Also, monumental, historical and cultural resources of Alentejo are quite impressive (see Table 8.2), including the recognition by UNESCO as World Heritage of two sites (the city of Évora, and the Fortifications of Elvas) and two intangible heritage ("Cante Alentejano", and the Craftsmanship Clay Figures of Estremoz). This entire heritage, either environmental or monumental and cultural, strongly contributes to the attraction of the region.

Furthermore, from the cultural point of view, the case of local gastronomy must be referred to, since the region is renowned due to its fairly simple and tasteful ingredients. The simplicity of the regional food, based mainly on bread, pork, olive oil, cheese, sausages ("enchidos") and local herbs (for example, coriander and oregano commonly feature in this cuisine), relates to the harsh past life of the region as the local population accessed only scarce resources and used whatever was to hand even if taste and enjoyment were never forgotten. Its desserts based on eggs, almonds and Siam pumpkin, typical of Alentejo, represent a very strong and varied tradition deriving from the religious convents here. The combination of all these features generates a very unique cuisine unlike those found elsewhere.

The tourism sector

As regards the positioning of Alentejo within the Portuguese tourism sector context, notwithstanding all the indicators identify significant growth rates over recent years, the region continues to register a low tourism score, compared with other tourism regions. According to Turismo de Portugal (2018), the number of hotel beds in Alentejo hotel industry has grown over this century, rising from 9,271 in 2004, 11,899 in 2010, to 15,900 in 2017, even though the region remains at the bottom position in terms of the national ranking (with only a 3.1% market share). The average length of stay does not exceed 1.8 nights, with residents representing the largest number of arrivals and overnight stays. The occupancy rate/room reached 52.3% in 2017 (growth of 5.3% over 2016) against 34.8% in 2004, with tourism revenues amounting to 100.1 M€, representing a growth of 18.4% over 2016 (INE, 2018). Although

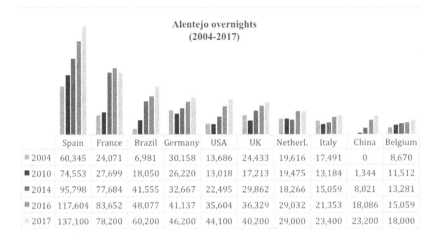

Figure 8.1 Overnights in Alentejo – "top international tourism markets", selected years, 2004–2017.

RevPar (Revenue Per available room) is also growing, it still remains very low (36.9% in 2017, from 20.6% in 2010), which is detrimental to the region's profitability and competitiveness as a tourism destination. All these indicators also convey the relevance of the development of Wine Tourism and its related activities given the boost made to usage of existing tourism capacities (Amaral et al., 2016).

We would also stress the top ten international source tourism markets for the Alentejo region (Figure 8.1). It is clear that between 2004 and 2017, there was a sharp increase in tourists arriving from new markets such as Brazil (3rd position in 2017) and China (9th), which contributed to a diversification in international demand.

After the previous analysis on Wine Tourism and the tourism sector in Alentejo, we need further information and reflection in order to put forward an accurate evaluation of these developments. In the next section, we deploy in detail the qualitative research methods used in this endeavour, taking particularly into account the views of those, public or private, that are directly involved in the process.

Research methodology

Even though Alentejo is made up of four sub-regions, as referred to above, our study solely focuses on three of these sub-regions: Higher Alentejo, Central Alentejo and Lower Alentejo. Such a deliberate selection is due to two specific reasons: on the one hand, Coastal Alentejo, as the name indicates, is mainly focused on sea and sun tourism activities, and it is knowingly associated with reduced wine production, when compared to all other sub-regions.

On the other hand, considering Coastal Alentejo in the study would lead to increasing difficulties in collecting and analysing data and would oblige the authors to make additional efforts in terms of costs.

Intending to understand the dynamics of the wine sector and its contribution to Alentejo's tourism development, our methodological approach was developed based on the following constructs:

1   Wine Tourism considers resources and equipment related to wine, such as wine producers, wineries, wine routes and other visitor support structures. This analysis is important for a better understanding of the factors that are truly relevant to the practice of Wine Tourism (Correia et al., 2004; Carlson and Getz, 2006). For this purpose, websites, brochures and studies promoted by Tourism of Alentejo, Alentejo Wine Route and by some municipalities were analysed. We also consulted several documents published by CCDRA ("Comissão de Coordenação e Desenvolvimento Regional do Alentejo") and IVV, namely with regard to financial support programmes to improve vineyards and wine, and tourist infrastructures as well.

2   *Economic Data* is based on the analysis about regional accommodation capacity, evolution of hotel beds, tourist revenues, occupancy rates, RevPar, as well as arrivals by the country of origin. Several authors propose the analysis of these indicators to study the dynamics of the tourism sector. For example, Soukiasis and Proença (2008) used accommodation capacity as a measure of tourism impact on regional growth. Kuznets (1966) points out that tourism growth is sustained when its evolution is supported by increase in arrivals. Eusebio et al. (2013) and Cortés-Jimenez (2008) focused their analysis on tourism revenues. Therefore, this analysis was based on a set of statistical data published by Turismo de Portugal, Instituto Nacional de Estatística (INE) and Banco de Portugal's websites.

3   *Resource Valuation*: Cunha (2017) points out that natural and environmental resources, including sites or classified World Heritage's resources, are made up of goods with no market value, i.e. they are neither bought nor sold. Thus, tourism is the only activity that allows transforming those resources into productive activities, because they are used without being consumed. Other perspectives are identified by Cracoli and Nijkamp (2008), when they refer that such resources contribute to create and develop competitive advantages, and Neves (2012) highlights its importance for the attractiveness of tourist destinations. Cunha (2017) further states that the transformation of these resources into economic goods when sold in the tourist market becomes part of the tourism supply. It means that they can be converted into "premium prices", offering advantages over competitors through differentiation. According to Hashimoto (2015), the preservation and restoration of built heritage, of traditional architecture, historical sites, handicrafts or

traditional products, all represent forms of past art that are stimulated and preserved by tourism. Therefore, they also constitute assets to the visited places. Other complementary resources such as typical gastronomy, cultural activities, fairs, festivals and exhibitions, as well as typical endogenous products' stores were considered in this analysis. All resources have been identified from diverse sources, such as websites, thematic brochures, cultural agendas and some documents of "Turismo do Alentejo", Municipalities, Tourism of Portugal, Ministry of Culture, Ministry of Environment and local travel agencies.

The inventory of resources, equipment and tourism services was duly structured by each of the three sub-regions under analysis (Table 8.2). Subsequently, we set out the assessment of those resources into three steps:

a   Evaluation of cultural resources through the official classification assigned by DGPC ("Direção Geral do Património Cultural"). This national public body holds responsibility for conserving and restoring those assets deemed part of the country's immovable, movable and intangible cultural heritage. Depending on their relative value, immovable property of cultural interest may be classified by the DGPC as of national interest, public interest or municipal interest. Considering that the DGPC classification has the three levels, we decided to apply a score of 6 points ("national interest"), 3 points ("public interest") and 1 point ("municipal interest"), respectively. We consider this analysis as important because it will allow the assessment of cultural resources in order to reduce their number to be used in the final evaluation.

b   Assessment by the authors of a global resources grid (i.e. wine facilities, monuments, cultural villages and sites, among others), including the final data about the cultural resources obtained after DGPC's assessment. This evaluation based on a Likert 5-point scale (1= not important; 5=very important) aims at understanding the potential of these resources for the Wine Tourism and inherently for Alentejo tourism development. It means that it will permit a deep evaluation about resources that could create value for the regional Wine Tourism, opening up, at the same time, insights generating deeper knowledge about this tourism segment.

c   Development of a final global resources grid (1= not important; 5=very important) consisting of the components obtained from the total of tables to convey a better understanding of the weighting of resources as regards their added value to Wine Tourism in Alentejo. Each table was calculated with the average values of the results from two axes (4 and 5 points) – only considered for the analysis. At the end of this process, we were able to obtain the overall assessment in terms of the critical assets for Wine Tourism in Alentejo.

Through this inquiry, we strove to ascertain stakeholder perceptions about the relevance of the main resources that matter to Wine Tourism, as well as their perspective in terms of its potential for tourism development.

The following stakeholders were invited to respond to our request employees and managers of the following organisations, both public and private: "Turismo do Alentejo"; Alentejo Wine Route; Estremoz, Évora, Reguengos de Monsaraz, Redondo, Borba, Vidigueira, Beja and Portalegre's municipalities, tourism information offices' desks of the referred municipalities; ADRAL – Regional Development Agency of Alentejo; D Viagens'; Agro-tourism Society of Monte Branco, Vadnature and Cervus (tourist animation agencies).

4 "Shared Leadership", to understand motivations, wishes and willingness of main local players to a common goal – development of the regional tourism based on Wine Tourism – is critical for our study. Perroux (1994) states that the development of a region happens when there is innovation and development of growth poles based on the agglomeration of their key strengths, contributing to the construction of its own identity. Telfer (2015) also points out that the links between economic activities in a given geographic space, namely production, service and marketing, all act as drivers of local development. This perspective is also sustained in Leick and Lang (2017) in the following terms: "it is symbolically of the highest importance for regional actors to actively shape the perception of 'their' city, town or region towards a positive and widely acknowledged basis for development".

In this context, it emerges as crucial to discuss the final results with regional players. Therefore, three face-to-face interviews were conducted with one Specialist of financial incentives for tourism development at CCDRA, with the President of "Turismo do Alentejo" and with the Adega Mayor's sales director (winery). A guide was elaborated, aiming to conduct in-depth interviews with the three regional actors who accepted our challenge. These interviews aimed at validating the results obtained by important regional players, to understand the impact of resources on the attraction of tourists with Wine Tourism motivations, as well as the importance of Wine Tourism for tourism development. The guide for evaluation is made up of two specific sections: i) impacts of endogenous resources on Wine Tourism in Alentejo and ii) impacts of Wine Tourism on regional tourism development.

Analysis of the results and discussion

This research aims at demonstrating the importance of Wine Tourism, which gains widespread recognition among the main local players as a major tourism product niche in Alentejo. This perspective also aligns with the

Table 8.2 Environmental and cultural heritage in Alentejo

Natura 2000 (sites)	514,000 ha
Natura 2000 (special protection areas)	368,000 ha
Natural network of protected areas	181,000 ha
Monuments	302
Cultural villages/historical places	58
Cultural sites	131
World heritage (UNESCO)	4*

* Two sites and two attributed to intangible heritage.
Source: Organised by the authors according to Turismo do Alentejo information and European Commission.

views expressed by other authors (e.g. Novelli, 2005; López-Guzmán et al., 2014), who argue that Wine Tourism is a new set of experiences interrelated to wine, food and other critical factors of success to destinations, with the capacity to attract demanding and specialised wine visitors, as well as different typologies of tourists.

After collecting and evaluating all data on tourist, cultural and other resources, a grid with a total of 1,131 resources was obtained. Let us begin with the cultural resources assessment results (Table 8.2) based on the DGPC classification, and we would note that many of these cultural resources are ranked as of national or public interest.

Therefore, cultural resources classified as municipal interest (1 point) were eliminated and resources that registered more than 2,000 visitors/year were considered for analysis. Crossing those data with the number of visitors registered in 2016 becomes even more evident when we analyse the higher incidence of visitors to those cultural facilities and resources (495 out of 1,131).

The other resources were selected as follows: 5 protected areas/natural parks (Ministry of Environment website); 65 wine cellars with Wine Tourism programmes (CRVA), 47 accommodation units, including hotels, Pousadas and TER – "Turismo no Espaço Rural" (Accommodation Guide of Alentejo Region); 85 restaurants (Alentejo Restaurants Certified Guide); 9 typologies of local handicraft; 12 Alentejo tourist packages promoted by travel agencies and national tour operators (sites of the municipalities). Regarding the tourist packages, it was not possible to separate them by sub-regions, considering that they include visits and/or wine tastings in Wine Tourism facilities among the three sub-regions under analysis. The authors examined the packages of the following tour operators and DMC (Destination Management Companies): Lusanova, Abreu, Maktour, Interpoint, Queensberry, Promptur, Flot Travel, Primetour, Evora Cultural Experience and Which Trip. Two online packages were also analysed (Alentejo Exclusive (NIT) and Visitacity). A grid with all the selected resources was produced for evaluation by stakeholders and by the main Alentejo main players, based on a scale with 5 points. In this way, it was possible to reduce the number of resources and get a global picture about the main critical success factors related to Alentejo (Table 8.3).

Table 8.3 Hotel industry in Alentejo – main data

Hotel industry (2004–2017)							
2004	*2010*	*2014*	*2017*	*2004*	*2010*	*2014*	*2017*
Bednights (thousands)				Occupancy rate (%)			
9.271	11.899	12.40	15.9	34.8	35.3	29.6	52.3
Overnights (thousands)				Revenues (million €)			
993.016	1,172.558	1,297.609	1,769.342	46.724	59.457	63.167	100.1
Guests (thousands)				RevPar (%)			
589.771	697.477	729.152	989.700	n.d.	20.6	21.1	36.9

Source: Turismo de Portugal; INE (2018).

This analysis was essential for the validation of the results and for a better understanding on the perceived critical success factors by the regional tourism, wine professionals and decision makers. We obtained 11 responses, representing 44% of the sample (Table 8.4). The all-partial results were added, which mirror the set of global resources/facilities valued by respondents as relevant to Wine Tourism. This entity recommends these tourism resources on the basis of their interest and quality for tourism-related purposes. We should also emphasise that the same table provides the average stakeholder percentage evaluation of the respective resources.

As far as wine facilities are concerned, as set out in Table 8.4, there were a total of 65 according to our data collection process (from "Rota de Vinhos

Table 8.4 Cultural resources after DGPC's evaluation

Cultural resources/ facilities sub-region	Monuments			Cultural villages & historical places		Cultural sites	
	CC	*HC*	*CM*	*AH*	*CV/HP*	*M/CS*	*CH*
	Church/ Chapels	Halls/ Castles	Convents/ Monasteries	Archaeological sites	Cult. villages/ hist. places	Museums/ cultural sites	UNESCO
Higher Alentejo	52	14	3	8	13	27	1
Central Alentejo	85	16	5	21	24	68	2
Lower Alentejo	62	6	1	29	21	36	1
Total	199	36	9	58	58	131	4

Source: Organised by the authors.

do Alentejo" and the CVRA). Their distribution throughout the sub-regions of Alentejo is as follows: Higher (10), Central (36) and Lower (19). We would duly note that outside of the main sub-regions capitals (Évora and Beja), these wine facilities cluster in some of the most traditional areas of production, such as Estremoz (9), Vidigueira (7), Reguengos de Monsaraz (5), Borba (4) and Redondo (4).

These global results seem to reflect a certain coherence regarding the perception of the various actors of the richness of Alentejo in terms of its resources and their impact on Wine Tourism, as well as on tourism development in general. Importantly, the main critical factors of success pointed out in various works carried out on Alentejo mainly focus on wine and related equipment, the specific attributes of Alentejo destination itself, as well as on tourism essentially interlinked with cultural motivations closely related to Wine Tourism.

With this valuable information, it was then necessary to discuss the overall results with relevant regional stakeholders. On the one hand, authors wanted to understand the perceptions of Alentejo's stakeholders in terms of the future and ways of improving regional tourism performance. On the other hand, critical issues such as planning, marketing, identity, financing, in short, regional governance, are highly important for Wine Tourism development and, above all, for regional development.

The result of the interviews was surprising. There is a general perception of all the interviewees of the improvement of the image of Alentejo as a result of the effort to integrate the region's endogenous resources, such as wine, handicrafts, cork and gastronomy, into the tourism route. There is also unanimity about the Alentejo's soul and uniqueness, and much that still has to be done for the Wine Tourism development and for the tourism development itself. However, some divergences arise, depending on the role that each actor must have to achieve such objective. For the representative of the regional tourism entity, it is only possible to have better results if there is more investment from public entities in order to improve marketing and communication initiatives. He also highlighted the necessity of coordination from all actors in the regional system, noting, "Coordination should be concentrated in the regional tourism entity". For the CCDR Alentejo's representative, tourism entities are not enough aware of other sectors operation, having even difficulties interacting with other economic agents. For him, *"it is unaccountable how tourist promotion campaigns do not involve, for example, wine or cork producers – key resources of the region".* The person in charge of the regional winery pointed out that tourists are increasing in Alentejo and one of the reasons is precisely the uniqueness of regional wines. He referred that the modernisation of vineyards and the strong economic dynamic ongoing in the region, allied to a new strategic vision by investors and regional and national entities, have been helping Alentejo tourism development. However, he also stressed that hotels and other kind of accommodations need to improve average-length stay in the region, as well as RevPar. For him, *"to pay less than 100 euros/night in a very unique and comfortable place is really hard to accept"*. This is only a small sample of the very interesting results of our inquiry to regional stakeholders.

Concluding remarks

In this chapter, we showed how Wine Tourism has developed in Alentejo during the last decades. For a long time, Alentejo was characterised by a peripheral economic status and stagnation; wine production in particular was quite limited and conditioned. Since the 1980s, this scenario gradually underwent major changes. Wine Tourism had a relevant contribution to this transformation. In fact, it has been closely linked to other regional advantages such as the environmental and cultural heritage, and the gastronomy. All this gave a broader base to the process, favouring an upgrade in regional tourism development. Our inquiry to local stakeholders confirmed the positive effects of this mix boosted by Wine Tourism. However, regional performance in tourism remains weak as compared to the rest of the country, providing unavoidable evidence of the need for further efforts of interaction among all parts involved.

Finally, we need also to recognise that in spite of the relevance of the subject to the region, this study constitutes only an introductory approach to the links between the wine sector and local stakeholders. Further research is needed to increase our knowledge of current and potential Wine Tourism demand in Alentejo, as well as to understand the kind of actions and promotion plans put into practice by stakeholders all across the territory. This represents the premise for any good assessment of this experiment, and consequently for improving the procedures enabling a better regional tourism performance. Additionally, only through such studies will we be able to provide an accurate evaluation of the role of Wine Tourism in the tourism industry capable of significantly contributing to the Alentejo's own development.

Note

1 During the dictatorial regime in effect in Portugal from 1926 to 1974, due to its self-sufficiency policies, characteristic of the interwar period but that here lasted until much later, Alentejo was deemed the ideal terrain for the production of cereals, especially wheat. Under these conditions, any increase in wine production through expansion into new spaces was highly discouraged and was effectively blocked. However, apart from very small areas, Alentejo was never geography-favourable to the competitive production of wheat, on the contrary. Moreover, such a policy only contributed to impoverishing its rural communities. Despite this, some limited and traditional areas remained linked to wine production (e.g. Borba, Reguengos and Vidigueira), even though a thorough and more rational restructuring of the sector took place in the 1980s and correspondingly only now bearing its fruits.

References

Alebaki, M., & Iakovidou, O. (2011). Market segmentation in wine tourism: a comparison of approaches. *Tourismos: An International Multidisciplinary Journal of Tourism*, 6 (1), pp. 123–140.

Alentejo Wine Route – "Rota dos Vinhos do Alentejo" (2018). Rota dos Vinhos. Available at: http://www.vinhosdoalentejo.pt/pt/rota-dos-vinhos/rota-dos-vinhos-do-alentejo/ [Accessed on: 12.03.2018].

Amaral, R., Saraiva, M., Rocha, S., & Serra, J. (2016). Gastronomy and wines in the Alentejo Portuguese Region: motivation and satisfaction of tourists from Évora. In M. Peris-Ortiz et al. (eds.), *Wine and Tourism*, chapter 13. doi:10.1007/978-3-319-18857-7_13.

Atout France (2010). *Tourisme et Vin: Les Clientèles Françaises et Internationales, les Concurrents de la France. Comment Rester Compétitif?* A. France (ed.). Paris: Marketing Touristique.

Barros, C. P., & Santos, J. C. G. (2007). Comparing the productive efficiency of co-operatives and private enterprises: the Portuguese wine industry as a case study. *Journal of Rural Cooperation*, 35 (2), pp. 109–122.

Bruwer, J. (2003). South African Wine Routes: some perspectives on the wine tourism industry's structural dimensions and wine tourism product. *Tourism Management*, 24 (4), pp. 423–435.

Cambourne, B., Macionis, N., Hall, M. C., & Sharples, L. (2000). The future of wine tourism. In M. C. Hall, L. Sharples, B. Cambourne, and N. Macionis (eds.), *Wine Tourism Around the World*, pp. 297–320. Oxford: Butterworth-Heinemann.

Carlson, J. & Getz, D. (2006). Strategic plan for a regional wine festival: the Margaret river wine regional festival. In J. Carlson and S. Charters (eds.), *Global Wine Tourism – Research, Management and Marketing*, pp. 209–224. Oxford: CA International.

Charters, S., & Ali-Knight, J. (2002). Who is the wine tourist? *Tourism Management*, 23 (3), pp. 311–319.

Charters, S., & Fontaine, J. (2006). Younger wine tourists: a study of generational differences in the cellar door experience. In J. Carlsen and S. Charters (eds.), *Global Wine Tourism: Research, Management and Marketing*, pp. 153–160. Oxfordshire: CAB International.

Charters, S., Fontaine, J., & Fish, N. (2009). Experiencing real service at the winery tasting room. *Journal of Travel Research*, 48 (1), pp. 122–134.

Chiorino, F. (2007). *Architettura e Vino*. Milano: Electa.

Comissão Regional Vitivinícola do Alentejo – CRVA (2018). Wines of Alentejo – Facts & Figures (November 2015). Available at: http://www.vinhosdoalentejo.pt/ [Accessed on: 17.02.18].

Correia, L., Ascensão, M. J. P., & Steve Charters, M. V. (2004). Wine Routes in Portugal: a case study of the Bairrada Wine Route. *Journal of Wine Research*, 15 (1), pp. 15–25. doi:org/101080/0957126042000300290.

Cortés-Jimenez, I. (2008).Which type of tourism matters to the regional economic growth? The cases of Spain and Italy. *International Journal of Tourism Research*, 10, pp. 127–139. doi.org/10.1002/jtr.646.

Cracoli, M.F. & Nijkamp, P. (2008). The attractiveness and competitiveness of tourist destinations: a study of southern Italian regions. *Tourism Management*, 30, pp. 336–344. doi:10.1016/jtourman.2008.07.006.

Croce, E., & Perri, G. (2010). *Food and Wine: Integrating Food, Travel and Territory.* Oxfordshire: CAB International.

Cunha, L. (2017). *Turismo e Desenvolvimento – realidades e perspetivas.* Lisboa: Lidel-Edições Técnicas.

Eusebio, C., Castro, A.D., & Costa, C. (2013). The economic impact of tourism in the Central region of Portugal: a regional economic impact study with marketing implications. In C. A. Tisdel (ed.), *Handbook of Tourism Economics, Analysis, New Applications and Case Studies.*University of Queensland (Australia): World Scientific.

Figueiredo, V., & Franco, M. (2018). Wine cooperatives as a form of social entrepreneurship: empirical evidence about their impact on society. *Land Use Policy*, 79, pp. 812–821.

Galloway, G., Mitchell, R., Getz, D., Crouch, G., & Ong, B. (2008). Sensation seeking and the prediction of attitudes and behaviours of wine tourists. *Tourism Management*, 29 (5), pp. 950–966. DOI: org/10.1016/j.tourman.2007.11.006.

Getz, D. (2000). *Exploring Wine Tourism: Management, Development and Destinations.* New York: Cognizant Communication Corporation.

Getz, D., & Brown, G. (2006). Critical success factors for Wine Tourism Regions: a demand analysis. *Tourism Management*, 27 (1), pp. 146–158.

Griffin, T., & Loersch, A. (2006). The determinant of quality experiences in an emerging wine region. In J. Carlsen and S. Charters (eds.), *Global Wine Tourism: Research, Management and Marketing*, pp. 80–92. Oxfordshire: CAB International.

Hall, C. M., Sharples, L., Cambourne, B., & Macionis, N. (2000). *Wine Tourism around the World.* Oxford: Butterworth-Heinemann.

Hashimoto, A. (2015). Tourism and socio-cultural development issues. In R. Sharpley, J. David, & J. Telfer (eds.), *Tourism and Development Concepts and Issues*, 2nd edition. Bristol/Buffalo/Toronto: Channel Views Publications.

Hashimoto, A., & Telfer, D. (2003). Positioning an emerging wine route in the Niagara region: understanding the wine tourism market in the Niagara region – Understanding the wine tourism market and its implications for marketing. *Journal of Travel and Tourism Marketing*, 14 (3/4), pp. 61–76. doi:10.1300/J073v14n03_04.

Henriques, P. D. S., Carvalho, M. L. S., & Fragoso, R. M. S. (2009). Technical efficiency of Portuguese wine firms. *NEW MEDIT*, no. 1, pp. 4–9.

Instituto Nacional de Estatística – INE (2018). Tourism Statistics. Available at: https://ine.pt/xportal/xmain?xpid=INE&xpgid=ine_base_dados [Accessed on: 17.02.18].

Instituto da Vinha e do Vinho – IVV (2018). A vinha e o vinho em Portugal. Available at: http://www.ivv.gov.pt/np4/47/ [Accessed on: 17.02.18].

Johnson, G. (1997). Surveying Wine Tourism in New Zealand. In G. Johnson (ed.), *Quality Tourism: Beyond the Masses*, Proceedings of the First National Tourism Students' Conference, pp. 61–66. Dunedin: Tourism Club.

Kuznets, S. (1966). *Modern Economic Growth: rate, structure and spread. An adaptation.* New York: Teffer and Simons.

Leick, B., & Lang, T. (2017). Re-thinking non-core regions: planning strategies and practices beyond growth. *European Planning Studies*, 26 (2), pp. 213–228. Doi:10.1080/09654313. 2017.1363398.

López-Guzmán, T., Vieira-Rodríguez A., & Rodríguez-Garcia, J. (2014). Profile and motivations of European tourists on the Sherry wine route of Spain. *Tourism Management Perspectives*, 11, pp. 63–68. doi:10.1016/j.tmp.2014.04.003.

Macionis, N. (1996), *Wine Tourism in Australia. Proceedings of Tourism Down Under II: A Tourism Research Conference*, pp. 264–286. Dunedin: University of Otago.

Metodijeski, D., Mitreva, E., Taskov, N., & Filiposki, O. (2017). Public-public partnership and tourism development strategy: the case of Municipality of Gazi Baba in Macedonia. *International Journal of Social, Behavioral, Educational, Economic, Business and Industrial Engineering*, 11 (4), pp. 846–850.

Morpeth, N. (2000). Diversifying wine tourism products: an evaluation of linkages between wine and cycle tourism. In C. M. Hall, L. Sharples, B. Cambourne, and N. Macionis (eds.), *Wine Tourism Around the World*, pp. 272–282. Oxford: Butterworth-Heinemann.

Neves, J. M. O. (2012). The attractiveness of Portugal as a tourist destination by mature domestic travellers. *World Review of Entrepreneurship, Management and Sustainable Development*, 8 (1), pp. 37–52. doi:10.1504/WREMSD.2012.044486.

Noonan, D. S., & Rizzo, I. (2017). Economics of cultural tourism: issues and perspectives. *Journal of Cultural Economics*, 41, pp. 95–107.

Novelli M. (2005). *Niche Tourism: Contemporary Issues, Trends and Cases*. Oxford: Elsevier.

O'Neil, M., & Charters, S. (2000). Service quality at the cellar door: implications for Western Australia's developing wine tourism industry. *Managing Service Quality*, 10 (2), pp. 112–122. doi:10.1108/09604520010318308.

Organisation for Economic Co-Operation and Development – OECD (2005), *Local Governance and the Drivers of Growth*. ISBN 92-64-01329-6. Available at: https:// books.google.co.ma/books [Accessed on: 11.12.17].

PCT – TendènciesEnotur (2011), European Wine Strategy, (1/3). Available at: http:// www.pct turisme.cat/intranet/sites/default/files/Tendencies_ENOTUR_1_eng_ wine_tourism.pdf [Accessed on 21.02.18].

Perroux, F. (1994). *L'économie du XXème siècle: ouvrage et articles*. Université de Grenoble.

Pikkemaat, B., Peters, M., Boksberger, P., & Secco M. (2009). The staging of experiences in wine tourism. *Journal of Hospitality Marketing and Management*, 18 (2), pp. 237–253. doi:pdf/10.1080/19368620802594110.

Proença, S., & Soukiasis, E. (2008). Tourism as an alternative source of regional growth in Portugal. *Portuguese Economic Journal*, 7 (1), pp. 43–61. doi:10.1007/ s10258-007-0022-0.

Santos, M., Galindro, A., Santos, C., Marta-Costa, A., & Martinho, V. (2019). Sustainability evolution of North and Alentejo Vineyard Regions. *Revista Portuguesa de Estudos Regionais*, 50, pp. 49–63.

Selwyn, T. (2000). An anthropology of hospitality. In C. Lashley and A. Morrison (eds.), *Search of Hospitality: Perspectives and Debates*, pp. 18–37. Oxford: Butterworth-Heinemann.

Silva, S.F.G.Q. (2012). Enoturismo no Alentejo: Visão global e perspetivas de desenvolvimento. Master Dissertation, Portugal: Escola Superior de Hotelaria e Turismo do Estoril.

Tassiopoulos, D., & Haydam, N. (2006). Wine tourism in South Africa: a demand-side study. In J. Carlsen and S. Charters (eds.), *Global Wine Tourism: Research, Management and Marketing*, pp. 141–152. Oxfordshire: CAB International.

Taylor, R. (2006). Wine Festivals and Tourism: Developing a longitudinal approach to festival evaluation. In J. Carlsen and S. Charters (eds.), *Global Wine Tourism: Research, Management and Marketing*, pp. 179–195. Oxfordshire: CAB International.

Telfer, D. (2015). Tourism and regional development issues. In R. Sharpley and D. J. Telfer (eds.), *Tourism and Development- Concepts and Issues*, 2nd edition. Channel View Publications.

Turismo do Alentejo (2018). Cante Alentejano. Available at: http://www.visitevora.net /encante-alentejano-unesco-portugal/. [Accessed on: 24.02.18].

Xu, J. B. (2010). Perceptions of tourism products. *Tourism Management*, 31 (5), pp. 607–610.

Yuan, J., Jang, S., Cai, A. L., Morrison, M. A., & Linton, J. S. (2006). Analysis of motivational and promotional effects of a wine festival. In J. Carlsen and S. Charters (eds.), *Global Wine Tourism: Research, Management and Marketing*, pp. 196–208. Oxfordshire: CAB International.

Websites

Alentejo Wine Route – "Rota dos Vinhos do Alentejo". http://www.vinhosdoalentejo.pt/pt/rota-dos-vinhos/rota-dos-vinhos-do-alentejo/

"Cante Alentejano". http://www.visitevora.net/en/cante-alentejano-unesco-portugal/

Cultural Heritage – "Património Cultural" (Source of the data: DGPC). http://www.patrimoniocultural.gov.pt/pt/recursos/

ERT – Regional Tourism. http://www.m.visitalentejo.pt/fotos/editor2/Quem%20 somos/pedpt_do_enoturismo_no_alentejo_e_ribatejo.pdf

Food and Certified Restaurants in Alentejo. https://www.visitalentejo.pt/pt/guiaderestaurantescertificadosdoalentejo/

Natura 2000 – Natural Parks. http://ec.europa.eu/environment/nature/natura2000/index_en.htm

PDO ("DOP") – Protected Designation of Origin. https://tradicional.dgadr.gov.pt/en/quality-products/pdo-protected-designation-of-origin

Wine Statistics – IVV ("Instituto do Vinho e da Vinha"). http://www.ivv.gov.pt/np4/estatistica/

Part III
Craft beer tourism

9 Tourism, authenticity, and craft beer

The case of West Virginia

Douglas Arbogast, Jason Kozlowski
and Daniel Eades

Introduction

Since the 1980s, craft beer sales have grown at a rapid rate in the U.S. According to the Brewers Association (2018), the number of craft breweries in the U.S. has grown from just over 500 in 1994 to over 6,000 in 2017 with sales reaching 12.7% of the U.S. beer market volume in 2017. In conjunction with the growth of craft breweries, many destinations are seeing a growth in craft tourism defined by Plummer et al. (2005, 449) as "visitation to breweries, beer festivals and beer shows for which beer tasting and experiencing the attributes of beer region." While there is a growth in craft beer consumption among all generations, millennials (22–37 years old in 2018) are leading the charge, rejecting Big Beer and seeking the diversity of styles and flavors offered by craft brewers (Reid 2018).

Craft breweries are increasingly located in rural or peripheral areas that offer unique settings. Despite the inconvenience of reaching rural/peripheral areas, tourists may see them as worth visiting because they are relatively unchanged and unspoiled; thus, rural/peripheral destinations should focus on distinctiveness and specialization (Chaperon & Bramwell 2013; Pezzi 2018). Beer tourism satisfies the demand the craft beer drinker has to experience a diversity of unique beers in unique settings (Reid 2018).

Just over 1.8 million people reside in West Virginia, making it the third most rural state in the nation (US Census Bureau 2010). While 2012 saw an explosion of craft breweries across the U.S., there were no reported openings of a craft brewery in West Virginia. This study informs rural communities, brewers, and destination leaders interested in cultivating craft beverages as a component of rural tourism, suggesting ways in which destinations can work cooperatively to attract travelers who seek an authentic experience. Additionally, the study provides critical insight into how craft beer can serve as a model for the growth of the tourism industry in West Virginia.

This study explores the tourism product mix in West Virginia, the role of craft breweries, and the evolution of the Wild and Wonderful brand. The study engages three central questions. (1) What role does craft beer play in the tourism product mix in West Virginia? (2) Is craft beer helping to redefine the state's identity as a destination? (3) Can craft beer tourism serve as a model for diversification of tourism in West Virginia while maintaining authenticity and sense of place?

Literature review

Authenticity, craft beer, and sustainable rural tourism development

According to Lane (1994), the retention of older ways of life and thinking is important in retaining rural 'character' for it is this residual character which, when combined with the scenic values and recreational opportunities of the countryside, attracts tourists from urban areas. More recently, several studies have identified a growing niche or "cohort" of tourists searching for the 'unspoiled' rural community in an attempt to find deeper and more meaningful experiences (Gartner 2004; George, Mair, and Reid 2009). Cohen (1972) described these travelers as "drifters," seeking to venture off the beaten track preferring to be almost wholly immersed. The mass tourist, on the other hand, prefers the package tour with familiarity at a maximum and novelty at a minimum. Cohen (1972, 182) predicted that "mass tourism, in developing countries, if not controlled and regulated, might help to destroy whatever there is still left of unspoiled nature and of traditional ways of life."

A primary challenge faced by rural destinations is to not succumb to the "commodification of culture" and allow cultural dimensions of their community to be transformed into commodities for exchange with consuming tourists (George, Mair, and Reid 2009). Rosenow and Pulsipher (1979) identified a sense of place as a key to the new tourism. They emphasized that a systematic means must be found for identifying, enhancing, and creating unique resources for it is these subtle elements that both give a community a sense of place and are often most susceptible to thoughtless destruction in the name of progress and growth. Rosenow and Pulsipher (1979, 36) pondered whether travelers would soon be asking the question, "why travel if what one will see or experience is no different than what is at home?" A study by Jepson and Sharpley (2015) in the rural Lake District of England determined that sense of place is a significant determinant of demand for tourism in this region and that promoting sense of place as a form of branding may strengthen customer loyalty.

Pine and Gilmore (2008) stressed the importance of genuine experiences in addition to low costs and high quality when providing services for consumers, as consumers increasingly seek the enjoyment of the experience of their purchase. MacCannell (1973) was one of the first authors to analyze the authenticity of tourist experiences identifying how tourists try to enter the "back regions" of the places they visit because these regions are associated with intimacy of relations and authenticity of experiences in contrast to the shallowness of their lives and inauthenticity of their experiences. According to Wang (1999), objective and constructivist accounts of authenticity relate to the nature of attractions being visited by the tourist, whereas an existential understanding of authenticity relates to the response that a particular tourism experience generates in the tourist. Existential authenticity describes the way in which tourists through their tourism experience can construct their identity to experience a more authentic sense of self (Wang 1999). Gatrell, Reid, and Steiger (2018, 362) contend that what becomes perceived and labeled as "authentic" imbues an object or service with deeper meaning carrying with it an almost sacred, cultural type of interpretation that conveys value.

Sims (2009) describes how local food initiatives offer an enhanced visitor experience by telling the 'story' of food production, making it possible to use the tourist's desire for authenticity to encourage the development of products and services that will boost sustainability and benefit rural regions for visitors and residents alike. Local foods and drinks are an asset to integrated and sustainable tourism because they enable host communities to capitalize on visitors' desire for some form of "authentic" experience that will enable them to connect with the place and culture of their destination (Sims 2009). It also allows destinations to use "iconic" local products to build a "brand" that can be used to distinguish the region from its competitors (Urry 2002).

The American beer market has seen a dramatic resurgence of microbreweries and craft beer is increasingly being recognized as a way for communities to attract rural tourists for their unique local and regional characters by showcasing their authentic and distinctive qualities (Eades, Arbogast, and Kozlowski 2017; Flack 1997; Plummer, Telfer, Hashimoto, and Summers 2005; Schnell and Reese 2003). Researchers are attributing the success of microbreweries to "neolocalism" (Debies-Carl 2018). According to Flack (1997), much of the appeal of a micro-brewed beer is that it is a rejection of national, or even regional, culture in favor of something more local. According to the neolocal perspective, consuming micro-beers gives consumers a sense of place, a means of supporting a local business, and a feeling of belonging to the local landscape and community (Debies-Carl 2018). A study by Murray and Kline (2015) of visitors to breweries in rural North Carolina concluded that making a community and local connection was the most important factor influencing brand loyalty followed by a desire for unique consumer products and satisfaction.

Gatrell, Reid, and Steiger (2018) suggest that the growth of the craft beer industry resides at the nexus between nature, place, and identity. The desire for unique consumer experiences is a concept that explores how consumers feel they define themselves by the products they purchase or consume (Ruvio, Shoham, and Brenčič 2008) and is a testament to this shift from organized mass tourism to more specialized, unique, and authentic experiences that breweries offer. Beer wandering is considered the new frontier for beer tourism and a very specific sub-culture related to craft beer consumption and appreciation, with strong linkages to forms of slow-tourism; territory discovery; educational purposes in terms of know-hows, materials, and production processes; ethical concerns in regard to sustainable and non-invasive forms of tourism; and the pursuit of a more authentic relationship with people, places, and products that does not see beer consumption as an end, but rather as a means of knowledge and of a particular form of "tourist gaze" (Urry 2002).

Methodology

Study area

West Virginia can be considered to be at early stages of Butler's (1980) Tourism Lifecycle. Longwoods International (2013 and 2010) identified outdoor recreation and visiting small towns and rural areas as primary activities for a large percentage of both day and overnight visitors to West Virginia. Although travel spending in West Virginia has consistently increased over the past decade, growing 6.3% annually (Runyan 2015), West Virginia ranks 45th nationally in visitor trip spending (U.S. Travel Association 2012).

West Virginia's Division of Tourism, "Wild and Wonderful West Virginia," launched the Real. campaign in 2015 in an effort to increase awareness of West Virginia's truly unique assets. The campaign created fresh content showcasing real people and authentic experiences in an attempt to capture the plethora of unique experiences available in the Mountain State, including lesser known attractions such as music, art, culinary, shopping, agritourism, and craft beer in an attempt to attract more visitors and generate additional economic impact from tourism (Industry Information 2016).

Although craft beer has proven to be a growth market for the tourism industry, West Virginia ranks just 44th by the number of breweries, 49th in total production (approximately 8,000 barrels a year), and 51st in per capita production (Brewers Association 2014); thus, it is no surprise that only a small percentage (6%) of overnight person-trips included a visit to a brewery (Longwoods 2013). Recent legislation allowing for expanded sales and increased ABV limits has had a dramatic effect on West Virginia's craft beer industry. The number of breweries in the state nearly quintupled between 2011 and 2015, from 5 breweries to 24; and seven additional facilities are slated to open in 2017 (West Virginia Craft Brewers 2017). In 2015, the state declared August 15–22 West Virginia Craft Beer Week, coinciding with several craft beer festivals and highlighting what Governor Tomblin identified as "one of the fastest-growing niche markets in the state" (Kabler 2015) (Table 9.1; Map 9.1).

Table 9.1 Description of West Virginia breweries and DMOs included in the study

#	Brewery	County	Year opened	DMO
1	Chestnut Brew Works Morgantown Brewing Co.	Monongalia	2013 1992/2009	Greater Morgantown CVB
2	Mountain State Brewing Co. Stumptown Ales	Tucker	2005 2015	Tucker County CVB
3	Big Timber Brewing Co.	Randolph	2014	Randolph County CVB
4	Greenbrier Valley Brewing Co.	Greenbrier	2014	Greenbrier County CVB
5	Bridge Brew Works	Fayette	2010	New River Gorge CVB
6	Bad Shepherd Brewing Co.	Kanawha	2015	Charleston, WV CVB
7	Berkeley Springs Brewing Co.	Morgan	2015	Travel Berkeley Springs
8	Wheeling Brewing Co.	Ohio	2014	Wheeling, WV CVB

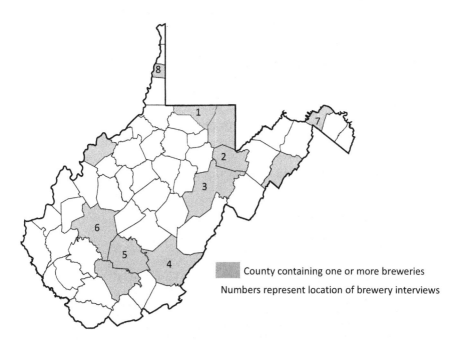

Map 9.1 Map of brewery and DMO interview locations.

Methodology

This study utilized a qualitative case study research design. According to Yin (2009, 16), "a case study is an empirical inquiry that investigates a contemporary phenomenon within its real life context especially when the boundaries between phenomenon and context may not be clearly evident." Yin (2009) also observes that a case study is a design particularly suited to situations in which it is impossible to separate the phenomenon's variables from their context. Interpretive research methods were utilized with the aim to collect rich and informed data. This included in-depth semi-structured individual interviews conducted within a two-month duration of fieldwork. The interviews were conducted with two principal groups of participants: breweries and destination marketing organizations (local convention and visitors bureaus, and the West Virginia Commissioner of Tourism). Destinations were selected in an attempt to cover a wide geographic range and diversity of destination characteristics throughout the state based on the researchers' knowledge of the craft beer and tourism industry in West Virginia. This technique yielded 19 interview candidates (10 breweries, 8 Convention and Visitor Bureau Directors, and the Commissioner of Tourism for Wild, Wonderful West Virginia) that serve as a representative sampling frame of the 15 total breweries in the state. Interviews were recorded and the data were transcribed as soon as possible afterward.

Data collection and thematic analysis occurred concurrently, with early analysis informing later interview protocols. Data analysis included coding of the data to explore the themes generated in the field and to group different aspects of the data to compare emerging categories with those already unearthed in the literature, ensuring the selection of the most representative and inclusive categories. Data analysis was conducted using Nvivo 11 software. The key themes to emerge from the analysis for each stakeholder group are presented in the results. Peer review, data triangulation across interview sources and between interviews and documents, and member checking strategies increased trustworthiness.

Results

Outdoor recreation and craft beer

As noted by Eades, Arbogast, and Kozlowski (2017), West Virginia is making a concerted effort to diversify its Wild and Wonderful brand to represent outdoor recreation as well as other authentic travel experiences. The state is positioned to redefine its brand and sustainably develop its product base to appeal to the growing market of venturers/drifters (Cohen 1972; Plog 2001). Craft beer is at the forefront of this evolution creating a potential model for the development of authentic tourism experiences by capturing the essence of what makes West Virginia a truly unique and authentic destination.

Amy Goodwin, the 2015 West Virginia Commissioner of Tourism, acknowledged the evolution of the brand and the role of craft breweries when she noted:

> Wild and Wonderful means different things to different people. Wild and Wonderful to me means black diamonds at Snowshoe. What my husband finds Wild and Wonderful is grabbing a craft beer at Black Sheep Burritos and going to watch Mountain Stage because it is very authentic and it is very real.

West Virginia's Division of Tourism [Wild and Wonderful West Virginia] has not only recognized this opportunity but also responded to the growing trend for authentic travel experiences and craft beer by investing significant marketing dollars in craft beer as a core component of their new marketing strategy. For example, they recently developed a video series for their Real. campaign and every video featured craft beer.

This roadmap for the development of the tourism industry in capturing, preserving, and sharing the authenticity and sense of place of West Virginia, driven in part by the craft brewers and the Division of Tourism's Real. campaign, is now being embraced across the state by local destination management organizations (DMOs) targeting new cohorts of travelers that are intently searching for deeper and more meaningful experiences and increasingly shifting from mass tourism activities to more specialized niche markets (Destination Analysts 2014; Gartner 2004; George, Mair, and Reid 2009; US Travel Association 2016).

The natural beauty of the Mountain State and opportunities for outdoor recreation on public lands embody the core component of the state's image and visitor base. Although recent studies demonstrate that a relatively small percentage of overnight visitors to West Virginia include a visit to a brewery (Longwoods 2013), the compatibility between outdoor recreation and craft beer has been demonstrated in states like Colorado, Oregon, and Pennsylvania (Bike Portland 2015; Longwoods 2014; Mowen, Graefe, and Graefe 2013). In fact, linking these assets is increasingly recognized as vital to attracting and retaining outdoor recreation enthusiasts and craft beer enthusiasts. This is evident in both Tucker County and the New River Gorge, the state's two most majorly visited destinations for outdoor recreation and adventure tourism.

Tucker County is a northern gateway to the Monongahela National Forest in the mountain highlands of West Virginia. Popular activities include winter sports, hiking, and mountain biking. The destination is now home to three breweries in two small towns of less than 1,400 permanent residents. According to the Executive Director of the Tucker County Convention and Visitors Bureau, "I think our primary attractions are our outdoor recreation, but we wouldn't be successful without the breweries. It helps to keep people coming back and staying longer." B.A., a co-owner of Mountain

State Brewing Company in Thomas, WV, noted the trend of travelers seeking out local products, "I think a lot of people are really interested in experiencing the places they visit and having something that's handmade or handcrafted is very appealing to people." Mountain State's beers give a nod to the state's natural beauty and coal mining heritage, including the Almost Heaven Amber Ale, Seneca IPA (named for Seneca Rocks), and Miner's Daughter Stout.

Stumptown Ales opened in 2015 in the town of Davis in Tucker County, WV. Once a lumber town, a picture on the brewery's wall shows a clear cut in Davis in 1885 when legend has it that you could jump around town from stump to stump and never touch the ground. According to J.R. and C.R., the brewery owners, the historic aspect of the brewery "ties it to the area and makes it unique to people and gives a sense of pride for the people that are already here."

Stumptown's owners spent time visiting Vermont and studying the breweries and beer styles that have emerged in Vermont. They were inspired by Vermont's commitment to authenticity and handcrafted, local products and its expansive craft beer scene, and appreciated the commitment to authenticity. According to the owners, "I guess we're just doing our part to kind of get a piece of Vermont down here to spread it, to be part of West Virginia."

The New River Gorge has long attracted outdoor enthusiasts for whitewater rafting on the New River Gorge National River, climbing in the Gorge, and more recently mountain biking. The destination is quickly becoming known for its unique culinary options as well. According to the New River Gorge Convention and Visitors Bureau Executive Director,

> Now we're a destination for foodies who may or may not be interested in going rafting but they definitely want to experience the different tastes of the area and that opens the door for I think the breweries as well as distilleries, it just all kind of goes together.

Bridge Brew Works in Fayetteville, WV is named for the famous New River Gorge Bridge and chose the location because of the owners' connection to the regions outdoor opportunities. Beer names and logos incorporate elements of the area's unique heritage and natural resource base, including the 3 River Tripel (named for the New River Gorge National River, Bluestone National Scenic River, and Gauley River National Recreation Area), Peregrine Porter (named for the reintroduced Peregrine Falcon), and Dun Glen Dubbel (named for the historic mining town of Dun Glen).

Craft beer and culture

Outdoor recreation and craft beer are becoming close companions in West Virginia and across the country. However, according to Lane (1994), rural tourism is a multi-faceted activity extending beyond outdoor recreation to include cultural and heritage, culinary attractions, and sports tourism. Travel reports show that while the majority of visitors seek out adventure and nature-related activities during their visit to West Virginia, a growing number are especially interested in other activities, including culture, heritage, and culinary (Longwoods 2013). A Virginia winery/distiller/brewery tour visitor profile identified 69% of those engaging in libation activities as also likely to engage in cultural activities including concert, dance, theater, festivals/event, historic sites, museums and art exhibits, and touring/sightseeing compared to just 34% likely to engage in nature-based activities and 28% in outdoor sports (Virginia Tourism Corporation 2013).

While Tucker County and Fayetteville, WV are known for world-class outdoor adventure, some destinations in West Virginia have a product mix that is not primarily reliant on outdoor recreation. These destinations also recognize the local breweries' importance as an attraction and service. With an attraction base less centered around outdoor and adventure travel, these destinations expressed some concern about the compatibility of their destination's identity and marketing campaign(s) with the state's Wild and Wonderful brand.

In the central region of the state, serving as a gateway to the Monongahela National Forest, Randolph County has a diverse product mix that has rapidly evolved over the past few years, including an excursion train, live theaters, traditional music, outdoor recreation, and now craft beer. The Convention and Visitors Bureau notes that visitors who are primarily drawn to the area for theater, heritage, music, and outdoor recreation are also interested in visiting the local brewery. Big Timber Brewing in Elkins is a member of the Mountain Music Trail and hosts live music performances. According to the Randolph County CVB Director, "the Wild and Wonderful, everybody is very familiar with, but they need something new and we are doing something new with the Mountain Music Trail and the brewery."

Sharing the culture and heritage of the state and the local area is very important to Big Timber Brewing. According to M.K., one of the co-owners, "We want to be known as a West Virginia brewery." Big Timber showcases the lumber heritage in the styles and names of their beers, including the Double Bit Imperial IPA (named for the double bit ax), Hatchet American IPA, and Logger Lager Pils.

Greenbrier County, WV is in the Greenbrier River Valley region of the state and the home of the Greenbrier Resort and the town of Lewisburg, WV, which boasts an eclectic art, music, culinary, and shopping scene. Lewisburg was recognized as one of West Virginia's coolest small towns in 2011. The destination primarily targets an older, more affluent visitor, not those seeking extreme outdoor adventure. According to the Marketing Director of the Greenbrier County Convention and Visitors Bureau,

> Actually we tend to be a little bit different. The state tends to push a little more the adventure side of West Virginia and we tend to be a bit

softer here and I think the market is a bit more affluent and probably a little bit older because of the Greenbrier and downtown Lewisburg. It's more of a cultural destination.

The Greenbrier Valley is now home to the Greenbrier Valley Brewing Company (GVBC), Smooth Ambler Spirits, and Hawk Knob Cidery. GVBC is located just north of Lewisburg, WV. According to W.L., one of the co-owners of the brewery, the location was appealing because "it's a unique part of the state with an established tourism economy near a major interstate with very supportive people." GVBC taps into the state's heritage by naming their beers after West Virginia folklore. They have the Devil Anse IPA named after Devil Anse Hatfield, the Steel Driving Stout named after John Henry, and the Mothman Black IPA named for the famous tale of the Mothman creature. They also feature the Wild and Wonderful series which celebrates the Mountain State as a special feature series of beers sold in 22 oz. bottles. The Greenbrier Resort has a bunker that was built for Congress in case of a nuclear attack in 1961 which the *Washington Post* exposed in 1992. The resort now offers tours of the declassified bunker (Bunker History 2016). GVBC taps into this unique local attraction with the bunker series which is intended to be a high alcohol series, "beers that are going to withstand the apocalypse." W.L., one of the co-owners, discussed the importance of GVBC's connection to West Virginia in an effort to improve the state's image:

> Having the West Virginia theme on the beer helps a lot. We're trying to leverage off of West Virginia because everyone's proud of this state and we're proud of what we do here. What we're trying to do is kind of bring out what's good about this state. West Virginia isn't known for craft beer. We're trying to change that.

Berkeley Springs, WV is located in West Virginia's Eastern Panhandle within approximately 100 miles of Washington, D.C. Spas capitalize on the famous Berkeley Springs water to attract visitors seeking to relax and unwind. In addition to the spas, the town is known for its artists, shopping, and fine dining. The Executive Director of Travel Berkeley Springs (TBS) described its attraction base and target demographic:

> It's a small town face-to-face experience kind of place and the town experience is important. Its relaxation and revitalization, people come after a hectic week in DC and they come here to soak in the waters, to relax, to do some shopping, have a nice dinner, and listen to some music in the evenings. It's not overly expensive which helps to attract both a younger and older demographic.

In contrast to the state's brand, TBS sees themselves as more of a cool and quirky destination than a wild and wonderful destination. According to the

Executive Director of TBS, "we're local, we're cool, we're quirky and it's cool to discover something that's locally based, so I think cool is the more predominant aspect as opposed to local." The cool and quirky aspect is allowing them to connect to and benefit from the Division of Tourism's Real. campaign. According to the Executive Director of TBS, "They [the West Virginia Division of Tourism] recently did a video for the Real. campaign here and we got a lot of great feedback. They focused on our quirkiness. It's a good campaign that will benefit us."

Established in 2015, Berkeley Springs Brewing Company (BSBC) was established in 2015 and is helping to expand this "cool and quirky" product mix. According to the brewery owner:

> Our visitors want to have that small town feel. What we hope to do is be able to just kind of be an accent to that, and we're trying to offer something different to do beyond the artsy stuff downtown. It's something new for the region and the fact that we play on the water and we use the water as our main ingredient that is a big draw in and of itself.

The names of their beers acknowledge the heritage of the area, natural features, and sense of place, including George's Toe Butter (named after George Washington's bathtub in Berkeley Springs), Cacapon Kolsch (named for nearby Cacapon river), Lover's Leap (named for a famous overlook), and the Toe Path Pale Ale (named for the nearby rail trail).

Millennials and craft beer

Charleston, WV, the state capitol, lies along the Kanawha River in the southwest region of the state. It was primarily a conference and convention destination before the Convention and Visitors Bureau conducted focus groups and determined that a creative class community, music, Mountain Stage, national performances, and rich performing arts and visual arts community are what differentiates them from other destinations. They began to focus on attracting millennials and created a new tagline, Charleston, WV – Hip, Historic, Almost Heaven. According to the CVB Director, "it's the arts, it's the events, it's the music, it's the downtown vibe, it's all about being real and authentic and the people."

One thing they recognized was that their target demographic [millennials] loves craft beer. A visitor in one of their focus groups commented on how they love the local brewery and wish Charleston had more. This prompted the CVB to put two men walking down the street with their growlers into their brand advertising. According to the CVB Director, "I don't think it's a fad. I think it's becoming ingrained into our everyday lives. People want it, and now we're seeing food and beer tastings."

Bad Shepherd Brewing Company (formerly the Charleston Brewing Company) was established in 2016 in downtown Charleston, WV. While Bad

Shepherd Brewing intends to incorporate unique aspects of Charleston and WV's culture and heritage into its product, it also sees the potential for a WV craft beer style to emerge as other states are becoming known for making exceptional versions of certain styles of beers.

Sense of place and craft beer

Located in the northern panhandle region of West Virginia, Wheeling was a transportation and industrial center in the late 1800 and early 1900s. It became known by locals and visitors for the "Wheeling feeling." Today, the "Wheeling feeling" is being defined by arts and culture. Primary attractions include Centre Market, Wheeling Island Hotel Casino and Racetrack, Oglebay Resort, Capitol Theater, Wesbanco Arena, and downtown shops and restaurants. The state of West Virginia was born in Wheeling's Independence Hall, and it served as the state's first capitol.

According to the Marketing Director for the Convention and Visitors Bureau:

> We have so many opportunities we can take advantage of. We've always worked towards making sure people know that we are different. We are wonderful. We are unique in our own way. I love to see that the state is finally accepting that it's okay to tell people that not every place here has whitewater rafting and you know huge zip lines and extreme sports and all that kind of stuff. It's okay because not everybody is into that.

The Centre Market area of downtown Wheeling dates back to 1853 and includes an eclectic mix of shops and eateries inviting visitors to reminisce the days of local corner stores, bakeries, and butcher shops when the local store owner knew your name (Centre Market n.d.). Centre Market helps to define the uniqueness of Wheeling by showcasing the heritage of a former era along with unique small businesses increasingly attracting millennials to the downtown district. Wheeling Brewing Company has become a key component of this growth and revitalization.

Wheeling Brewing Company was established in 2014 and is owned and operated by young professionals who were born and raised in Wheeling and have a love for the town. They felt that they could spearhead the movement in Wheeling with good craft beer; Centre Market is an obvious location to open a brewery, since it showcases locally owned businesses which draw both residents and visitors to the business district.

Wheeling Brewing Company tries to accentuate Wheeling's history. Their beer names capture the rich heritage of the area with their Route 40 Red (named for historic U.S. Route 40, the National Road), Panhandle Pale Ale, Nail City Porter (Wheeling was once the largest producer of hand cut nails in the country), and Old Ryeman's Amber Ale (named for a historic brewery that once operated in Wheeling).

Morgantown, WV is in the northern part of the state and is the home of West Virginia University. Its primary attraction base is closely tied to the University and local sporting events, although it sits at the foothills of Coopers Rock State Forest with nearby hiking and biking trails.

Morgantown Brewing Company (MBC), which operates as a brewery and brew pub, started as the One Onion Brewing Company in 1992 and then became the West Virginia Brewing Company until 2009 when the current owner acquired the business and it became the MBC. A.G., the current owner, sees the business as an integral part of the downtown community in Morgantown:

> It's a small, close-knit community, and we really feel like we're part of a small downtown cultural district and I think a brew pub in any city is a good anchor. My wife and I travel around the country, that's the first place we look to. You're going to get a flavor of the town that's going to be something unique and authentic. It comes from the people. It's nothing you can manufacture. I don't think I could put this in a strip mall somewhere and get the same feel.

Although visitors are often attracted to Morgantown for West Virginia University and WVU sports, MBC would like to see more emphasis placed on the community's local and unique small businesses which have traditionally been overshadowed by the University and its sports teams. According to A.G.:

> I think we do our small part to add to what makes Morgantown unique. And I think there's a lot more room for it. I think Morgantown's pretty far behind a lot of other towns. I think keep it local and keep local ownership because that's where you get the personalities. We're the outdoors, white water rafters, mountain bikers, people that are outdoors people. They appreciate a good quality locally made product that is made in an environmentally friendly way.

Chestnut Brew Works (CBW) started in 2013 in the owner's garage. In 2015, it moved to its current location which features the brewery and a taproom in the South Park neighborhood of Morgantown. Local pride and West Virginia pride are important parts of CBW. The chestnut tree was a major timber species in West Virginia before being decimated by a fungal blight in the early 20th century. The brewery owner saw correlations between the demise and resurgence of both the chestnut and craft beer. According to B.R., the owner, "there's been a lot of work to bring the chestnut back and it's kind of the same thing with craft beer, it kind of disappeared for a while but it's coming back."

CBW views the connection to the local neighborhood, region, and state as a key to their success. According to the brewery owner:

> My best selling beer is called Halleck Pale Ale based on the street that I lived on. In businesses I like genuineness. I think that's so much of what makes a brewery, like a local craft brewery, a really good local craft brewery, is being local. People, when they travel, they like that local thing, or that local flavor.

CBW incorporates various levels of local identity into its product. The local neighborhood identity is captured in the South Park Porter. They've collaborated with Gene's Beer Garden, another South Park neighborhood bar. They try to capture and share the Morgantown identity and the West Virginia identity at various levels and see it as key to enhancing the tourist experience.

> I think craft beer in West Virginia and our tourism definitely go hand in hand. I think craft beer and tourism go hand in hand regardless of what the attractions are that bring tourists in. If we can promote the craft beer industry, we can make the tourists happier, at least give them a better experience when they come into West Virginia.

Discussion and conclusion

This study has revealed an increasing role that craft beer is playing in the tourism product mix in West Virginia as destinations across the state continue to evolve. Craft beer has proven to be complementary to both outdoor recreation and other visitor attractions including art, music, and heritage, and an important component of the visitor experience in West Virginia. Its importance to tourism in West Virginia was noted by Amy Goodwin, Tourism Commissioner, "we just lit the flame for craft beer, lit the flame, and now we're on." Its growth and popularity are proving that developing a quality product, along with a commitment to incorporating and showcasing the unique qualities of the destination, can create a competitive advantage and attract a growing market of travelers seeking authentic experiences.

While West Virginia will always be known for its mountains, natural beauty, and opportunities for adventure, local and state industry leaders have recognized that a key to West Virginia's success as a competitive and sustainable destination is to maintain a focus on unique, authentic, local products and services, and a sense of place. DMOs are endorsing the Real. campaign in extending the Wild and Wonderful brand to represent unique and authentic experiences available in the state. As noted by Eades, Arbogast, and Kozlowski (2017), craft beer has been recognized as a growth industry in West Virginia and embraced by the Governor and numerous leaders within state government quickly moving from a secondary to a core component of the Wild and Wonderful brand.

Diversifying the tourism product base and extending the brand while maintaining a commitment to authenticity and real experiences will not be without challenges. The state appears to be in a position to extend its tourism product base, enhance its brand identity, and capture a growing market share and craft beer has proven to be helping to lead the charge (Eades, Arbogast, and Kozlowski 2017). With many destinations at early stages of the Tourism Lifecycle (Butler 1980), West Virginia is in a unique position to enhance the visitor experience without succumbing to the commodification of culture as cautioned by George, Mair, and Reid (2009).

This study confirms that in West Virginia, as well as other states, the development of the craft beer industry is increasingly recognized as a way for destinations to showcase their unique local and regional characters by emphasizing authenticity and distinctiveness (Eades, Arbogast, and Kozlowski 2017; Flack 1997; Plummer, Telfer, Hashimoto, and Summers 2005; Schnell and Reese 2003). The destinations highlighted in this study can be considered to be in the involvement stage of Butler's (1980) Tourism Lifecycle where visitors and locals share spaces, visitor-community interaction is high, and brand and destination identities are developing. Increased visitor-resident interaction allows these destinations to attract visitors seeking authentic rural tourism experiences by showcasing and preserving rural life, art, culture, and natural beauty, thereby benefiting the local community economically and socially and enriching tourism experiences for visitors.

The state's challenge moving forward will be to avoid succumbing to pressures for the development of attractions that cater to the commercial/mass tourism market with less commitment to authenticity and sense of place. If destination managers/planners understand the psychographic curve, it is possible for them to control development and maintain ideal positioning (Plog 1974). Planning and control is imperative at this stage because many unplanned destinations face a declining future as uncontrolled growth discourages venture-type travelers.

While the Tourism Commissioner and local DMOs have expressed a commitment to developing and promoting authentic experiences, the lack of a specific tourism development function to ensure that effective planning and control occur within these destinations with mechanisms to prevent unwanted forms of tourism development could pose some concern for the future of these destinations. The state's Tourism Office maintains a budget for marketing and advertising, yet lacks a specific tourism development function. While Oregon has achieved success with outdoor recreation and craft beer (Anderson 2013), the state also funds the Oregon Rural Tourism Studio program which demonstrates Oregon's commitment to maintaining an authentic tourism product. It is a robust training program designed to assist rural communities in sustainable tourism development in hopes that the program will increase high-value, authentic experiences for travelers, thereby strengthening Oregon's position as a premier North American tourism destination (Rural Tourism Studio 2017).

The introduction of the Real. campaign demonstrates an intent to evolve the Wild and Wonderful brand, while preserving the state's identity characteristics and protecting its sense of place and, in turn, strengthening customer loyalty among the drifters/venturers following the recommendations of Jepson and Sharpley (2015) and Smith (2012). Forty years later, there exists a renewed opportunity for what Rosenow and Pulsipher (1979) called a broader-based new tourism that finds its roots in all of what is America, especially in those subtle elements of the diverse American experience that have not often been thought of as tourism resources that can bring the economic benefits of tourism to a much larger segment of American life, providing economic reasons for perpetuating that which is unique, special, and different in the various regions of the country, things which may otherwise be lost forever.

West Virginia appears to be on the path of developing a sustainable rural tourism industry by leveraging the opportunities identified through this analysis of the state of craft beer and tourism in West Virginia. Enhancing and showcasing these assets and opportunities should enhance the state's brand identity, attract a growing niche market of responsible travelers, protect its unique assets, and serve as a model for other rural destinations.

Limitations

While this study provided insight into the relationship between craft beer and the tourism industry from the perspective of destination leadership in West Virginia, it did not analyze resident attitudes toward and support for craft beer or visitors preferences in regard to local craft beer, including styles and price points in West Virginia. Further research is needed to better understand to what extent local residents support local craft breweries as well as visitor preferences in regard to beer styles, prices, and importance in the local attraction and service mix to provide further insight into the growing importance of craft beer to rural tourism. This study also did not analyze destination management practices in West Virginia. More research is required to better understand destination management practices and growth management opportunities.

References

Anderson, M. (2013). New brewery in Cascade Locks hopes to bank on bike tourism. Bike Portland. Accessed September 17, 2018. http://bikeportland.org

Bike Portland (2015). "New brewery in Cascade Locks hopes to bank on bike tourism." Accessed May 1, 2015. http://bikeportland.org

Brewers Association. (2014). "State craft beer sales and production statistics." Accessed May 1, 2015. https://www.brewersassociation.org/statistics/by-state/

Brewers Association. (2018). "National beer sales and production statistics". Accessed October 15, 2018. https://www.brewersassociation.org/statistics/national-beer-sales-production-data/

Bunker History. (2016). "The Greenbrier's bunker history". Accessed May 1, 2016. http://www.greenbrier.com/activities/the-bunker/bunker-history

Butler, R.W. (1980). "The concept of a tourist area cycle of evolution: implications for management of resources." *Canadian Geographer/Le Géographe canadien* 24, no. 1, 5–12.

Centre Market. (n.d.). Accessed May 1, 2015. http://www.centremarket.org/

Chaperon, S. & Bramwell, B. (2013). "Dependency and agency in peripheral tourism development." *Annals of Tourism Research* 40, no. 1, 132–154.

Cohen, E. (1972). "Toward a sociology of international tourism." *Social Research* 35, no. 1, 164–182.

Debies-Carl, J.S. (2018). "Beyond the local: places, people, and brands in New England beer marketing." *Journal of Cultural Geography* 36, no. 1, 1–33.

Destination Analysts. (July 2014). "State of the American traveler", no. 16. Accessed May 1, 2015. http://www.destinationanalysts.com/the-state-of-the-international-traveler-study/the-state-of-the-american-traveler-study/

Eades, D., Arbogast, D., & Kozlowski, J. (2017). "Life on the 'beer frontier': a comparative case study of sustainable craft beer tourism in West Virginia". In *Craft beverages and tourism, Volume 1: the rise of breweries and distilleries in the United States*, edited by Carol Kline, Susan L. Slocum, and Christina T. Cavaliere. Springer: Switzerland, 57–74.

Flack, W. (1997). "American microbreweries and neolocalism: "Ale-ing" for a sense of place." *Journal of Cultural Geography* 16, no. 2, 37–53.

Gartner, W. C. (2004). "Rural tourism development in the USA." *International Journal of Tourism Research* 6, no. 3, 151–164.

Gatrell, J., Reid, N., & Steiger, T.L. (2018)."Branding spaces: place, region, sustainability and the American craft beer industry." *Applied Geography* 90, 360–370.

George, E. W., Mair, H. & Reid, D.G. (2009). *Rural tourism development: localism and cultural change.* Channel View Publications: Bristol, UK.

Industry Information. (2016). "Tourism Reports". Accessed May 1, 2015. http://gotowv.com/industry-information/

Jepson, D., & Sharpley, R. (2015). "More than sense of place? Exploring the emotional dimension of rural tourism experiences." *Journal of Sustainable Tourism* 23, no. 8–9, 1157–1178.

Kabler, P. (2015). "Craft beer predicted to grow under new WV law." Charleston Gazette-Mail. Accessed May 11, 2015. http://www.wvgazettemail.com/article/20150511/GZ01/150519858/1176

Lane, B. (1994). "What is rural tourism?" *Journal of Sustainable Tourism* 2, no. 1–2, 7–21.

Longwoods International. "2010 Day Visitor Study." Accessed May 1, 2015. http://www.wvcommerce.org/travel/industryinformation/default.aspx

Longwoods International. "Colorado travel year 2014: final report." Accessed May 1, 2015. http://www.colorado.com/sites/default/master/files/Colorado2014Visitor-FinalReportonline.pdf

Longwoods International. *West Virginia 2013 Visitor Report.* Accessed May 1, 2015. http://www.wvcommerce.org/travel/industryinformation/default.aspx

MacCannell, Dean. (1973). "Staged authenticity: arrangements of social space in tourist settings." *American Journal of Sociology* 79, no. 3, 589–603.

Mowen, A.J., Graefe, A.R. & Graefe., D. A. (2013). "Research brief: results from the Pennsylvania craft beer enthusiast study." *Unpublished report to the Brewers of Pennsylvania Association.*

Murray, A. & Kline, C. (2015). "Rural tourism and the craft beer experience: factors influencing brand loyalty in rural North Carolina, USA." *Journal of Sustainable Tourism* 23, no. 8–9, 1198–1216.

Pezzi, M.G. (2018). "From Landscapes to Drinkscapes, Craft Beer Tourism in Peripheral/Rural Areas." Paper presented at the RSAI/GSSI Workshop The Geography of Craft Beer Brewing and Consumption: Local Entrepreneurialism and Tourism Development, L'Aquila, Italy, July 2018.

Pine, B.J., & Gilmore, J.H. (2008). "The eight principles of strategic authenticity." *Strategy and Leadership* 36, no. 3, 35–40.

Plog, S. C. (1974). "Why destination areas rise and fall in popularity." *Cornell Hotel and Restaurant Administration Quarterly* 14, no. 4, 55–58.

Plog, S. (2001). "Why destination areas rise and fall in popularity: an update of a Cornell Quarterly classic." *Cornell Hotel and Restaurant Administration Quarterly* 42, no. 3, 13–24.

Plummer, R., Telfer, D., Hashimoto, A., & Summers, R. (2005). "Beer tourism in Canada along the Waterloo–Wellington ale trail." *Tourism Management* 26, no. 3, 447–458.

Reid, N. (2018). "Craft Beer Tourism: Sampling Unique Beer in Unique Spaces." Paper presented at the RSAI/GSSI Workshop The Geography of Craft Beer Brewing and Consumption: Local Entrepreneurialism and Tourism Development, L'Aquila, Italy, July 2018.

Rosenow, J.E., & Pulsipher, G.L. (1979). *Tourism the good, the bad, and the ugly.* Nebraska: Century Three Press.

Runyan, D. (2015). "Economic impact of travel on West Virginia 2000–2014p detailed state and county estimates." Accessed May 1, 2015. http://www.wvcommerce.org/travel/industryinformation/default.aspx

Rural Tourism Studio (2017). Accessed May 15, 2017. http://industry.traveloregon.com/industry-resources/destination-development/rural-tourism-studio/

Ruvio, A., Shoham, A., & Makovec Brenčič, M (2008). "Consumers' need for uniqueness: short-form scale development and cross-cultural validation." *International Marketing Review* 25, no. 1, 33–53.

Schnell, S.M., & Reese, J.F. (2003). "Microbreweries as tools of local identity." *Journal of Cultural Geography* 21, no. 1, 45–69.

Sims, R. (2009). "Food, place and authenticity: local food and the sustainable tourism experience." *Journal of Sustainable Tourism* 17, no. 3, 321–336.

Smith, V. L. (Ed.). (2012). *Hosts and guests: The anthropology of tourism.* University of Pennsylvania Press: Philadelphia, PA.

Urry, J. (2002). *Consuming places.* Routledge: Abingdon, UK.

U.S. Census Bureau. (2010). "Census of Population." Accessed May 23, 2015. http://www.census.gov/geo/www/ua/2010urbanruralclass.html

U.S. Travel Association. (2012). "The economic impact of the travel industry." Accessed May 15, 2015. http://traveleffect.com/economy

U.S. Travel Association. (2016). "Changing demographics: current trends that drive American travel." April 23. Accessed June 1, 2017. https://www.ustravel.org/research/changing-demographics-current-trends-drive-american-travel-2015

Virginia Tourism Corporation. (2013). "Winery/Distillery/Brewery tour visitor profile 2011–2013."

Wang, Ning. (1999). "Rethinking authenticity in tourism experience." *Annals of Tourism Research* 26, no. 2: 349–370.

West Virginia Craft Brewers. (2017). Accessed June 30, 2017. http://www.wvbrewersguild.com/

Yin, R. K. (2009). *Case study research: design and methods (applied social research methods)*. 5th ed. London and Singapore: Sage.

10 Beercations

A spatial analysis of the U.S. craft brewery and tourism sectors

Andrew Crawley and Todd Gabe

Introduction

Over the past several decades, the U.S. craft beer industry has experienced substantial growth. The number of craft breweries increased by a remarkable 3,500% between 1981 and 2011—from 48 to 1,700 establishments (McLaughlin et al., 2014). By 2016, there were over 6,300 craft breweries in operation in the U.S.[1] These establishments manufactured over 24 million barrels of beer, and they employed over 425,000 U.S. workers in 2016. Craft beer sales exceeded $24 billion in 2017, which represents an 8% increase over the sales revenue generated by the industry just one year earlier. This makes the craft brewery sector one of the fastest growing industries in the U.S. However, despite the robust growth that is currently occurring in the industry, the craft beer sector has experienced successively lower growth rates of industry sales over the last three years.

The growth and location patterns of U.S. craft breweries have been examined in academic studies (Elzinga et al., 2015; Nilsson et al., 2018), but an area that has received less attention is the connection between local tourism and the presence of craft breweries. There is anecdotal evidence that newly opened breweries become major attractions that draw visitors to an area. As the tastes and preferences of consumers have shifted toward craft beer (Aquilani et al., 2015), the demand generated by tourists and local residents alike has supported significant growth in the industry. High tourism areas offer fertile ground for the emergence of a type of beer tourism, also termed "beercations," which are holidays built around visiting as many breweries as possible. Culinary tourism is a topic of interest to academics and it has been shown to be a driver of economic growth in some regions (Horng and Tsai, 2010; Mason and Paggiaro, 2012; Stone et al., 2018). This raises the question of whether craft breweries also go hand in hand with a vibrant tourism sector.

This chapter provides a spatial analysis of the U.S. craft brewery and tourism industries, with a particular interest in identifying regions that specialize in both of these sectors. Such places are likely to have tourism that is supported, at least in part, by the presence of craft breweries. To date, academic studies have focused on explaining—in a dichotomous way—the location of the craft beer industry and tourism in the U.S. This chapter attempts to fill a hole in the literature by considering craft breweries and tourism using similar spatial analytics to uncover potential patterns of location and development that have not been considered in past studies. The analysis of craft breweries is based on an establishment-level dataset provided by the U.S. Brewers Association, which is used to assign almost all of the U.S. craft breweries to their counties of location. This allows for a finer-grained spatial analysis than performed in previous studies. For the purposes of this work, we use a broad definition of craft breweries and include brew-pubs and brew-restaurants. The tourism industry is measured—using data from County Business Patterns—as the total number of lodging establishments, restaurants, and arts and recreation businesses located in a county.

Craft breweries

The U.S. Federal tax code classifies breweries by the size of production unit, and craft breweries are defined as breweries that produce less than two million barrels in total annual sales (Elzinga, et al., 2015). By comparison, large breweries—such as Anheuser-Busch and MillerCoors—produced and sold about 124 million and 10 million barrels of beer in 2015, respectively.[2] The exceptional growth of the craft brewery sector in recent decades has generated substantial interest across several academic fields (Carroll and Swaminathan, 2000; Swinnen, 2011; Olajire, 2012; Elzinga et al., 2015). One area of research has explored the location patterns of craft breweries. For example, Florida (2012) examined the key factors that might explain the location of U.S. craft breweries. Using state-level data, he found a positive and significant relationship between the number of craft breweries (per capita) and areas with higher levels of education and well-being. Florida (2012) also found a lower concentration of craft breweries in areas that are more conservative and religious.

Baginski and Bell (2011) focused their study of craft brewery location patterns at the level of the MSA and found that, similar to what Florida (2012) uncovered in the analysis of states, craft breweries are associated with the presence of high-quality educational services and a higher quality of life. The MSA-level analysis, however, suggests that the presence of craft breweries is associated with higher degrees of wage inequality, and a less vibrant arts and culture scene. Baginski and Bell (2011) also found that the growth of craft breweries in the U.S. occurred at a much slower pace in the southeast as compared with the rest of the country. Focusing on supply-side factors that might affect the location of microbreweries, Cortright (2002) studied the U.S. Pacific Northwest and found that the emergence of microbreweries in this region was primarily the result of the large hops growing industry present in this area more so than by consumer tastes.

One of the first studies to explicitly look at the spatial distribution of craft breweries in the U.S. was conducted by McLaughlin et al. (2014). This study provides numerous insights into the geography of craft breweries from a detailed analysis of the temporal changes in the volume of production, the number of breweries across states and the country as a whole, and per capita beer production. This research found that there is significant unevenness in the spatial distribution of craft breweries and that states with a history of brewing beer are still the areas with the greatest growth.

Another main result uncovered by McLaughlin et al. (2014) is that breweries, which originally had more of a concentration in major urban centers, have begun to increase in numbers in non-urban locations. This supports the contention suggested in the tourism work of Sidali et al. (2015) and Schnell and Reese (2003), which posited that craft breweries are beginning to increase in more rural areas. Other research on the locational patterns of breweries found a spatial clustering among craft breweries, which leads to the emergence of brewery districts (Nilsson et al., 2018).

Likewise, Elzinga et al. (2015) find a similar pattern of clustering in states, as well as results suggesting that higher income and, interestingly, an older population are determinants of craft brewery locations.

Beer tourism

The term "beer tourism" was coined by Plummer et al. (2005, p. 449), and it is described as "visitation to breweries, beer festivals and beer shows for which beer tasting and experiencing the attributes of beer regions are the prime motivating factors for visitors." Beer tourism falls under a broader category of "niche tourism," in which destinations are designed around the motivation of a subgroup or market segment (Robinson and Novelli, 2005). Although Nilsson et al. (2018, p. 114) suggest that some communities support breweries as a way to "boost tourism and economic development," there has been surprisingly little academic work exploring the challenges and opportunities of tourism associated with the craft beer industry (Alonso and Sakellarios, 2017). Dunn and Wickham (2016) have suggested the need for more academic research on the growth trajectory of craft brewery tourism to provide information that might allow regions to capitalize on the benefits of this recent growth.

In contrast to the lack of research on the connection between breweries and tourism, there is a relatively more extensive literature on tourism aspects of the wine and whisky industries. Both have a rich academic history in tourism research going back over the last 25 years. Indeed, in the case of wine tourism, Alonso and O'Neill (2011) find that wineries in rural areas are one of the key sectors attracting visitors and, thus, increasing economic vibrancy. However, both the wine and whisky industries tend to be concentrated in places with physical and natural environments that are sought after by tourists (Getz and Brown, 2006).

In contrast, craft beer operations are more associated with urban and light industrial areas (Plummer et al., 2005) and, in some cases, these operations are viewed as a driver of urban gentrification (Mathews and Picton, 2014; Chapman et al., 2017). These location patterns, however, have begun to change in the past decade as craft breweries are spreading out beyond the traditional postindustrial areas to more rural communities. For example, Sidali et al. (2015) found evidence of a growing number of breweries in small towns and rural areas. Likewise, Schnell and Reese (2003) use the term beer tourism when describing visitation to breweries in "small local communities." Murray and Kline (2015) find that a desire of consumers to connect with the community, an interest in unique products, and product satisfaction have driven the growth of rural breweries. As an example of the role that breweries play in connecting consumers to their communities, Holtkamp et al. (2016) identified many breweries that have adopted local images and names of places to link their beers to specific locations, with an emphasis on local communities or destinations.

Over the past decade as the craft beer sector has experienced substantial growth, the influence of neo-localism has led some to draw connections between the industry and tourism. For example, research by Eades et al. (2017) has begun to explore the link between craft beer and tourism in formal ways through a case study analysis of U.S. regions. Francioni (2012) and Murray and Kline (2015)—also focusing on visitors—have explored the motivation of tourists visiting North Carolina breweries and have noted their impressive growth as tourist attractions. Likewise, Dunn and Kregor (2017) found that facilities such as tasting rooms, craft beer festivals, competitions, and social media have allowed avenues for tourists to better enjoy breweries in Oregon and Washington states—two states that we find to have specializations in craft breweries. Finally, the connections between craft breweries and sustainable tourism have been explored by Lorr (2018) and Eades et al. (2017).

Numerous stories about craft breweries and tourism have appeared in the popular press, with particular attention given to the potential regenerating effects of craft breweries in areas that have suffered recent economic struggles.[3,4] For example, the highly publicized craft beer trail in Michigan cuts through areas devastated by industrial decline and has provided much needed employment.[5] Likewise, many areas have used extensive marketing about their craft beer pedigree as a way to attract visitors (Myles and Breen, 2018). A very practical example of such marketing efforts is evident in the collaborative project between the U.S. Brewers Association and Travelocity, which surveyed people on craft beer tourism.[6] These organizations developed an index of craft beer tourism locations and it is available in downloadable map form to encourage tourists to visit these areas. Some of the areas noted for beer tourism include Portland, Oregon; Colorado Springs, Colorado; Santa Rose-Petaluma, California; and Portland, Maine.

Empirical analysis and findings

Previous research on the spatial distribution of craft breweries has focused on locational patterns at the national, state, and MSA levels. However, to date, there has been little analysis examining the spatial patterns of craft breweries at the U.S. county level. Using establishment-level data provided by the U.S. Brewers Association and employing a variety of geocoding techniques (e.g. matching the latitude and longitude of the establishment's location to its address, matching the address to a county), we were able to estimate the number of craft breweries in each U.S. county as of 2016. Having information at this level of spatial disaggregation offers a number of distinct benefits, compared to an analysis of state- or MSA-level data, such as the ability to observe and discern differences among structurally diverse counties. The ability to explore craft breweries at such a localized level also allows the exploration of the connection between craft breweries and tourism, which is a focus of our analysis below.

We use a multiple-step approach to analyze the spatial distribution of craft breweries, and the link between these establishments and local tourism. First, a high-level analysis of the current and changing spatial patterns of U.S. craft breweries is carried out at the state level. This analysis uses data on the number of craft breweries in 2016, with comparisons to similar information from 2011. State-level regional specialization in craft breweries is measured using location quotients (LQs), and locational Gini coefficients are calculated to measure the geographic concentration of craft breweries across states. Following the examination of state-level patterns, the second part of the analysis focuses on county-level specialization in craft breweries—also using LQs. The final part of the analysis looks at spatial patterns in the location of tourism-related businesses and this information, combined with the county-level data on craft breweries, is used to identify counties with an abundance of craft breweries and tourism establishments.

State-level craft brewery location patterns

Figure 10.1 shows the number of craft breweries by state in 2011 and 2016.[7] Overall, the number of U.S. craft breweries increased from 2,047 to 6,372 over this five-year period. In the map using data from 2011, the darkest-shaded states indicate the highest number of craft breweries, with amounts between 136 and 270. Although the states with the darkest shading do not change very much when comparing the maps from 2011 and 2016, the darkest shading represents state-level counts of between 369 and 764 in the 2016 map. In both years, the maps show the largest numbers of craft breweries in states such as California, Colorado, Florida, Michigan, Oregon, Pennsylvania, and Washington.

Figure 10.2 shows state-level LQs for craft breweries in 2011 and 2016. The LQs measure the share of total establishments (from County Business

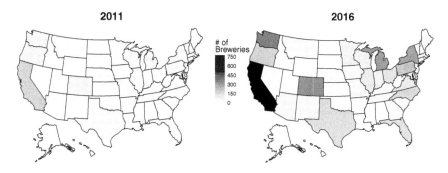

Figure 10.1 Number of craft breweries by state in 2011 and 2016.

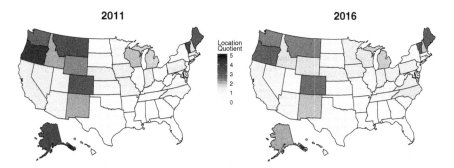

Figure 10.2 State-level location quotients (LQs) for craft breweries in 2011 and 2016.

Patterns of the U.S. Census Bureau) that are craft breweries in each state, relative to the share of all U.S. establishments that are craft breweries. While the counts of craft breweries shown in Figure 10.1 are, to some extent, influenced by population size (e.g. large states such as California, Florida, and Texas tend to have more of all sorts of businesses), the LQs measure a state's specialization in the sector as a percentage of all businesses. The LQs indicate regional specialization of craft breweries in states of the Pacific Northwest such as Oregon and Washington, as well as Colorado, Massachusetts, Michigan, Montana, and Virginia. The darkest-shaded states in 2011 and 2016 have LQs ranging from 2.36 to 4.31 and 2.21 to 3.21, respectively. This decrease in the LQs characterizing the states with the highest specializations, along with an increase in the lowest state-level LQs (e.g. from 0.13 to 0.25) between 2011 and 2016, suggests that the craft brewery sector has become more geographically dispersed across states in recent years.

We can further examine this trend of a dispersion of the craft brewery sector by calculating and comparing locational Gini coefficients (Krugman, 1991; Kim et al., 2000), which measure the geographic concentration of

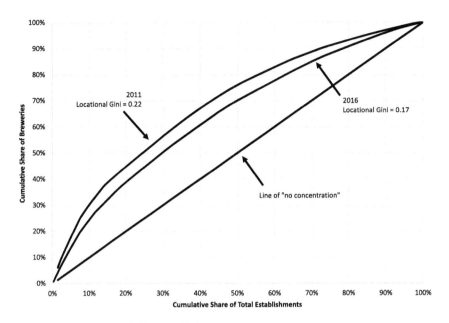

Figure 10.3 Locational Gini coefficients.

industries. Figure 10.3 shows locational Gini coefficients for the craft brewery sector in 2011 and 2016. The Y- and X-axes plot the cumulative shares of breweries and total establishments, in descending order of the state's LQ. The 45-degree line, labeled as the line of "no concentration," would depict an industry that was dispersed across states in proportions similar to the shares of all establishments. In other words, the 45-degree line would represent industries that are ubiquitous and "equally available" everywhere.

The locational Gini coefficients shown in Figure 10.3—along with the corresponding curves—indicate that craft breweries became more geographically dispersed across states between 2011 (Gini of 0.22) and 2016 (Gini of 0.17). For example, the top states for specialization in craft breweries (i.e. in descending order by LQ) that had about 30% of all establishments (X-axis) accounted for about 56% of craft breweries in 2011. The top craft brewery states with about 30% of all establishments accounted for only 49% of craft breweries in 2016. This decrease, along with the overall pattern represented by the locational Gini coefficients, is a fairly large change over such a short time period. These patterns showing that craft breweries have become more geographically dispersed across states—between 2011 and 2016—are different than the earlier results of McLaughlin et al. (2014), which found higher growth in states with a history of brewing beer.

County-level craft brewery location patterns

Now moving to an analysis at a more disaggregated geographic scale, Figure 10.4 shows the spatial patterns of county-level specialization in the craft brewery sector. As mentioned earlier, the county-level figures are based on the latitudes and longitudes of individual establishments that were geocoded to their physical addresses. The locations of U.S. craft breweries were provided (with permission to use in this study) by the U.S. Brewers Association. The original dataset of establishment-level records had 6,430 observations and, after cleaning the data and removing businesses that could not be assigned to a physical location, we were left with just over 6,100 useable observations.

The county-level map shows the highest levels of regional specialization in the Western U.S.—between the Pacific Coast and Rocky Mountains—as well as the northeast and around the Great Lakes. By contrast, the lowest levels of specialization are found in the Southeastern U.S. and across vast swathes of Texas, Oklahoma, and Kansas. Most of New England's 67 counties have a significant presence of craft breweries, and the state of Maine has craft breweries in all 16 of its counties. Our results showing relatively low specializations in the Southeastern U.S. are similar to those of Baginski and Bell (2011), which found slower growth rates (as compared to the country as a whole) of craft breweries in the southeast.

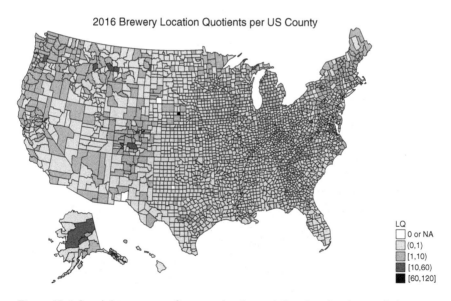

Figure 10.4 Spatial patterns of county-level specialization in the craft brewery sector.

Local tourism and craft breweries

With information on the county-level locations of craft breweries, we can now examine the link between the tourism and the craft brewery sectors. The tourism sector is made up of the accommodation (NAICS 721); restaurants and other eating places (NAICS 7225); and arts, entertainment, and recreation (NAICS 71) industries. The combined count of establishments in these three sectors was calculated for all U.S. counties (using data from County Business Patterns) and, similar to our county-level analysis of craft breweries, we use LQs as a measure of regional specialization in tourism.

Figure 10.5 shows the geographic patterns of county-level specialization in tourism businesses. While the craft brewery sector is characterized by a pattern where some counties have a high specialization and others do not have any craft breweries at all, the tourism industry is more evenly dispersed across U.S. regions. The locational Gini coefficient for the craft brewery sector is 0.40, compared with a county-level tourism locational Gini coefficient of 0.09. Relatively high pockets of tourism exist in the counties between the Pacific Coast and the Rocky Mountains, as well as in the Northeastern U.S. and in coastal counties. Although the composite tourism variable might be capturing some economic activity that is not related to tourists (i.e. restaurants, which also serve local residents, are counted as tourism businesses), it provides a reasonable representation of the counties that are over- or underrepresented in the infrastructure and attractions that are desired by visitors.

Figure 10.5 Geographic patterns of county-level specialization in tourism businesses.

The final part of the analysis uses the county-level LQs for the craft brewery and tourism sectors to examine the connection between these industries. Following an approach used by Tian (2015), the LQs are transformed into logarithms. This reduces our sample size from an analysis of 3,142 counties in Figures 10.4 and 10.5, to 1,209 counties in the analysis of "beer tourism." Figure 10.6 shows a scatterplot of the transformed craft brewery and tourism sector LQs, and these two county-level variables have a correlation of −0.025. This suggests that—across the U.S. counties that have at least one craft brewery and one tourism establishment—there is very little connection between these two sectors. The scatterplot is separated into four quadrants based on the counties' specializations in craft breweries and tourism and, in the present analysis, the quadrant of primary interest is the upper right. The counties in this quadrant are characterized as having high specializations in craft breweries and tourism.

The counties that reside in the upper-right quadrant of Figure 10.6 can be used as a first cut for the regions that might be described as "beer tourism centric" (Plummer et al., 2005)—or places where visitors might enjoy "beer-cations." But given that LQs are sensitive to the size of the region considered (e.g. a place with one craft brewery could have a very large LQ if the county has a small number of overall establishments), we use an additional criterion to identify places with high amounts of tourism and craft breweries. More

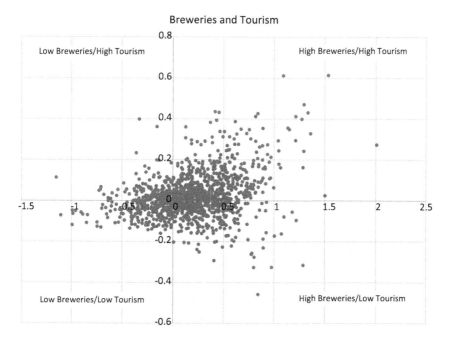

Figure 10.6 Relationship between breweries and tourism.

specifically, along with using the LQs for craft breweries and tourism businesses, we also include information on the count of craft breweries in each county. Places that rank in the top one-half of the 1,209 counties considered in terms of the log(LQ) of tourism businesses, the log(LQ) of craft breweries, and the raw number of craft breweries are characterized as having brewery-related tourism.

When these three criteria are applied to our dataset of 1,209 U.S. counties, 60 places are identified as having high levels of beer tourism. These 60 regions are indicated in Figure 10.7, and the top 10 counties for beer tourism are listed in Table 10.1. The map shows counties that are hospitable to

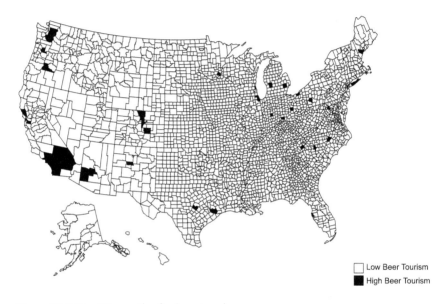

Figure 10.7 Top 40 counties for beer tourism.

Table 10.1 Top 10 countries for beer tourism

FIPS code	Top 10 high beer and tourism counties	Number of breweries
6037	Los Angeles County, California	93
41051	Multnomah County, Oregon	76
6001	Alameda County, California	35
37021	Buncombe County, North Carolina	34
6065	Riverside County, California	32
23005	Cumberland County, Maine	31
6071	San Bernardino County, California	25
45019	Charleston County, South Carolina	24
42101	Philadelphia County, Pennsylvania	20
47037	Davidson County, Tennessee	19

craft breweries and tourism across seven states. The information presented in Table 10.1 also suggests that California is home to many of the top places for beer tourism, with 4 of the top 10 counties located in the Golden State. These results are not surprising given that California has about 12% of all the U.S. craft breweries. Outside of California, hotspots for beer tourism include counties located in the metropolitan areas of Portland, Oregon; Asheville, North Carolina; Portland, Maine; Charleston, South Carolina; Philadelphia; and Nashville. Overall, our list of the top places for beer tourism are similar to those identified by the U.S. Brewers Association and Travelocity in their collaborative project on the best places for "beercations."

The top 10 counties noted in Table 10.1, along with the map showing all 60 counties uncovered by our analysis, suggest that having a large urban population is not a prerequisite for supporting a beer tourism sector. Along with counties that are 'part of the Los Angeles, Philadelphia, and Nashville MSAs—which are among the nation's largest—smaller metropolitan areas such as Asheville, North Carolina; Charleston, South Carolina; and Portland, Maine are identified as having specializations in both sectors. Although these metropolitan areas differ in size—e.g. Los Angeles is one of the largest; Portland, Maine is one of the smallest—many of them rank high for artistic and cultural amenities. Los Angeles and Nashville are well known for music and entertainment, while Asheville and Charleston are noted in the arts.

Discussion

The growth of the U.S. craft beer industry has been an astounding success story by almost all measures. An industry that was barely in existence 15 years ago has evolved into a multi-billion-dollar sector of the U.S. economy. However, despite the recent success of the industry and the promise it holds, there is very little information about its detailed locational patterns. This chapter sought to fill this void, and we also present a first look at the spatial patterns of craft beer tourism. Although the economic geographies of these sectors are interesting on their own, future research will examine some of the regional characteristics that are associated with a strong beer tourism sector.

The first part of our research focused on state-level patterns, and uncovered a changing spatial distribution of craft breweries between 2011 and 2016. The main result found in this analysis is that craft breweries have become more dispersed across states. However, in spite of this, and as an example of the current strength of the industry, states such as California and Pennsylvania have seen dramatic increases in the number of breweries—with these states home to, respectively, 747 and 550 craft breweries as of 2016. All 50 states experienced an increase in the number of breweries between 2011 and 2016, and some states saw particularly impressive growth (e.g. Virginia went from 45 to 225 craft breweries; South Carolina grew from 11 to 52; and Florida saw an increase from 45 to 243).

Unsurprisingly, New England is densely covered in craft breweries—possibly as a result of its long brewing history in some of the region's densely populated urban areas—but the location of craft breweries in rural areas of the northeast is also quite intense. Vermont, New Hampshire, and Maine have several counties that specialize in craft breweries, and the latter has at least one brewery in every county. These rural areas of the northeast are well known as tourist destinations, offering activities such as skiing, hiking, "leaf pepping," and—in the cast of Maine—coastal pursuits such as sailing. Some areas around the Great Lakes, also rich in amenities that are desired by visitors, provide other examples of tourist destinations that also have a large number of craft breweries. For example, Lake Michigan is entirely surrounded by craft brewery-intensive counties.

With the advent of beer tourism vacation packages like those offered through Travelocity, the potential for an area with significant numbers of breweries to attract more tourists has grown sharply.[8] This chapter has shown that it is not just the big cities or large metros where the craft beer industry has a stronghold, but these businesses are also in abundance in some small rural areas without, in some cases, a history of brewing. This is similar to the findings of Sidali et al. (2015) and Schnell and Reese (2003). A continuation of this trend could help craft breweries become a contributing factor to regional development in some rural areas. Given that the craft brewery industry is perhaps reaching maturity, although still exhibiting growth, future avenues for expansion of the craft brewery sector should be welcomed and supported. However, the recent slowdown in industry growth rates should be seen as a warning to those regions and cities which have purely seen craft beer as some form of regional development panacea.

Summary and conclusions

The goal of this chapter was to examine spatial patterns of the U.S. craft brewery sector, along with its connection to local tourism. The review of background data and previous academic studies revealed an impressive growth of craft breweries, and suggested some linkages to tourism. Our initial analysis of the state-level economic geography of craft breweries shows that—along with its substantial growth—the sector became more geographically dispersed. In other words, some of the states with lower specializations of craft breweries in 2011 grew faster than states with higher initial specializations. In particular, places in the Southern and Western U.S. fared particularly well between 2011 and 2016, with steady increases in numbers in New Mexico, Texas, Arizona, and Florida.

To undertake a spatial analysis at a more disaggregated scale, we used establishment-level records to assign craft breweries to U.S. counties. A composite tourism variable was constructed by combining the numbers of establishments in the accommodation; restaurants and other eating places; and arts, entertainment, and recreation industries in each county. These two measures were then analyzed to provide insight into where the largest relative numbers of craft breweries and tourism businesses are located. In particular, we found concentrations of these types of businesses in New England, around the Great Lakes and along the U.S. coasts. With this information, and applying three criteria—(1) the county has a higher number of breweries than the U.S. average, (2) the LQ for breweries is higher than the U.S. average, and (3) the LQ for tourism is higher than the U.S. average—we identified 60 counties that are leaders in beer tourism. The counties identified in this analysis are similar to those found in the Travelocity craft beer index, with some subtle variations particularly capturing more southern areas such as Davidson, Tennessee, and Charleston, South Carolina.

The county-level spatial analysis presented in this chapter provides a way of identifying those counties with the necessary conditions for craft beer tourism. The craft beer industry has been a phenomenal success story but, as it matures and growth rates begin to decline, more information is needed about potential avenues for future development. Previous academic literature and articles in the popular press have praised the virtues of "craft beer trails" and "beercations"; yet—to date—very little work has explored the U.S. regions that specialize in craft breweries and tourism. This chapter has provided some initial empirical evidence on areas of high beer tourism and regions that might be able to attract visitors that are seeking out "beercations." An interesting extension to this study would be to examine the changes over time in the county-level patterns of craft breweries, as our current approach focusing on a single year of data poses somewhat of a limitation. Likewise, future research could explore the regional characteristics that impact the state- and county-level growth of craft breweries. Finally, future research could broaden the focus of study to include social and cultural dynamics associated with craft beer tourism.

Notes

1 The craft brewery sector figures are from the U.S. Brewers Association: https://www.brewersassociation.org/statistics/economic-impact-data/
2 https://www.marketwatch.com/story/these-11-brewers-make-over-90-of-all-us-beer-2015-07-27
3 https://www.curbed.com/2017/6/13/15788960/brewing-economic-development-craft-beer
4 https://www.citylab.com/life/2017/08/can-craft-breweries-transform-americas-post-industrial-neighborhoods/536943/
5 http://www.mibeer.com/beer-tourism
6 https://www.brewersassociation.org/communicating-craft/travelocity-debuts-new-beer-tourism-index/
7 This information is from the U.S. Brewers Association.
8 https://www.travelocity.com/things-to-do/theme-best-us-brewery-tours

References

Alonso, A.D., and O'Neill, M.A., 2011. Climate change from the perspective of Spanish wine growers: a three-region study. *British Food Journal, 113*(2), 205–221.

Alonso, A.D., and Sakellarios, N., 2017. The potential for craft brewing tourism development in the United States: a stakeholder view. *Tourism Recreation Research, 42*(1), 96–107.

Aquilani, B., Laureti, T., Poponi, S., and Secondi, L., 2015. Beer choice and consumption determinants when craft beers are tasted: An exploratory study of consumer preferences. *Food Quality and Preference, 41*, 214–224.

Baginski, J., and Bell, T.L., 2011. Under-tapped? an analysis of craft brewing in the southern United States. *Southeastern Geographer, 51*(1), 165–185.

Carroll, G.R., and Swaminathan, A., 2000. Why the microbrewery movement? Organizational dynamics of resource partitioning in the US brewing industry. *American Journal of Sociology, 106*(3), 715–762.

Chapman, N.G., Lellock, J.S., and Lippard, C.D., 2017. *Untapped: Exploring the Cultural Dimensions of Craft Beer*. West Virginia University Press, USA.

Cortright, J., 2002. The economic importance of being different: regional variations in tastes, increasing returns, and the dynamics of development. *Economic Development Quarterly, 16*(1), 3–16.

Dunn, A., and Kregor, G., 2017. Tourism as a business strategy for growth in Oregon and Washington craft breweries. In Kline, C., Slocum, S., and Cavaliere, C. (eds.), *Craft Beverages and Tourism, Volume 1* (pp. 105–118). Palgrave Macmillan, Cham.

Dunn, A., and Wickham, M., 2016. Craft brewery tourism best-practices: a research agenda. *Annals of Tourism Research, 56*, 140–142.

Eades, D., Arbogast, D., and Kozlowski, J., 2017. Life on the "Beer Frontier": A case study of craft beer and tourism in West Virginia. In *Craft Beverages and Tourism, Volume 1* (pp. 57–74). Palgrave Macmillan, Cham.

Elzinga, K.G., Tremblay, C.H., and Tremblay, V.J., 2015. Craft beer in the United States: History, numbers, and geography. *Journal of Wine Economics, 10*(3), 242–274.

Florida, R., 2012. The geography of craft beer. *The Atlantic Cities*.

Francioni, J.L., 2012. *Beer Tourism: A Visitor and Motivational Profile for North Carolina Craft Breweries*. The University of North Carolina at Greensboro.

Getz, D., and Brown, G., 2006. Critical success factors for wine tourism regions: a demand analysis. *Tourism Management, 27*(1), 146–158.

Holtkamp, C., Shelton, T., Daly, G., Hiner, C.C., and Hagelman III, R.R., 2016. Assessing neolocalism in microbreweries. *Papers in Applied Geography, 2*(1), 66–78.

Horng, J.S., and Tsai, C.T.S., 2010. Government websites for promoting East Asian culinary tourism: A cross-national analysis. *Tourism Management, 31*(1), 74–85.

Kim, Y., Barkley, D.L., and Henry, M.S., 2000. Industry characteristics linked to establishment concentrations in nonmetropolitan areas. *Journal of Regional Science, 40*(2), 231–259.

Krugman, P., 1991. Increasing returns and economic geography. *Journal of Political Economy, 99*(3), 483–499.

Lorr, M.J., 2018. Pure Michigan Beer? tourism, craft breweries, and sustainability. In *Craft Beverages and Tourism, Volume 2* (pp. 49–64). Palgrave Macmillan, Cham.

Mason, M.C., and Paggiaro, A., 2012. Investigating the role of festival scape in culinary tourism: The case of food and wine events. *Tourism Management*, *33*(6), 1329–1336.

Mathews, V., and Picton, R.M., 2014. Intoxifying gentrification: brew pubs and the geography of post-industrial heritage. *Urban Geography*, *35*(3), 337–356.

McLaughlin, R.B., Reid, N., and Moore, M.S., 2014. The ubiquity of good taste: A spatial analysis of the craft brewing industry in the United States. In Patterson M., and Hoalst-Pullen N. (eds.), *The geography of Beer* (pp. 131–154). Springer, Dordrecht.

Murray, A., and Kline, C., 2015. Rural tourism and the craft beer experience: Factors influencing brand loyalty in rural North Carolina, USA. *Journal of Sustainable Tourism*, *23*(8–9), 1198–1216.

Myles, C.C., and Breen, J.M., 2018. (Micro) movements and microbrew: on craft beer, tourism trails, and material transformations in three urban industrial sites. In Slocum, S. L., Kline, C., & Cavaliere, C. T. (eds.), *Craft Beverages and Tourism, Volume 2* (pp. 159–170). Palgrave Macmillan, Cham.

Nilsson, I., Reid, N., and Lehnert, M., 2018. Geographic patterns of craft breweries at the Intraurban Scale. *The Professional Geographer*, *70*(1), 114–125.

Olajire, A.A., 2012. The brewing industry and environmental challenges. *Journal of Cleaner Production*, *275*(2), 234–245.

Plummer, R., Telfer, D., and Hashimoto, A., 2005. The rise and fall of the Waterloo-Wellington Ale Trail: a study of collaboration within the tourism industry. *Current Issues in Tourism*, *9*(3), 191.

Robinson, M., and Novelli, M., 2005. Niche tourism: an introduction. In Novelli, M. (ed.), *Niche Tourism: Contemporary Issues, Trends and Cases* (pp. 1–14). Oxford, Elsevier Buterworth-Heinemann–.

Schnell, S.M., and Reese, J.F., 2003. Microbreweries as tools of local identity. *Journal of Cultural Geography*, *21*(1), 45–69.

Sidali, K.L., Kastenholz, E., and Bianchi, R., 2015. Food tourism, niche markets and products in rural tourism: Combining the intimacy model and the experience economy as a rural development strategy. *Journal of Sustainable Tourism*, *23*(8–9), 1179–1197.

Stone, M.J., Migacz, S., and Wolf, E., 2018. Beyond the journey: the lasting impact of culinary tourism activities. *Current Issues in Tourism*, *22*(2), 1–6.

Swinnen, J.F. ed., 2011. *The economics of beer*. Oxford University Press, Oxford, UK.

11 Caring for community through crafted beer

Perspectives from Northern Sweden

Wilhelm Skoglund
and Annelie Sjölander-Lindqvist

Introduction

Localized small-scale agricultural production and entrepreneurship, including tourism efforts, are increasingly being promoted as means to sustain rural economies, cultures, and ecosystems (McAreavey and McDonagh 2011). In effect, local–regional natural and cultural resources are increasingly exploited in pursuing revitalized and sustainable rural development. Sweden, where the culture of food and drink has changed dramatically since the 1950s, exemplifies this trend. Old traditions have been replaced by new 'solutions', closely following the evolution of food production in the USA (Lee 2009). This has meant the rapid modernization of the entire range of agricultural customs and food production, all the way from the producer to the dinner table (Beckeman 2004). This development led scholars to claim that Swedish culinary traditions had been lost, turning the countryside into a 'food desert' (Bonow and Rytkönen 2012). A plausible background to this interpretation is the rapid rationalization of the food industry in Sweden since WWII, marked by efficient retailers and a packaging industry that standardized product output, reducing the size and scope of traditional food markets. Today, food is seen as a social and cultural heritage, and a potential 'vehicle' for innovation and knowledge creation that can support and drive regional development. This development follows a general discourse: gastronomy has become a preeminent component of contemporary tourism promotion, forming the foundation of many regional, national, and international policies and agendas (Seyfang 2006; Lin et al. 2010), and increasingly acknowledged as an opportunity for cultural policy and the hospitality industry to support a viable connection between various human activities and the characteristics of particular cultural landscapes (Richards 2011).

The case of the northern Swedish region of Jämtland is no exception, and tourism is considered vital to the region's economy. As in many other rural areas, a shrinking agricultural sector and increased market globalization have affected the possibility of maintaining local food distribution. Moreover, outmigration, high rates of unemployment, urbanization, industrial transformation, ill health, an ageing population, labour shortages in certain sectors, tourism pressure, and environmental challenges all hamper regional sustainability. Finding ways to diversify the economy to increase employment, enlarge the tax base, and support sustainable business revenue growth is therefore critical to such regions (Johns and Mattsson 2005). With over 4,300 people working in the sector (Lundqvist 2018), the role of gastronomy in increasing the value of tourism (Regionförbundet Jämtlands län 2013, 24) should be seen against this background.

Starting from these circumstances, we turn our sights to the craft beer sector to explore it as a locus of interaction between heritage, tourism, and creative entrepreneurship, influencing the way gastronomic initiatives work in rural regions. The highly rural and peripheral region of Jämtland has rapidly changed its character in terms of beer production and today is home to 13 small-scale craft beer producers, making it a compelling case for study. By interrogating the motives underlying the producers' engagement with beer, we can discuss how a 'sense of belonging' (Trubek 2008) supports local industry, building on the cultural and experiential economy instead of the traditional industrial economy. This study, combining business administration and social anthropology perspectives, concentrates on the producer perspective (Dunn and Wickham 2015), product heritage and identity (Sjölander-Lindqvist and Cinque 2014), and linkages to tourism strategies and associated hindrances and opportunities (Murray and Kline 2015). As gastronomy is increasingly relevant to tourism (Slocum 2016) and is considered a way for peripheral rural areas to promote local and regional products and services, we find it important to examine and reflect on the perspectives of the small-scale producers themselves: How do they make sense of their actions? What does beer mean to them as a food item? What are the symbolic and cultural properties of the beer produced in the region? Finding out how the producers understand their work, products, and reasons for doing business casts light on the entrepreneurial core of the sector.

Research approach

The focus of this case study is on cultural industries, gastronomy, and the growing number of craft breweries in the peripheral region of Jämtland in Northern Sweden. Located in central–northern inland Sweden, geographically encompassing almost 50,000 km², Jämtland is significantly larger than countries such as Switzerland or Belgium. The region is sparsely populated and rural, with a population of only 129,000 – fewer than three inhabitants per km² – and only one city, Östersund (62,000 inhabitants) (Regionfakta n.d.). The region is characterized by small-scale farming and forestry. Many hillside farms are still in operation, and the region's skilled culinary artisans and farmers produce both innovative and inventive food, as well as use more ancient methods and recipes passed from one generation to another. Tourism has long been a growing contributor to the economy, and mountain resorts, primarily located in the western, mountainous part of the region

(Rolén and Thomasson 1990), welcome many tourists in both winter and summer to practise sports and enjoy nightlife.

To enhance our knowledge and understanding of conditions that may create and sustain localized, traditional food production, and of how such food production and distribution can support the development of rural areas, we employed a qualitative research approach, combining the perspectives of business administration and social anthropology. The study was undertaken in 2016–2017 within a larger research project interrogating the opportunities and limitations associated with gastronomic initiatives at regional levels in different peripheral locations in Europe, and identifying what is needed – from the entrepreneurial to the policy levels – to encourage sustainable community and tourism development. For this study, we conducted semi-structured interviews with all brewers ($n = 10$) then operating in Jämtland that were able to provide interviews. The interviews were carried out on site, and complemented with tours of the brewery facilities. Informal conversations during festival, restaurant, and pub visits, and studies of documents and websites complemented the interviews.

Specifically, the study started in social-anthropological food theory, considering food and drink as connecting people, society, and place (Trubek 2008). This line of interrogation is supported by Rodman (1992), who emphasized place as a node of physical, emotional, and experiential realities rooted in, and constructed by, time and space. This argument can be compared to the thought of Low and Lawrence-Zúñiga (2003), who considered places as locations for speaking about and acting on the world. From a symbolic perspective, food and drink labelled 'local' can be said to hold 'discursive currency' (Leitch 2003), situated on the divide between localization and globalization (Badii 2013). In contrast to globalization, which fosters cultural homogenization and disrupted places, localism resolves places (Wilk 1995), for example, when both the production and consumption of food encompass people's experiences of living in a culturally relative and historically specific place. The business administration dimension complements these perspectives by providing value-adding entrepreneurship perspectives on production and developmental issues. Here, the cultural and creative industries can be seen and approached as a 'new' form of economy using human and creative capital instead of limited physical resources or marked by a changed consumption paradigm placing customers' preferences ahead of producers'. In other words, the cultural and creative industries bring new dimensions to creative development and entrepreneurial dynamics, in turn, enabling businesses to develop and create new employment opportunities and economic growth as a consequence (Johannisson and Rylander 2010). Further arguments in line with this reasoning are provided by Pine and Gilmore (2014), who stated that the sector provides opportunities to reduce customer 'sacrifice' in consumption, meaning that businesses, to be competitive, now must customize products and charge them with authenticity, a development that will eventually transform business behaviour throughout the advanced economy.

The cultural and creative economy as a foundation for the craft beer movement

The creative economy framework is understood as a way to stimulate and revitalize economic development, and promoting the creative and cultural industries and economy has emerged as a more or less unavoidable approach to redirecting the future of deindustrialized places and regions (Florida 2002; Hesmondhalgh 2002; Pine and Gilmore 2014). UNESCO (n.d.) has defined the creative economy as a sector consisting of organized activities whose principal purpose is the production or reproduction, promotion, distribution, and/or commercialization of goods, services, and activities of a cultural, artistic, and heritage-related nature. While the creative economy approach is criticized for lacking conceptual rigour (Galloway and Dunlop 2007), it is also valued because it can unite passionate people in striving to reshape places, work, art, and regions. The approach stresses individual determination and promotes the idea that for an industry to be competitive, it needs to communicate, reproduce, and explore something 'more' and 'new', so consumers will be interested in buying its products or services (Pine and Gilmore 2014). Along these lines, the European Union is addressing how economic growth is dependent on progressive and 'smart' ideas in order to overcome structural weaknesses, improve competitiveness, and increase productivity (European Union 2010), and the UNESCO Creative City Network (UCCN) has been initiated to promote sustainable development via culture and creativity (Hosagrahar 2017). Businesses are increasingly striving to integrate culture, creativity, and experience into their offerings, and cities and regions are identifying new and unique ways to attract residents and competent labour, to respond to changes in the competitive landscape. Examples from the tourism sector can be seen in gastronomic-oriented regional tours, where visits are made to farms and production sites, and to the restaurants where the finished products are served, or in the viticulture and wine sector, where the soil, production processes, and even storage facilities attract visitor interest (Lin et al. 2010; Bonow and Rytkönen 2012).

Hesmondhalgh (2002), building on William's notion of a 'signifying system' (1981, 11), wrote about how creative industries produce social meaning by adding experiential dimensions and symbolic values to products or services. To be competitive in the globalized economy, producers need to create products and services that provide vivid and memorable experiences. Champagne is perhaps the most famous example of this. Through the creation of 'aristocratic genealogies and myths of patrimony' (Trubek 2008, 25), champagne was made an eloquent marker of civilized life among the international bourgeoisie during the belle époque (Guy 2003). A more recent example is the American 'pale ale movement', in which the local community context is obvious in the breweries' operations and products, and local mythology and nature are vividly used in company names, product stories, and product names to build competitive edge (Murray and Kline 2015). This links to the work of Florida (2002), Landry (2015), and Scott (2006), who all spoke of how creative economies are led by a 'creative class', i.e. people who strive to create new ideas or technology by endowing symbolic and cultural capital. These people can also break new ground as their decisions to settle in particular places are not determined primarily by available job opportunities, but rather by the experienced capacity of places to offer 'something more', such as quality of life, tolerance of alternative ways of life, and proximity to university education (Florida 2002).

The craft beer segment

The craft beer movement exemplifies this development. From a global, Western perspective, the production and consumption of beer took a radical turn starting in the mid-19th century when brewing became industrial. From being dominated by local, often small, and plentiful brewers in each town, larger and larger companies started evolving, reducing the number of small-scale producers to virtually zero (Faxälv and Olofsson 2007; Pascua et al. 2016). Not only did brewing become industrial, but the types of beer produced also often developed into mass-produced commodities with little or no character, tradition, or culture. In the USA, only 44 brewing companies remained by the end of the 1970s (Brewers Association n.d.). The same trajectory was evident in Sweden: in the 1950s, a few gigantic breweries emerged, and the concentration continued into the 1990s when only around 20 breweries remained in the entire country (Faxälv and Olofsson 2007). However, demand has increased for more complex and distinctive types of beer (Nilsson 2007). This growing interest in 'local' food and drink, in celebrating and fostering authenticity, has been referred to as a counter-movement to globalization (Wilks 1995; Leitch 2003). As a favoured way to enlist every day, small-scale agricultural practices and handcrafted food preparation in regional development, this trend, which some call 'normative localism' and others 'neolocalism' (Flack 1997; Pezzi 2017), refers to a desire to 'reconnect' producers and consumers (Kneafsey et al., 2008), and to find associations between particular products or services and their producers through place, landscape, and cultural identities (Flack 1997; Kneafsey et al. 2008).

The craft beer segment comprises small and independently owned breweries producing ale, stout, porter, and lager made entirely or mostly from malt, and not diluted with adjuncts such as corn or rice (Brewers Association n.d.). For the consumer, craft beer is largely associated with small brewing facilities such as microbreweries selling through distributors or retailers, brewpubs selling directly to the consumer at the production site, and even home brewing or nanobreweries whose production is on a very small scale (Elzinga et al. 2015). Today, craft beer is understood as a concept symbolizing a localized response to the stale brands and tastes of macrobrewery beer, emphasizing quality, flavour, diversity, and limited production quantities

(Gatrell et al. 2018). The segment is adding new taste signatures to beer and new packaging (Elzinga et al. 2015), building on imagery of anthropomorphism, insiderness, personification, and environmental embeddedness (Hede and Watne 2013). Much of the movement appears to be driven by millennial producers and consumers coming together in a commitment to social causes and environmental sustainability (McWilliams 2014).

A symbolic turning point in the transformation of the craft beer segment was the Great American Beer Festival in Boulder, Colorado, in 1982 (Pascua et al. 2016). In Boulder, brewers gathered, and still gather, to sample and compete for the best beer. Today, the festival offers over 3,500 types of beer to over 60,000 visitors, hosting competitions in a multitude of beer categories (Great American Beer Festival n.d.). For city officials, the festival has been a positive experience from the outset because the visitors to the event, centring on craft beer as food more than liquid, did not generally become drunk and cause damage to municipal property (Elzinga et al. 2015). The numbers of craft brewers in the USA grew from eight in 1980, to 537 in 1994, and to over 4,000 in 2015 (Brewers Association n.d.). The US experience, leading in terms of consumption, production, and research, shows the craft beer segment peaking around the turn of the millennium, but increasing again after 2010 (Elzinga et al. 2015). The segment's growth has been higher in less religious regions, and it has been shown that its consumers are in a higher average income category (Barajas et al. 2017).

Developments in Sweden have trailed those in the USA. In the early 1990s, the production and consumption of beer began to change, with small-scale craft brewers again emerging, and increasing consumer interest in high-quality English or American-style ales and pale ales. In Sweden as a whole, the number of craft brewers has been growing continuously, from around 50 in 2007 to over 170 ten years later (Sveriges Mikrobryggerier, n.d.). In 2016, the average turnover of a craft brewer was SEK 5.4 million with a median of SEK 2.3 million. Selling craft beer to pubs and restaurants is important, as is distribution through Systembolaget, a government-owned chain of liquor stores in Sweden, the only retailer allowed to sell alcoholic beverages containing over 3.5% alcohol by volume, and craft breweries supplement these sales channels by operating pubs and restaurants of their own (Föreningen Sveriges Oberoende Småbryggerier and Lantbrukarnas Riksförbund 2018).

As is evident from this overview of beer production, the craft beer trend has taken a strong hold in the leading craft beer nation, the USA, as well as in Sweden. After a downturn around the turn of the millennium, the number of craft beer producers increased again, and the sector now also encompasses beer tourism, as travellers increasingly seek local and authentic experiences. In their study of visitors to North Carolina breweries, Kraftchick et al. (2014) considered how the innovative tendencies of brewers, who often experimented with new styles and flavours, contributed to the tourism experience. An Australian study by Argent (2018) highlighted that rural craft beer entrepreneurs value place and embeddedness, and desire to advance local or regional development. In comparison, the 'typical' beer tourist is interested in visiting a brewery, beer festival, or beer show to taste and experience the beer, its making, and roots in place and local heritage (Murray and Kline 2015; Fletchall 2016). The social status of consuming 'real' beer, or rather ale, was further stressed by Thurnell-Reed (2016), who described how more intellectual beer consumption has recently blossomed in the UK, both emerging from and simultaneously attracting localism movements and hipster culture.

The reinvention of beer brewing in Jämtland

Until the early 1900s in Jämtland, beer was produced in brewing cottages on small farms, mostly producing top-fermented ale and stout types of beer. At the end of the 19th century, low fermentation processes were introduced from Germany, eventually making lager and pilsner types the most popular local beers (Faxälv and Olofsson 2007). Industrialization, taxation, and the rise of the sobriety movement in the early 1900s changed the preconditions of brewing, and small-scale breweries were gradually replaced by larger ones, until only one brewery remained in the entire region by the early 1990s, and even it closed in 1992 (Berglund 2007; Faxälv and Berglund 2007).

It was not until 1996 that organized microbrewing began re-emerging in Jämtland, and now there are ten small-scale breweries in the region, and more that are planning to start up. New breweries are steadily opening, and all are thriving on the strong demand for local, craft beer: 'The beer trend in Sweden is really strong today – it wasn't like this five, or even two years ago – nowadays people keep asking for locally produced beer' (Local craft beer producer, 33).

The first small-scale brewery was Jämtlands Bryggeri, which opened in the small village Pilgrimstad, outside Östersund, in 1995. The brewery was inspired by the pilgrims who, on their way to the holy grave of Olav in Trondheim, Norway, stayed at the site and drank the clean water there. The brewery played a pioneering role in the Swedish craft beer sector by aiming for high quality, using English malt, and concentrating on brewing English types of ale, while headed by an English brewmaster. The brewery, one of the first small-scale craft beer producers in Sweden, used local mythology and stories to inspire its product names. It had a big impact on local consumers, and achieved a quality that made beer drinkers elsewhere interested as well. The brewery has won 133 medals at the annual Stockholm Beer and Whiskey Festival. 'We are by far the most award-winning brewery in Sweden', is a fair claim made by the CEO, who has been an inspirational voice for a rising generation of beer producers in Jämtland. The brewery continues producing widely popular ales, sold throughout Sweden and branded using local legends for inspiration and marketing. Jämtlands Bryggeri now produces around 1,000,000 L of 16 types of beer every year, as well as seasonal beers for the Christmas and Easter holidays.

It took an additional 15 years before the next brewery, Klövsjö Gårdsbryggeri (KGB), was established in 2010. This brewery produces 15 types of ale for a total production run of 15,000 L a year, using small amounts of hops produced on its own farm and local honey to flavour some beers. It started as a home brewery after the founder became inspired by taking a course in the art of making craft beer. Inspiration also came from the USA, as the founder explained: 'It spread from the US, [the idea] that it was possible to make really good beer at home'. In addition to brewing, KGB also runs an ambitious Jämtlandish–Mexican crossover restaurant in conjunction with the brewery. The beer is brewed in a converted barn from the 1850s, where 'looking through the windows, you see parts of the mountains of Jämtland extending in the background'. Today, it is part of the Économusée Artisans at Work network, intended to showcase traditional trades and knowhow around the world.

Another of the small breweries, Jemtehed & Brandes nanobrewery, which is rapidly growing and aims to increase its output from today's 20,000 to 80,000 L per year in a few years, production was initially oriented towards ales, but has since expanded to include several types of lager as well, such as the top-selling Östersund City Lager. Åre Bryggcompagni, which sold its first beer in 2013 and only recently moved into a new and larger brewery, has grown to produce around 25,000 L per year in the short time since its start-up. It also focuses on ale-type beers, but has added lagers and lambic-type beers to its output. Other craft brewers in the region have outputs similar to, or smaller than, those of KGB, Jemtehed & Brande, and Åre Bryggcompagni, and most of them focus on ale-type beers, whereas several also have attempted to start producing lagers.

Most of the brewers refer to the American craft beer movement as an important source of inspiration, but many also talk of the importance of the national resource centre for artisan food, located outside Östersund. This centre, Eldrimner, has expert advisors and runs courses and field trips to support artisan food producers in Sweden. The centre also arranges a food fair every two years to spread ideas and knowledge, certifies products, recognizes high-quality products, and distributes a magazine four times a year. Eldrimner's activities have been relevant to Swedish artisan food production, particularly in Jämtland, whose geographical proximity to the centre has been an advantage since it opened in 1995 (Eldrimner, n.d.; von Friedrichs and Skoglund 2012). Several of the local brewers would like to work more closely with Eldrimner, although its focus on primarily using local ingredients may be difficult for the brewers:

> They push for local ingredients ... and I feel they don't support us that much. It's difficult for us to be entirely local ... we need ingredients that cannot be grown here.
>
> (Local craft beer producer, 61)

Most of the brewers do not cite increasing revenues, profits, or size – i.e. the traditional economic growth motives of entrepreneurs and businesses – as basic motivations for their activities. Instead, they are often driven by passion, sometimes to produce high-quality beer, and by a desire to contribute to local development. Few of them earn large profits from brewing, and several are the so-called *combinateurs*, i.e. having another job on the side so they can run their brewing business, combining brewing with running a restaurant, or bundling tourism activities into package deals:

> Initially I wasn't particularly interested in beer ... but then I went to the US, also Stockholm, visited some really good bars, then, my brother-in-law, he is a sommelier, and this other guy, he was very interested in cooking. So you know, food and drink came together ... so we decided to go for that combination.
>
> (Local craft beer producer, 40)

We don't have the ambition to brew volume, but we want to combine beer brewing with a café and nature tourism excursions (Local craft beer producer, 46).

Among the breweries, there are even cases of owners turning down outside investment, from local as well as large national investors, in order not to lose control of the artisan dimension. As one owner explained: 'It's this drive to find better and better recipes, make better beer, get a good response from people ... we never really had any financial motivations'. Another brewer explained: 'You can call it a passion ... we made lots of beer on a hobby level ... we had this urge to develop, come up with new recipes, improve our beer. And then, this positive response from people, that too. But financial? ... No, not really' (Local craft beer producer, 41)!

Establishing a business in such a rural location as Jämtland has its difficulties, for example, transporting and distributing beer to consumers and lack of a large local customer base. To overcome the difficulties of geographic isolation, the brewers strive to cooperate as much as possible. This strategy is traceable to the cooperative attitude of the pioneering Jämtlands Bryggeri brewery, which believed that it was important to support the growing interest in craft beer production, even if it meant competition. Mutual support occasionally entails exchanging ideas and recipes, but mostly means helping one another with transportation and distribution and, if someone is lacking an ingredient, supplying it from one's inventory. The brewers visit one another and run courses to increase all their brewing 'know-how'. Cooperation is not restricted to fellow brewers, but also extends to other local producers, such as local bakeries, dairies, butchers, and fishermen.

Beyond working hard to produce high-quality beer, many of the producers conceive their local connections as vital for their business. Place and locality, they say, are important for their credibility, and locally known places have inspired the names of beers such as Östersund City Lager, Great Lake

Monster beer (referring to a monster claimed to live in the 90-m-deep lake Storsjön in Jämtland), Klövsjöbrygd, and the beers Brakk, Klumpen, and Sielken, named after nearby mountains. To strengthen the local connections, the brewers use old photographs or short historical narratives on the bottle labels. Even friends' names are used as inspiration, as in the case of the Oppistuggu beers, referring to the tradition of brewing farm beer in small *bryggstu* cottages, or the Mighty Mofaza beer: 'We try to come up with stories about old friends, beer drinkers – we turn them into superheroes who drink our beer' (Local craft beer producer, 41). The brewers also use natural scenery as a source of inspiration: 'There's a jagged mountain peak seen from our window that is called Santa, and this inspired us to make the Christmas beer Santa' (Local craft beer producer, 46). Although some of the brewers have moved from other parts of Sweden, or even from elsewhere in the world, most of them were born and raised in the region, and they display a strong desire to contribute to local identity and development. The locality is therefore not only a source of inspiration for the products and brand names, but also encompasses an end in itself. The goal is to create something positive for the local community of which they are part, and for the environment. One of the CEOs explained: 'The idea was to generate something sustainable, to generate something that supports others in our locality ... providing more opportunities for people locally' (Local craft beer producer, 46). Another illustration of this local commitment is the 'community beer' produced by one of the breweries, a portion of the sales of which goes to fund local ventures: 'From each Community Beer [sold], we donate a part to local development projects – that's sort of part of our philosophy of how to act as a business' (Local craft beer producer, 40).

Regarding their target market, most of the craft beer produced in Jämtland is delivered to the national alcohol monopoly of Sweden, Systembolaget, for national distribution. Some see this as an opportunity, while others see Systembolaget as complicated to deal with and hindering their development. This means that if the local producers of alcoholic beverages want to distribute their products to a wider customer base outside their region, they must transport their products to the central warehouse of Systembolaget, located some 600–800 km from the breweries in Jämtland. The logistics and transportation involved are difficult for some, so local producers may choose to deliver directly to local or regional high-end restaurants and pubs. They can also distribute via local Systembolaget stores (three in Jämtland), in effect creating a restricted and regionalized market segment.

Five of the brewers also run their own restaurants where they serve their beer, mostly as the main attraction. This naturally associates these producers with tourism, since many of them cater to tourists. Some also offer tours of their breweries and see great potential in further developing the tourism connection to their breweries, for example, through offering study visits and brewing courses. Also, a beer festival is held every year in Östersund, when the brewers present their products at local restaurants, and locals and visitors have the chance to taste the latest malts. In 2017, another beer festival was held in east Jämtland, as well as a 'slow food'-inspired 'Beerstock' in Östersund. Although many of the brewers are aware of the challenges of being located in the periphery – difficult transport and logistics, few restaurants, and a small customer base – they still see themselves as contributing to the local and regional brands, and as tourist attractions. Some even call tourism a prerequisite for their beer production: 'Without tourism, we would never have been able to open a brewery here!' (Local craft beer producer, 33).

Successful beyond profits?

As illustrated earlier, creativity can be expressed through narratives of identity and social differentiation as well as through one's priorities (Waitt and Gibson 2009). In this framing, local food and food production are entangled in complex webs of significance, and imagined elements guide both the production and marketing of craft beer in Jämtland. Connected to locality and place, craft beer offers meanings and specific relationships to its producers and consumers. Great Lake Monster, Östersund City Lager, and other local beers express the role of heritage and social and cultural identities. In line with this, the brewers adhere to an alternative economic approach when describing how their work does not primarily target growth in a traditional business sense. Instead of increasing revenues, profits, or turnover, the producers take an alternative road, centring their work on other dimensions, namely, the social, cultural, and ecological.

This is, in business terms, a rather unusual perspective, linked to the concept of community entrepreneurship in which the local and immediate environment of the entrepreneurs motivates and legitimizes activity (Johannisson 1990). The creative economy framework, increasingly used to elevate the operations and actions of businesses and entrepreneurs at different levels in society, does not necessarily contribute to economic change at a local or regional scale (Trubek 2008), but may instead enhance the sustainable development potentials of localities and places in the margins.

This is vividly illustrated by the brewers in Jämtland, who take inspiration in local history and context, using nicknames of childhood friends or local places with a kind of 'mythological' value in branding. They celebrate the locally unique, entangled within a framework of care in order to 'make a difference' (Massey 2005, p. 11). Instead of globalization fostering cultural homogenization and disrupted places (Ritzer 2011), distinctiveness is promoted through local entrepreneurship, policy measures, as well as tourism development efforts (de Jong and Varley 2018). Through the practices of production and consumption, a web of images and feelings associated with the locality is woven, and a sense of belonging to the area is created or reinforced when fellowship, solidarity, and relationships are established in upholding local history and distinctiveness (Sjölander-Lindqvist and Cinque 2014).

In other words, the marketing of the beer is closely connected with place and with the framework of local cultural identity, as locally produced foodstuffs are envisioned as traditional, rooted in time and place, forging a binding connection between people, society, and place (Hede and Watne 2013). By addressing these aspects in their products, the brewers clearly invoke the symbolic and experiential dimensions singled out by Pine and Gilmore (1998), and the creative place aspects of the creative economy (Florida 2002).

Embedded neolocalism (Flack 1997; Pezzi 2017) is here evident in the promoted uniqueness of the beer, with local geography and stories being sold as distinct features enabling consumers to reconnect with the specificities of the places where the breweries are located. The producers' networks, competence-raising measures, and investments they put into their production are motivated by a desire to produce high-quality beer for the satisfaction of making good beer and living a good life, and to establish and strengthen links with local history, and natural and cultural heritage (cf. Argent 2018; McWilliams 2014). These factors are at the heart of craft beer production in Jämtland. Most brewers are not primarily seeking profit. Rather, their work is a way of life driven by enthusiasm for beer and a desire to help create sustainable local communities in the margins of northern Europe, even though it is difficult to be completely local, organic, or ecological due to the difficulties of finding all the right ingredients for such a product at this latitude.

Although much of the inspiration in Jämtland may have come from the dramatically growing craft beer scene, primarily in the USA and the UK, courses run by Eldrimner – the national resource centre for artisan food – and the brewers themselves have contributed greatly to the steady growth of local artisanal food production, including beer. Together with its ambition to recover old traditions and recipes, Eldrimner can be said to be collaborating in elevating the role of local and regional heritage in gastronomic efforts. While the 'local' can be idealized, despite sometimes actually defending elitist and reactionary sentiments (DuPuis and Goodman 2005), celebrations of the local can also been said to support more authentic relations between consumers and producers as well as being used as a tool to counteract homogenization. While Leitch (2003) suggested that food labelled as 'local' has 'discursive currency' in that we, through foodstuffs, debate the implications of globalization for cultural identity, Wilk (1995) defined the global–local dynamic as comprising 'structures of common difference'. By adapting and preserving local traditions, he argues, the impact of globalization can be defeated.

As suggested, tourists are seeking gastronomic experiences, ranging from eating and drinking locally produced food to wider experiences, such as meeting local producers, studying production processes, learning about local customs, traditions, and products, and learning how to prepare food in local ways (Bonow and Rytkönen 2012; Fletchall 2016; Slocum 2016). Although the brewers are aware of the tourism potential, which some of them try to exploit to support their livelihoods, business politics and policies are

understood as hindrances. For example, transport and logistics are complicated when shipping the products, particularly given the – from the brewers'
standpoint – problematic national alcohol legislation. This leaves some of
them disappointed at the lack of support from their regional and municipal
business support systems, which cannot see the actual or potential contribution of beer making to local and regional development. These business
support systems are simply not aligned with craft beer production and its
potential to promote regional development. The area's rurality is in many
senses a problem to overcome, but in another sense, this rurality also provides a foundation for cooperation and networking. It is evident that the
beer producers see the value and necessity of rural social bonds in managing
the distance to consumers. To overcome these barriers, the brewers have
opted for close-knit networks and cooperation, both among one another
and between themselves and other gastronomy actors in their respective
communities.

Concluding remarks: the way forward?

Our case study of the northern Swedish region of Jämtland, where small-
scale breweries have proliferated, regaining market power after the local
brewing business had become more or less extinct, provides a critical examination of craft beer and related tourism in a peripheral and sparsely
populated area where gastronomic development has been comparatively
successful. By focusing on the Jämtland case, we have expanded examination of the craft beer movement beyond its US origins and have learned
more about the brewers' motives for crafting beer. We have illustrated how
craft beer production is contextually situated, and how gastronomic efforts
can link people, places, and businesses. Today, there are 13 thriving breweries in the Jämtland region, taking inspiration from local traditions and the
craft beer movement in the USA and the UK. Though small in scale and
mostly not run primarily to seek profit, they still provide the brewers with
pride and identity; they also provide incentives for tourism, although this
is not a key motivator of the brewers themselves. The conclusions concern
several key themes, connecting local cultural heritage, local craft beer brewing, and the possible impact of such brewing on regional tourism within
an ethical framework centred on care for the local community and natural
environment.

In line with Argent's (2018) line of reasoning, craft beer brewers often
wish to contribute to holistic local development, which is why their businesses, given growing interest in craft beer (Fletchall 2016; Slocum 2016),
can be important drivers of tourism. This is relevant not least to rural areas
where the integration of culture, creativity, and experience can strengthen
touristic attractiveness. Because foodstuffs are not only essential commodities but also objects of social and cultural heritage, they can serve as potential 'vehicles' for innovation and knowledge creation that can support and

drive regional development. From a policy perspective, it would be beneficial for Jämtland to extend its support systems for the tourism, cultural, and creative industries to cover gastronomy, including craft beer production. This could include support in providing the sector with a common transport and logistics system, arranging traditional business courses, and inspiring further knowledge exchange and collaboration opportunities among gastronomy actors. Some of the studied brewers rely on tourism and have explored tourism opportunities by developing local community concepts through networks, for example, by packaging gastronomic experiences with other small-scale food producers. Meanwhile, many producers are yet to connect to or develop tourism strategies, leaving great potential for further development of rural tourism concepts. The Jämtland region indirectly benefits from the breweries as well as from their brand names and individual beer names. There would seem to be further potential in using heritage to increase craft beer demand and promote tourism. In these times, when gastronomes are interested in food and drink beyond their actual consumption, incorporating the connection between taste, local culture, and production in extended producer cooperation could prove essential.

Drawing on the results, it can be concluded that the context of the local community matters. While American pale ales may be a source of inspiration, local mythology and nature matter even more, as they are vividly used in company names and brands, product stories, and product names. Some of the brewers rely on tourism and exploit tourism opportunities by developing local community concepts through producer networks. For the producers, place and its qualities enrich practice, which is why decision makers and planners should be aware of the potentials and implications of the 'localism' turn. The producers' emphasis on place and care for community, evident in their everyday practices, in the memories and experiences embedded in the brewing of craft beer, and in the mobilization of these tangible and intangible imaginings, can, if not properly consolidated into policy and planning, cause unnecessary tension (Healy 2018).

Meanwhile, many producers are yet to connect to and develop tourism strategies, leaving great potential for the further development of rural tourism concepts. The present findings would be applicable to many similar rural regions where gastronomy, craft beer production in particular, is gathering momentum and producing direct and indirect opportunities for employment and new business development, as well as strengthening community bonds and benefits (Bessière 2017). Furthermore, as the brewers are putting considerable emphasis on sustainability, the beer sector, together with many other local food producers and local gastronomy actors, has the capacity to serve as a role model in business development, increasing its attractiveness and symbolic value among local and external consumers, as well as strengthening tourism development opportunities.

Finally, the small-scale production of beer and other food types is thriving in the region of Jämtland, a development that has utilized local and regional cultural heritage as an inspirational asset (cf. von Friedrichs and Skoglund 2011). This study illustrates how the beer producers have used a sense of place as an important departure point. Driven by passion and enthusiasm for craft beer production and sustainable livelihoods, they have advanced local livelihood opportunities at the same time as contributing to local community development through joint networks and efforts building on an ethical framework. Drawing on the symbolic and cultural capital of place, the brewers' creativity has enhanced the quality of life in this peripheral locality.

References

Argent, Neil. 2018. "Heading Down to the Local? Australian Rural Development and the Evolving Spaciality of the Craft Beer Sector." *Journal of Rural Studies*, 61: 84–99.

Badii, Michela. 2013. "Traditional Food Heritage in Contemporary Tuscany: Local Networks and Global Policies Around the Zolfino Bean." *Ethnologies*, 35 (2): 129–145.

Barajas, Jesus, Geoff Boeing and Julie Wartell. 2017. "Neighborhood Change, One Pint at a Time: The Impact of Local Characteristics on Craft Breweries." In: *Untapped: Exploring the Cultural Dimensions of Craft Beer*, edited by Nathaniel. G. Chapman, J. Slade Lellock, and Cameron D. Lippard, 155–176. Morgantown, WV: West Virginia University Press.

Beckerman, Märit. 2004. "Development of Successful Food Packaging and Logistics in Sweden since 1945." In: *Logistics Research Network Conference Proceedings*, edited by Edward Sweeney, John Mee, Bernd Huber, Brian Fynes, and Pietro Evangelista, 58–66. Chartered Institute of Transport and Logistics. Dublin.

Berglund, Anna. 2007. "Introduktion." In *Öl och dricka – dryckestillverkning i Jämtland*, edited by Anna Berglund, 5. Eldrimner, Ås.

Bessière, Jacinthe. 2017. "Tourism as a Strategy for Redeployment in the Local Agrifood Supply: The case of Midi-Pyrénées." *Gastronomy and Tourism*, 2 (4): 273–285.

Bonow, Madeleine and Paula Rytkönen. 2012. "Gastronomy and Tourism as a Regional Development Tool – The Case of Jämtland." *Advances in Food, Hospitality and Tourism*, 2 (1): 2–10.

Brewers Association. n.d. "History of Craft brewing". Accessed March 20, 2018. https://www.brewersassociation.org/brewers-association/history/history-of-craft-brewing/

De Jong, Anna and Peter Varley. 2017. "Food Tourism Policy: Deconstructing Boundaries of Taste and Class." *Tourism Management*, 60: 212–222.

Dunn, Alison and Mark Wickham. 2015. "Building Product Awareness and Distribution Channels in Crowded Markets: An analysis of craft breweries in the USA." *Academy of Taiwan Business Management Review*, 11 (1): 60–67.

DuPuis, E. Melanie and David Goodman. 2005. "Should We Go 'Home' to Eat? Toward a Reflexive Politics of Localism." *Rural Studies*, 21 (3): 359–371.

Eldrimner, n.d. "Om Eldrimner." Accessed March 20, 2018. https://www.eldrimner.com/om-eldrimner/31374.eldrimner.html.

Elzinga, Kenneth, Carol Horton Tremblay and Victor J. 2015. "Craft Beer in the United States: History, Numbers, and Geography." *Wine Economics*, 10 (3): 242–274.

European Commission. 2010. Communication from the Commission to the European Parliament, the Council, the European Economic and Social Committee and the Committee of the Regions. Regional Policy contributing to smart growth in Europe 2020. European Commission.

Faxälv, Anna and Berglund, Anna. 2007. "Dagens öl i Jämtland och Härjedalen." In *Öl och dricka – dryckestillverkning i Jämtland*, edited by Anna Berglund, 33. Eldrimner, Ås.

Faxälv, Anna and Olofsson, Björn. 2007. "Ölets historia." In *Öl och dricka - dryckestillverkning i Jämtland*, edited by Anna Berglund, 42–47. Eldrimner, Ås.

Flack, Wes. 1997. "American Microbreweries and Neolocalism: "Ale-ing" for a Sense of Place." *Journal of Cultural Geography*, 16 (2): 37–53.

Fletchall, Ann M. 2016. "Place-making through Beer Drinking: A Case Study of Montana's Craft Breweries." *Geographical Review*, 106 (4): 539–566.

Florida, Richard. 2002. *The Rise of the Creative Class: And How it's Transforming Work, Leisure, Community and Everyday Life*. New York: Basic Books.

Föreningen Sveriges Oberoende Småbryggerier & Lantbrukarnas Riksförbund. 2018. Svenska Småbryggerier i Siffror 2018. Accessed September 15, 2018. https://www.lrf.se/globalassets/dokument/mitt-lrf/nyheter/2018/svenska-smabryggerier-i-siffror-2018-liten-fil.pdf.

Galloway, Susan and Stewart Dunlop. 2007. "A Critique of Definitions of the Cultural and Creative Industries in Public Policy." *International Journal Public Policy*, 13 (1): 17–31.

Gatrell, Jay, Neil Reid and Thomas L. Steiger. 2018. "Branding Spaces: Place, Region, Sustainability and the American Craft Beer Industry." *Applied Geography*, 90: 360–370.

Great American Beer Festival. n.d. www.greatamericanbeerfestival.com. Accessed May 10, 2017.

Guy, Kolleen. 2003. *When Champagne Became French*. Baltimore, MD: Johns Hopkins University Press.

Healy, Patsy. 2018. "Creating Public Value through Caring for Place." *Policy & Politics*, 46 (1): 65–79.

Hede, Anne-Marie and Torgeir Watne. 2013. "Leveraging the Human Side of the Brand Using A Sense of Place: Case Studies of Craft Breweries." *Journal of Marketing Management*, 29 (1–2): 207–224.

Hesmondhalgh, David. 2002. *The Cultural Industries*. London: Sage Publications.

Hosagrahar, Jyoti. 2017. "Culture and Creativity for Sustainable Urban Development." In *Proceedings of Valuing and Evaluating Creativity for Sustainable Regional Development*, edited by Daniel Laven and Wilhelm Skoglund, 20–22. Östersund: Mid Sweden University.

Johannisson, Bengt. 1990. "Community Entrepreneurship – Cases and Conceptualization." *Entrepreneurship & Regional Development*, 2 (1): 71–88.

Johannisson, Bengt, and David Rylander. 2010. *Entreprenörskap i regioners tjänst. Ingångar till nya näringar genom design, upplevelser, kulturarv*. Jönköping: Jönköping International Business School.

Johns, Nick and Jan Mattsson. 2005. "Destination Development through Entrepreneurship: A Comparison of Two Cases." *Tourism Management*, 26 (4): 605–616.

Kneafsey, Moya, Rosie Cox, Lewis Holloway, Elizabeth Dowler, Laura Venn and Helena Tuomainen. 2008. *Reconnecting Consumers, Consumers and Food: Exploring Alternatives*. Oxford: Berg.

Kraftchick, Jennifer Francioni, Erick T. Byrd, Bonnie Canziani and Nancy J. Gladwell. 2014. "Understanding Beer Tourist Motivation." *Tourism Management Practices*, 12: 41–47.

Landry, Charles. 2015. *Cities of Ambition*. UK, Gloucestershire: Comedia.

Lee, Jenny. 2009. "The Market Hall Revisited: Cultures of Consumption in Urban Food Retail During the Long Twentieth Century." PhD diss., Linköping University.

Leitch, Alison. 2003. "Slow Food and the Politics of Pork Fat: Italian Food and European Identity." *Ethnos*, 68 (4): 437–462.

Lin, Yi-Chin, Thomas E. Pearson, Liping A. Cai. 2010. "Food as a Form of Destination Identity: A Tourism Destination Brand Perspective." *Tourism and Hospitality Studies*, 11 (1): 30–48.

Low, Setha M. and Denise Lawrence-Zúñiga. 2003. "Locating Culture." In *The Anthropology of Space and Place: Locating Culture*, edited by Setha M. Low and Denise Lawrence-Zúñiga, 1–48. Malden, MA and Oxford: Blackwell.

Lundqvist, Evelina. 2018. *Att öka exporten i Jämtland Härjedalens kreativa och kulturella företag – förutsättningar, utmaningar och möjligheter*. Stockholm: The Good Tribe.

Massey, Doreen. 2005. *For Space*. London: Sage Publications Ltd.

McAreavey, Ruth and John McDonagh. 2011. "Sustainable Rural Tourism: Lessons for Rural Development." *Sociologia Ruralis*, 51 (2):175–94.

McWilliams, James. 2014. "The Ecological Creed of Craft Beer." *Conservation Magazine*, March 14, 2014. http://conservationmagazine.org/2014/03/sustainable-practices-in-craft-brewing.

Murray, Alison and Carol Kline. 2015. "Rural Tourism and the Craft Beer Experience: Factors Influencing Brand Loyalty in Rural North Carolina, USA." *Journal of Sustainable Tourism*, 23: 1198–1216.

Nilsson, Mats. 2007. *Den hemlige kocken: Det okända fusket med maten på din tallrik*. Stockholm: Ordfront.

Pascua, Michael, Scott Guehne, and Mdsadaf Mondal. 2016. "History of Craft Beer." Master Thesis., California State University San Marcos.

Pezzi, Maria Giulia. 2017. "From Peripheral Hamlet to Craft Beer Capital: Appechio and the 'Alogastronomia'." *Italian Journal of Planning Practice*, 7 (1): 154–185.

Pine II, B. Joseph and James H. Gilmore. 1998. "Welcome to the Experience Economy." *Harvard Business Review*, July–August, 97–105.

Pine, B. Joseph and James H. Gilmore. 2014. "A Leader's Guide to Innovation in the Experience Economy." *Strategy and Leadership*, 42 (1): 24–29.

Regionfakta, n.d. Jämtlands län. "Fakta och perspektiv." Accessed March 20, 2018. http://www.regionfakta.com/jamtlands-lan.

Regionförbundet Jämtlands län. 2013. "Prioritering hållbar tillväxt" In *Regional Utvecklingsstrategi 2014–2030*, 23–25. Östersund: Regionförbundet Jämtlands län.

Richards, Greg. 2011. "Creativity and Tourism: The State of the Art." *Annals of Tourism Research*, 38 (4): 1225–1253.

Ritzer, George. 1993. *The McDonaldization of Society*. Thousand Oaks, CA: Sage.

Rodman, Margaret C. 1992. "Empowering Place: Multilocality and Multivocality." *American Anthropologist*, 94 (3): 640–656.

Rolén, Mats, and Lars Thomasson. 1990. *Jämtland/Härjedalens historia 1880–1980*. Östersund: Jämtlands läns museum.

Scott, Allen J. 2006. "Creative Cities: Conceptual Issues and Policy Questions." *Journal of Urban Affairs*, 28: 1–17.

Seyfang, Gill. 2006. "Ecological Citizenship and Sustainable Consumption: Examining Local Organic Food Networks." *Rural Studies*, 22 (4): 383–395.

Sjölander-Lindqvist, Annelie and Serena Cinque. 2014. "Locality Management Through Cultural Diversity: The Case of the Majella National Park, Italy." *Journal of Food, Culture and Society*, 17 (1): 143–160.

Slocum, Susan L. 2016. "Understanding Tourism Support for a Craft Beer Trail: The Case of Loudoun County, Virginia." *Tourism Planning and Development*, 13 (3): 292–309.

Sveriges Mikrobryggerier. n.d. Accessed May 8, 2018. http://www.sverigesmikrobryggerier.se.

Thurnell-Reed, Thomas. 2018. "The Embourgeoisement of Beer: Changing Practices of 'Real Ale' Consumption." *Journal of Consumer Culture*, 18 (4): 539–557.

Trubek, Amy B. 2008. *The Taste of Place: A Cultural Journey into Terroir*. Berkeley, CA, Los Angeles, CA and London: University of California Press.

UNESCO. n.d. "Creative Industries." Accessed March 23, 2018. http://www.unesco.org/new/en/santiago/culture/creative-industries/.

Von Friedrichs, Yvonne and Wilhelm Skoglund. 2011. "Gastronomi som kraft för regional utveckling." In *Gastronomins politiska geografi*, edited by Bonow, Madeleine and Paulina Rytkönen, 19–43. Motala: Svenska sällskapet för antropologi och geografi.

Waitt, Gordon and Chris Gibson. 2009. "Creative Small Cities: Rethinking the Creative Economy in Place." *Urban Studies*, 46 (5–6): 1223–1246.

Wilk, R. 1995. "Learning to be Local in Belize: Global Systems of Common Difference." In *Worlds Apart: Modernity through the Prism of the Local*, edited by Daniel Miller, 110–133. London: Routledge.

William, R. 1981. *Culture*. London: Fontana.

12 From landscapes to drinkscapes

Craft beer, tourism, and local development in the Italian Apennines

Maria Giulia Pezzi

Introduction

How local actors and communities respond to the implications of peripherality through a variety of tourism-related strategies is a topic of increasing importance. Peripheral areas, indeed, are generally considered to be endowed with a wealth of key environmental and cultural resources of many different kinds, which could be seen as a means to potentially attract tourists. Therefore, seeking local development through rural/mountainous tourism destination development is a strategy that has been widely adopted (and pursued) in recent decades. Indeed, peripheral-area tourism, although not always right, has often been seen as a viable answer to the negative effects of progressive depopulation or lack of essential services, as many studies from a variety of theoretical perspectives have evidenced (Andreoli & Silvestri, 2017; Biddulph, 2015; Brown & Hall, 2000a; Chaperon & Bramwell, 2013; Christaller, 1963; Gannon, 1994; Hall, Harrison, Weaver, & Wall, 2013; Pröbstl-Haider, Melzer, & Jiricka, 2014; Salazar, 2010; Wanhill, 1997).

This contribution seeks to insert itself into the wider debate on the topic, by focusing on a peculiar declination of peripheral-area tourism in general, and of food tourism in particular, by analysing, through a descriptive approach, the case of a peripheral area of the Marche region (Italy), which has decided to develop a territorial marketing strategy based on the nascent craft-beer-related industry. The research sets itself within a wider project that has been ongoing since 2015, designed to investigate *in itinere* the implementation of the so-called Italian National Strategy for Inner Areas (Barca, Casavola, & Lucatelli, 2014)—hereafter referred to as SNAI. The strategy is aimed at seeking, through a participative and bottom-up approach, the drafting and implementation of targeted policies that could help a selected number of peripheral areas to trigger forms of endogenous social and economic development. One of the pilot areas is the "Appennino basso-pesarese e anconetano", where most of the research here presented was carried out, specifically in the village of Apecchio, located on the central Italian Apennine at the border between the Marche and Umbria regions, in a territory that is mainly hilly and rural.

The village of Apecchio, in the last five years, has had a prominent role in the drafting of the development strategy for the SNAI area "Appennino basso-pesarese e anconetano", thanks to the presence of three craft beer breweries in its territory, which have led to the creation of a national association of craft beer cities, and a related festival, which will be here denominated the "Alogastronomia Festival".

While the tight relationship between SNAI, its policy aims, and the prospect development path launched by the area has been widely analysed in a previous publication (Pezzi, 2017a), this chapter seeks to analyse the ongoing process based on the most current academic debate on food tourism as a trigger for regional development, intersecting it with data collected through various periods of ethnographic fieldwork undertaken between 2016 and 2017.

The chapter is, therefore, structured as follows: the first section provides an overview of the key elements of food tourism in relation to regional development, cross-referencing insights from anthropology and other disciplines, such as geography and regional science; the second section sets the context and main features of the so-called craft beer revolution in Italy; the third section expands the previous two, highlighting why and how it is possible to understand the contribution of craft beer tourism to regional development; and finally, the last section deals with Apecchio, its gastronomic heritage, and the related "Alogastronomia Festival", introducing the concept of "drinkscapes" in relation to craft beer and peripheral tourism.

In the following pages, therefore, I aim to demonstrate how anthropology can be a useful lens through which to understand the growth and success of the craft beer industry in the Italian peripheral areas, using the case of Apecchio as a prominent example, on the basis of the concurring identity construction and bottom-up local development processes, for which the craft beer industry and its related tourism expansion are playing a pivotal role.

Food tourism and regional development: some preliminary accounts on a complex relationship

Peripheral areas, being subject to a series of issues directly linked with their distance from urban hubs providing essential services, and their relative difficulty to be reached (Pezzi & Urso, 2016, 2017), are often not well equipped to undergo profound economic, social, and structural changes, and, therefore, the relation between peripheral areas and prospect tourism development is not an unproblematic one.

First of all, the so-called *tourism transition* in peripheral areas is a much swifter process in theory than in practice. In a recent study on tourism transition in Italian rural areas, Salvatore, Chiodo, and Fantini (2018) questioned whether tourism can actually play a role as drivers of change in peripheral areas, through the enhancement and revitalisation of countryside capital.

They start their analysis by acknowledging the fact that, until recently, when tourism has emerged as a relevant economy in the Italian peripheral areas, it has been developed through a hierarchical core-periphery model that has more often created tourism enclaves that served as extended leisure resorts for urban hubs and metropolitan areas (ibid., p. 42).

Moreover, peripheral tourism destinations soon find themselves confronted with what Brown and Hall (2000b) have defined as the paradox of peripheral tourism and development: first, peripherality and the attributes linked to it can be considered as triggers for tourism development; second, if peripheral-area tourism prospers, they may encounter a quick decline owing to the fact that they could be considered as "too touristy" and not peripheral enough.

Indeed, peripheral-area tourism has acquired its own raison d'être through the emergence of various forms of tourism (see, i.e. Cohen, 1979 for experiential tourism), focusing on proximity and encounters between locals and tourists, which are made possible specifically because of the peripheral character of such tourist destinations.

Among the different forms of experiential tourism that are becoming more and more relevant in peripheral areas, gastronomic tourism is definitely one that is witnessing a fast and steady growth (see, i.e. Dixit, 2019; Hall & Gössling, 2016a). The recent emergent popularity of food, cuisine, and travel-related programmes on TV, radio, and streaming platforms is surely demonstrating that the social significance of food consumption is not only impacting everyday life, but also consumers' habits and tourists' motivations to visit a certain place: food choices, as Guigoni (2009) maintains, are identity-making mechanisms that reflect both on the self of individuals and on their social projections, and are mirrored in travel motivations and destination choices.

From the locals' point of view, agricultural systems, and local or localised products and cuisines, constitute an opportunity to generate value in areas otherwise marginalised by the lack of other economic assets. Focusing on the role of local actors and their entrepreneurial ability is pivotal in understanding how forms of tourism based on local food systems, their products and their production methods, can contribute to the social and economic wellbeing of peripheral areas, within a more generalised regional development perspective that also takes into account the interrelation with bottom-up practices and the related policies.

Few clarifications on the current stance on studies on food tourism, and their possible declinations, are necessary in order to proceed to the analysis of the case study.

Hall and Mitchell (2000, p. 308) defined food tourism as "visitation to primary and secondary food producers, food festivals, restaurants and specific locations for which food tasting and/or experiencing the attributes of specialist food production region are the primary motivation for travel". Food tourism and local products, indeed, constitute good leverage for the creation of a tourism niche[1] market by establishing closer relationships between local producers and tourist-consumers. In fact, 'rural areas with their specific history, traditions and eno-gastronomic heritage seem suitable for the development of successful food niches' (Sidali, Kastenholz & Bianchi, 2015, 2).

On the one hand, food tourism can be considered as based on *local food systems*, which are deliberately formed systems that are characterised by a close relationship between producers and consumers, within a certain place or locality. On the other hand, when coupled with (international) tourism, these systems peculiarly create a paradoxical effect, as evidenced by Hall and Gössling (2016b, p. 12): "while the local food system is often regarded as a device to counter some of the negative elements of globalization, tourism by its very nature is a potent force for encouraging globalization".

It is beneficial, moreover, to recall the existing distinction between local and localised food products, for which *Vitterso and Amilien (2011) have evidenced a fundamental categorisation*: the former are short-travelled products featuring a close relationship between consumer and producer. The latter, instead, are 'products from a particular geographical area in which they have strong spatial and culture roots' (ibid., pos. 3), which can serve as added values in the scope of tourism marketing.

The focus on locality, as Pratt (2008, p. 289) states, requires more discussion, particularly when linked with another core concept—that of quality: "almost all food considered high quality [...] has a territorial designation. As a result, it is easy to reverse the equation and assume that local produce immediately connotes good quality, a logical fallacy encouraged by marketing techniques". Grasseni (2012, p. 198), drawing on her research on mountain cheese in the Italian Alps, has made some very clear stances on the (re) invention of local food products, focusing on the "local conflicts that can ensue from the transformation of marginal rural areas into locations for the production of typical [the common designation for 'local' in Italy, through an interesting linguistic turn] food". Grasseni (ibid., 199), moreover, relies on works by other authors (Papa, 2002; Bourdieu 1987; Bauman 1998, as cited in Grasseni 2012) to sustain the thesis that in fact, typical products are comparable to oxymorons: they attempt to serve as signs of distinction and, at the same time, they are high-quality foods with a mass-market attainment. In this sense, although this process may be seen as forecasting standardisation, local tastes and global phenomena lead to 'glocal' strategies, as well as the creation of niche markets.

Moreover, as pointed out by Ellis et al. (2018, p. 261), "food functions as a metaphor for the construction and expression of ethnicity and cultural identity". Food, in general, and food tourism, in particular, can therefore be considered as highly socially constructed objects, whose construction involves social actors (i.e. tourists and locals), politics, policies, and production/consumption practices that concur in creating what Grasseni defines the re-invention of food: "a process that often entails a transformation of the production, perception, representation and consumption of food" for tourism purposes (2012, p. 198).

Studies on gastronomic tourism supporting regional development (see, i.e. White & Gasser 2001, as cited in Hall & Gössling, 2016b, p. 10) have evidenced the existence of four features that influence local development strategies: participation and dialogue; territorial focus; mobilisation of local resources; and the local ownership or management of existing resources.

These features are to be found, as a matter of fact, in the recently launched National Strategy for Inner Areas (2014–2020, in its first implementation phase) (Barca et al., 2014), which sees tourism and local food systems as one of its structural pillars and is aimed at fostering local development through a place-based approach (Barca, McCann, & Rodríguez-Pose, 2012) that is highly reliant on local human, cultural, economic, and territorial resources.

Setting the context: the craft beer revolution in Italy

Craft beer brewing is a relative novelty in the Italian context, as the emergence of this phenomenon can be dated back to the mid-1990s, which is around ten years after the beginning of the so-called craft beer revolution in the US (Fastigi, Esposti, & Viganò, 2015; Kline, Slocum, & Cavaliere, 2017) (Figure 12.1).

The peculiarity of the Italian craft beer panorama is that the country doesn't have a long history, or tradition, of beer production and consumption, aside from some of the northern regions, which were under the Austrian-Hungarian Empire's influence until the 19th century (Fastigi, Esposti, & Viganò, 2015, p. 71). Craft beverage production in Italy has, indeed, more often involved the making of wine and other distillates, such

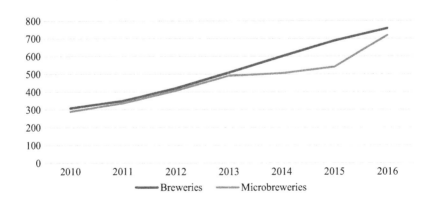

Figure 12.1 Breweries and microbreweries in Italy (2010–2016).
Data from: https://brewersofeurope.org/

as *grappa* (schnapps) or *limoncello* (lemon liquor), just to name some of the most well-liked ones.

The growing popularity of the craft beer industry in Italy must have, therefore, been influenced by other factors, not related to traditional beverage consumption habits and to the availability of raw materials and specific production know-how, but rather to more global consumption trends and the emergence of the neo-localism movement in the latest years (see, i.e. Gatrell, Reid, & Steiger, 2017; Hede & Watne, 2013; Holtkamp et al., 2016; McLaughlin, Reid, & Moore, 2014; Reid & Gatrell, 2017). Nevertheless, it can be argued that craft beer brewing in Italy, although not specifically linked with a previously existing industry, has been able to rely on other specificities of the Italian territory, such as the high number and variety of typical and local food products available, of the Slow-Food movement (Petrini, 2003), and on the recognition of the Mediterranean diet by UNESCO World Heritage Centre (Pfeilstetter, 2015), as well as on social and cultural dimensions that foster the creation of small-medium enterprises and creativity, which this contribution seeks to unravel.

While most craft breweries in Italy seem to be located in urban centres, recent trends have evidenced a growing number of small microbreweries[2] in rural/peripheral assets (Fastigi, Esposti, Orazi, & Vignanò, 2015), as well as of the so-called "agricultural craft breweries", a national peculiarity regulated by Ministerial Decree (DM) n. 212/2010, which includes beer in the goods to be considered as agricultural products. In this sense, agricultural craft breweries are typically agricultural firms that produce the barley that is later employed for the production of craft beer, although some exceptions may apply: the DM, in fact, has been later subject to a multiplicity of interpretations and implementations, which have led to a more complex diversification of agricultural craft breweries. Three subtypes of "agricultural craft breweries" have been identified: existing craft breweries that acquire or rent land in order to cultivate their own raw material inputs and, therefore, become an agricultural holding; agricultural firms that harvest barley and then subsidise their craft beer productions to other existing plants, becoming an agricultural beer firm; agricultural firms that acquire a craft beer production plant and create their own beer using their harvested crops (Fastigi, Esposti, & Viganò, 2015, p. 78). According to an empirical study by Fastigi, Esposti, and Viganò (2015, 84ff), the main motivation for the creation of an agricultural craft brewery is the desire to diversify the agricultural production, while other craft beer owners have usually started as homebrewers and then turned to entrepreneurs in the craft beer sector.

From craft beer tourism to "beer-wandering": unravelling the components of a relatively new phenomenon

Craft beer tourism can be ideally considered as a sub-niche of food tourism and defined as trips made to destinations where the local craft beers are the main motivating factor for travel. Beer drinkers and craft beer enthusiasts are usually keen to visit other locations on the basis of their interest in trying new craft beer types, visiting breweries, and collecting beer-related souvenirs, such as glasses, bottles, and coasters. Craft beer tourism, though, does not only include leisure activities, but it can also entail gaining a broader knowledge of the visited region, getting in contact with the local population, and learning about typical products and localised production methods. In this sense, craft beer tourism is growing more and more as a means to produce and reinforce niche tourism based on beer production and consumption but is also to be considered as the result of local development strategies that specifically leverage on local products to attract tourists, as we will see in the next paragraph.

Bujdosó and Szűcs (2012), in their analysis of beer tourism (Plummer, Telfer, Hashimoto, and Summers (2005)), identified two sub-groups on the basis of tourists' main motivations for travel, and their categorisation seems to fit the peculiarities of craft beer tourism as well.

The first sub-group is that which sees *beer as a primary motivation for travel*, and includes different forms of "encounter" with beer types, breweries, and local communities, in particular: beer tasting (consumption of beer produced in a given location); beer-themed lunches (menus created to accompany a given list of beer); beer tours (i.e. along dedicated trails or routes, which include other general tourist attractions, as the landscape and the local heritage); beer weekends (packages that enable the acquisition of the know-how or beer brewing, i.e. through courses) (ibid., 106–107).

The second sub-group, on the other hand, sees *place as a primary motivation for travel*, involving activities like breweries and brew-pubs visits (as a result of their distinctiveness, atmosphere, historical heritage, originality, etc.); festivals and events (where the sold beer may be another force of attraction or the focus of the events themselves); beer museums (i.e. breweries and/or brew pubs that are important for their architectural value as industrial heritage); beer houses, brewery visits (where the main motivation is not beer consumption, but visiting a brewery that constitutes a form of tourist attraction); and gastropubs (bars and restaurants that serve high-end beer and food) (ibid., 107–109).

In the case of craft beer tourism, we can observe the coexistence of all of the abovementioned kinds of tourism practices, although literature and direct observation suggest that "place" is actually a transversal driver for tourism, both in urban and peripheral assets. Indeed, as Gatrell et al. (2017) highlight, the concept of "sense of place is critical to the understanding the growth of the craft beer sector" (ibid., p. 4), and for extension of craft beer tourism, leveraging on historical heritage, authenticity, identity, and narratives. In this sense, we would like to draw on the definition of sense of place provided by Low and Laurence-Zúñiga (2003), who see places as socially constructed through particular interactions, in this case though, the encounter between tourists' travel motivations and local craft beer production.

Hede and Watne (2013), analysing craft beer branding strategies, maintain indeed that sense of place "has potential to address the relationship gap between brands and humans" (ibid., p. 208) through very specific narrative forms that humanise beer brands and beer destinations, and through references to local history, heroes, tales, myths, folklore, and landscape, incorporating concepts such as place identity and place attachment, while at the same time focusing "on people's own experiences and how they feel about places" (ibid., p. 211).

There is another element of craft beer tourism that has been developing in recent years, and that has not only a very important spatial connotation, but is also very much linked with forms of mobility, which Salazar and Smart (2011) would define as "deviations from [...] discourses of globalization, and cosmopolitanism" that "seem to have shifted the pendulum in the opposite direction, mobility being promoted as normality, and place attachment as a digression or resistance against globalizing forces" (ibid., p. ii): *craft beer wandering*. While the word "beer wandering" seems to not have gained great popularity in English (as observable through a Google search on the topic), apart from a few blogs referring to it, the literal translation "birrovagare" (beer wandering) and "birrovago" (beer wanderer) is becoming rather popular among Italian craft beer enthusiasts and, indeed, is solely used in reference to craft beers. The Italian Blog *A Scuola di Gusto*, for example, in a recent post has defined *beer wandering* as the new frontier for food tourism,[3] next to the emerging beer trails. "Birrovagare", although an evocative term, as of now seems to not have reached a univocal definition and accounts of beer wanderers include multiple activities and experiences. What can be observed is that it seems to refer to a very specific sub-culture related to craft beer consumption and appreciation that has strong linkages with forms of slow-tourism; territorial discovery; educational purposes in terms of know-how, materials and production processes; ethical concerns in regard to sustainable and non-invasive forms of tourism; and the pursuit of a more authentic relationship with people, places, and products, which does not see beer consumption as an end, but rather as a means of knowledge and of a particular form of "tourist gaze" (Urry, 2002).

It is then interesting to observe current and future developments of such niche-tourism experiences and their relevance for the craft beer sector, particularly in peripheral regions. In doing so, the case of the mountainous and peripheral village of Apecchio is trying to contribute to, and drive local development from, a tourism strategy revolving around craft beer production and consumption.

Apecchio: the beer city

Apecchio is a small village situated on the Italian Apennine in central Italy at about 500 metres above the sea. It had a population of a little over 1,800 inhabitants in January 2018, which is about half of the population residing in the municipality only 50 years ago (Source: DEMOistat.it). Located in the outmost part of the province of Pesaro and Urbino, in the Marche region, the village can be considered as peripheral because of its distance from urban hubs and service centres. This condition has been acknowledged by the Department for Territorial Cohesion, which, in 2014, included Apecchio in one of the pilot areas of the previously recalled SNAI development strategy, namely "Appennino Basso Pesarese e Anconetano" (see, i.e. Pezzi, 2017a). As an inner area municipality, Apecchio suffers from many of the negative aspects of peripheralisation, i.e. population decline—as we have seen—population ageing, a decrease in the available essential services, such as health, mobility and transport, and economic marginalisation.

Tourism is the sector that has seen the higher degree of expansion in the latest years, thanks to the presence of various attractors in the area, such as Mount Nerone, a popular hiking destination, and the rich variety and beauty of its agroforestry system, which calls wanderers and tourists not only from nearby areas, but also from other Italian regions and European countries, allowing many recreational activities, including fruit and chestnut picking.

The area is also historically popular for the quality of its soil, which allows white and black truffle grounds. Restaurants offering truffle-based menus and recipes are a peculiarity of the region, and truffle festivals have been held in neighbouring villages (i.e. in Acqualagna) for over 30 years. Agro-pastoral activities, gastronomy, and tourism are, therefore, tightly interwoven aspects of the local economy. The emergent territorial marketing strategy in Apecchio has been selected by the pilot area as one of the pillars of its future development strategy within the wider SNAI framework (Pezzi, 2017a; 2017b; 2018), both in relation to tourism and heritage and to agro-pastoral activities and entrepreneurship.

The village of Apecchio is, in fact, home to three craft breweries, very different from each other for what regards history, entrepreneurial path, and characteristics. The linking peculiarity is that all three produce their beers using the water spring from Mount Nerone, which is apparently very suitable for this purpose because of its organic composition and its purity.

The oldest brewery is Tenute Collesi, established in 1870, initially producing spirits such as grappa, gin, and vodka, and that only in recent years has been expanding its business by entering the craft beer market, and producing both bottled and draft beers. In 2018, at the World Beer Awards, its Collesi Ubi was declared the "World's Best Dark Beer"[4]—a very prestigious award for this sector. Moreover, late 2018/beginning of 2019, Tenute Collesi launched a cosmetic line (for both men and women), in which the products contain craft beers on the basis of their organic composition, which is apparently beneficial for skincare purposes.

The second craft brewery is Amarcord, established in 1997 in another city, Rimini, and later moved to Apecchio. The brewery has been named after the Academy Award-winning film by Italian director Federico Fellini.

Their first produced beers were named after the most famous characters of the movie, and they were later followed by four other lines. What is interesting to notice is that the brand identity of this brewery remained linked with its city of origin, regardless of its current geographical location. Its name, "Amarcord", is the dialect form of the Italian "I remember", and contributes to maintaining its linkage with the city of Rimini in a nostalgic yet innovative way, as the blog Amarcordlife seeks to portray, although it is now one of the pillars of Apecchio's territorial brand, as we will see below.

The newest addition to the village of Apecchio is microbrewery Birra Venere, established in 2014, and pertaining to the category of agricultural craft breweries, as they do produce their own barley. The brand and its image rely on the famous painting "The birth of Venus" by Sandro Botticelli. The produced beers are also named after the goddess, i.e. Blonde Venus, Red Venus.

What is interesting to notice here is that although local in effect, none of the breweries have connected their brands and their image with local elements that could recall their linkages with the territory and its peculiarities, which is a fact that is in contrast to much of the literature on craft beer branding (see, i.e. Hede and Watne 2013). Nevertheless, in 2014, the municipality of Apecchio worked on the establishment of the association "Apecchio Città della Birra" ("*Apecchio the beer city*") with the aim of indissolubly linking the city, its produced craft beers, and the territory through a series of activities created in partnership with other craft breweries in the same region (Marche).

The main event promoted by the association is the so-called "Mostra mercato del tartufo e dei prodotti del bosco – Alogastronomia", which, for brevity reasons, will be here denominated "Alogastronomia Festival".

Before getting into detail on how this festival is important for this case study, a few clarifications on the term Alogastronomia[5] are necessary.

'*Alogastronomia*': when beer creates culture and tourism, and tourism creates the beer culture

According to an interviewed member of Apecchio's local administration, the term 'Alogastronomia' is a neologism and, since recently, a registered trademark, which aims to connect two pivotal features of the territorial marketing strategy that lies behind it: food and craft beer. The etymology of the word gastronomy derives from Ancient Greek and literally means "the art of regulating the stomach". While the term originally was all-encompassing, referring to a variety of aspects, from cooking techniques to taste and other related senses such as smell, nutritional aspects, and food-related knowledge, in modern times, it has come to signify a close relationship between culture and food, as well as between food and place (Ellis et al., 2018, p. 253). The prefix "Alo", on the other hand, was picked by Apecchio's local administration because it resembled "ale" (a kind of beer) but was easier to pronounce in Italian once connected to "gastronomia". The composed term Alogastronomia should, therefore, be interpreted as "the art of regulating the stomach through craft beer".

Alogastronomia, in the way it was intended by its creators, has strong linkages both with the community and gastronomic culture, and with tourism. Indeed, one of the advertising campaigns created to support the territorial marketing strategy in Apecchio relies on the sentence "Beer creates culture, beer creates tourism" (interview, 25th July 2016).

First, this is because of the fact that Alogastronomia has been set to encompass different aspects of the local gastronomic culture in Apecchio through its matching with recipes and foods typical of the area, such as *Bostrengo*, a Christmas cake, and *Salmì del Prete*, a dish traditionally prepared with game and herbs. These dishes can be tasted in the trattorias and inns located in Apecchio together with a selection of local craft beers to reflect the tight interconnection between local cuisine and craft beers.

Second, other tourism-based activities have been implemented in order to allow tourists to get in touch with Alogastronomia, i.e. cooking courses with local chefs, during which tourists can learn how to cook dishes using local products, and how to pair them with the locally produced craft beers. Getting in touch with Alogastronomia, and Apecchio's typical products, requires, therefore, the tourist and the visitor to engage in "gastronomic performances" that construct a culture of alogastronomic discernment.

In Apecchio, therefore, the current tourism development strategy is aimed at making craft beers *and* place as a primary motivation for travel, in an interrelated strategy that sees Alogastronomia as the connecting thread, through the involvement of sensorial activities that are not only related to taste but to all basic five senses, more than on sight (seeing).

The Alogastronomia Festival

Apecchio's Alogastronomia Festival came to its 6th edition in 2018, and it is habitually held between the end of September and the beginning of October, when other *typical* gastronomic products of the area become available, i.e. truffles and chestnuts (Pezzi, 2017a, p. 173ff). The festival is celebrated in the ancient citadel, where historical buildings, such as Palazzo Ubaldini (est. 14th century), are opened to the public and host a variety of events, as photo exhibits that depict the old and traditional way of life in Apecchio and its agrarian heritage. Gazebos are built in the little squares and around the alleys to host local producers selling their products, but most interestingly also non-local food producers from neighbouring regions in central Italy, that sell similarly 'typical' products, like truffles and honey. A relevant number of gazebos are devoted to tasting and retail activities focused on the three craft beer brands produced in Apecchio, while in the trattorias, visitors can have a try of Alogastronomia, combining food and beer tasting.

Through observation carried out during the 2016 and the 2017 editions, it was possible to witness that quite a large number of people[6] visit Apecchio during the festival, though these are mainly locals residing in the same area. The presence of people coming from afar is partly hindered by the fact that tourism facilities in the area are still rather limited and finding a place to stay in Apecchio is, consequently, quite difficult. Moreover, the festival is held in a period that is already outside of the typical tourist season in the area that mostly relies on sea-sand-sun tourism on the Adriatic coast, and a growing component of rural tourism, which goes mostly between May and September. The decision to host a festival at the beginning of autumn relied on the desire for de-seasonalisation of tourism, in an attempt to draw visitors in the area in other periods as well, but obviously this had the dis-advantage of lower numbers of potential tourists to attract and even lower facilities able to host them.

Nevertheless, the fact that the festival is mostly directed to the local commu-nity (in its broadest sense) is not necessarily a negative outcome, but quite the contrary. It actually serves an unanticipated purpose: it helps create a sense of community among the local population on the basis of the festival's perfor-mance and performative function, that once a year turns the *imagined commu-nity* inhabiting the village of Apecchio into an existing community of "the beer city". At the same time, the symbolism linked with craft beers, Alogastronomia, and traditional food recipes becomes—literally—incorporated through a beer and food consumption "ritual" that entails "tasting the place" and its "Apec-chiosità" (roughly translatable as *Apecchiosity* in English).

This is in accordance with the existing literature on the relationships be-tween local gastronomies and tourism activities, which seems to paraphrase the theorisation of the existence of '-scapes'[7] by Appadurai (1996). For ex-ample, Vittersø and Amilien (2011) analysed the senses involved in the tour-ist experience (such as sound, smell, taste, etc.), which, according to them, produce 'sensed environments' within the tourism industry and conclude that talking about 'landscapes' within tourism consumption necessarily in-volves considering the existence of the relative 'soundscapes', 'smellscapes', 'tastescapes', etc. (ibid., pos. 16). These, indeed, constitute further declina-tions of 'foodscapes' as already analysed by Guigoni (2004; 2009, p. 166). Other authors, such as Hall and Gössling (2016b), acknowledge that food-scapes are not a homogeneous entity that includes the production methods of the food that people eat, and their embeddedness with the landscape. According to the authors, foodscapes are a significant attractor for tourism when it comes to food tourism. These inputs, in relation to craft beer con-sumption, would allow us to talk about "drinkscapes". As a consequence of that, by looking at the case of Apecchio and its Alogastronomia movement, we could imply that the same process is currently ongoing for craft beer tourism, to the extent that it may be beneficial to refer to it as Aletourism.

Conclusions

The case of Apecchio and its "Association of Beer Cities", with all their relative events, is not a *unicum* in the gastronomic tourism panorama.

Indeed, Hall and Gössling (2016b, p. 28) have evidenced a similar recent trend in the US:

> many rural towns [...] often proclaim themselves as the 'capital' of various food types as a way of celebrating their heritage and food production, while simultaneously using the food as a way of differentiating themselves as a place to visit.

In Apecchio, the relative novelty of the craft beer phenomenon does not allow us to predict whether the heritage (re)generation component of the localised craft beer production will effectively be adopted and confirmed by the local population as an identity-making strategy.

Nevertheless, for what concerns the local development strategy, it is possible to evidence that there are a number of advantages in the creation of a tourism-led development path that heavily relies on what is perceived as a high-quality, local, and "typical" product, as Apecchio's craft beers have come to be. The first advantage is that both Apecchio and Apecchio-produced craft beers are becoming recognisable in the craft beer panorama, such as the success by Tenute Collesi in recent competitions has shown. This *recognition* constitutes good leverage for the whole area in which they are produced, in a mutually reinforcing strategy, where craft beer creates tourism, and tourism creates craft beer consumption. This *attraction* factor constitutes the second advantage.

The third factor is *differentiation*. Apecchio's craft beers are very different from one another, in terms of history, raw materials, packaging, and sales volumes, but also in terms of flavour profiles, with each brewery's beer reflecting the creativity and preferences of the brewmaster. Nevertheless, in the marketing strategy pursued by the area, they all seek to portray the *Apecchiosity* of their character, endowed in the fact that all three craft beers are produced using spring water from Mount Nerone, a mountain that has a high identity component for the local population. This fact differentiates Apecchio from other craft breweries, as well as a tourism destination.

A fourth advantage is represented by *identification*. Food festival and events, apart from serving their obvious marketing and income purposes, can be considered as challenges to build sense of places (Low & Lawrence-Zúñiga, 2003) on the basis of the existing cultural and material heritage, on the one hand, and of collective identities presented in a way that is also usable for outsiders and tourists, on the other. While representing their culture and gastronomic heritage through food events, communities reinforce their sense of belonging to a particular place, which acquires new relevance on the basis of its newly built centrality. This is particularly important for peripheral areas, which, as recalled at the beginning of this chapter, are often suffering from a hierarchical relationship with their urban cores, which turns them into tourist enclaves (Salvatore et al., 2018).

In this sense, it can be maintained that through the linkages between craft beers and other local gastronomic products, as effectively portrayed by the Alogastronomia neologism, Apecchio is seeking to leverage on already existing cultural resources through a creative approach. This is in line with what Bujdosó et al. (2015) evidenced in their study on the relationships between cultural heritage and tourism development:

> Culture can serve as an excellent and favourable tool of competitiveness strategies in many regions because it 'only' requires the exploration and creative utilisation of local capabilities. Its most important resource requirements are human capital and creativeness.
>
> (p. 309)

Following a similar approach, food events can be said to have both a centripetal and centrifugal force: they globalise their products through a focus on locality and tradition, picking up on the postmodern tension between global homogeneity and local heterogeneity. Indeed, what seems to be happening at the moment is that through the Alogastronomia Festival, both locals and tourists have a chance to *incorporate* the taste of the place (Trubek, 2008) in which the beers are produced.

All these factors can be considered as concurring in shifting from a territorial branding strategy that focuses on the material heritage (i.e. landscape) to a place-making strategy that focuses on a renewed and innovative approach to a sense of place. Given its focus on craft beer tourism, the tourism development strategy adopted in this area of the Marche region is seeking to turn the landscape into a drinkscape, thanks to the signs and symbols attached to the craft beer experience through a variety of place-making strategies.

Notes

1 Robinson and Novelli (2005) define a niche market as a group where the individual members are identifiable by the same specialised needs and, consequently, have a strong desire for related products on offer (ibid., p. 5). Hence, niche tourism can be defined as a market 'breaking down into still relatively large market sectors (macro-niches—i.e. cultural tourism, rural tourism, sports tourism, etc.), each capable of further segmentation (micro-niches—i.e. geo-tourism, gastronomy tourism, cycling tourism, etc.)' (ibid.; Novelli, 2005).
2 Production <1000 hl per year.
3 http://www.ascuoladigusto.it/birrovagare-la-nuova-frontiera-del-turismo-del-gusto/ [accessed on May 31st 2018].
4 https://www.collesi.com/world-beer-awards-2018-la-finale-decreta-collesi-ubi-miglior-birra-scura-al-mondo/ [accessed 23/10/2018].
5 The word would translate as "Alegastronomy" in English.
6 No official record of the number of visitors for any of the Festival editions is available. According to the organisers, around 4,000 people visit Apecchio within the two or three days of the event [personal communication, 25th July

2016]. As a consequence of the observations carried out, this number of *unique* visitors should probably be adjusted downwards.

7   A. Appadurai, in his book *Modernity at Large* (1996), suggested the use of the suffix '-scape' (typically accompanied by either of these five prefixes: ethno-, media-, techno-, finance- and ideo-) as a framework to examine the 'new global cultural economy as a complex, overlapping, disjunctive order that cannot any longer be understood in terms of existing centre-periphery models' (ibid, 32).

References

Andreoli, A., & Silvestri, F. (2017). Tourism as a driver of development in the Inner Areas. *IJPP – Italian Journal of Planning Practice, VII*(1), 80–99.

Appadurai, A. (1996). *Modernity at Large: Cultural Dimensions of Globalization.* Minneapolis: University of Minnesota Press.

Barca, F., Casavola, P., & Lucatelli, S. (Eds.). (2014). *A Strategy for Inner Areas in Italy: Definition, Objectives, Tools and Governance.* Roma: UVAL.

Barca, F., McCann, P., & Rodríguez-Pose, A. (2012). The case for regional development intervention: Place-based versus place-neutral approaches. *Journal of Regional Science, 52*(1), 134–152. http://doi.org/10.1111/j.1467-9787.2011.00756.x

Biddulph, R. (2015). Limits to mass tourism's effects in rural peripheries. *Annals of Tourism Research, 50*(January 2015), 98–112. http://doi.org/10.1016/j.annals.2014.11.011

Brown, F., & Hall, D. (2000a). Introduction: The paradox of peripherality. In F. Brown & D. Hall (Eds.), *Tourism in Peripheral Areas: Case Studies* (pp. 1–6). Clevedon: Channel View Publications.

Brown, F., & Hall, D. (Eds.). (2000b). *Tourism in Peripheral Areas: Case Studies.* Clevedon: Channel View Publications.

Bujdosó, Z., Dávid, L., Tőzsér, A., Kovács, G., Major-Kathi, V., Uakhitova, G., ... Vasvári, M. (2015). Basis of heritagization and cultural tourism development. *Procedia – Social and Behavioral Sciences, 188*, 307–315. http://doi.org/10.1016/j.sbspro.2015.03.399

Bujdosó, Z., & Szűcs, C. (2012). Beer tourism – From theory to practice. *Academica Turistica, 5*(1), 103–111.

Chaperon, S., & Bramwell, B. (2013). Dependency and agency in peripheral tourism development. *Annals of Tourism Research, 40*(1), 132–154. http://doi.org/10.1016/j.annals.2012.08.003

Christaller, W. (1963). Some considerations of tourism location in Europe: The peripheral regions – Underdeveloped countries – Recreation areas. *Regional Sciences Association Papers, 12*(1), 95–105. http://doi.org/10.1111/j.1435-5597.1964.tb01256.x

Cohen, E. (1979). A phenomenology of tourist experiences. *Sociology, 13*(2), 179–201. http://doi.org/10.1177/003803857901300203

Dixit, S. K. (2019). *The Routledge Handbook of Gastronomic Tourism.* Oxon: Routledge.

Ellis, A., Park, E., Kim, S., & Yeoman, I. (2018). What is food tourism? *Tourism Management, 68*(March), 250–263. http://doi.org/10.1016/j.tourman.2018.03.025

Fastigi, M., Esposti, R., Orazi, F., & Vignanò, F. (2015). The irresistible rise of the craft brewing sector in Italy: can we explain it? In *4th AIEAA Conference "Innovation, productivity and growth: towards sustainable agri-food production" 11–12 June, 2015 Ancona, Italy* (pp. 1–22).

Fastigi, M., Esposti, R., & Viganò, E. (2015). La craft beer revolution in Italia e i birrifici agricoli: traiettorie evolutive e principali criticità. *Argomenti, Terza Seri* (2), 67–92.

Gannon, A. (1994). Rural tourism as a factor in rural community economic development for economies in transition. *Journal of Sustainable Tourism, 2*(1–2), 51–60. http://doi.org/10.1080/09669589409510683

Gatrell, J. D., Reid, N., & Steiger, T. L. (2017). Branding spaces: Place, region, sustainability and the American craft beer industry. *Applied Geography*, 90, 1–32.

Grasseni, C. (2012). Re-inventing food: The ethics of developing local food. In J. G. Carrier & P. G. Luectchford (Eds.), *Ethical Consumption: Social Value and Economic Practice*. New York and Oxford: Berghahn Books.

Guigoni, A. (Ed.). (2004). *Foodscapes. Stili, mode e culture del cibo di oggi.* Milano: Polimetrica.

Guigoni, A. (2009). *Antropologia del mangiare e del bere.* Torrazza Coste (PV): Edizioni Altravista.

Hall, C. M., & Gössling, S. (2016a). *Food Tourism and Regional Development: Networks, Products and Trajectories* (C. M. Hall & S. Gössling, Eds.). London and New York: Routledge.

Hall, C. M., & Gössling, S. (2016b). From food tourism and regional development to foood, tourism and regional development: Themes and issues in contemporary foodscapes. In M. C. Hall & S. Gössling (Eds.), *Food Tourism and Regional Development: Networks, Products and Trajectories* (pp. 3–58). London and New York: Routledge.

Hall, C. M., Harrison, D., Weaver, D., & Wall, G. (2013). Vanishing peripheries: Does tourism consume places? *Tourism Recreation Research, 38*(1), 71–92. http://doi.org/10.1080/02508281.2013.11081730

Hall, C. M., & Mitchell, R. (2000). "We are what we eat": Food, tourism, and globalization. *Tourism, Culture & Communication, 2*(64), 29–37.

Hede, A.-M., & Watne, T. (2013). Leveraging the human side of the brand using a sense of place: Case studies of craft breweries. *Journal of Marketing Management, 29*(1–2), 207–224. http://doi.org/10.1080/0267257X.2012.762422

Holtkamp, C., Shelton, T., Daly, G., Hiner, C. C., & Hagelman, R. R. (2016). Assessing neolocalism in microbreweries. *Papers in Applied Geography, 2*(1), 66–78. http://doi.org/10.1080/23754931.2015.1114514

Kline, C., Slocum, S. L., & Cavaliere, C. T. (Eds.). (2017). *Craft Beverages and Tourism. Volume 1.* Palgrave MacMillan.

Low, S. M., & Lawrence-Zúñiga, D. (Eds.). (2003). *The Anthropology of Space and Place.* Oxford: Blackwell Publishing Ltd. http://doi.org/10.1525/can.1992.7.1.02a00050

McLaughlin, R. B., Reid, N., & Moore, M. S. (2014). The ubiquity of good taste: A spatial analysis of the craft brewing industry in the United States. In M. Patterson & N. Hoalst-Pullen (Eds.), *The Geography of Beer: Regions, Environment, and Societies* (pp. 131–154). Springer Science+Business. http://doi.org/10.1007/978-94-007-7787-3

Novelli, M. (Ed.). (2005). *Niche Tourism: Contemporary Issues, Trends and Cases.* Oxford and Amsterdam: Elsevier. http://doi.org/10.1016/S0262-4079(07)60814-8

Petrini, C. (2003). *Slow Food: The Case for Taste.* New York: Columbia University Press.

Pezzi, M. G. (2017a). From peripheral hamlet to craft beer capital: Apecchio and the 'Alogastronomia'. *Italian Journal of Planning Practice, 7*(1), 154–185.

Pezzi, M. G. (2017b). When history repeats: Heritage regeneration and emergent authenticity in the marche's peripheral areas. *Almatourism, 8*(7), 1–20. http://doi.org/https://doi.org/10.6092/issn.2036--5195/6747

Pezzi, M. G. (2018). Home away from home: Landscape as a mediator between place and belonging in the peripheral areas of the Marche region in Italy. *International Journal of Tourism Anthropology, 6*(4), 340–356.

Pezzi, M. G., & Urso, G. (2016). Peripheral areas: Conceptualizations and policies. Editorial note. *Italian Journal of Planning Practice, VI*(1), 1–19.

Pezzi, M. G., & Urso, G. (2017). Coping with peripherality: Local resilience between policies and practices. Editorial note. *Italian Journal of Planning Practice, 7*(1).

Pfeilstetter, R. (2015). Heritage entrepreneurship. Agency-driven promotion of the Mediterranean diet in Spain. *International Journal of Heritage Studies, 21*(3), 215–231. http://doi.org/10.1111/j.1467-8330.1974.tb00606.x

Plummer, R., Telfer, D., Hashimoto, A., & Summers, R. (2005). Beer tourism in Canada along the Waterloo–Wellington Ale Trail. *Tourism Management, 26*(3), 447–458. http://doi.org/10.1016/J.TOURMAN.2003.12.002

Pratt, J. (2008). Food values: The local and the authentic. *Research in Economic Anthropology, 28*, 53–70. http://doi.org/10.1016/S0190-1281(08)28003-0

Pröbstl-Haider, U., Melzer, V., & Jiricka, A. (2014). Rural tourism opportunities: Strategies and requirements for destination leadership in peripheral areas. *Tourism Review, 69*(3), 216–228. http://doi.org/10.1108/TR-06-2013-0038

Reid, N., & Gatrell, J. D. (2017). Creativity, community, and growth: A social geography of urban craft beer. *Region, 4*(1), 31–49. http://doi.org/10.18335/region.v4i2.144

Robinson, M., & Novelli, M. (2005). Niche tourism: An introduction. In M. Novelli (Ed.), *Niche Tourism: Contemporary Issues, Trends and Causes* (pp. 1–11). Oxford, Amsterdam: Elsevier.

Salazar, N. B. (2010). The glocalisation of heritage through tourism: Balancing standardisation and differentiation. In *Heritage and globalisation* (pp. 130–147). Routledge. http://doi.org/10.4324/9780203850855

Salazar, N. B., & Smart, A. (2011). Anthropological takes on (Im) mobility. *Identities: Global Studies in Culture and Power, 18*(6), 1–11. http://doi.org/10.1080/1070289X.2012.683674

Salvatore, R., Chiodo, E., & Fantini, A. (2018). Tourism transition in peripheral rural areas: Theories, issues and strategies. *Annals of Tourism Research, 68*(218), 41–51. http://doi.org/10.1016/j.annals.2017.11.003

Sidali, K. L., Kastenholz, E., & Bianchi, R. (2015). Food tourism, niche markets and products in rural tourism: Combining the intimacy model and the experience economy as a rural development strategy. *Journal of Sustainable Tourism, 23*(8–9), 37–41. http://doi.org/10.1080/09669582.2013.836210

Trubek, A. B. (2008). *The Taste of Place. Journal of Chemical Information and Modeling* (Vol. 53).

Urry, J. (2002). *The Tourist Gaze* (2nd ed.). London: Sage.

Vittersø, G., & Amilien, V. (2011). From tourist product to ordinary food? *Anthropology of Food* [Online], *8*(http://aof.revues.org/6833).

Wanhill, S. (1997). Peripheral area tourism: A European perspective. *Progress in Tourism and Hospitality Research, 3*, 47–70. http://doi.org/10.1002/(SICI)1099-1603(199703)3:1<47::AID-PTH38>3.0.CO;2-F

Conclusion

Tourism in peripheral regions: some challenges

*Neil Reid, Maria Giulia Pezzi
and Alessandra Faggian*

Introduction

Agritourism, wine tourism, and beer tourism are growing in popularity (Jensen et al. 2013; Shoup 2017, Peregrine 2018). For example, market projections suggest that the global agritourism market size will increase by almost US\$54.63 billion between 2019 and 2023. This represents a compounded annual growth rate of almost 18% (Yahoo Finance 2019). In Italy, interest in gastro-tourism grew 48% between 2017 and 2018, with visiting farms and wineries being the most popular activities among such tourists (Fes 2019). In the United States, over half of the ten million visitors to craft breweries each year are beer tourists (Baran 2017). Many places are recognizing the economic opportunities associated with growing consumer interest in visiting farms, wineries, and breweries. This includes peripheral places. Peripheral places are often geographically distant from urban centers, making them less accessible when measured in terms of the cost, time, and convenience of traveling there. The geographic isolation of peripheral places can create unique socio-economic challenges that can be extremely difficult to overcome. As a result, peripheral places perhaps have much to gain from developing a successful tourism industry that includes agritourism, wine tourism, and beer tourism in its portfolio of attractions.

The 12 chapters that comprise the main body of this volume examine the phenomena of agritourism, wine tourism, and beer tourism in peripheral regions. The peripheral regions are located across a number of different countries and the perspectives presented come from a number of different academic disciplines. As such, we hear the voices of scholars in anthropology, agricultural and resource economics, business administration, economics, environmental science, geography, human ecology, and political science. The geographic coverage of the chapters includes Greece, Italy, Mexico, Sweden, Portugal, and the United States. The geographic spread and disciplinary breadth of these contributions lead us to make two observations. First, recognition of the potential benefits afforded by these types of tourism is not geographically restricted to one region of the world; peripheral communities in a wide variety of places view agritourism, and wine and beer tourism as an opportunity to address at least some of their socio-economic challenges. Second, no single academic discipline has a monopoly on helping us understand the challenges and opportunities associated with these types of tourism for peripheral areas. The diversity of disciplinary perspectives, we believe, is a good thing. Having said that, our primary goal in this chapter is to identify common and recurrent themes that manifest themselves across the various contributions.

The various chapters in this volume identify some of the challenges faced by peripheral regions. These include:

- the decline of traditional (mainly agricultural) industries
- population decline due to net out-migration
- high rates of unemployment
- an aging population
- a lack of essential services
- geographic isolation and socio-economic marginalization.

Addressing these challenges is not easy. There are no simple solutions. Moreover, we do not expect agritourism and wine and beer tourism to be the silver bullet that can address all of these challenges. As noted by Giordano (Chapter 3), "tourism is certainly not a panacea able to solve the problems of economic and social marginalization of marginal rural areas". While recognizing the wisdom contained in these words of caution, we do believe that, for some peripheral regions, tourism can be part of the solution. In other words, the residents of a peripheral community can benefit, individually and collectively, from a carefully crafted tourism strategy that includes leveraging its agricultural, winemaking, and beer brewing assets.

The chapters in this volume identify some of the benefits that tourism may bring to a peripheral area. These include:

- diversifying the economic base
- providing additional sources of employment for residents
- providing additional sources of revenue for local businesses
- creating a market for new business opportunities
- increasing awareness and promoting the quality of local products to a wider market
- enhancing the quality of life for local residents
- enhancing the stock of social capital among local residents
- strengthening the social and business fabric of the local community
- reducing out-migration
- preserving a place's local cultural heritage and sharing it with visitors.

If successful, the "transfer of funds through tourism could help to bring apparently neglected peripheral regions back into the mainstream of economic development (Murphy and Andressen 1988, 32)". For some peripheral areas, developing its potential tourism assets may be its best option. As noted by Wanhill and Buhalis (1999, 296):

> where the alternatives, such as agriculture, fishing and light manufacturing and repair, are already in decline, then the community may be faced with stark choices between tourism and living off the public purse. The latter relies on an expenditure based system of transferring tax revenues, which is inefficient in the use of resources and generates a low income economy.

In this chapter, we identify four themes that seem important to tourism in peripheral areas – overcoming geographic isolation, fostering collaborations, retaining authenticity, and promoting sustainability. These are by no means the only four challenges faced by tourism in peripheral regions. They are, however, the ones that appeared to resonate with the contributors to this volume.

Overcoming geographic isolation

The study of core-periphery relationships has a long tradition among scholars interested in the development of peripheral regions. This includes a sizeable literature focused specifically on the applicability of core-periphery ideas in understanding the challenges faced by peripheral tourism destinations (see, for example, Murphy and Andressen 1988, Schmallegger et al. 2010). The challenges include a lack or tourist infrastructure, a lack of investment capital (public and private), a lack of appropriate education and training, and a lack of entrepreneurial culture and distance to markets (Wanhill and Buhalis 1999).

One challenge faced by peripheral areas is their geographic isolation. Geographic isolation means that potential tourists often have to commit more time, effort, and money to reach a peripheral region than they would in traveling to a more accessible location. Vickerman (1995, p. 29) suggests that "the problem of peripherality is essentially one of accessibility", while Davis and Michie (2011, p. 12) note that "peripherality is the opposite of accessibility".

In conceptualizing peripheral tourism, Reilly's Law of retail gravitation provides a useful framework (Reilly 1931). Developed within the context of trying to understand consumer travel to retail centers, Reilly's Law states that potential customers are willing to travel longer distances to larger retail centers, as such centers offer a larger number and diversity of retail opportunities. Reilly's Law is clearly applicable to the potential attractiveness to peripheral regions to tourists. The more opportunities for engagement that a peripheral region offers to potential tourists, the greater its potential attractiveness. As noted by Mitchell and Murphy (1991, p. 66), however, the disadvantages of geographic isolation may be offset if a place can develop a reputation for offering visitors an outstanding tourist experience:

> a zonal pattern of decreasing tourism volumes around a core metro-politan region which has much in common with agricultural bid rent curves. This zonal pattern is influenced by increasing travel costs and declining knowledge of distance locations, but can be modified by the hierarchy of resort destinations, the spatial advantages offered by major transport routes, and locations with outstanding (unique) reputations.

Other useful set of ideas are those of the Edward Ullman (1954). Ullman, a geographer, coined the term *spatial interaction*, which refers to the flow of people, goods, information, etc., between two places. Ullman identified what he termed the three bases for spatial interaction, two of which, com-plementarity and transferability, seem apropos to the theme of this volume. Discussing complementarity, Ullman (1954, p. 867) noted, "in order for two regions to interact there must be demand in one and supply in the other". Ullman's concept of transferability is also important in understanding tour-ist flows. Transferability refers to the idea that spatial interaction involves a cost. Cost is typically viewed in real economic terms of time and/or travel cost. The cost of overcoming distance is referred to as the *friction of dis-tance*, and if that cost is too high, then the spatial interaction will not oc-cur (or will occur to a lesser extent), in spite of any existing complementary supply-demand relationship (Hay 1979). Peripheral locations are, by defini-tion, geographically isolated, resulting in what can be thought of as a spatial mismatch between tourists and the amenities that they wish to enjoy.

In Chapter 5, Myles et al. provide a compelling example of the problem of spatial mismatch between potential tourist and peripheral vineyards. In their case study of the wine industry of the Arizona, they note that the ideal growing locations are located in the southern part of the state, while the wineries and tasting rooms that market the final product to consumers are located in and around urban population centers in the central and northern parts of the state. Their peripheral location and the fact that potential tour-ists do not have to visit their vineyards to taste Arizona wine are particu-larly challenging.

In Chapter 1, Van Sandt et al. provide a nice exposition of the variation between rural regions in the Western United States in terms of demand curves and price sensitivities. They clearly demonstrate that not all periph-eral regions or all activities are equal in this respect. For example, they find that "travelers coming with a goal of primarily participating in agritourism activities that are enhanced by the natural assets of the Western US are the least price sensitive". Furthermore, they suggest that "agritourism sites tend to earn more revenues when they are surrounded by a cluster of other agritourism sites to draw visitors to an area". The latter observation by Van Sandt et al. suggests that agritourism, wine tourism, and beer tourism in peripheral regions may benefit from agglomeration economies. In particular, they may benefit from being in close geographic proximity to other tourism assets. As noted by Van Sandt et al. (Chapter 1):

> Geography is important to agritourism and the potential success of agritourism in a region may be enhanced if agritourism activities are geographically clustered in space and/or they are in geographic proximity to other activities (e.g., heritage sites or National Parks) that may be attractive to the agritourist . . . Visitors are attracted by the choice of multiple activities within a small travel radius.

Many of the chapters in this volume highlight the advantages to peripheral areas of having a variety of tourism assets and activities that will increase their destination's appeal to visitors. In their analysis of tourism potential in the fishing community of Las Arenitas (Mexico), De Jesus Izábal de La Garza and Contreras Loera (Chapter 4) suggest that "the aims of the rural tourism as a development strategy must start from the integration with the rest of the economic activities of the communities to achieve a productive diversification of the rural area".

Myles et al. (Chapter 5) note the difficulty of attracting visitors "without the appeal of other nearby tourist sites or amenities". Indeed, there is considerable evidence in wine tourism literature suggesting that visitors to wineries are rarely just interested in tasting wine. Rather, they would like to participate in other locally focused activities such as exploring the rural landscape, attending events that highlight local culture, sampling local food, and meeting local people (Charters & Ali-Knight 2000; Alant & Bruwer, 2004; Getz et al. 2008).

With respect to beer tourism, Arbogast et al. (Chapter 9) noted that the Convention and Visitors Bureau of West Virginia recognizes that while visitors to the state "are primarily drawn to the area for theater, heritage, music, and outdoor recreation are also interested in visiting the local brewery".

Fostering collaboration

In trying to understand the competitive success of particular places, Michael Porter emphasizes the importance of the existence of what he calls industrial clusters. Porter (2000, 15) defines industrial clusters as "geographic concentrations of interconnected companies, specialized suppliers, service providers, firms in related industries, and associated institutions (e.g., universities, standards agencies, trade associations) in a particular field that compete but also cooperate". As noted by Porter (1988, 88), "the mere colocation of companies, suppliers, and institutions creates the potential for economic value; it does not necessarily ensure its realization". One of the keys to the success of an industrial cluster is collaboration among its various stakeholders. Without collaboration, the businesses in a region may reap the benefits of co-location from agglomeration economies (external economies of scale). However, collaboration allows them to access the benefits of what is termed collective efficiency (Nadvi 1999). Collective efficiency is the competitive advantage attained from the combined benefits of external economies of scale and collaboration or joint action (Reid and Gatrell 2016). As noted by Reid and Gatrell (2016, 196), "external economies of scale are passive in that they are a natural outcome of geographic concentration of businesses. Joint action, in contrast, requires conscious and deliberate collaboration".

There is a small literature examining the tourism from the perspective of industrial cluster theory (see, for example, Fundeanu 2015, Novelli et al. 2006, Jackson and Murphy 2002). For tourism in peripheral areas, two types of collaboration would appear to be important. First, there is collaboration between businesses that may be viewed as being in competition with one another, such as craft breweries located in the same geographic region. Second, there is collaboration among the various parts of the larger tourism infrastructure. This includes, for example, collaboration between agritourist businesses, hotels, destination marketing organizations (DMOs), etc. There is ample evidence from the chapters in this volume that both of these types of collaborations are important to the success of tourism in peripheral regions.

Within the context of tourism in peripheral areas, there is a strong argument to make that, due to their geographic isolation, collaboration local stakeholders are particularly important. Skoglund and Sjölander-Lindqvist (Chapter 11), in their analysis of the craft beer industry of northern Sweden, capture this sentiment very nicely:

> The area's rurality is in many senses a problem to overcome, but in another sense, this rurality also provides a foundation for cooperation and networking. It is evident that the beer producers see the value and necessity of rural social bonds in managing the distance to consumers. To overcome these barriers, the brewers have opted for close-knit networks and cooperation, both among one another and between themselves and other gastronomy actors in their respective communities.

Wine trails and, increasingly, craft beer trails are being developed as a way to promote wineries and craft breweries. A craft beer trail is a "collaboration of breweries, located in close proximity to each other, and often involves joint marketing efforts to promote beer consumption as a tourist activity" (Slocum 2018, 85). Many craft beer trails have websites where the prospective tourists can access information, including maps and suggested itineraries (Reid 2019, forthcoming). There is evidence that craft beer trails attract tourists to a destination (Plummer et al. 2005, 2006). In addition to creating additional revenue for wineries and craft breweries, Brandano et al. (Chapter 6), in their study of wineries in Sardinia (Italy), found that wineries that were part of a formal wine route realized gains in technical efficiency that were not enjoyed by wineries that did not participate in a wine route. This suggests that the benefits of collaboration may extend beyond financial ones.

In marketing a peripheral region to tourists, it is important to sell the destination. As suggested by Jackson and Murphy (2002, 40), "individual businesses can only hope to attract tourists if those tourists are visiting their particular destination". In other words, all the tourism assets of a peripheral region (wineries, hotels, restaurants, etc.) can benefit from collaboration and coordination. As noted by Augustyn and Knowles (2000, 341), "the fragmented nature of tourism supply at destinations, combined with the need for the provision of total tourism products that satisfy the visitors' needs calls for cooperation within tourism regions". A common barrier to collaboration is the lack of an overarching coordinating authority to "initiate appropriate projects, as well as lowering the transaction costs of cooperation for the partners" (Pechlaner et al. 2009). Very often, a lack of trust is a major barrier to collaboration. For example, in Loudon County, Virginia (USA), Slocum (2018) found that craft breweries do not trust large tour operators and corporate hotels to promote the region's craft breweries (Slocum 2018). The challenge to effective collaboration may be competing priorities. Jackson and Murphy (2002, 37) suggest that as "each tourist destination is an agglomeration of businesses each with its own agenda and priorities, it is a difficult industry to coordinate and manage at the destination level".

A number of the contributions to this volume echo some of these challenges to effective collaboration. While Constantoglou et al. (Chapter 7) find evidence of collaboration between wineries and with local restaurants, hotels, retailers, and transport companies in peripheral areas of Greece, they note that these relationships can be strengthened. They suggest that improved "co-operation and coordinated actions are required between the wine industry, tourism agents, hospitality and catering industry, to create an attractive and competitive tourism product". In their analysis of wine tourism in Alentejo, Portugal, Neves et al. (Chapter 8) find similar room for improvement, noting that those responsible for promoting the region's tourism assets do not do enough to promote the region's wine assets in their marketing initiatives. At least one of the officials responsible for promoting the region's tourism assets recognized the importance of this omission, stating, "it is unaccountable how tourist promotion campaigns do not involve, for example, wine or cork producers – key resources of the region".

The contributions to this volume do provide us with some examples of effective collaboration. Pezzi (Chapter 12) presents a particularly successful example of collaboration. In her case study of craft breweries in Apechio, Italy, the local administration worked in tandem with the town's three craft breweries and others in the local food sector to establish the annual Alogastronomia Festival that highlights local beer and food.

Retaining authenticity and promoting sustainability

Many of the chapters in this volume invoked the concept of authenticity as a major factor driving the attractiveness and success of tourism in peripheral regions. Indeed, authenticity is a pervasive and recurring theme in much of the broader tourism literature (e.g., see Hughes 1995, Taylor 2001), including within the more specific field of gastronomic tourism (Sims 2009). A recent study of visitors to heritage site in South Korea found that "tourist satisfaction from experiencing constructive and existential authenticity is a strong indicator of their intention to revisit" (Park et al. 2019). In discussing the growing popularity of heritage tourism in the United States, Hargrove (2003) made the dual observation that "experience is now more important than destination" and "increased competition requires cultural heritage sites and events to provide high quality, authentic experiences".

Discussing tourism in West Virginia (USA), Arbogast et al. (Chapter 9) suggest that its primary role should lie in "capturing, preserving, and sharing the authenticity and sense of place of West Virginia". Neves et al. (Chapter 8) suggest that the wineries of Alentejo (Portugal) "may serve as an instrument for the rebirth of local festivities and traditions". In short, as they develop, a peripheral tourist destination should "not lose its essence" (De Jesus Izabal de la Garza and Contreras Loera, Chapter 4).

Arbogast et al. (Chapter 9) suggest that a major challenge faced by peripheral regions is to resist the temptation to "succumb to the commodification of culture". Doing so has the potential to transform the cultural dimensions of their community into "commodities for exchange with consuming tourists". Hargrove (2003) agrees, noting that "when authenticity is compromised cultural heritage tourism loses what differentiates it from sanitized theme park adventures and recreate (rather than real) attractions".

A potential challenge faced by many peripheral tourism destinations is identifying and maintaining the appropriate balance attracting a desirable number of tourists and attracting too many. As stated by Pezzi (Chapter 12), "if peripheral areas tourism prospers . . . they could be considered as 'too touristy' and not peripheral enough". In extreme cases, as a peripheral location grows in popularity as a tourism destination, there is a danger that it "gradually acquires the features of the core" (Papatheodorou 2004). The availability of accommodation may limit tourist volumes. This appears to be the case in Apechio, Italy (Chapter 12) whose "tourism facilities in the area are still rather limited and finding a place to stay in Apecchio is consequently quite difficult". Whether Apecchio should increase its available accommodation is a decision that should be made by the locals living there. As suggested by Murphy and Andressen (1988, 41), "tourism and regional economic development in the peripheral regions should be sensitive to residents' preferences and priorities" and should "fulfill the needs and desires of those affected by that development".

Despite the benefits tourism can bring to peripheral regions, the dangers or dark side of this phenomenon should be noted. She cites the "trade-off between economic benefits and environmental and social costs, congestion in the use of resources and possible conflicts of use between local population and guests" and warns that "rural and natural areas are easily damaged, and tourism can be a powerful agent for a negative change". In maximizing the potential benefits and minimizing the potential negative impacts, Giordano suggests that region must develop a place-specific strategy that reflects and protects the interests of local stakeholders. As noted by Arbogast et al. (Chapter 9), part of the attraction of peripheral areas is that they "are relatively unchanged and unspoilt". As noted by Giordano (Chapter 3), tourism in peripheral areas must be sustainable. Catering to tourists and remaining relatively unchanged and unspoiled can be a challenging balancing act. As noted by Hargrove (2003), however, "the real focus must be on balancing the needs of three assets: the resource, the resident, and the visitor". Successfully performing that balancing act involves minimizing "the damage, both cultural and environmental, caused by unmanaged tourism" while ensuring "the satisfaction of visitors and above all an economic growth for the hosting region" (Giordano, Chapter 3). As noted by Hargrove (2003) in discussing the challenges faced by heritage tourism, "one of our unique challenges is to manage the external demands that place pressure on fragile assets", for "if the resource is not protected then the very opportunity to attract visitors with authentic experiences vanishes".

Conclusion

Not only should peripheral areas develop a tourism industry that is fundamentally different from a traditional mass tourism model, but also each place may best be served by developing a policy and set of strategies that meet their unique vision, needs, and aspirations. As noted by De Castris and Di Gennaro (Chapter 2), a "one-size-fits-all approach does not work". As De Jesus Izabal de la Garza and Contreras Loera observe (Chapter 3), "the definitions and conceptualizations of local and regional development differ geographically and change with time and historical context". Furthermore, De Jesus Izabal de la Garza and Contreras Loera (Chapter 3) suggest that "not all areas are suitable for economic development, not all communities wish to be developed or are suitable for development, and not all forms of tourism activity are acceptable in every location". It is entirely feasible, after a careful and thoughtful assessment, that a peripheral area may decide to not pursue tourism as a development opportunity. In the end, not all peripheral areas will view tourism as the answer to their development challenges, and even those that do may face challenges that prove to be insurmountable. In Chapter 4, De Jesus Izabal de la Garza and Contreras Loera highlight the challenges, which to date have proven insurmountable, to the development of tourism in the fishing community of Las Arenitas

(Mexico). These challenges include insufficient financial support from governments, a poorly developed entrepreneurial culture, and a lack of trust and willingness to collaborate among local stakeholders.

References

Alant, K., and J. Bruwer. 2004. Wine tourism behaviour in the context of motivational framework for wine regions and cellar doors. *Journal of Wine Research*, 15(1): 27–37.

Augustyn, Marcjanna M., and Tim Knowles. 2000. Performance of tourism partnerships: A focus on York. *Tourism Management*, 21(4): 341–351.

Baran, Michelle. 2017. Tourism on tap: Beer-related travel. TravelWeekly.com. April 26. https://www.travelweekly.com/North-America-Travel/Tourism-on-tap-Beer-related-travel.

Charters, S., and J. Ali-Knight. 2000. Wine tourism – A thirst for knowledge? *International Journal of Wine Marketing*, 12(3): 70–81.

Davies, Sara, and Rona Michie. 2011. Peripheral regions: A marginal concern. Paper prepared for the 32nd Meeting of the EoRPA Regional Policy Research Consortium at Ross Priory, Loch Lomondside, October 2–4.

Fes, Nik. 2019. Italian gastro-tourism registers growth. ToursimReview.com. February 4. https://www.tourism-review.com/gastro-tourism-in-italy-still-very-attractive-news10928.

Fundeanu, Daniela Doina. 2015. Innovative regional cluster, model of tourism development. *Procedia Economics and Finance*, 23: 744–749.

Getz, D., J. Carlsen, G. Brown, and M. Havitz. 2008. Wine tourism and consumers. In: A.G. Woodside & D. Martin (Eds.) *Tourism Management: Analysis, Behaviour and Strategy* (pp. 245–268). Wallingford: CABI.

Hargrove, Cheryl. 2003. Authenticity in cultural heritage tourism. *Forum Journal*, 18(1): 45–52.

Hay, Alan. 1979. The geographical explanation of commodity flow. *Progress in Human Geography*, 3(1): 1–12.

Hughes, George. 1995. Authenticity in tourism. *Annals of Tourism Research*, 22(4): 781–803.

Jackson, Julie, and Peter Murphy. 2002. Tourism destinations as clusters: Analytical experiences from the New World. *Tourism and Hospitality Research*, 4(1): 36–52.

Jensen, Kim, Megan Bruch, Jamey Menard, and Burt English. 2013. A snapshot of Tennessee agritourism: 2013 update. Knoxville: Department of Agricultural & Resource Economics, The University of Tennessee. https://ag.tennessee.edu/cpa/CPA%20Publications/2013%20Agritourism%20Study%20Final%20Report%206%2020%2013.pdf.

Mitchell, Lisle S., and Peter E. Murphy. 1991. Geography and tourism. *Annals of Tourism Research*, 18: 57–70.

Murphy, Peter E., and Betty Andressen. 1988. Tourism development on Vancouver Island: An assessment of the core-periphery model. *The Professional Geographer*, 40(1): 32–42.

Nadvi, K. 1999. Collective efficiency and collective failure: The response of the Sialkot surgical instrument cluster to global quality pressures. *World Development*, 27(9): 1605–1626.

Novelli, Marina, Birte Schmitz, and Trisha Spencer. 2006. Networks, clusters and innovation in tourism: A UK experience. *Tourism Management*, 27: 1141–1152.

Papatheodorou, Andreas. 2004. Exploring the evolution of tourism resorts. *Annals of Tourism Research*, 31(1): 219–237.

Park, Eunkyung, Byoung-Kil Choi, and Imothy J. Lee. 2019. The role and dimensions of authenticity in heritage tourism. *Tourism Management*, 74: 99–109.

Pechlaner, Harald, Frieda Raich, and Elisabeth Fischer. 2009. The role of tourism organizations in location management: The case of beer tourism in Bavaria. *Tourism Review*, 64(2): 28–40.

Peregrine, Anthony. Why wine tourism is booming in 2018 – and the best destinations to visit. *The Telegraph*, February 1. https://www.telegraph.co.uk/travel/food-and-wine-holidays/best-destinations-for-wine/.

Plummer, Ryan, David Telfer, Atsuko Hashimoto, and Robert Summers. 2005. Beer tourism in Canada along the Waterloo–Wellington Ale Trail. *Tourism Management*, 26: 447–458.

Plummer, Ryan, David Telfer, Atsuko Hashimoto, and Robert Summers. 2006. The rise and fall of the Waterloo-Wellinton ale trail: A study of collaboration within the tourism industry. *Current Issues in Tourism*, 9(3): 191–205.

Porter, Michael. 1988. Clusters and the new economics of competition. *Harvard Business Review*, 76(6): 77–90.

Porter, Michael. 2000. Location, competition, and economic development: Local clusters in a global economy. *Economic Development Quarterly*, 14(1): 5–34.

Reid, Neil. 2019. Craft beer tourism: The search for authenticity, diversity, and great beer. In Özge Öner, Mauro Ferrante, and Oliver Fritz (Eds.) *Regional Science Perspectives in Tourism and Hospitality*. Dordrecht: Springer (forthcoming).

Reid, Neil, and Jay Gatrell. 2016. Cluster-based economic development: 4 cases for context in developing regions. In Ashok K. Dutt, Allen G. Noble, Frank J. Costa, Rajiv R. Thakur, and Sudhir K. Thakur (Eds.) *Spatial Diversity and Dynamics in Resources and Urban Development (Urban Development – Volume II)* (pp. 195–207). Dordrecht: Springer.

Reilly, William J. 1931. *The Law of Retail Gravitation*. New York: Knickerbocker Press.

Schmallegger, Doris, Dean Carson, Dean, and Pascal Tremblay. 2010. The economic geography of remote tourism: The problem of connection seeking. *Tourism Analysis*, 15(1): 125–137.

Shoup, Mary Ellen. 2017. Beer tourism boom brews up across the US, showing no signs of slowing. January 24. BeverageDaily.com. https://www.beveragedaily.com/Article/2017/01/24/Beer-Tourism-boom-brews-up-across-the-US-showing-no-signs-of-slowing.

Sims, Rebecca. 2009. Food, place and authenticity: Local food and the sustainable tourism experience. *Journal of Sustainable Tourism*, 17(3): 321–336.

Slocum, Susan L. 2018. Developing social capital in craft beer tourism markets. In Susan L. Slocum, Carol Kline, and Christina T. Cavaliere (Eds.) *Craft Beverages and Tourism, Volume 2* (pp. 83–100). Cham: Palgrave Macmillan.

Taylor, John P. 2001. Authenticity and sincerity in tourism. *Annals of Tourism Research*, 28(1): 7–26.

Ullman, E. L. 1954: Geography as spatial interaction. Reprinted, in Eliot Hurst, M. E. 1974: Transportation geography, New York: McGraw-Hill, 29–39. 1956: The role of transportation and the bases for interaction. In W. L. Thomas (Ed.) *Man's*

Role in Changing the Face of the Earth (pp. 862–880). Chicago: Chicago University Press.

Vickerman R. 1995. Accessibility and peripheral regions. In H. Coccossis and P. Nijkamp (Eds.) *Overcoming Isolation. Advances in Spatial Science* (The Regional Science Series). Berlin, Heidelberg: Springer.

Wanhill, Stephen, and Dimitrios Buhalis. 1999. Introduction: Challenges for tourism in peripheral areas. *International Journal of Tourism Research*, 1(5): 295–297.

Yahoo Finance. 2019. Global agritourism market will grow at a CAGR of 18% during 2019–2023. YahooFinance.com. February 5. https://sg.finance.yahoo.com/news/global-agritourism-market-grow-cagr-124300246.html.

Index

Printed in the United States
by Baker & Taylor Publisher Services